For Steven Marcus

for Magi

____ , with
my strong respect.

Keats's Life of Allegory
The Origins of A Style

Marjorie Levinson

Basil Blackwell

Basil Blackwell Ltd
108 Cowley Road, Oxford, OX4 1JF, UK

Basil Blackwell Inc.
432 Park Avenue South, Suite 1503
New York, NY 10016, USA

British Library Cataloguing in Publication Data

Levinson, Marjorie
The origins of Keats's style: a life of allegory.
1. Keats, John, *1795–1821* – Criticism and interpretation
I. Title
821'.7   PR4837

ISBN 0–631—14509–5
ISBN 0–631–14511–7 Pbk

Library of Congress Cataloging in Publication Data

Levinson, Marjorie
The origins of Keats's style: a life of allegory / Marjorie Levinson
p. cm.
Bibliography: p.
Includes index.
1. Keats, John, 1795–1821 – Critism and interpretation.
I. Title.
PR4837.L48   1988   87–29388   821'.7 – dc19
ISBN 0–631–14509–5: $49.95 (U.S.).
ISBN 0–631–14511–7 (pbk.): $24.95 (U.S.)

Typeset in 11 on 13 pt Ehrhardt
by Hope Services, Abingdon, Oxon.
Printed in Great Britain

Whereas in the symbol destruction is idealized and the transfigured face of nature is fleetingly revealed in the light of redemption, in allegory the observer is confronted with the *facies hippocratica* of history as a petrified, primordial landscape. Everything about history that, from the very beginning, has been untimely, sorrowful, unsuccessful, is expressed in a face – or rather in a death's head. And although such a thing lacks all 'symbolic' freedom of expression, all classical proportion, all humanity – nevertheless, this is the form in which man's subjection to nature is most obvious and it significantly gives rise not only to the enigmatic question of the nature of human existence as such, but also of the biographical historicity of the individual.

Walter Benjamin, *The Origin of German Tragic Drama*,
trans. John Osborne

Cockney: egg: lit. 'cocks'' egg
1. An egg: the egg of the common fowl . . . or perh. one of the small or misshapen eggs occasionally laid by fowls . . . 2. 'A child that sucketh long' . . . a squeamish or effeminate fellow, 'a milksop' . . . 3. A derisive appellation for a townsman, as the type of effeminacy, in contrast to the hardier inhabitants of the country. 4. One born in the city of London . . . Always more or less contemptuous or bantering, and particularly used to connote the characteristics in which the born Londoner is supposed to be inferior to other Englishmen.

Oxford English Dictionary

For my parents, Sylvia and Alfred Levinson, and for Laurie, my sister

Contents

Acknowledgements

Jerry McGann, Marilyn Butler and Terry Eagleton read this book as it grew, and encouraged it in their very different ways. The final product looks nothing like a book that any of those writers would have made, a fact that troubles me but seems not to disturb them. For their liberality, I thank them.

I thank Joe Valente, who talked with me passionately about this book in its early stages, and Stanley Shapiro, who helped me talk of other things.

I am deeply grateful to the Guggenheim Foundation for its gift of a year's freedom to write, and also for its vote of confidence.

All Keats's texts as well as textual information are from Miriam Allott ed., *The Poems of John Keats* (London and New York: Longman and Norton, 1970). Variants preferred by Jack Stillinger (ed., *The Poems of John Keats*, Cambridge, Mass.: Belknap Press of Harvard University, 1978) are noted in brackets (see Appendix).

All quotations from Keats's letters are from *Letters of John Keats*, ed. Robert Gittings (Oxford: Oxford University Press, 1970; reprinted 1979).

1

Introduction

The true cause of Mr. Keats's failure is, not the want of talent, but the misdirection of it . . . [T]here is a sickliness about his productions, which shews there is a mischief at the core. He has with singular . . . correctness described his own case in the preface to Endymion [*sic*]: 'The imagination of a boy', he says, 'is healthy, and the *mature* imagination of a man is healthy; but there is a space of life between, in which the soul is in a ferment, the character undecided, the way of life uncertain, the ambition thick-sighted: thence proceeds mawkishness'. The diagnosis of the complaint is well laid down; his is a diseased state of feeling arising from the want of a sufficient and worthy object of hope and enterprise, and of the regulating principle of religion.

Josiah Conder, *Eclectic Review*, September 1820

He outhunted Hunt in a species of emasculated pruriency, that . . . looks as if it were the product of some imaginative Eunuch's muse within the melancholy inspiration of the Haram.

Blackwood's, January 1826

There is a cool pleasure in the very sound of the word vale. The English word is of the happiest chance . . . It is a sort of Delphic Abstraction – a beautiful thing made more beautiful by being reflected and put in a mist.

Keats, marginal note on *Paradise Lost* I: 321

[Keats] says he does not want ladies to read his poetry: that he writes for men . . .

Richard Woodhouse to John Taylor, letter, 20 September 1819

The Argument

There's no need, I think, to defend the statement that our commitment to a canonical Keats runs deep. Anyone who has

Introduction

thought critically about Keats in the past five years must appreciate
the difference between the Keats commentary and the kinds of
inquiries conducted on the poems of the other Romantics. This
business of a canonical Keats is not a matter of explicitly idealizing or
redemptive readings.[1] I'm talking about the assumptions that
organize our practical understanding of the relations between Keats's
life and writing and the social context in which they both materialized.

Keats, like Shakespeare, is a name for the figure of the capable
poet. The best Keats criticism (Lionel Trilling, John Bayley,
Christopher Ricks), and the smartest (the Harvard Keatsians), mark
out the canonical extremes and define a range of problems, many of
which are addressed in this study.[2] These greatly disparate critiques,
sketched toward the end of this chapter, are both founded on a single
premise, one which opposes *tout court* the governing thesis of the
contemporary criticism of Keats's poetry. We all agree to know the
man and his writing by their eminent authenticity: Bayley's 'Gemeine',
Ricks's 'unmisgiving' imagination, Eliot's epistolary *idiot savant*,
Vendler's true craftsman. In order to produce this knowledge, we put
what the contemporary reviews called Keats's 'vulgarity' under the
sign of psychic, social, and textual unself-consciousness: roughly, the
sign of sensuous sincerity. Further, by the providential tale of
intellectual, moral, and artisanal, development we find coded in
Keats's letters, we put the vulgarity which cannot be so sublimed in
the early verse and show its gradual sea-change into the rich,
inclusive seriousness that distinguishes the great poetry. Thus do we
rescue Keats's deep meanings from his alluring surfaces, his poetic
identity from his poetical identifications. By and large, we read the
poetry as a sweet solution to a bitter life: a resolution of the actual
contradictions. The writing is not, we say, an escape from the real but
a constructive operation performed upon it so as to bring out its
Truth, which is also a new and deeply human Beauty. We describe, in
short, a transformation of experience by knowledge and by the
aesthetic practice which that knowledge promotes. The word that
best describes this critical plot is romance: a march from alienation to
identity. The governing figure of this narrative is the Coleridgean or
Romantic symbol and its rhetorical device the oxymoron: irreducibly
syncretic ideas. The hero of our critical history is a profoundly
associated sensibility and his gift to us is the exemplary humanism of
his life and art.

Trilling, Bayley and Ricks have discriminated a stylistic 'badness' that occurs throughout Keats's poetry: a certain remove whereby Keats signifies his *interest* in his representations and, we might add, in his own expressiveness. In so doing, these critics approximate the response of Keats's contemporaries, analyzed below. However, by emphasizing the psychic investment rather than the social remove which prompts it (and, by focusing mimetic and rhetorical rather than subjective disorders), Bayley and Ricks bring Keats's discursive alienations into the dominant romance.[3] Following these powerful writers, we read Keats's lapses from the good taste of innocent, object-related representation and transparent subjectivity as a determined consent to his own voluptuous inwardness *and* to the self-conscious recoil. By this willed abandon, Keats transcends both enthrallments, thereby releasing the reader into a more generous (in today's parlance, 'intersubjective') relational mode. In other words, those critics who acknowledge the stylistic vulgarity of Keats's writing put it in the redeemable field of creaturely instinct and defense, and not in the really unsettling category of externality, materiality, and ambitious reflexiveness. When Keats nods, we say, it is because he *dares* to nod ('swoon', 'sink', or 'cease'), not because he tries too hard.

The early reviews tell a different story. The most casual survey of this commentary (1817–35) reveals a response so violent and sustained, so promiscuous in its blending of social, sexual, and stylistic critique, and so sharply opposed to mainstream modern commentary as to imply a determinate insight on the part of Keats's contemporaries and a determined oversight on the part of his belated admirers. While we're all familiar with *Blackwood*'s Cockney School attack (Lockhart's rebuke of Keats's literary presumption ['so back to the shop Mr. John, back to "plasters, pills, and ointment boxes, . . ."']), we have not attended very closely to the sexual invective, and not at all to the relation between those two discourses. Time and again, the poetry is labelled 'profligate', 'puerile', 'unclean', 'disgusting', 'recklessly luxuriant and wasteful', 'unhealthy', 'abstracted', and 'insane'.[4] More specifically, it is graphed as a stylistically self-indulgent verse: prolix, repetitive, metrically and lexically licentious, overwrought. The diatribes culminate in the epithet 'nonsense'.

We have always related the savaging of the early poetry to the anomaly of Keats's social position and to the literary blunders which follow from that fact: generally, problems of diction, rhetoric, and subject matter, all of them reducible to the avoidable (and, finally, avoided) misfortune of Keats's coterie. Because we situate these blunders at a certain level and within a very contained biographical field, and because we isolate them from the beauties of the so-called great poetry, we have not understood the deeper insult of Keats's writing, that which explains the intensity and displacements of the early response and the equal but opposite distortions of the twentieth-century view.

From the distance of today, one can detect in those vituperative catalogues a governing discursive and even cognitive model. Keats's poetry was characterized as a species of masturbatory exhibitionism, an offensiveness further associated with the self-fashioning gestures of the petty bourgeoisie.[5] The erotic opprobrium pinpoints the self-consciousness of the verse: its autotelic reflection on its own fine phrases, phrases stylistically objectified as acquired, and therefore *mis*acquired property. The sexual language of the reviews was, of course, an expedient way to isolate Keats, but it is also a telling index to the social and existential project outlined by Keats's style. In his overwrought inscriptions of canonical models, the early readers sensed the violence of Keats's raids upon that empowering system: a violence driven by the strongest desire for an authorial manner and means, and for the social legitimacy felt to go with it. In the alienated reflexiveness of Keats's poetry, the critics read the signature of a certain kind of life, itself the sign of a new social phenomenon. Byron's famous epithet for the style of the Cockney writers, 'shabby genteel', puts the matter plainly.

> The grand distinction of the under forms of the new school of poets is their *vulgarity*. By this I do not mean that they are *coarse*, but 'shabby-genteel', as it is termed. A man may be *coarse* and yet not *vulgar*, and the reverse . . . It is in their *finery* that the new under school are *most* vulgar, and they may be known by this at once; as what we called at Harrow 'a Sunday blood' might be easily distinguished from a gentleman . . . In the present case, I speak of writing, not of persons. (Extract from letter to John Murray, 25 March 1821)

If we were not already convinced of Byron's ear for social nuance, we would only have to recall Keats's confession, 'I look upon fine Phrases like a Lover'.

Like our own criticism, the early reviews read in Keats's poetry 'a life of Allegory', but the meaning they develop by that allegory lies in the realm of social production, not aesthetics, metaphysics, or humanistic psychology. To those early readers, 'Keats' was the allegory of a man belonging to a certain class and aspiring, as that entire class was felt to do, to another: a man with particular but typical ambitions and with particular but typical ways of realizing them. A world of difference separates this hermeneutic from the 'poignantly allegorical life', an adventure in soul-making, which has become today's John Keats.[6] By respecting the social-sexual compounding evidenced by those reviews, we recover the sense of danger underlying our formalist and rhetorical readings of Keats's middling states: his adolescence, his literariness, his stylistic suspensions, his pronounced reflexiveness. We focus Keats's position – sandwiched between the Truth of the working class and the Beauty of the leisure class – not as a healthy both / and but as the monstrous neither / nor constructed in the reviews. We see that the problem of Keats's early poetry is not its regressive escapism (its instincts, so to speak), but its stylistic project: a social-ego enterprise. The deep contemporary insult of Keats's poetry, and its deep appeal (and long opacity) for the modern reader, is its idealized enactment of the conflicts and solutions which defined the middle class at a certain point in its development and which still to some extent obtain. We remember that Keats's style can delineate that station so powerfully because of his marginal, longing relation to the legitimate bourgeoisie (and its literary exemplars) of his day. In emulating the condition of the accomplished middle class (the phrase is itself an oxymoron), Keats isolated the constitutive contradictions of that class. The final fetish in Keats's poetry is precisely that stationing tension.

By the stylistic contradictions of his verse, Keats produces a writing which is aggressively *literary* and therefore not just 'not Literature' but, in effect, *anti*-Literature: a parody. We will see that Keats's most successful poems are those most elaborately estranged from their own materials and procedures and thus from both a writerly and readerly subjectivity. The poetic I describe, following the lead of Keats's contemporaries, is the opposite of 'unmisgiving'.[7] The triumph of the great poetry is not its capacious, virile, humane authenticity but its subversion of those authoritarian values, effects which it could not in any case, and for the strongest social reasons, realize. This is the triumph of the double-negative. The awfulness of the early work, by contrast, is explained as an expression of the *single*, or suffered negative: a nondynamic reflection of Keats's multiple estrangements and of the longing they inspired. The accomplished poetry may be considered the negative knowledge of Keats's actual life: the production of his freedom by the figured negation of his given being, natural and social. To say this is not to consecrate Keats a precocious post-modernist, only to take seriously the social facts and meanings embedded in his representations and in the contemporary reception. It is to see in 'the continuous manner in which the whole is elaborated' a parodic reproduction of the social restrictions that marked Keats as *wanting*: unequipped, ineffectual, and deeply fraudulent.[8]

Keats did not accomplish by this greatly overdetermined stratagem the goodness he craved: that plenitude of being he worshipped in the great canonical models and which he images in Autumn's breeding passiveness. What he did produce by what Shelley called 'the bad sort of style' was a truly *negative* capability. I call this power 'virtual' to bring out its parodic relation to authorized forms of power, 'virtuoso' to suggest its professional, technically preoccupied character, and 'virtuous' by reference to its imposed and contrived limitations. (See chapter 2, p. 45 and note 2, and chapter 3, pp. 103–8). To generate this verbal sequence is also, of course, to put as the ruling stylistic and social question the question of Keats's virility: to begin, that is, where the early commentary leaves off. We will take Keats's own phrase, the 'wreathed trellis of a working brain', as a figure for Keats's negative power: his inside-out, thoroughly textualized and autotelic accomplishment. In the celebrated poise of Keats's poetry, we read the effect of the impossible project set him by his interests and circumstances: to become by (mis)acquiring; to become by his writing at once authorized (properly derivative) and authorial (original); to turn his suffered objectivity into a sign of his self-estranged psyche, and to wield that sign as a shield and an ornament.

The project of this book is to read the meaning of a life in the style of a man's writing, and then to read that writing, that style, and that life back into their original social context. What I describe is a self-consciously distanced and totalizing study on the order of Sartre's *Saint Genet.*

The Life

The facts of Keats's life are too familiar to bear recounting here. I refer the reader to Aileen Ward's unsurpassed biography and to the important work of Walter Jackson Bate and Robert Gittings.[9] Below, I elaborate those aspects of the story that bear directly on Keats's stylistic development.

To observe that Keats's circumstances put him at a severe remove from the canon is to remark not only his educational deficits but his lack of those skills prerequisite to a transparent mode of appropriation: guiltless on the one side, imperceptible on the other. He knew some French and Latin, little Italian, no Greek. His Homer was Chapman, his Dante was Cary, his Provençal ballads translations in an edition of Chaucer, his Boccaccio Englished. Keats's art education was largely by engravings and, occasionally, reproductions. His absorption of the accessible English writers was greatly constrained by his ignorance of the originals upon which they drew and by his nonsystematic self-education. To say all this is to observe Keats's literally corrupt relation to the languages of poetry: his means of production.

We might also consider a more mundanely mechanical aspect of Keats's composition. Throughout his life, Keats felt compelled *physically* to escape his hard, London reality in order to write. A great deal of the poetry was conceived or composed at a number of modest, middle-class and, as it were, publicly designated resorts: Margate, Shanklin (the Isle of Wight), Burford Bridge (Surrey). Keats could afford only the leanest accommodations, of course, and often he adjourned to these spots alone and off-season. When even these small excursions were not possible, Keats sought his escape on Hampstead Heath, in the British Institution, or in a friend's well-furnished living room. In short, the graciously conformable bowers and dells enjoyed by Wordsworth and Coleridge were no more available to Keats than were the glory and grandeur of Greece and Rome, Byron's and Shelley's enabling resorts.

'Romantic retirement' gains a whole new dimension with Keats. Imagine the solitude of a young man in a seaside rooming house in April, a borrowed picture of Shakespeare his only companion: a man with nothing to do for a set period of time but write the pastoral epic which would, literally, *make* him. Compare this withdrawal to the seclusion of a writer musing in his garden, deserted by his wife and literary friends of an afternoon; or to the isolation of two English aristocrats, recognized poets both, galloping along the Lido and relishing their escape from the cant of high society and from its official voices. Better yet, imagine a conversation poem, a social verse, or a lyrical ballad by Keats; project from Keats's pen a sublimely inspired ode on the order of Shelley's 'Mont Blanc', or a *Defence of Poetry*, or a pamphlet on the Convention of Cintra. The experiment should point up the problematic nature for Keats of those elementary and, in the period, normative literary effects: authority, authenticity, and ease.

Apropos that last and deeply Romantic effect, ease, we recall that Keats hadn't the luxury for a 'wise passiveness'. His early detection of his disease, Tom's condition, the time constraints imposed by his medical training, his assumption of responsibility for his sister, his haste to make a name so he could marry Fanny: all these familiar facts precluded the meditative quiescence which enabled in the other Romantics a rhetoric of surpassing naturalness.[10] Wordsworth's compositional program was simply not an option for a man who could not wait upon memory's slow digestive processes. Nor could Keats draw upon his everyday life, a monotonous struggle to get by and get ahead, for the interest, surprise, and suggestiveness which Byron and Shelley found in their large circumstances. Keats's necessary writing trips were hasty and purposive; the work of this simulated leisure was the production of pleasure, precondition for the rich, selfless, and suspended literary exercise which was Keats's dream of art. The result of these sad, self-vexing outings is a poetry evincing the paradoxes by which it is made. A poetry too happy by far, too full by half. When Shelley disdainfully rejected Keats's advice, 'load every rift with ore', he knew what he was about. He registered the class implications of Keats's plenitude, and knew that he, for one, did not have to plump his poems to the core.

Before we can begin re-reading Keats, we must really imagine what we know. We must see very clearly, as John Bayley saw, that Keats was a man whose almost complete lack of control over the social code kept him from living his life. He could not write his poetry in the manner he required, marry the woman he loved, claim his inheritance, hold his family together, or assist his friends. He could not, in short, seize any of the appurtenances of manhood. Keats was as helplessly and ignominiously a 'boy' poet as Chatterton, and Byron's 'Mankin' was a viciously knowing insult.

The range of paradoxes which Byron and his contemporaries observed in Keats's poetry is ultimately referrable to the fact that it was not given to Keats, a poet in Shelley's 'general sense', to be a poet in the most pedestrian, professional, 'restricted' sense. Keats had to make for himself a life (the training at Guy's; then, getting by on his allowance; finally, when the money ran out, the projected career of ship's surgeon), while writing a poetry that was, structurally, a denial of that life.[11] At no time did Keats make any money from his writing. (One wonders *how*, exactly, Keats applied the title of 'poet' to himself. How did he introduce himself in ordinary social interactions?) The oddly abstract materialism of the poetry – its overinvestment in its signs – takes on a new look when we remember both Keats's remove from his representational manner and means, and also his want of those real things that help people live their lives. Is it any wonder that the poetry produced by this man should be so autotelic, autoerotic, so fetishistic and so stuck? Should it surprise us to find that his dearest fantasy – a picture of somebody reading, a window on the one side, a goldfish bowl on the other – takes the form of a multiply framed, *trompe-l'oeil* still life? 'Find the subject', we might call it; or, what is the same thing, 'Find the frame'.

Keats's poetry was at once a tactical activity, or an escape route from an actual life, and a final construction: the concrete imaginary to that apparitional actual. What was, initially, a substitute *for* a grim life became for Keats a substitute life: a real life of substitute things – simulacra – which, though they do not nourish, neither do they waste. At the very end of his career, Keats began, I believe, to position this parodic solution as part of the problem. 'Lamia' is Keats's attempt to frame the problematic of his life and writing and thus to set it aside.

It is crucial to see, as Bayley saw, that the deep desire in Keats's poetry is not for aesthetic things or languages *per se* (that is, Byron's 'finery'), but for the social code inscribed in them, a code which was, to Keats, a human transformational grammar. Indeed, all Keats's meditations on art and identity (typically, plasticity), should be related to his abiding desire, to live. The real perversion of Keats's poetry is not its display of its cultural fetishes but its preoccupation with the system felt to organize those talismanic properties. Keats could have had all the urns, Psyches, nightingales, Spenserianisms, Miltonisms,

Claudes, and Poussins he wanted; he was not, however, permitted possession of the social grammar inscribed in that aesthetic array, and this was just what Keats was after.

We illuminate Keats's legitimacy problem by way of the originality anxiety that seems to have beset most of the Romantic and what used to be called pre-Romantic poets. The past only lies like a weight on the brain of those who inherit it. Or rather, the past imposes a special *kind* of burden on those individual talents who feel themselves disinherited by the Tradition, and, thus, excluded from the dialectic of old and new, identity and difference. Wordsworth's celebrated defense of his poetical innovations – 'every author, as far as he is great and at the same time *original*, has had the task of *creating* the taste by which he is to be enjoyed' – must be understood as the statement of a man so assured of his entitlement that he can trust his originality to be received as intelligible and valuable. (That Wordsworth's confidence was not always confirmed is not the issue here.) Keats, by contrast, could not begin to invent an original voice without first and *throughout* establishing his legitimacy: roughly, his derivativeness.

Chatterton, the poet with whom Keats felt the strongest affinities, developed a most economical solution to this problem. By his perfect reproduction of 'the medieval', Chatterton not only established that epochal concept as a normative style, thereby sanctioning his persona, Rowley, and that figure's verse; he produced as well and dialectically, *for the knowing reader*, the originality of the entire *oeuvre* (viz. poems, charts, maps, coins). Theoretically, Rowley's canon at once created the taste, which it represented as already venerable and prestigious, and offered itself as the only artifact capable of satisfying it.

Practically speaking, however, Chatterton couldn't begin to fashion the readership he needed. Indeed, the logic of his enterprise compelled him to do all he might to malform – *misinform* – his audience. The literariness of his poetry was strictly a function of its documentary, antiquarian presentation. The aesthetic dimension of the writing only materialized under the pressure of a fundamentally historical interest, and in that case, of course, the literary credit was Rowley's. Chatterton's successful negotiation of the technical imperatives set him by his social facts required his entire self-effacement, as a man and a writer. A rare intuition of this paradox surfaces in the controversy prompted by the hoax poems. We find considerable puzzlement among Chatterton's detractors, and ingenuity on the part of his defenders, regarding the anomaly of a writer who would seem to have preferred the inferior reputation of translator-editor to the glory of proper poetic genius: that is, originality.[12] To us, of course, Chatterton's perversity indicates how completely over-determined a choice he faced. His election of the lesser fame, scholarly authority, was in fact an embrace of the bad originality of the counterfeiter. In that vexed ideal, we read the situation of the writer whose mastery consists exclusively in his self-violation.

Keats sidestepped Chatterton's final solution. By the self-signifying *imperfection* of his canonical reproductions (a parodic return upon his own derivativeness), Keats drew upon the licensing primacy of the code even as his *representation* of that total form changed the nature of its authority. The pronounced badness of Keats's writing figures the mythic goodness of the canon and, by figuring, at once exalts and delimits it. Thus did Keats plot for himself a scene of writing. By the double unnaturalness of his style, Keats projects the authority of an *anti*-nature, stable by virtue of its continuous self-revolutionizing and secured by its contradictions. The proof of these claims is the rest of this book, but let me offer as a critical instance a reading of 'Chapman's Homer'.

On First Looking into Chapman's Homer

Much have I trevelled [travell'd] in the realms of gold,
    And *many goodly* states and kingdoms seen;
    Round *many* western islands have I been
Which bards in fealty to Apollo hold.
Oft of one wide expanse had I been told
    That deep-browed [brow'd] Homer ruled as his demesne;
    Yet did I never breathe its pure serene
Till I heard Chapman speak out loud and bold.[:]
Then felt I like some watcher of the skies
    When a new planet swims into his ken;
Or like stout Cortez when with eagle eyes
    He stared [star'd] at the Pacific, [—] and all his men
Looked [Look'd] at each other with a wild surmise –
    Silent, upon a peak in Darien.

I have accented several words in the first three lines by way of amplifying the tone of Keats's address. Even if we were ignorant of

Keats's social disadvantages, this fulsome claim to literary ease would give us pause. The very act of assertion, as well as its histrionically commanding and archly literary style, undermine the premise of natural authority and erudition. The contemporary reader might have observed as well some internal contradictions; not only *is* Homer the Golden Age, but not to 'have' Greek and not to have encountered Homer by the age of twenty-three is to make one's claim to any portion of the literary empire suspect. (Keats's acquaintance with Pope's translation is suppressed by the sonnet.) Keats effectively assumes the role of the literary adventurer (with the commercial nuance of that word) as opposed to the mythic explorer: Odysseus, Cortes, Balboa. More concretely, he advertises his corrupt access to the literary system and to those social institutions which inscribe that system systematically in the hearts and minds of young men. To read Homer in translation and after having read Spenser, Coleridge, Cary, and whoever else is included in Keats's travelogue, is to read Homer badly (in a heterodox and alienated way), and to subvert the system which installs Homer in a particular and originary place. Moreover, to 'look into' Chapman's Homer is to confess – in this case, *profess* – one's fetishistic relation to the great Original. Keats does not *read* even the translation. To 'look into' a book is to absorb it idiosyncratically at best, which is to say, with casual or conscious opportunism. Similarly, the substitution of 'breathe' for the expected 'read' in line 7 marks the rejection of a sanctioned mode of literary acquisition. To 'breathe' a text is to take it in, take from it and let it out, somewhat the worse for wear. It is, more critically, to miscategorize the object and in such a way as to proclaim one's intimacy with it. Both the claim and the title of Keats's sonnet are, in a word, vulgar.

One is reminded of Valéry's appraisal of museum pleasure: 'For anyone who is close to works of art, they are no more objects of delight than his own breathing'.[13] Keats, we observe, rejoices in his respiration and goes so far as to fetishize the very air he admits. I single out the phrase 'pure serene' not only because it is structurally foregrounded but because it reproduces in miniature the method – the working contradiction – of the sonnet. What Keats 'breathes' is, of course, anything but pure and Homeric (since he reads in translation and perversely with respect to canon protocol), and the phrase formally exposes that fact. We cannot help but see that 'pure serene', a primary reification, further calls attention to itself as a fine phrase, that Keats clearly looks upon as a lover. Not only is the phrase a Miltonic construction, but more recent usage would have characterized it as a sort of translator-ese. One thinks of Pope's 'vast profound' and indeed, of Cary's own 'pure serene', a description of Dante's ether (1814). Coleridge uses the phrase in his 'Hymn before Sunrise in the Vale of Chamouni', 1802. Keats's reproduction of the phrase designates both his access to the literary system and his mode of access – that of translator to Original. In effect, he intentionalizes the alienation he suffers by his social deficits. By signifying the restriction, he converts it into restraint: 'might half-slumbering on its own right arm'. Let me note here that the translation of an adjective into a noun, while etymologically justifiable, transforms Homer's pure and therefore insensible atmosphere – his aura – into a palpable particular: a detached literary style and a self-reflexive one at that. What figures in Homer as a natural and epochal expressiveness is in Keats, and first, a represented object. Only by performing that office does the Homeric value assume for Keats an expressive function.

The thing to remark is the way Keats produces the virtues of his alienated access to the canon. The consummate image of the poem – that which accounts for its overall effect of 'energetic . . . calmness' – is, obviously, that of Cortes / Balboa 'star[ing] at the Pacific' while 'all his men / Looked [Look'd] at each other with a wild surmise – / Silent, upon a peak in Darien'. Cortes, we notice, is a 'stout' and staring fellow: a solid citizen. 'Stout' means, of course, 'stout-hearted', but in the context, where Cortes's direct stare at the object of his desire is juxtaposed against the 'surmise' of his men (and the alliteration reinforces these visual connections), one feels the energy of the men and the stuck or frozen state of their leader. By their surmise – a liminal, semi-detached state – the men are 'wild', a word which in the Romantic idiom means 'free'. We clearly see that the relation of the men to that (etymologically) literal 'pure serene', the Pacific, is indirect and perverse. Who in that situation would avert his gaze?

Claude Finney has reminded us that according to Keats's sources, Balboa's men were forbidden the prospect until their leader had had his full gaze.[14] We can see that the social discrepancy vividly sketched by Keats's original gets translated in the sonnet into an existential and self-imposed difference, and one that inverts the given power ratio by rendering the men, not the master, free and vital. One does not, I think, go too far in associating Keats with those capably disenfranchised men.

It is the stillness and strangeness of the men – their peculiar *durée* – which stations Keats's sonnet, all the gregarious exploration metaphors notwithstanding. Homer enters the poem as the Pacific enters the sensibilities of Cortes's men: through Chapman's / Cortes's more direct possession of / by the object of desire. Odysseus's extrovert energy animates Keats's sonnet but, again, perversely. In the Keatsian space, that energy turns self-reflexive, reminding us perhaps of Tennyson's 'Ulysses'. The poem looks at itself as the men look at each other. The virtue of both looks is their impropriety; what they refuse by that gesture is the Gorgon stare, the direct embrace of and by the authorizing Original. Keats's poem 'speak[s] out loud and bold' by not speaking 'out' at all. We finish the sonnet, which seems to be predicated on such a simple *donnée*, and we wonder where we have travelled. What happened to Homer, and to Keats for that matter? Why does Keats interpose between himself and his ostensible subject Chapman, Cary, Coleridge, Gilbert, Robertson, Herschel, Balboa, Cortes, and Cortes's men? Why does Keats leave us with this off-center cameo, an image of turbulent stasis among the extras of the cast when what we expect is a 'yonder lie the Azores' flourish by the principal? What *is* this poem? By the conventions it sets, it should strike us as a graceful display of literary inspiration and gratitude. But it seems other, and otherwise. How do we explain the real power of its slant rhyme?

Let me recall Hunt's comment on the sonnet: 'prematurely masculine'. By emphasizing the adverb for a change, we begin to see that Keats's unnatural (illicit) assumption of power, signified by the 'poetical' octet, does not *qualify* the 'masculinity' of the sestet, it constitutes it. The direct and natural compression of the sestet is the stylistic effect of the displayed disentitlement that is the functional representation of the opening eight lines. The pivot which constructs this before-and-after dynamic (the coordinates for a range of ratios: imitation–genuine, protest–power, struggle–ease) is, of course, the experience of reading Chapman. The experience takes place, significantly, in the breach between the two movements of the sonnet. Rather than imitate Chapman, Keats reproduces Chapman's necessarily parodic (that is, Elizabethan) inscription of Homer. The queerness of Chapman's 'mighty line, loud-and-bold' version is rewritten in Keats's own parodic Elizabethan*ism*, and, through the queerness of the Cortes / Balboa image. It is the self-reflexive, fetishistic inscription of the canon – the display of bad access and misappropriation – that emancipates Keats's words. Keats's sonnet breaks free of Homer and Chapman by mis-giving both. By the English he puts on Homer's serenity (he reifies it) and on Chapman's 'masculine' extrovert energy, Keats produces the perpetual imminence which is the hero of his sonnet. In the Keatsian idiom, we could call that imminence or suspension a 'stationing', with an ear for the full social resonance of Keats's aesthetic word.[15]

The instance of this poem would suggest that Keats's relation to the Tradition is better conceived as dialogic (Bakhtin) than dialectic (Bloom).[16] The poetry does not clear a space for itself by a phallic agon; it opens itself to the Tradition, defining itself as a theater wherein such contests may be eternally and inconclusively staged.[17] The authority of this poetry consists in its detachment from the styles or voices it entertains. By this detachment, these styles become *signatures*: not audible voices but visible, material *signs* of canonical voices. These signs – like all such marks, inauthentic and incomplete – are *not*, ultimately, mastered by the master-of-ceremonies. And because they remain external to authorial consciousness, theirs is the empowering virtue of the supplement. In these magic supplements, 'Things semi-real', lies the terrific charm of Keats's poetry.

The contained badness of 'Chapman's Homer' constitutes its goodness, which is to say, its rhetorical force. The paradox hinges, naturally, on the word 'contained'. When Keats is great, it is because he *signifies* his alienation from his *materia poetica*, a fact that modern criticism and textual studies have suppressed.[18] This alienation – inevitable, given Keats's education, class, and opportunities – was highly expedient. By it, Keats could possess the 'stuff of creativity' without becoming possessed by it. By 'stuff', I do not mean Bloom's primary, inspirational matter but the means and techne for exercises in literary production. Keats's poetry, inspired by translations, engravings, reproductions, schoolroom mythologies, and Tassie's gems, delivers itself through these double and triple reproductions as the 'true, the blushful Hippocrene'. That phrase describes, ironically, *precisely* a substitute truth. Again, Byron understood these things; 'You know my opinion of *that second-hand* school of poetry.'

Discussion

The early commentary has more to teach us. Byron's vivid epithets – 'a Bedlam vision', a 'sad abortive attempt at all things, "signifying nothing"' – suggest that the masturbation trope was a most economical way of designating the poetry nonsense: not bad Literature but *non*Literature. In practical terms, it would seem that the association of Keats's poetry with masturbation was a way to isolate Keats without agonizing him.

We make sense of this tactic in two ways. First, the commonplace alignment of masturbation with madness suggests that whereas homosexuality was part of the normative heterosexual configuration – either a standard deviation or binary Other – masturbation was outside the curve: the age's $1/0$, 'signifying nothing'.[19] This speculation is consistent with the class affronts (revelations of practical and ideological projects) leveled by Keats's poetry and explored below. Second, while 'nonsense' attacks always suppress unwanted sense, this particular noncognition additionally implies a response to the subjective irreality of Keats's self-reflexive poetry. 'Frigging [one's] *Imagination*' is one thing; frigging an imagination tenanted by other minds is another and a double-perversity. ('Frig' means 'to chafe or rub', 'to agitate the limbs' [OED], and most commonly, of course, to copulate. The '*Imagination*' to which Byron refers is, thus, a male and female property; or, Keats was accused of masturbating / fucking a Nothing.) Byron's contempt for Keats's fetishistic relation to his acquired literary languages – borrowed 'finery' – masks a fearful insight into the subjective vacancy of Keats's writing. The 'Bedlam' association registers Keats's want of a proprietary subject-form: a voice distinct from the entertained canonical echoes and offering itself as a point, however 'bad', of readerly identification and authorial control. In Keats's poetry, the diverse cultural languages which we call the Tradition are both the means and the *manner* of representation, both object and subject. The 'self' upon which the verse reflects is, precisely, 'not-self': a fetishized, random collection of canonical signatures. One can see that this bad imitation of that earnest Romantic exercise, self-reflection, was, in effect, a burlesque. Keats's operations objectified the naturalness (originality, autonomy, and candor) of all writerly origins, putting those transparencies at risk. Even Byron, that determinedly mad bad man, was threatened;

Byronic irony, no matter how inclusive, is always recuperated by the biographical subject-form coded in all the poems. Keats's poetry is differently, but no *more* masturbatory than Wordsworth's or Byron's, the largest, most virile poets of the age. We could say that Keats offended his generation so deeply by practicing one of its dominant modes of literary production while showing his hand. The sexual slander developed in the reviews registers Keats's relation to the Tradition, understood as a limited-access code with powerful social functions, and the class contradictions which that relation stylistically defined. At the same time, the critique displaces those contradictions to the sphere of private life and pathology: a safety zone. Thus was a serious, or materially designing sensuousness converted into a grave sensual disease.

A juxtaposition of two professional responses to Keats's poetry gives us a practical purchase on the meaning of Keats's style. Wordsworth and Byron agreed on very little; their consensus on Keats argues their glimpse of that in his poetry which challenged a common interest or which exposed a contradiction at the center of both their very different practices.

Wordsworth's brisk dismissal of Keats's 'Hymn to Pan' – 'a Very pretty piece of Paganism' – concisely maps the manifold of impressions I've been describing. By 'pretty', with its resonance to 'fancy' (Imagination's weak sister), and its evocation of the ingenious, the trivial, the overcultivated *and* infantile, Wordsworth suggests both the mechanical elegance of Keats's writing and its servility to an imperfectly discriminating appetite. The adjective describes a taste at once immature and effete, under- and overrefined, and in both cases unhealthy: an appetite for 'dainties' or for 'luxuries', baby-food or caviar.[20] Wordsworth's disgust is the revulsion of a plain-eating, water-drinking man for a connoisseur of pulpy strawberries and claret. It is the contempt of a man who *transcends* class – an *essential* man addressing his peers in a language as limpid and restorative as mountain streams – for a man to whom class is a fetish, and whose language, impure and overcharged, must spoil the taste and the constitution of his readers. Putting the critique on the side of production, and with an ear to that 'Paganism', we might describe Wordsworth's Keats as a purveyor of substitute pleasures: real signs that provide lacks and differences.

Wordsworth's 'piece', while it describes, of course, the formal self-containment of the Hymn within *Endymion*, also marks out the thingness, partiality, and externality of Keats's attempt at an archetypal discourse of presence.[21] The word suggests the *essentially* extraneous character of Keats's writing, if we can allow that solecism for a moment. Wordsworth is out to imply the sheer factitiousness of the verse, an interested representation of what is already for Keats a received idea or, following Wordsworth, a 'poeticism': 'the Pagan'. Wordsworth's 'ism' is his way of naming this double fetish. The singsong alliteration of the phrase, an imitative tactic, contrastively conjures the austere, holistic, deeply qualitative hedonism which is Wordsworth's Pagan: 'the pleasure which there is in life itself'. The conceptual resonance amplifies the ontological corruptness of Keats's partial, purposive, and mechanical self-pleasuring. In a phrase (Wordsworth's), Keats's is a poetry of 'outrageous stimulation'; we might say, the pleasure of the ornament.

By the memorable epithets Byron coined for Keats and his poetry ('a sort of mental masturbation – frigging his *Imagination*', 'Johnny Keats's *piss a bed* poetry', 'the drivelling idiotism of the Mankin', 'dirty little blackguard Keates', 'Self-polluter of the human mind'), Byron crystallized the sexual associations diffused throughout the more modulated responses. A more interesting phrase, however, is Byron's 'shabby genteel', quoted above, an expression which seems to emerge from a different perceptual field. In context, the phrase identifies Keats's vulgarity less with his motives (cheap thrills; supplemental delights), than with his methods. Specifically, Byron censures Keats's display of his literary entitlement. 'It is in their *finery* that the new under school are *most* vulgar . . . I speak of writing, not of persons'. Byron's 'finery', like Wordsworth's 'Paganism', designates those elements in the poetry which are perceptible *as* styles ('ery', 'ism'), because imperfectly appropriated, heaped heterogeneously together, and reflected on by an 'author' who is but the alter ego to those styles. 'I don't mean he is *indecent*, but viciously soliciting his own ideas into a state, which is neither poetry nor any thing else but a Bedlam vision . . .' By his three-way equation, linking self-reflection, masturbation, and middle-class acquisition and display, Byron clarifies the broad social offensiveness of Keats's poetry. As Byron well knew, a good deal of his own poetry and that of his contemporaries solicits its own ideas into a state. Byron had, of course, his quarrel with those serious self-reflectors, the Lakers, and his attack on Keats is no doubt part of that quarrel. *But*, Keats was a figure from the 'Mediterranean' side of the great North–South, serious–sensuous divide: Byron's side, that is. It would seem that Keats owes his rare achievement – at once Byron's and Wordsworth's whipping boy – to the manifest *subject* disorders of his discourse.[22]

Byron is repelled by Keats's psychic fane first, because it is filled with false things: not human qualities or even authorial properties, but *props*, or material signs of literary reality. Worse, everything acquired by the Keatsian consciousness, no matter how 'good' originally, gets falsified within that precinct. Fine becomes 'finery', cultivation becomes Culture, whole and living speech is rendered a quotation, and everything is as an artifact in an overwrought cabinet: framed, spotlighted, exhibited as possessions that are also signs *of* possession.[23] Keats's 'solicitation' of his ideas was manifest because practiced *on* false-consciousness, and 'vicious' because tending to *falsify* (that is, reify) some privileged *forms* of consciousness. Keats's canonical 'abstractions' (the word recurs obsessively in the reviews) effectively exposed the canon as a construct, as authoritarian, and as subject to violation. This is to say, Keats's scavenging replaced the authority of Authority, a natural and internal quality, with that of a more literal, original author-ity: with the figure of the literary entrepreneur. No poetic style could have been more abhorrent to the respectively private and public transparencies of Wordsworth and Byron, or rather, to the class subject-forms projected by those good manners. Returning to Byron's 'nonsense' verdict: when self-reflection is projected as reflection on other poets' selves, when 'frigging [one's] *Imagination*' describes a dalliance with other men's surmises, when a signally autotelic poetry exposes the real interests served by its display of disinterest, and an autoerotic verse betrays the busyness – and business – of a working brain, then accusations of 'nonsense' make perfect sense.

Keats's strangely alienated reflexiveness carried, I believe, an even stronger social charge than the one I've just identified. We get at this meaning by setting Keats's methods against the Wordsworthian model, which we read as an exemplary Romantic form, and by glossing that comparison with another of Byron's colorful commentaries. The governing antinomy here is not legitimacy / originality but pleasure / work.

Wordsworth's poetry, like so much of Keats's, typically represents its coming *into* being as its reason *for* being, and also its chief delight. What distinguishes the Wordsworthian from the Keatsian method are its defenses against a mechanically divisive – analytic, one might say – reception. The devices of Wordsworth's poetry fend off a reading which would dissociate the verbal means from authorial and rhetorical ends, and, thus, set 'poet' against both 'human being' and reader, writing against speaking and reading. Wordsworth discourages this kind of attention first, by figuring the poem's formal materialization as a generically idealized human process: a development independent of authorial design and direction. Wordsworth's narrators loudly proclaim their passivity; and, their unself-consciousness invites us to identify narrator with poet. By these techniques, the work's semiotic center of gravity gets displaced to the reader, a postulated activity center. The narrator's encounter with an object, memory, or event is the condition of a narration which claims to be nothing but a self-accounting, offered to the reader as a humanizing opportunity. 'It is no tale; but, should you think, / Perhaps a tale you'll make it' ('Simon Lee'). One is meant to translate this disclaimer as follows: this *is* a tale, a tale of telling, but like all discourse, it is also a contract, a 'Thing semi-real'. To actualize the form, the reader must take it 'kindly', or according to the usage of *essential* humankind. Any suggestion of distinct and divisive purposiveness – 'particular', *interested*, or class-specific self-consciousness – is neutralized by the textual gesture toward, if not a communicative, then a shared existential and social circuit. Wordsworth's pleasure becomes *our* delight when we cast off our minute particulars and make ourselves him; thus, of course, do we also discover the *essential* being within our historical being.

The framing devices of Keats's poetry do not, like Wordsworth's preemptive techniques, usher us into the poem, they frame us out. Think of the 'Ode on a Grecian Urn'. The final, bracketed epigram – formally, a parody of Wordsworth's closing, intersubjective immediacies – puts the entire poem and all its apparently human and authorial anguish in aesthetic space: museum space, to be precise. The triumph of this ode is its transformation of poetry into scripture, sound into silence, relief (the Truth of fantasy) into Relief (an art of surfaces: Beauty). 'End-stopped feel' is as good a phrase as any to describe the alienating closure of Keats's poetry.[24]

Moreover, Keats's poems tend rather to distinguish than to identify narrator (or lyric 'I') and writer. Rarely do we hear his verse as the utterance of an unmediated human voice. Even in so magical, so historically *sincere* a poem as 'La Belle Dame', one must remember than an anonymous working brain is continuously engendering and overhearing the reciprocally exclusive languages of the balladeer and 'knight-at-arms', low and high languages that can only engage within the artificial space of a sentimental ballad.[25] Keats, like Wordsworth, teases us out of thought by making his method of representation his representational *object* in the sense of 'purpose'. The difference is that by fetishizing this purpose, Keats makes of it an 'object' in the material sense and a 'subject' in the philosophic sense. With these transformations, self-reflexiveness crystallizes as a mode of production with determinate social meanings and purposes, some of them having no immediacy for the reader, others possessed of the most threatening and, thus, rejected immediacy. Keats's double alienation, from the textual interior and from his audience, outlines the contradictions which make the work, contradictions invisibilized by subject-related writing and object-related sex. Keats's pleasure stands revealed as his work.

Again, consider the phenomenology of the Wordsworthian narration. The poet effortlessly reaps his memory of its rich and naturally integrated meanings. Indeed, by emphasizing both the strain of those lives which are often the originals of his mnemonic experience and the wise unconsciousness which fashions the inner verse, *and*, by arousing his readers to the challenge of their high and arduous calling, Wordsworth underscores the pure pleasure which is the poet's special gift: his character, even. The poet

> is a man speaking to men: a man, it is true, endued with more lively sensibility, more enthusiasm and tenderness, who has a greater knowledge of human nature, and a more comprehensive soul . . . a man pleased with his own passions and volitions, and who rejoices more than other men in the spirit of life that is in him; delighting to contemplate similar volitions and passions as manifested in the goings-on of the Universe, and habitually impelled to create them where he does not find them. (Preface to *Lyrical Ballads*, 1802)

By contrast, Keats's careful inventories of his overdecorated psychic interiors are at once pointless and busy, giving us something very like an inversion or parody of Wordsworth's wise passiveness. Keats's authorial exercise seems unrelated to the reader's imagined enjoyment, and to any of the more familiar forms of expressive gratification. The early readers, who recognized in Keats's ease a *display* of ease, experienced the verse as entirely dis-eased. Again, it is Byron who clarifies the social offensiveness of the Keatsian difference.

Here is the strange little fable Byron produced for the purpose of characterizing Keats's poetry.

> The *Edinburgh* praises Jack Keats or Ketch, or whatever his names are: why, his is the *Onanism* of Poetry – something like the pleasure an Italian fiddler extracted out of being suspended daily by a Street Walker in Drury Lane. This went on for some weeks: at last the Girl went to get a pint of Gin – met another, chatted too long, and Cornelli was *hanged outright before she returned*. Such like is the trash they praise, and such will be the end of the *outstretched* poesy of this miserable Self-polluter of the human mind. (Extract from letter to John Murray, 4 November 1820)

We recall that during the Regency, as before, 'Jack Ketch' was an appellation for the common hangman, and, that the name and character were strongly associated with the puppet-play of Punchinello (OED). With this double-dangling as his starting point, Byron goes on to explore, as it were, the social and sexual nuances of the resonance attaching to Keats's name. The fiction he unfolds describes a particularly laborious form of masturbation, *le coup de corde*, a trick that requires the technical assistance, here, of a prostitute. The 'Italian fiddler's' busy contrivance is emphasized by his partner's fecklessness, and the comedy of the story (literally, a 'hoist by one's own petard' narrative) involves the exposure of a work–pleasure ratio where we least expect to find it, at the center of an autoerotic activity. (The joke is perhaps more pointed yet; Byron involves a distinctly lower-class character in a perversion associated with aristocratic refinement, *ennui*, and unself-consciousness – dare we say, *hauteur*. Presumably, one's valet would not leave one hanging. Byron's aspiring fiddler is punished for his violation of *social*, not sexual proprieties.) Byron's '*outstretched*', a comment on the ambitiousness, elaboration and sexual tension of Keats's poetry, says it all. So does this extract from an 1820 review appearing in the *London Magazine and Monthly Critical and Dramatic Review*: 'he says nothing like other men, and appears always on the stretch for words to shew his thoughts are of a different texture from all other writers.' The reviewer recommends to the clever but overwrought lad, suffering from a sort of literary priapism, some country air, a change of diet, and an introduction to 'the *retreat* at York', a private madhouse.

What Byron is driving at is the contradiction which organizes both masturbation and the reproductive habits of the middle class. Below, I propose that the dream or the concept of masturbation is one of conscious unconsciousness: 'the feel of not to feel it', or, as in the Nightingale Ode, sensible numbness. (Here again, we detect a debased because reified version of that Wordsworthian paradigm, 'wise passiveness'.) Inasmuch as one is both worker and pleasurer, giver and receiver, subject and object in masturbation, the act should produce a rare psychic consolidation. However, both the technical groundplot (a part of the body is fetishized and overworked), and the absence of a distracting other to absorb the purposiveness of the activity and naturalize the techne, install with unusual force the divided psyche, which must know itself busy for luxury.

No one cared, of course, about Keats's exposure of the contradiction which informs masturbation. What did concern Wordsworth and Byron was the poetry's exposure of the relation between 'working brain' and the 'spontaneous overflow' or 'rattling on exactly as I talk' of Romantic poetry: that is, Keats's demystification of a prestigious idea of literary production. In the case of Wordsworth, we might call this method 'natural selection': a darkling deliberation effected by memory and emerging as a spontaneous, strictly processual value. Byron's worldliness, the counterpart to Wordsworth's naturalism, establishes authorial purpose within a psyche so profoundly socialized (so *inherited*, one might say), and *accomplishes* those purposes through audience reciprocities so exact, that calculation has no place to surface. Both protocols are commonplaces of Romantic criticism. Less obvious, perhaps, is the fact that while these myths of production negate what the poets conceived as the age's dominant *material* productive mode, the mechanical, they also *rehearse* a mode of social and ideological production.

In order to constitute its structural betweenness (a neither-nor, 'Nothing' state), an 'existence', the middle class had to expose the historicity of value, clearing the ground as it were for its own violation of inherited and naturalized values. At the same time, and so as to sanction this originality and safeguard its middling position, threatened on the lower front by imitation, and the upper by assimilation, the class in the middle had to represent its own, invented values as either ahistorical or as history's telos. The trick was to look valuably and essentially ambitious – history's coming class – and also eternal: a class dreamed by Adam, who awoke and found it real. One logical solution to this stylistic problem (we will see it in Keats) was the phenomenology of the *nunc stans*, or the look of an *eternally coming* class, in motion / in place forever. The display of ease, a contradiction in terms, was another device for converting nothingness into prolific tension. By its self-identification as a profitably consuming class, the bourgeoisie imitated the *ontologically* productive condition of the aristocracy. At the same time, the rhetorical orientation of this mimesis, as well as its fetishism (the effect of its semiotic interests), marked it as an ambitious gesture: literally, as *wanting*. The power of this mark, a negative originality, was, of course, its determined negativity. A class that is *self*-violating makes itself inviolable. That which has no center cannot be seized; what has no character cannot be defamed, and what is always and by definition moving is not easily removed.

I am describing a 'bad' solution to an ideological bind: on the one hand, the middle-class commitment to a program of social mobility (Keats's 'camelion poet': an ethic of becoming, or, less Romantically, a work ethic), and on the other, its longing for the authority connected with the generative passivity, stable identity, and 'quiet being' which was an influential fantasy of the leisure class. Keats, we shall see, motivates the contradiction in the style of the middle class but, because this was not 'naturally' *his* solution, and because it was, for him, greatly polyvalent, that style gets reified. Keats works at his pleasure and stations himself by that oxymoron. Wordsworth, as we saw, tends to suppress that conflictual figure which is no less the agency of his art than of Keats's. Wordsworth's genius is to operate a kind of double-standard. Even as he identifies poet (for him, *speaker*) with reader-listener as both essential men, he splits apart production and consumption into respectively passive and active moments. The poet easily overflows with his own pre(*consciously*) meditated verse. The reader, however, is forbidden the spontaneous, inward delight which is the poet's prerequisite and prerogative. Indeed, the reader cannot emulate that noble ease without degrading it and himself, becoming but a seeker after 'the pleasure of Frontiniac or sherry'.

Wordsworth's readers are instructed to *work* at their meanings, to 'find' tales in the things which the poet effortlessly makes available to them. By contrast, Keats's ambitiously masturbatory poetry correctly positions the work–pleasure contradiction in the act of production. Is it any wonder that Byron, a poet who reaped such profits by producing himself as an aristocrat for the delectation of the middle class, and Wordsworth, who did well enough by his 'habits of meditation', should have been so shaken by Keats?

To explore the virtues of Keats's bad stylistic solution, we move to a more abstract register. Oddly enough, this is the way we proceed to the most concrete textual place. Christopher Ricks's interest in the Keatsian pathology makes an excellent guide.

Ricks's Keats is a poet who abolishes his own and his readers' self-consciousness by a poetics of conscious discomfiture. Through its aurally and visually embarrassing representations, Keats's poetry induces in its readers a painful, but, since this is art, a contained self-consciousness. By *entertaining* what is, in its natural form, a consuming state of mind, the reader learns to surpass rather than suppress his embarrassment. This is what Ricks means by his accolade, taken from Keats: 'unmisgiving'. Keats constructs a canon so psychically capacious that it accommodates even self-consciousness, which it thereby deconstructs. To use the idiom of the theory from which Ricks's argument implicitly derives, the acting-out is also a working-through for both the poet and his reader.

By setting Ricks's psychological construct in social space, we find within his own argument the shadow of an answer to the question we have raised. Why did Keats's early readers find the poetry so precisely *mis*giving: solipsistic, fraudulent, falsifying, and perverse? Ricks studies Keats as a 'blushing' poet: a poet of adolescence and its special self-consciousness. We are reminded that blushing and genital engorgement, as by masturbation, are only nominally distinct processes. By reference to the social meanings we've teased from the early response to Keats's style, we associate one sort of self-consciousness (adolescent, sexual) with another: middle-class, social. Or, just as self-consciousness is the salient symptom of adolescence (signified by the blush and at once a cause and effect of masturbation), so does it signify the complex identity problems of a middle class in a middling stage, securing itself *and* its anxiety by its fetishistic possessive style. I'm suggesting that we draw an analogy between the marginal, insecure, or immature bourgeoisie of Keats's day and the modern state of adolescence. Both those middle classes are defined by memory (the longing for a childhood, working-class, 'gemein', or 'primitive' unself-consciousness: for example, Wordsworthian authenticity), and desire (a state beyond self-consciousness: Byron's adult, aristocratic coolness). Both, moreover, are *constituted* by that contradiction. In the accomplished bourgeois poet, this self-division translates into a 'high', philosophic self-consciousness, which is, we have seen, a good solution to two such identity problems (legitimacy / originality, pleasure / work). In Byron, the self-consciousness is also 'high', not in an intellectual sense but in a social register, where it signifies the political mastery that comes of self-possession. By the analogy, the 'low' self-consciousness of Keats's poetry – something like the awkwardness we feel in social situations – cannot be read as only the luckless effect of his ambitiousness, or as a reflection of ideal psychic processes. We must also construe this effect, the rhetorical form of a contradiction, as part of a project in its own right. Thus did Keats go about the business of making himself into that nonsense thing, the middle class.

Keats's poetry blushes more radically and purposively than Ricks suggests. It blushes at the level of style. This is a discourse which 'feeds upon' but does not assimilate its sources. It *engorges* – a transitive operation – in such a way as to make itself permanently, gesturally, *intransitively* engorged: 'stationed', in Keats's phrase. Keats's discursive procedures rehearse that protocol whereby the middle class of his day produced itself as a kind of collective, throbbing oxymoron: achieved by its ambitiousness, hardworking in its hedonism, a 'being' that defined itself strictly by its properties, or ways of having. In the style of Keats's poetry, we read the dream of masturbation: the fantasy of 'the perpetual cockstand', that solution to castration anxiety.[26] In both the dream and the anxiety, we, like Byron, discern the genetic code of the middle class.

Derrida has taught us that the supplemental or additive character of masturbation is also its substitutive character.[27] Derrida's word, '*le supplément*', describes that which adds its own difference and subtractiveness: masturbation, writing. Derrida's fabulously suggestive concept is more deeply antinomial than I've made it sound. I naturalize the idea slightly with an eye toward summarizing the practical charm of the supplement for Keats. In the readings to come, we shall recover the more irrational, more precisely functional dimension of Keats's substitutions.

Masturbation may be conceived as a fantasy of pleasure without the death of perfect gratification: or, meaning / value without the loss of reflexive consciousness *or* the object. The fantasized masturbatory experience is one of energy *and* luxury; giving and receiving; high (cerebral) and low (genital); infinite metamorphosis contemplated by a center of consciousness keen to enjoy that lability. Ideally, or in imagination, masturbation establishes a psychic wholeness which *knows itself* to be dialectically contingent. Thus is it also vitally, *capably in*complete.[28] The defensive virtue of masturbation, understood as a fantasy *of* (in place of / in addition to) proper sex, is its protection against the drive which, correctly enacted, must obliterate the consciousness which would *own* that pure pleasure, that death. 'Now more than ever seems it rich to die, / To cease upon the midnight with no pain . . . . Still wouldst thou sing, and I have ears in vain – / To thy high requiem become a sod.' Masturbation – the part for / in addition to the whole, the fantasy for / plus the actual, the oblique for / with the direct, the sign for / alongside the thing – is a holding action: a way of holding on to a holding off. The formula could be recast in temporal terms. Masturbation, that unnaturally hasty act, dreams of a 'slow time': a duration which neither wastes nor realizes, at once history's negation and its fulfillment. 'Deathwards progressing / To no death was that visage'. (Or, for a categorical association, 'purposiveness without purpose', Kant's definition of aesthetic experience.) Many of our fondest moments in Keats's poetry describe this condition: 'Their lips touched [touch'd] not, but had not bade adieu.' (The very time signature of 'To Autumn' is a code for this kind of *durée*; it is also the subject and object of this *undying* poem.) Many describe a fantasy wherein the sign (let us say, the Tradition: an empowering reproductive apparatus), and the thing (John Keats, an author-original) are simultaneous but distinct: a metonymic dream, or a fantasy of *being*, put under erasure by *having* and, thus, violated, idealized, effectuated, and *possessed*. Another way to frame this fantasy is as an instant(iation) wherein Beauty (the sign of legitimacy: the signifying possession) and Truth (the natural, unspeaking attribute) do not antithesize or succeed one another, neither do they coalesce.

They exist, rather, side by side: parallel, mutually delimiting total systems, value *and* 'existences', Symbolic *and* Imaginary zones. In class terms, a logical category, all these couplings describe a conjunction of *having*, a function of distance, difference, and loss, and *being*, the form of presence, identity, and plenitude. In class terms, a *social* category, this conjunction describes·a proprietary style and function. Nowhere is this coincidence so clearly and economically expressed as in Keats's typically ambiguous 'of' locutions, where the preposition is used both partitively (or genitively), and descriptively (for example, 'bride of quietness': belonging to quietness [having], and characterized by quietness [being]).

I have been describing a masturbation fantasy: the *concept* shadowed forth by Keats's strong practice. The special offensiveness of Keats's very early writing arises from its *incomplete* perverseness: its failure, thus, to realize that concept. (Byron's qualification, 'I don't mean he is *indecent* . . .', should be taken as part of the criticism; regarding the sexuality of Keats's writing, more *would* have been less.) The early poetry is bad in the commonplace colloquial sense: accidentally or passively imperfect. What vitiates it is the innocence of its self-consciousness, the intimacy of wish and word.

The poetry we call great is that which *signifies* – indeed, fetishizes – its alienation from its representational objects and subjects, and, thus, from its audience. This poetry is a discourse whose self-possession is a function of its profound structural *dis*possession; its pleasure is its knowledge of a 'wished away' / unavailable workaday world. 'Pleasant pain', 'a drowsy numbness pains / My sense', 'ditties of no tone', 'unheard' melodies. Each of these phrases, fetishized negations, captures the (il)logic of Keats's masturbatory exercise and of its social objective: a state of being at once 'first, and last, and midst, and without end' – a fair definition, that, of a state of nullity.

Finally, 'Lamia' evinces a badness that indicates a new scene of writing. Keats's bold plot in this last romance is to analyze materially and conceptually his own mode of literary production. The romance undoes itself even as it unfolds, and there is no interest in recuperating this deconstruction at another level. Neither are the contradictions motivated in the manner of the canonically central romances. 'Lamia' is the closest thing we have in the Romantic repertoire to a scientific poem.

To grasp these bad varieties, we must appreciate both the binding nature of Keats's social circumstances and the special opportunities he found in those binds. Even as we say this, we should remember what life, as opposed to proverbs, likes to teach us: that 'opportunities' are always part of the factual web, not breaks in that binding fabric. The virtues we make of necessity were there all the time, waiting to be released. Our virtuous inventions are necessity's best friend.

I'd like to sketch a critical opposition which, while it organizes much of our thinking about Keats, is not clearly developed in the scholarly literature. I use the names Ricks and Vendler to designate John Bayley and Christopher Ricks on the one hand, and Walter Jackson Bate, Douglas Bush, David Perkins, Helen Vendler, and Earl Wasserman on the other. Obviously, the scheme is a drastic reduction. What get dropped (Blackstone, Dickstein, Jones, Muir, Sperry) are those arguments which mediate Keats's sensuousness and seriousness, reinforcing Ricks's and Vendler's models at different moments and according to the interests and bias of the reader. I would also note that while the oppositional framework implies comparable influence, Ricks (the name names a very small body of commentary: one long essay and a book) is, in the practical academy, not nearly so powerful a bloc as Vendler.

Ricks's critique is a finer-tone repetition of Keats's poetry; Vendler's is a reification.[29] When I say 'repetition', I mean that Ricks, like Keats, situates vulgarity at the heart of the literary action, and also like the poetry (a question of manner: practical, disjunctive, antisystematic), Ricks converts the low vulgarity of factitiousness into the high vulgarity of strategy. But what is best about Ricks's work is its badness, or that which not only *escapes* the liberal, humanistic model of the book, but which is then cornered, framed, displayed. When we encounter in *Keats and Embarrassment* an unfortunate and rather nonsequitur quotation from Bob Dylan ('Her mouth was watery and wet'), a line offered as an illustration of some characteristically Keatsian usage, we sense a characteristically Ricksian usage. We feel, with some embarrassment, the presence of an actual writer, a manifold of interests and assumptions, some of which can be trained to perform critically, some of which cannot. This is not a distracting revelation. When we feel the life of a critic in his writing, then we feel again Keats's author-izing presence: not the figure of the capable poet but the whole, and sometimes incapable, and sometimes negatively capable man. Thus, while Ricks sublimes the social and ideological vulgarity of Keats's poetry, his writing is, like Bayley's, alive with betrayals, and these release us from an obsequiously 'end-stopped' consumption. Perhaps no one but men in Bayley's and Ricks's situations, professors at Oxford and, when he wrote about Keats, Cambridge, *could* so release us.

Vendler's critique, a most academic enterprise, leaves no rift unfilled. The canon figures in Vendler's discourse as at once means, manner and end of the critical representation, but where this writing differs from Keats's is in the systematic and abstract character of its appropriations and display. Everything is suave and seamless: end-stopped think. One is left admiring all that this scholarly body has 'got' (Chaucer, Boccaccio, Spenser, Shakespeare, Milton, Poussin, Greek, Latin, Provençal), and with what expertise, how disinterestedly, these properties are used. Vendler's is a virtuoso critique and the clear, humanistic doctrine it advances is perfectly consistent with that professionalism.

To set Ricks against Vendler (I do not think either critic would accept the opposition) is to focus in our scholarship some of the social issues with which Keats and his first readers struggled. I suspect that the position of today's American critic with respect to Keats's poetry is not unlike Keats's relation to the canon. That 'Swiss perfection' (the phrase is Stevens's) which characterizes Vendler's critical labor is, as it were, a parody of Keats's stylistic *nunc stans*. One feels in this critical ideal the eternal return Kermode so crisply articulated in the figure of clock-closure: unending alternation between tick and tock. It is to this sort of posthumous existence, this sort of myth that we reduce ourselves *and* Keats when we subtract from the poetry its own, liberating self-consciousness. The concrete analogue to our stuck criticism is the deadly arrest we feel in 'To Autumn', probably the only one of Keats's poems where the self-consciousness – the class and personality line – gets overwritten. We want to approximate the style of Bayley and Ricks: to become easy enough with our subject to forget ourselves and, more important, to have the bad taste to *represent* that lapse.

Barbara Everett, reviewing *The Odes of John Keats*, sharply observes 'the difficulties Vendler gets into throughout her book in her treatment of the historical'.[30] Everett explains that Vendler's 'reverence for the poet', which motivated her to 'rewrite his life as a story of consciousness triumphant', effectively deadens the poetry and the life. As the corrective to Vendler's hagiography, Everett introduces 'the haphazard', that which was so telling a fact in Keats's life and so compositionally invasive. I have suggested, and will demonstrate textually, that attention to contingency (those 'Clouds continually gathering' and suddenly, absurdly bursting) will only realize Keats's poetry in the way Everett envisions if we stand far enough back to perceive the historical front, a weather necessity, which those clouds both constitute and signify. From Keats's point of view, of course, life was a matter of isolated storms; he survived those upsets by inventing a distinctive and functional style. That style, separated from the conditions which determined it, assumes the look of the purely aesthetic, like those wind-sculpted trees on the California coast. A critical knowledge of the early response to Keats's poetry brings those conditions to our attention, and by clarifying our lucky remove from the canon, it enables the sort of total understanding Keats could not produce. By reading Keats in this way, and by reading our own critical configurations through the instance of Keats's poetry, we cannot but illuminate 'the social production of texts as Literary and . . . the effects which thus accrue to them in the light of the position which they occupy in relation to other texts and the uses to which they are put within the social process'.[31] We might also, by this inside-out, absorbed-alienated, Anglo-American reading of Keats's style, come to appreciate the uses which his poetry *puts* in process.

Procedure

Two facts, both of them requiring some explanation, will become obvious to the reader of this book. First, I provide no sustained discussion of any of Keats's odes. This omission was not conceived as a political or even a critical decision. (It is, of course, both.) I wrote about poems that I'd found awkward to teach. Like most readers, I had luxuriated in the language of 'St. Agnes', conjured with the marked allusiveness of the text, and framed the poem by a number of allegorical systems. Always, however, there remained a felt abyss between discourse and meaning: always a clear impression of violence perpetrated upon that still unravished bride. Because the critical effort seemed at once overpowering and ineffectual, the pedagogical task felt distinctly guilty.

What attracted me, then, to the romances treated here was their peculiar transparency, a quality that renders them strangely opaque.[32] Because there seem to be no real 'meaning' questions to ask of a poem such as 'St. Agnes', everything about the poem becomes questionable at the deepest level. This kind or impression of intentionality puts us outside the pale of both history and form, as these ideas have developed in the practice of Romantic scholarship. The very norms for critical production become part – but not, typically, a privileged part – of the textual problem. (We're not dealing with meta-poetry.) Whereas there's always a tendency to overread the odes – a tendency that is textually and semantically rewarded – the reader of the romances finds very little to say that isn't descriptive or metaphysical. Neither of those discourses comes close to locating the *point* of these very vexed pleasure-poems. Some might argue that since the odes are, in the largest sense, *about* those vexations (pleasure–pain, sensation–knowledge, art–life, beauty–truth), they represent the ideal critical counterpoint to the romances. We can see, however, that the odes, which *thematize* those polarities rather than enact them, cannot easily work as a critical instrument, one that might move us beyond the margins of aesthetic (formalist) and philosophic (thematic) understanding. The working contradictions of the odes, framed (arrested) at the level of form and idea, do not expand into their full antinomial expression, and it is only at this extremity that those social facts, images, and projects I've been sketching materialize. Because this social and material dimension is where we must always seek the answer to that first and final question – why did *Keats* write Keats's poetry – the romances constitute a privileged body of texts. In these works, we find a sort of categorical imperative for the production of literary experience, our own and Keats's.

It may be said, with some justice, that I jettison the odes in order to construct the perverse Keats who figures in this book. In defense, let me say first that this setting-aside looks so dramatic because of the massive foregrounding undergone by the odes in this century; and second, that my exclusion of the odes represents an attempt to ease that imbalance. The early critical commentary is, by and large, less occupied by the odes than the romances. When the odes *were* discussed, they were largely approved, whereas with the exception of 'Hyperion' (which is decidedly *epic* romance anyhow), the romances tended to prove both problematic and authorially 'typical'. So, if I unfairly scuttle one portion of the canon, I do so not just by way of reclaiming another, but also to reproduce – parodically, to be sure – the tone of the early reception.

The question of the odes must also be the question of Helen Vendler. It is easy to find Vendler's formalism politically disturbing and, at this late date, intellectually meagre. The more interesting task is to locate the special virtue of her masterfully totalizing exercise. *The Odes of John Keats* releases a multitude of meanings from the works studied and their literary field of operation, meanings that we may consider by way of raw material, to be positioned in and worked upon by the many other fields that do not interest the author. Vendler gives us something to read, and more important, something to read against. Indeed, her book is so firm in its persuasions, so pure and exhaustive in its execution of them – so heavenly, in short – that it practically writes its own Bible of Hell. For these reasons, I did not feel compelled to discuss Keats's odes.

Finally, I came up against an astonishing fact while writing this book. Our criticism has almost nothing to say about *Romantic* romance. The historical meaning of the form – both its causes and purposes, and the levels of real dynamics binding those dimensions – is nowhere addressed in a sustained fashion. What Jameson does with the 'magical romance' of middle and late nineteenth-century French fiction needs doing for early nineteenth-century English poetry.[33] It was not, obviously, my aim in this book to write that critique. But by attending exclusively to Keats's romances, and to the multiple realities of their linguistic fictions, I have hoped to situate the romantic practice of Keats's contemporaries in a differently conceived generic field.

One does not talk about authors these days without bowing to the irony of the times. The basic method of this book might be described as post-structuralist; its governing ideology, historical-materialist. What, then, *is* this 'John Keats' – 'the Creature has a purpose and his eyes are bright with it' – of whom I speak as a meaningful origin? It will be noted that in this book, the meaningfulness of Keats's purposes and of the acts that embody them develops only and always in the field of social facts and meanings. In other words, the psyche that motivates my John Keats is a dynamic reflection of social configurations. The 'dynamic' aspect is, to an extent which is rather de-emphasized here, *unique*; to some extent, also unaccented, *ahistorical*; and by and large, a finer-tone repetition of the very forces Keats was resisting. This becomes clear in the final section of this book, where 'Lamia' is discussed.

Second, this critique is, like Vendler's, a totalizing study. Elsewhere I have elaborated my version of Sartre's progressive–regressive method, a method employed in my fashion in this book and based on the belief that 'the concrete is concrete because it is a synthesis of many particular determinants.'[34] Basically, my Keats is a reconstruction of the problem (and from that, a problematic) from the style of the solution. Keats, as developed by this book, is the system of wishes and resistances that had to exist in order to explain a poetry of this kind. The formalism of the method is opposed throughout by the highly material investigation of isolated discursive forms, as by the constant attempt to relate those forms to what were once called 'extrinsic' orders of determination.

Historicist readers will judge this an ahistorical book. My failure to attend not just to the larger poetic canon but to the letters, as to the everyday of Keats's life and that of his circle, will betray to these readers the modernity of the exercise. This is a just observation. A criticism like this could not have been conceived until late in this century and I do not regret that fact. Indeed, whatever truth gets produced by this study will emerge from its belatedness. What is lost in one kind of immediacy (knowledge), is gained in another (meaning). I like to think that a more comprehensive book on Keats would not necessarily have been a better one, and, if the continuity compromised the interpretive model, it would have been worse. What I've attempted is to amplify the silenced voices in Keats's poetry and in the response to that poetry, voices whose tone we catch in the conflict between the material language of the *text*, which cannot *but* speak the truth, and the *poem* – the total form – which can't and won't. (The *work*, we could say, is the compromise between text and poem.) The investigation of this conflict which is only *conceived* through a late and totalizing hermeneutic must be conducted in the most scrupulously local and disjunctive fashion. From the results of these pinpoint investigations, one builds the model of a problem that is nowhere (not in Keats's writing, not in nineteenth-century documents and histories, not in twentieth-century historiography), defined systematically because our intervention is part of its being.

Canons *are* things but they are also ways of reading and arranging things. Not to read in the manner of this book – 'sideways', piecemeal, and as Blake says, *through* the eyes – is, for the student of Keats, to read canonically. And that is a mode of meaning-production which definitely suppresses those text–poem conflicts I spoke of: a suppression, this, of the literary work.

But these things do not really need arguing today. What does is the fact that throughout long sections of this book, one finds very few references to politics and social life in their topical behaviors, so to speak. I am less than zealous in refiguring the immediate rhetorical situation of Keats's poetry because I do not believe Keats *had* such a situation. This is a dangerous statement for any kind of materialist critic to make, and I'd like to take some time to explain it.

Above, I called attention to the transparency of Keats's romances. By observing the transparency of Wordsworth's and Byron's poetry, we produce a resemblance–difference model that should illuminate my inattention to the occasional matter of Keats's poetry. Somewhere in chapter 5, I designate Wordsworth – the discursive origin constructed by his writing – the age's healthy authorial subject: as it were, the subjective mean. No one could describe Byron's persona as 'healthy', but we must all feel in his unparalleled niceness of address the innocence with which he bears his psyche. The tonal perfection of both poets' verse – Wordsworth in the private mode, Byron in the public – is a function of their assimilation of, by, and to the age's dominant structures of feeling: the ideological subject-forms underlying its diverse political positions. Both poets owe the marvellous structure, differentiation, and dialecticity of their writing to their primary, *constitutive* internalization of much that is consciously positioned by them and us as 'outside'.[35] One might even relate that very accomplished dialecticity to the fact that for both poets, the immediate social dimension of that most primal of dialectics, self / other, was historically resolved for them before they sat down to write. Because their poetry is so easily and deeply dialogic, its intonation is barely audible: its style, we might say, hardly perceptible. This is indeed a poetry written to be 'overheard'. It has nothing to conceal: no designs upon its audience that are not at the same time designs upon itself. (Perhaps this is what we have always meant by the 'self-reflexiveness' of Romantic poetry.) Moreover, its whole history of readers is already included in the conversation. We must work very hard to recover the intonation of this verse, to reconstruct the determinate purpose in its amorphous 'purposiveness', to set aside this gift of inclusion, of innocence. We must *make* ourselves hypocrite readers of poems that assure us of our excellent faith.

Jerry McGann has said much the same thing and more elegantly, as usual. 'When we say that Byron's is a highly rhetorical poetry we mean . . . not that it is loud or overblown, but that it is always, at whatever register, elaborating reciprocities with its audiences.'[36] To accept McGann's distinction is also to realize that Wordsworth's greatly sincere and spontaneous discourse makes of these reciprocities and their elaboration its means, manner, and end. Surprisingly, Wordsworth's poetry is not just *as* rhetorical as Byron's, but in some ways more so.

I have already talked about the special and disturbing self-reflexiveness of Keats's poetry, one that brings out the difference between the subject and its internalized models, not their identity. To 'overhear' Keats's poetry is to hear nothing *but* intonation, to feel nothing but style and its meaningfulness. The effect is explained, of course, by the problematic nature of Keats's subjectivity, which we would call 'authorial' if Keats had had any other kind, and if that were not exactly his problem. Throughout this book, I try to show the terribly *dynamic* character of Keats's inner representations of those particular 'outsides' we call 'audience': both 'the public' (an idea of the present), and the People, philosophically characterized (the Tradition, a past and future thing). To read Wordsworth or Byron is to feel that the style is accessory to the subject or content of the writing. To read Keats is to focus the 'aboutness' of the verse as the vehicle for a stylistic design.

This impression of interestedness is just what we usually mean when we say that a poem is 'rhetorical'. Yet with Keats we are treating of something we can't really call rhetoric at all. While his poetry 'elaborates reciprocities at all registers', the elaboration is definitely laborious: more in the way of primary production than reflection. Moreover, where the textual labor does develop reciprocities already in place, these are not, typically, *audience* reciprocities – not, that is, engagements with institutionally mediated forms – but reciprocities with the structures and relations of production. If we are willing to give up the security of the graduated exegesis – an inductive or deductive advance from level to level until such time as the text–

context distinction, which one had dissolved, reappears – we may begin to feel the shocking directness of Keats's engagement with the profoundest orders of determination. That Keats was an anomalous subject is the subject of this book; it does *not* follow that our articulation of this subject must therefore proceed irregularly. But, in that we have so deeply and for so long identified with Keats – so taken his subject-form for our own – it would seem that we can only start seeing him *clearly in the idea of him* by an act of self-estrangement. We must try to make ourselves anomalous subjects – 'bad' critics – in order to read Keats properly, even while remembering that this metamorphosis is also an effect of such a reading.

Rhetoric

This book was commissioned as part of a series designed for undergraduate and graduate students and for the general literary public. It quickly became clear to me, as to my editor, that I was writing not just for a professional audience but for a period-bound one, Romanticists.

Unfortunately, this is also the group most likely to be offended by the method and the findings of the book. The doctrinal insults are obvious and need no explaining. As for method, I shall say by way of extenuation that reading Keats against the grain is not so easy as the comparable reading of Wordsworth or Shelley. There, without too much trouble and with the help of several generations of strongminded criticism, we can at least *find* the grain. The critical corrosive for the Wordsworth copperplate is derived from the history that is accessible to us through historiography and primary documents and that is clearly designated *by* Wordsworth's code as its key. The acid for Shelley and Byron comes from social and cultural reconstruction of a fairly concrete and immediate kind. To inquire into the various audiences Byron intended for his 'Fare Thee Well', to investigate the political resonance of the Prometheus myth in the Enlightenment and early nineteenth century, to research the concept and the prospect presented by Tintern, the town and Abbey, in 1798, and to underline the neoclassical iconography and diction of a central Romantic ode, is to go far toward explaining the transparency of Byron's lyric, Shelley's poetic drama, and Wordsworth's two sublime meditations.[37] Because

Keats's social relations were so much more primitive than that of the other Romantics, one learns very little through inquiries into mimetic manners and objects (present, distorted, or unaccounted for), and not too much from research into reception, actual and anticipated. With Keats, we cannot say with any confidence where the poetry draws *its* line between inside and outside, discourse and life. That line is one of the things Benjamin means by 'the grain'. We recall the infinite anteriority and also exteriority of Keats's little dream, the multiply framed 'picture of somebody reading', and we see that any kind of 'antithetical' approach to this nonthetic poetry must be reductive, which is alright, and also textually disengaged, which isn't. (Of course, this complete resistance to binary critique is also the great gift of Keats's poetry. It does not allow us the luxury of imagining ourselves to be good readers *and* good critics at the same time.) With Keats, the fire that refines must be kindled not just within the poetry but at the level of its style: its total apparatus for realizing and derealizing its several worlds. Only a reader familiar with Keats's poetry, with Keats criticism, and with those works of contemporary and of nineteenth-century theory that are always teaching us to hear toneless ditties and to see viewless things will, I'm afraid, kindle to this flame.

Notes

1 Alan Bewell's essay 'The Political Implication of Keats's Classicist Aesthetics' (*Studies in Romanticism*, 25, Summer 1986, pp. 220–9) represents the beginning of a departure from the critical norm for Keats studies. Bewell's sensitivity to the special political discourse of the writer situated by the *polis* on its *under*side or *between* its categorical positions, intimates a criticism beyond the margins of formalist, thematic, biographical, and metaphysical inquiry as these have developed in Romanticist scholarship over the past thirty years, *and also*, beyond the 'new historicism'. This last observation is part of an argument about the new historicism in Romantic studies (see Levinson, 'The New Historicism: What's in a Name', in *Critical Readings of Romantic History: Four Literary Essays*, ed. Levinson, forthcoming Blackwell's, 1988).
2 Walter Jackson Bate, *John Keats* (Cambridge, Mass.: Harvard Univ. Press, 1963); John Bayley, 'Keats and Reality', *Proceedings of the British Academy*, 1962, pp. 91–125; Douglas Bush, *John Keats* (New York: 1966); David Perkins, *The Quest for Permanence* (Cambridge, Mass.: Harvard Univ. Press, 1959); Christopher Ricks, *Keats and Embarrassment* (Oxford: Clarendon Press, 1974); Lionel Trilling, 'The

Fate of Pleasure' in *Beyond Culture* (London: Secker and Warburg, 1955); Helen Vendler, *The Odes of John Keats* (Cambridge, Mass.: Harvard Univ. Press, 1983); Earl Wasserman, *The Finer Tone* (Baltimore, Md: Johns Hopkins Univ. Press, 1953).

3 John Bayley shrewdly divines that Keats's badness *is* his goodness. Had Bayley pushed his *aperçu* a little further, he would have come up against the meanings shadowed forth by the contemporary criticism. He would, perhaps, have associated the vulgarity of Keats's poetry with the situation, activities, and interests of the burgeoning middle class. As it is, Bayley's interpretative construct neatly registers this association by negation. 'Das Gemeine' – a postulate of healthy, earthy, Elizabethan (that is, sociologically and psychically nonstratified) consciousness – is the mirror image of the nineteenth-century Keats, or of a poetry experienced as sick, pretentious, horribly contemporary, and thoroughly mannered. To the early readers, Keats's poetry was the expression of a 'folk' degraded by a bad eminence: the petty bourgeoisie.

4 All excerpts from contemporary notices are drawn from Donald Reiman, *The Romantics Reviewed: Contemporary Reviews of British Romantic Writers* (New York: Garland Publishing, 1972), C, I, 91–3; C, I, 95; C, I, 330–3; C, I, 339; C, I, 344–5; C, I, 385; C, I, 423–4; C, II, 470; C, II, 479; C, II, 531; C, II, 587–90; C, II, 614; C, II, 768–9; C, II, 807–8; C, II, 824–5; C, II, 829–30; and from G. M. Matthews, ed., *Keats, The Critical Heritage* (London: Routledge and Kegan Paul, 1971), pp. 35, 129–31, 150, 208–10, 248, 251. Censored Byron material checked against Leslie Marchand, *Byron's Letters and Journals*, vol. 7, 1820 (Cambridge, Mass.: Belknap Press, 1977), p. 217 (from letter to John Murray, 4 November 1820; Matthews lists it as 4 September).

5 The association of masturbation with the individualism and materialism of the early middle class is something of an established literary theme. Swift's Master Bates, the physician to whom Gulliver is apprenticed, teaches his student more than a middle-class trade, he teaches him the principles of acquisition and display (in Gulliver's case, anthropological), which constitute the middle class an *ideological* phenomenon over and above its economic being.

6 The much-quoted phrase 'poignantly allegorical life' is Bate's allusion to Keats's own observation that Shakespeare led 'a life of Allegory' (*Letters of John Keats*, ed. Robert Gittings, Oxford: Oxford Univ. Press, 1970; 1979, p. 218).

7 'Unmisgiving' is Ricks's class term, taken from Keats, for the social, psychic, and rhetorical generosity of the poetry.

8 Fredric Jameson, *Sartre: The Origins of a Style* (New York: Columbia Univ. Press, 1961; 1984), p. vii.

In the course of my current research, I've discovered two books, both marvels of textual and theoretical exposition, that coincide closely with my reading of Keats's strategic defenses against, as well as his longing for, social and canonical majority. I refer to Louis Renza's *'A White Heron' and the Question of Minor Literature* (Madison, Wisc.: Univ. of Wisconsin Press, 1984), pp. 11–19; and David Lloyd's *Nationalism and Minor Literature: James Clarence Mangan and the Emergence of Irish Cultural Nationalism* (Berkeley, Calif.: Univ. of California Press, 1987), pp. 19–26. I thank Renza for refreshing my memory of Leslie Brisman's

Romantic Origins (Ithaca: Cornell Univ. Press, 1978): specifically, Brisman's derivation of George Darley's originality from his 'posture of weakness'.

9 Aileen Ward, *John Keats, the Making of a Poet* (New York: Viking, 1963); W. J. Bate, *John Keats*, R. Gittings, *John Keats* (London: Heinemann, 1968). All source information from Claude Finney, *The Evolution of Keats' Poetry*, 2 vols. (New York: Russell & Russell, 1963); George Ridley, *Keats's Craftsmanship* (Oxford: Clarendon Press, 1933); Ian Jack, *Keats and the Mirror of Art* (Oxford: Clarendon Press, 1967); Miriam Allott, *The Poems of John Keats* (London and New York: Longman and Norton, 1970; 1972).

10 See Georg Lukács, *History and Class Consciousness*, trans. R. Livingstone (Cambridge, Mass.: MIT Press, 1971), pp. 164–72. See also Fredric Jameson, *Marxism and Form, Twentieth-Century Dialectical Theories of Literature* (Princeton, NJ: Princeton Univ. Press, 1971), on the worker's negative privilege: the lack of that leisure needed to 'intuit [the outside world] in the middle-class sense'. By the adjective 'middle-class' Jameson means the static and contemplative immediacy required by industrial capitalism's productive structures and relations.

11 Apropos Keats's medical training, see n. 22, ch. 6.

12 Marjorie Levinson, *The Romantic Fragment Poem* (Chapel Hill, NC: Univ. of North Carolina Press, 1986), pp. 41–3, 239–40.

13 Quoted in Theodor Adorno, *Prisms*, trans. Weber and Weber (Cambridge, Mass.: MIT Press, 1967; 1983). The essay from which that quotation derives, 'Valery Proust Museum', deeply informs my discussion.

14 Finney, *The Evolution of Keats' Poetry*, vol. 1, p. 126: 'When, with infinite toil, they had climbed up the greater part of that steep ascent, Balboa commanded his men to halt, and advanced alone to the summit, that he might be the first who should enjoy a spectacle which he had so long desired'. From Robertson's *History of America*.

15 In his notes on Milton, Keats comments on 'what may be called his stationing or statuary. He is not content with simple description, he must station . . .', quoted in Jack, *Keats and the Mirror of Art*, p. 142.

16 To the extent that the inner voices in Keats's poetry tend to be maintained as signs, and also as signs of otherness, the 'we' experience central to Vološinov's dialogic analysis is missing. Keats's dialogism conforms more to the Bakhtinian model.

17 Allusions to the indeterminacy of Keats's gender (for example, 'Mankin', 'effeminate', 'boyish') should be taken as responses to Keats's mode of literary production or to the androgyny thereby implied. Keats's discourse 'mans' itself by a self-consciously autotelic receptivity, at once 'unmanning' the Tradition and, paradoxically, feminizing itself as well. Indeed, we might illuminate some of the more mysterious female figures in Keats's poetry by identifying them with the code or languages at once feared and desired by Keats: a phallic order. Aileen Ward's compelling defense of Fanny Brawne – her insistence that Keats loved Fanny precisely for the unpoetical distinctness of her character – is not contradicted by Keats's fascination with women like Isabella Jones: protean women who seemed, in addition, capable of transforming others, and, by liberating them from themselves, freeing them from their self-consciousness as

well. Keats could love Fanny; he could *use* the Isabella Joneses of his life. What I'm suggesting is a loose association in Keats's poetry binding the phallic fetish-woman and the social code which Keats sought indirectly and defensively to embrace.

18 Jerome McGann, 'Keats and the Historical Method in Literary Criticism', *MLN*, 94 (1979), pp. 988–1032. McGann's discussion of the textual history of 'La Belle Dame' and of the Paolo and Francesca sonnet is an invaluable lesson in the ideological uses of textual scholarship.

19 See Tristram Engelhardt, Jr, 'The Disease of Masturbation: Values and the Concept of Disease', in *Bulletin of the History of Medicine*, 48 (1974), pp. 234–48; Engelhardt, 'Ideology and Etiology', *Journal of Medicine and Philosophy*, I (1976), pp. 256–68; Michel Foucault, *The History of Sexuality, An Introduction*, vol. 1, trans. R. Hurley (New York: Random House, 1978).

Louis Crompton's fine study, *Byron and Greek Love* (Berkeley: Univ. of California Press, 1985), has opened our eyes to the homophobia of the early nineteenth century. The special ignominy I confer upon 'the masturbator' is not meant to contest or in any way qualify Crompton's representation. I am only elaborating the lesson we first learned from the Romantics. Namely, that Satan is always God's product, structural complement, and support system; that which *threatens* divinity because it reveals the *machina* in the *deus* is either not named, or it is named as a nonphenomenon. Not evil, but monstrous.

20 'Pretty' implies an imitation of 'nice', in the sense of 'exact' or 'appropriate'. 'Pretty' misses the mark, however, erring on the side of deficiency or excess, precisely because it imitates a fetishized Idea of the middle. Hence, perhaps, the adverbial usage: for example, 'pretty good', 'pretty warm'.

Apropos what Shelley called Keats's 'false taste' – its resonance for Wordsworth – here is Hunt's synopsis of Wordsworth's famous Preface (from Notes on *The Feast of the Poets*, 1814): 'the taste of society has become so vitiated and so accustomed to gross stimulants . . . as to require the counteraction of some simpler and more primitive food, which should restore to readers their true tone of enjoyment, and enable them to relish once more the beauties of simplicity and nature' (pp. 90, 91).

21 Wordsworth's critique of Macpherson runs along the same lines (see Essay, Supplementary to the Preface, 1815). Wordsworth does not attack Macpherson's hoax *per se*; in the Essay, he is careful to indicate his awareness of the doubtful authenticity of Percy's *Reliques*, and also his great admiration for that anthology. What he condemns in the Fingal collection is its fraudulent expressiveness. Macpherson's failure to feel his subject, and thus to communicate in a quick and quickening manner, is for Wordsworth the intolerable flaw.

22 The poetry's lack of intrinsic reference, its deep insincerity, was its great and largely unmet generic challenge.

> But when the . . . arts have reached the period of more refined cultivation, they cease
> to be considered as means through which to convey to other minds the energies of
> thought and feeling: the productions of art become themselves the ultimate objects of
> imitation, and the mind is acted upon by them instead of acting through them from

itself ... [W]hen imitative skill has brought an art the nearest to perfection, it is then that its cultivation is the least allied to mind: its original purpose, as a mode of expression, becomes wholly lost in the artificial object, – the display of a skill. (Josiah Conder, *Eclectic Review*, September 1817)

On one level, this criticism marks out the difference between a classically mimetic and a Romantic-expressive mode. But this difference was, by 1817, a familiar one, and it seems not to trouble the writer unduly. The damaging fact of Keats's poetry was its expressive falseness. Where Wordsworth, for instance, offers himself *in propria persona*, Keats was felt to provide a tissue of received, heterogeneous, and often conflicting manners. That this was the source of the generic confusion is something Keats seems to have guessed. One feels in his penetrating characterization of Wordsworth's mode, 'the egotistical sublime', an implicit reading of his own style, the egotistical bathetic. Or, where ego should be, there is alienated, interested reproduction.

23 This discussion is informed throughout by Jean Baudrillard, *For a Critique of the Political Economy of the Sign*, trans. C. Levin (St Louis: Telos Press, 1981); *The Mirror of Production*, trans. M. Poster (St Louis: Telos Press, 1975); and *Simulations*, trans. Foss, Patton, and Beitchman (New York: Semiotext(e), 1983).

24 John Jones, *John Keats's Dream of Truth* (New York: Barnes and Noble, 1969), p. 111. For the context of my phrase 'museum space' see Philip Fisher, 'A Museum with One Work Inside: Keats and the Finality of Art', *Keats–Shelley Journal*, 33 (1984), pp. 85–102.

25 Aileen Ward writes of 'La Belle Dame', 'One hesitates to press this poem for any meaning beyond itself, for it is poetry of a kind that, as Keats said of his favourite passage in Shakespeare, "One's very breath while leaning over these pages is held for fear of blowing these lines away"'. (*The Making of a Poet*, p. 273).

26 Steven Marcus, *The Other Victorians* (New York: Basic Books, 1964; 1974). My understanding of the early response to Keats's poetry, and my argument for the complex purposes of that poetry, began with a reading of Marcus's extraordinary book.

27 Jacques Derrida, *Of Grammatology*, trans. G. Spivak (Baltimore, Md: Johns Hopkins Univ. Press, 1974; 1976), p. 155 and *passim*, and pp. 141–64; *Dissemination*, trans. B. Johnson (Chicago: Univ. of Chicago Press, 1981), pp. 75–171.

28 To recast the model in a familiar philosophic idiom, one may conceive the dream or the concept of masturbation along the lines of self-enriching alienation.

29 Jerome McGann, *The Romantic Ideology* (Chicago: Univ. of Chicago Press, 1983), see the discussion of Coleridge and Hegel, Part I.

30 Barbara Everett, 'Somebody Reading', a review of Helen Vendler's *The Odes of John Keats, London Review of Books* (6), 11 (1984).

31 Tony Bennett, *Formalism and Marxism* (London: Methuen, 1979), p. 174.

32 My omission of *Endymion* is explained by my interest in narrational procedures, as opposed to narrative structures. The shorter, less coherent or 'bound' narratives of *Endymion*'s compositional period afford better access to that material.

33 Fredric Jameson, *The Political Unconscious* (Ithaca: Cornell Univ. Press, 1981), pp. 103–50. Patricia Parker's *Inescapable Romance, Studies in the Poetics of a Mode* (Princeton; NJ: Princeton Univ. Press, 1979), makes available some of the formal materials we would need for the historical critique I've proposed.

34 Marx, quoted in Lukács, *History and Class Consciousness*, p. 9. A fuller quotation of Lukács's own interpretation of Marx's conclusion is in order:

> As the products of historical evolution, [the facts] are involved in continuous change. But in addition they are also *precisely in their objective structure the products of a definite historical epoch, namely capitalism.* Thus when science maintains that the manner in which data immediately present themselves is an adequate foundation of scientific conceptualisation and that the actual form of these data is the appropriate starting point for the formation of scientific concepts, it thereby takes its stand simply and dogmatically on the basis of capitalist society. It uncritically accepts the nature of the object as it is given and the laws of that society as the unalterable foundation of science . . . Thus we must detach the phenomena from the form in which they are immediately given and discover the intervening links which connect them to their core . . . [thus] we shall arrive at an understanding of their apparent form and see it as the form in which the inner core necessarily appears. It is necessary because of the historical character of the facts . . . This twofold character, the simultaneous recognition and transcendence of immediate appearances is precisely the dialectical nexus. (pp. 7, 8)

Here is my version of Sartre's progressive–regressive method (see *Search for a Method*, trans. H. Barnes (New York: Random House, 1963; 1968), part 3, especially pp. 133–66. One begins with an extensive (that is, 'progressive') move. One reads out from the formally disturbing textual feature – an isolated and, it would appear, unmotivated contradiction – toward a determining contextual domain which is at this point a received and abstract order. In this phase, one 'give[s] to each [discursive] event, in addition to its particular signification, the role of being revealing' (*Search for a Method*, p. 26). By this allegorical analysis, one articulates a *positionally* objective ensemble subtending the particular discursive case. By these abstractive procedures, the work begins to assume a more situated and concrete aspect. One now reorganizes the work in the mode of 'structural difference and determinate contradiction' (Jameson, *The Political Unconscious*, p. 56). In this 'regressive' stage, what had appeared as an isolated deviation from the textual logic operates as the governing principle of the subtextual thought. By conceiving the surface–depth discrepancy as a compromise formation, we reconstruct in the form of a social problem the conditions that had to obtain for this 'solution' to take shape. Specifically, we are interested in the 'lacks and "oversignifications"', which seem to define this solution (*Search for a Method*, p. 26). We show that what is Keats's is also and specifically *not* Keats's: indeed, anti-Keats. By bringing out that within his language which is dynamically opposed to the interests *he* would pursue, the negations *he* would accomplish, we also reveal that what is *not* his – not represented as such – is also his. Thus, even as we deconstruct his projection, we enrich it by the discourses that work alongside, within, and across it. By comparing the work's private logic to that social logic which overdetermines the work's presented relations, we derive a model of internal–external, individual–social dynamics for the period (or subset thereof) in question. We use this model to reinterpret that objective ensemble installed uncritically at the outset of the critique. (See Lukács, *The Ontology of Social Being, 2: Marx*, trans. D. Fernbach [London: Merlin, 1978], pp. 27–31.

The method *is* circular. The individual element – an illusory concrete particular – is raised to the level of general, conceptual and social signification. That dimension is in turn realized – interrogated – by the element it has engendered in the mode of difference, distance, and deformation. In short, and as my rhetoric must have suggested, this two-stage exercise (progressive–regressive, reconstructive–deconstructive) is a dialectically totalizing critique.

35 V. N. Vološinov, *Marxism and the Philosophy of Language*, trans. M. Matejka and I. R. Titunik (New York: Seminar Press, 1973), pp. 83–106, especially p. 89.

36 Jerome McGann, 'Byron and the Truth in Masquerade', public lecture, University of Pennsylvania, 1986.

37 McGann, ibid.; Stuart Curran, 'The Political Prometheus', *Studies in Romanticism* (25), 3 (1986), pp. 429–55; Levinson, *Wordsworth's Great Period Poems* (Cambridge: Cambridge Univ. Press, 1986), pp. 14–57, 80–100.

2

'La Belle Dame Sans Merci'

Hegel remarks somewhere that all facts and personages of great importance in world history occur, as it were, twice. He forgot to add: the first time as tragedy, the second as farce.

Karl Marx, *The Eighteenth Brumaire*

Treason doth never prosper, what's the reason?
For if it prosper, none dare call it Treason.

Sir John Harington, *Of Treason (Epigrams)*

Throughout his book, Steven Marcus highlights his period-piece portrait of the masturbator with excerpts from Romantic poems. While the figure of the masturbator only achieves its full mythic dimensions in the pornography and medical literature of the Victorian period, Marcus's literary associations develop a kind of preliminary sketch. Nowhere does the outline emerge so plainly as in Marcus's allusions to Keats; and nowhere does the Romantic canon provide so concentrated a symptomatology as in Keats's representation of the knight, hero of 'La Belle Dame Sans Merci'.[1] Simultaneously pallid and blushing, moist and feverish, anxious and languid, occupied and vacant, 'here' (l. 43) and 'there' (l. 34), Keats's knight is a figure of psychic, social, and physiological contradiction.

By the argument sketched in the Introduction, masturbation figures an enabling contradiction. I call this contradiction 'virtuous' by way of likening its imitativeness to that of the virtual image, and also to underline its *virtuoso*, or professionally managed, technically accomplished character.[2] We shall trace the defensive virtue of masturbation as well as its special constructive properties to both characteristics. I have outlined in this virtuous contradiction, mythically projected, a dynamic, problem-solving reflection of some structural problems peculiar to the early nineteenth-century middle class. We might even say that the age's horror of masturbation in the flesh, so to speak, marks the phenomenon as an instance of a cultural uncanny: an image registered as a terrible strangeness precisely because it tropes in so naked a way the structural conflicts – the skeletal identity – of the dominant class. The Victorian invention of the disease, by which I mean the medical discourse of masturbation, represents, by this logic, one of many, socially absorptive inscriptions of the dilemmas facing the middle class at a particular point in its development. By these inscriptions, the necessitous contradictions were valorized and activated; that which was suffered was seized. Roughly, the axes along which we interpret this figure of virtuous contradiction, the hero of the masturbation myth, are part–whole, work–pleasure, legitimacy–originality, ownership–possession. We read the figure of masturbation as an image of productive self-alienation. What the masturbator, like the middle class, produces is himself as an internally fissured, eternally hungry space: a market that consumes but does not assimilate. The dis-ease promoted by this activity describes a specifically functional identity.

By situating Marcus's trenchant associations within the conceptual field I have plotted for Keats, we focus the knight's anguishing middleness, a state of animated suspension, as a highly determined posture. In his canonical, topographical, and discursive placement, we discover an image of that telos toward which masturbation and some characteristically middle-class life and writing styles tended. To register this image is to put ourselves in position to investigate those formal procedures and compositional projections in 'La Belle Dame' which situate Keats as Keats situates his hero. The knight's liminal, conflicted stance is, we shall see, a *nunc stans*. Or, respecting the temporal mood of 'La Belle Dame' and Keats's own usage, we shall call that stance a 'stationing', remembering the social meaning hidden in Keats's sculptural term.

To seize this position on Keats and his knight is to cease concerning ourselves with the genealogy, motivations, and allegorical affiliations of the Lady. By abandoning our own enthrallment with that creature, we free the knight from her critical spell. Further, by putting the knight, his strange tension, at the center of our inquiry, we start explaining some curious patterns in our criticism. Most readers of 'La Belle Dame' remark the glamour of the knight's interlude, and although its nonconsummation is not explicitly linked to that magic, it certainly informs our response. We are, after all, readers of the 'Ode on a Grecian Urn' as well; forever loitering, like forever panting, has its charm. We have also seen that the poem disallows an abstractly contrastive reading: the logic of this vs. that, engagement vs. escape. Or, to use the more familiar language of character, few critics are willing to identify la belle dame as a wicked enchantress *tout court*. While her effect is typically regarded as baleful, her motivations, or the extent to which she intends her effect, are, we allow, problematic.

What we have missed is the connection between the poem's and the knight's respective charms, both of them the effect of a contrived contradiction. We have overlooked the special virtue of what appears to be a punishing and narratively compelled representation: the knight's limbo. Rather than construe this state by reference to the commonsense, creaturely norms inscribed in the opening interrogation or by way of what must be highly conjectural arguments about the Lady's interests, we might conceive the knight's betweenness in terms of authorial imperatives.

Let me backtrack a bit so as to orient this suggestion more clearly within our scholarship. I do this not only to articulate the critical problems I hope to engage, but in order to suggest that these binds reproduce certain formal and genetic facts about 'La Belle Dame', facts which our finished arguments suppress. What must initially seem a perverse reading of the anguishing knight – a man whose self-contradiction constitutes his identity and his endurance – is only the result of a decision to take those facts and binds seriously.

By critical consensus over the past thirty years or so, 'La Belle Dame' is a cautionary faery tale addressed to a more or less professional audience: us. We read the knight's ordeal across our own literary histories, those that sandwich the Romantic era between the healthy, sociably engaged literatures of the Restoration and the Augustan age, and the equally though more critically committed discourses of the Victorian and the modern periods. The knight, by nearly all our interpretations Keats's authorial persona, is found to suffer the effects of his solipsism: concretely, his refusal of the organic sociality figured by the opening stanzas. These stanzas (1–3) are read as the utterance of a minstrel contemporary with the knight and sharing, roughly, his universe of discourse. Typically, we read the poem as an archetypal narrative sequence (enchantment, betrayal, devastation), animated by archetypal agents (knight, faery, common-sense foil), the whole package telling a tale about Romantic poetry and, specifically, so-called escapist poetry. The knight's limbo, which we treat as qualitatively identical to and devolving toward the destiny of the starved kings, princes, and warriors, is seen to objectify and requite his perverse self-indulgence: his rejection of the matter-of-fact established by the opening stanzas. Discursively, it would seem that the knight's posture figures a negation (derivative, ineffectual, possessed), as opposed to a critique: enlightened, unimplicated, effective.

And here we begin to encounter those critical problems mentioned above. By the minstrel's lights, the knight's poise is plainly pathological. Inasmuch as our criticism likes to take those lights as a commonsense independent of time and place, we too find in the knight an image of deprivation. He is, we say, a hero deflected from his proper ambitiousness and its rewards: namely, militant Christianity, the knightly equivalent of the organic purposiveness inscribed by the opening stanzas. Ironically, the knight's generic perversity equally estranges him from his ideal object, or from the full, melancholic satisfaction she promises. By the curious tastes of this unnatural hero, the Romantic bower becomes a tomb, the beautiful lady a lamia, the idyll a withering. Or so the practical wisdom of stanzas 1–3 has persuaded us.

Surely, however, the critical power we all find in 'La Belle Dame' does not inhere in any simple way in the quotidian discourse of stanzas 1–3. (Nor, as I suggested above, is the poem's charm unrelated to the spellbound knight.) Certainly Keats, whom we identify with the knight by their mutual attraction to that empowering Otherness, the Lady, does not plant in the minstrel's univocal, prosaic, and manifestly inappropriate interrogation the critical salient that exposes the false *and* genuine consciousness of the authorial persona.

What we have is a poem that, like its hero, hangs fire. The frame device, while it seems formally to resolve the work's doctrinal and dramatic contradictions, only recapitulates them. It is not, after all, the minstrel who concludes, as is customary in a framed ballad. *Were* this the case, we might properly find in the poem an image of requited exchange, equilibrium, and complete formal gratification. As it stands, however, the frame effect is produced by the knight's closing repetition, a bad translation, of the minstrel's opening speech. To the minstrel's verb 'loiter', the knight adds 'sojourn'; for 'has withered [wither'd]' he substitutes 'is withered'. In this, linguistic way, Keats juxtaposes the categories of the minstrel's organic world – where nothing *lives* because nothing really dies – against those of the world of finished histories or romance: a dimension which is always present because always already gone. There, nothing *dies* because it never really lives. Or, to anticipate myself, the meaningless, divinely determined closure of Nature, brought over into Culture, a closure overdetermined by history, engenders Keats's knight: an image of radical self-determination.

'La Belle Dame', a poem which does not *release* its critique, appears to be a melancholy and possessed reflection on its own mode of production. Or, from a slightly different angle, the ballad ends, as do so many of Keats's poems, on what someone has excellently called 'a knife edge of uncertainty'. It situates its existential and aesthetic judgments as a practical, local response to a set of unmarked narrative conditions: a *donnée*. Because the critique does not develop as a removed authorial reflection, no doctrinal position can take shape. We have something more like a critical posture, a standing rather than a stance. Readers of 'La Belle Dame' like to rationalize this reticence by suggesting that the poem offers itself as an object-lesson. We say that this 'distilled and disengaged' piece of poetic magic recommends by its negative example an engaged, humane, and richly contradictory verse.

Once we observe that the knight's suspension objectifies the poem's formal procedures and effect, we are committed to framing the unnaturalness of both suspensions as an *anti*-nature and a critical form. The victim starts looking like an anti-hero; his discomposure appears to describe a special kind of composure. The strong charm of this oddly arrested poem invites us to find in the knight's arrest a comparable virtue: a securing magic. In other words, by relating the formal to the dramatically figural patterns, we begin to articulate what we have always at some level known: namely, that 'La Belle Dame' is not an instructively flawed escape, the negative *précis* for a poetry of experience, but a work that describes at every register a rare kind of experience.[3] If we must call that experience 'escape', then we must also acknowledge the practicality of this vacation.

A more obvious problem with the received readings of 'La Belle Dame' is their canonical circularity. We like to read in the ballad Keats's encoded farewell to 'flowery bowery' poetry, a phrase that describes the regressive, wish-fulfilling verse that dominates the 1817 volume. In 'La Belle Dame', the flower is withered, the bower a barren hillside, the fulfillment a famishing. As I observed, most critics agree that these negative accents whisper the results of a new, toughminded, and 'unmisgiving' humanism on Keats's part. But because 'La Belle Dame' develops its critique in so queer and reluctant a fashion – because its formal procedures seem to set it within the rejected romance world – we must specify the new poetics by isolating those works subsequent to the ballad that seem to exemplify its emergent humanism. We look back to 'The Eve of St. Agnes' with its wintry intimations, and forward to the death-defying Odes for the text of this lesson. Naturally, we find what the canon has already found for us: a poet who evolves from faeryland to fact, from the poetry of escape (*Endymion*), to an ethical science ('The Fall of Hyperion'). Or, in the idiom of the early commentary, from 'Johnny Keats' to Keats the poet, 'Mankin' to man.

I do not believe Keats made, could have made, *believed* he could make, or entirely wanted to make this journey.[4] There is a terrific critical power in 'La Belle Dame', that enthralled and enthralling poem. That power does not derive from a manly critique of escape but from the definition of a special kind of escape, something between and also partaking of an 'effeminate' self-indulgence and a 'virile' humanism, or something between and partaking of romance and minstrelsy: healthy consumption and healthy production, and their dead ends. That 'between-partaking of' space describes what I call a sojourn, a word I explain more fully below. By investigating this sojourn, a living end, we also start accounting for the judgments (for example, sick–healthy, regressive–responsible, sensuous–serious, effeminate–virile) that judge Keats and us. We see how such judgments get made, and what additional meanings their makings introduce.

We want to know, for example, by what logic we read the minstrel's discourse as a commonsense: an eternal formal category and a critical prospect available to any reader of 'La Belle Dame' at any moment. One of the facts we might grasp about 'La Belle Dame' by this line of skepticism is that to seize the minstrel's world as *essentially* that of contemporary life and values, Keats's and ours, is to forget the complex relations of appetite to satisfaction, 'creation of the taste' to taste-specific production in the early nineteenth century and today. It is to forget that for Keats, healthy harvests and organic communities were as much a literary feature as knights and belles dames, and that insofar as these features inscribe strongly vexed social and professional themes, they get charged with class-authorial ambivalence.[5]

Certainly there is no reason why ideology should operate more self-critically in art than anywhere else. There are, however, practical and circumstantial reasons for these critical differences, or the exposure potential of particular artworks. In Keats's case, generally, class facts make the difference.[6] These facts, which necessitate the knight's strange poise, produce as well the virtue of that state which we have for so long and with such unanimity read either as a punishment or as a sign of some morbid debility. For an explanation of Keats's class situation, reviewed in chapter 1, I refer the reader to the entire discussion, chapters 4 through 6 (especially pp. 230 ff.) and to notes 4 and 6, chapter 2, and note 22, chapter 6. A general, existential analysis is found in chapter 3, pp. 126–7.

A good introduction to the project of 'La Belle Dame' is provided by Keats's Paolo and Francesca sonnet, 'As Hermes once took to his feathers light'. This poem was written five days before 'La Belle Dame' and, like that ballad, was printed in Hunt's *Indicator* and signed 'Caviare'. In the sonnet, Keats describes an escape from this 'dragon-world' to Dante's second circle, a place of perpetual, end-stopped motion. Dante's punishing figure of eternal frustration serves the narrator as an explicitly *authorial* resort (viz. 'So on a Delphic reed . . .'). As if to identify more forcefully the perverse virtue of that terrible poise, Keats refuses 'pure Ida', an Olympian figure; by a pun on 'idea', Keats seems to reject philosophy, that pure place, as well. On the other, *lower* side, as it were, he dismisses Tempe, here as in the 'Grecian Urn', designated a mortal resort by reference to Arcadia's intimations of immortality. By a second pun (Tempe–tempus), Keats banishes 'fast' or historical time: a consummative and therefore consuming duration. Finally, and most emphatically, Keats projects himself into the eternal sad suspension which the lovers iconically describe, a condition which translates into permanent body language their initial sin: a willing suspension of disbelief. We recall that Paolo and Francesca fall in love over their reading of the Lancelot–Guinevere episode. Their lovemaking is an act 'after' the original.

The draft of this sonnet appears on the fly-leaf of Keats's gift copy to Fanny Brawne of Cary's translation of *The Inferno*. Two false starts, one on the blank lining of the front board and one on the back board, provide a sort of frame for Cary's text. The textual situation is illuminated by another poem of the same periòd, 'Written on a blank space at the end of Chaucer's tale, "The Floure and the Leafe"', 1817. Keats inscribes the first twelve lines of the sonnet in the space immediately below the conclusion to Chaucer's 'Floure and Leafe'. He completes the poem at the bottom of the next page, just below the opening to 'The Court of Love'. Keats concludes his sonnet with a paean to the 'power [of] white simplicity', a reference to Chaucer's 'Leafe', symbol of Chastity. The ascription of power, however, seems also to include the whiteness of the page or 'leaf' following Chaucer's text, a 'blank space' which enables Keats's equal but opposite version. Keats's poem, which celebrates Chaucer's power 'to keep the reader in so sweet a place', presents itself not as a complimentary imitation, but as a complementary translation: a substitute, or a scriptural standing in that same sweet place Chaucer marked out. The difference is Keats's self-consciousness. The pronounced relation to Chaucer is, obviously, a self-authorizing device; at the same time, Keats's honorific and secondary discourse graphically upstages Chaucer's words. What had looked centered and stable on its page and within the field of the canon, emerges now as above to Keats's below, left to his right, and earliest to his latest.

As I noted, Keats signed this poem as he signed 'La Belle Dame', 'Caviare'. The pseudonym, an allusion to Hamlet's contempt for palates rude, is Keats's way of asserting his literary authority: his easy access to the canon and his easy address to a *cognoscenti*. At the same time, the substitute name suppresses Keats's real name – judging by the changes rung upon it in the reviews, a low, regional name – and, of course, his actual authorship.[7] Moreover, Keats's slick pseudonym – effectively, a parody of literary ease – discredits his professed authority. Where there is display, there is no true possession: insolence, not indolence. Or, where there is literariness – here, a representation of a supremely canonized (that is, Shakespeare's) representation of ease – there is no Literature.

Keats's cryptic 'Caviare' might well characterize the text, along with its author and notional audience. Caviar is, of course, and was in Keats's day (and, apparently, Shakespeare's), what Keats would call a luxury and what we might designate a supplemental food. No one eats caviar from hunger. This is not to say that caviar lacks nutritional value or that a hungry person couldn't be satisfied by a soupbowl of the stuff, only that its food status is to indicate indifference to nutritional and appetitive interests. One eats caviar to show that one need not eat at all, and this, obviously, is to signify an ontologically replete character. Caviar stands in for proper food, reproducing the gratification value of that original in a finer tone. What was the transparency of a primary, organic value is represented *as such* and, thus, reconstituted by the caviar. Its special negativity – a figured distance from need and desire – at once idealizes the primacy it represents, and depreciates it by reference to its own valorized perverseness: its semioticity, we might say.

Keats's signature, which, with his titles, frames the two poems under discussion, highlights the function of those titles and the canonical status of the works they introduce. 'La Belle Dame' is, as Hunt's note explains, the title of a poem written by the fourteenth-century French court poet, Alain Chartier, and translated by Chaucer, the version to which Keats's title alludes. (The Chaucerian narrator refers to Chartier's 'boke' as 'La bel Dame sans Mercy'. Chaucer renders 'bel' as 'Belle' in his title.) Most of the narrative content – I refer to forms, not functions – derives from two slightly earlier works, the Scottish True Thomas and Thomas Rymer ballads which Keats had read 'Englished', or in translation in Jamieson's and Scott's editions.[8]

The original printed title of the Paolo and Francesca sonnet is 'A Dream, After Reading Dante's Episode of Paolo [Paulo] and Francesca'. That title, like 'La Belle Dame', signifies inherited entitlement. This is to say, both names are titles in a social as well as literary sense. Both identify the poems that follow as scions of greatly canonized and already illustriously translated (that is, 'descended') Originals. Keats's titles, we observe, do not identify the mediating translations between those first words and Keats's own, latest version. The *poems*, however, by their accented inscriptions of the source translations, and of Originals situated as translations, come across as works at two removes or more from the Original. They 'present', so to speak, as profoundly substitutive as opposed to imitative utterances.

It is Chaucer, we notice, not Chartier, who gets brought over, and Cary, not Dante.[9] The Original, installed in these works as a sort of 'fairy's song', is seductively absented. Thus, while 'La Belle Dame' and the Paolo and Francesca sonnet are authorized by their displayed ownership of powerfully signifying Originals, they are at the same time *originated* by their corrupt relation to those first and dangerously absorptive texts.[10] This corruption, coming as it does under the sign of translation, is rendered a respectable form of difference.

In both cases, Keats develops his originality, the differential between his 'latest dream' and all its precursors, as a certain literariness: a matter of authorial self-consciousness. This value is produced and signified by the textual apparatus described above, and by a self-reflexive, end-stopped narration. Neither 'La Belle Dame' nor the Dante sonnet releases its meanings or its readers; both disallow an engaged reception, critical *or* sympathetic. Both, moreover, are works *after* the Original, where 'after' means belated and different (original), and 'like' or equivalent (canonically authorized). Both poems, like the 'Floure and Leafe' sonnet, position themselves canonically and rhetorically as facing-page translations. Keats's translational poetics, which legitimate his inventions by canonical genetics, situate those inventions as 'not-Literature', or, as *writing*: participial, partial, and perverse. Capable negativity is my phrase for this effect.

We can all see that the knight is a still point by virtue of the equal and opposite forces which pull him backward and downward (to the Lady, the sinister dreaming space), and onward and upward, toward the world which is the place of all of us. These conflicting interests – neither extrinsic weathers nor eternal psychic drives – are, we shall see, historically marked modes of social production. They meet within and constitute the knight a kind of spiral or whirlwind, a figure clearly presented in the Paolo and Francesca sonnet as the condition of an erotic and literary immortality. The point of rest which the knight occupies is, then, something of an illusion, insofar as it is constituted and maintained at every moment by a violent contradiction, like the eye of a tornado. We have always attended to the knight's stillness. What we sometimes forget is that 'still' is always and literally a loaded word for Keats, denoting a stasis which is the effect and appearance of an interpenetrative tension. (Example: 'Thou still unravished [unravish'd] bride . . .': or, you who are eternally undergoing unravishment, whose virtue *is* perverseness [since brides *should* be ravished], whose presence *is* absence.) As for the Lady, let us read her as no more than the necessary and sufficient cause of the knight's poise, in which we find the poem's *raison d'être* and the poet's *raison d'écrire*. This poise offers itself as a representation of Keats's own, comparable relation to the canon, and, as a figure of social production. Where Keats's situation differs from that of the knight is in the self-consciousness with which the poet entertains the contradictions of his station.

_____

Before developing this reading, I'd like to broach a related argument, one that raises the issues I've laid out to meta-proportions. It is my feeling that Keats reproduces his relation to the canon (a mode of acquisition and display), and precipitates that critical difference, his self-consciousness, by translating his own Original. I refer to the two authorized versions of 'La Belle Dame': the fair copy which is our standard text (the so-called *Brown*, or 1848 text), and the revision Keats himself published in 1820, the *Indicator* text. Just as Keats's initial text, *Brown*, fetishistically translates the canon (a deconstructive idealization), so does the *Indicator* revision parodically rewrite *Brown*, reconstituting *it*, thus, a naive, self-identical expression. Both latest dreams – *Brown* vis-à-vis the canon, *Indicator* vis-à-vis *Brown* – work the contradictions produced but not presented by their Originals. In both cases, we see a liberation by indiscreet reproduction; literary effects are split off from authorial and semantic causes, styles separate out from the representations which should support them. Thus are certain properties acquired, and thus are certain easeful deaths resisted.

We cannot start proving this argument before reviewing the compositional facts. First, we consider the strange textual history of 'La Belle Dame'. Jerry McGann, in an article that changed the shape of Keats studies, raises an old but distinctly marginalized question.[11] He asks us to reconsider the authority of that 'La Belle Dame' text which is our standard version of the poem. McGann does not argue for the restoration of the rejected, *Indicator* version; which is to say, he does not *dismiss* Keats's initial words, the *Brown* text. He simply situates at the center of any critical inquiry into the poem the existence and the comparable authorizations of the two texts. Moreover, he locates the salient of the *Indicator* version – its effective difference from *Brown* and thus, one might say, the intention of the revision – in the authorial self-consciousness which its literariness, a distinctly parodic value, brings out. McGann registers for us the social overtones of Keats's 'Caviare' autograph. More critically, he identifies Keats's substitution of 'wretched wight' for 'knight-at-arms [knight at arms]' as the poet's arch allusion to his own literary pretensions. Keats's 'wight', that burdened literary word, flaunts Keats's access to a particular and an elitist literary language, and his freedom to ironize that language.

McGann's general argument should direct our attention to the social myths inscribed throughout the poem, meanings less or differently accessible to Keats than those embedded in 'wight' and 'caviare'. I read these meanings more intensively than McGann, whose interest is methodological, not, in this essay, closely critical. By 'intensively', I mean that I move beyond what we may infer to have been Keats's determined revisionary intentions. In his textual decisions, I locate certain social and psychic tropes: objectifications of conditions *not* logically articulated precisely because they defined Keats's sense of the actual, or constituted his cognitive field.

I cull these features from a rather unusual study text: the two authorized versions of 'La Belle Dame' plus, as a third discourse, their intertextuality. The critical power which we observe in the *Brown* text is, as I've implied, a function of its bad incorporation of canonical Originals: a nonsystematic, fetishistic reproduction. The knight's peculiarly restricted possession of / by the Lady – that is, his possessive *style* – exemplifies the text's orientation toward its beloved properties. The contradictions that station the knight by their tension are reproduced in the poem's perverse inscription of its literary sources. By that inscription, Keats produces the medieval*ism* of the *Brown* 'La Belle Dame': a 'latest', in the sense of most belated, stylized, sentimental, and therefore *original* dream.

The *Indicator* text, Keats's translation of his own first but canonically 'latest dream', *thematizes* the contradictions embedded in the *Brown* original. By this double parody (conscious badness / bad consciousness), the *Indicator* cancels the canon preceding *Brown*, and bestows upon that work the aura of the *Original*: a first, or literally *latest* – most remote – dream. A relic from the tragic world, it appears wonderfully closed upon itself: not medievalist, but medieval, a cause rather than an effect, a substance not a style, an 'existence' rather than an abstraction, a Truth rather than a Beauty. Keats produces in this manner an origin that is not an origin; in effect, he translates the translation. By the designated fraudulence of the *version*, he produces a genuine *verse*: a model of literary authority, propriety, closure, and timelessness. One could say that Keats negates his own negation, producing, thus, a position: concretely, a new ·phenomenology of textual time and space.[12]

We can be more specific about the way in which the *Indicator*'s literariness consecrates *Brown* by parody. When we read the *Indicator* in *Brown*'s echo, we feel the falseness of that latest dream, the *Indicator* revision. We see that Claude Finney's astonishing source study is not nearly so misguided a critical venture as it first seems. The poem, described by a very good reader of Keats as so magical we dare not breathe upon it lest it disintegrate, emerges as a fetishized exhibition of other men's words: Chaucer's, Spenser's, Shakespeare's, Wordsworth's, Coleridge's, Hunt's.[13] We see that what we took to be an unmarked expressive manner is also the represented material means. In the most literal sense, Keats takes his subjectivity for an object, and also an object of display (a second reification, this). However, even as we contrast the two texts along the lines of transparency and self-presence, we must notice their essential identity. That observation must characterize *Brown* as itself a parody of genuine discourse, or Literature. Thus is the subversiveness – the badness – of the Original exposed. *And*, by the capable negativity argument, thus is *its* Originality effectuated, its *originality* engendered.

The psychic dissonance that the Lady precipitates in the knight is mirrored by the textual dissonance produced by the poem when it is read as a threefold form. In both cases, the dissonance – a dissociation and reorganization of manner and means, quality and quantity – is a discursive prerequisite. By his bad translation of the Lady, her actions and speech, the knight acquires the wherewithal for his exercise in self-expression. Clearly, however, his designated alienation from the 'self' he expresses, as well as the obvious interestedness of the expression, mark the exercise, Keats's and the knight's, as an aggressively ironic affair.

Next in the order of business is a look at the actual making of 'La Belle Dame'. We want to consider more closely the kind of reception which this process, or its representation, solicits. In 'The Eve of St. Agnes' (composed January–February 1819), Porphyro sings to Madeline as she sleeps, and so as to bring her over from her own dream into his. The particular unheard melody Keats has his hero sing is 'an ancient ditty, long since mute, / In Provence called [call'd], "La belle dame sans mercy"'. The ditty was not, we know, *really* mute, or not mute in anything but a technical sense. It was, in 1819, not only a chanson in print but canonized by its inclusion in Chaucer's *oeuvre*, and readily available in the cheap popular Chaucer edition where Keats read it. 'La Belle Dame' is situated in that edition among a collection of poems about difficult women, thematically emphasizing, as it were, Chaucer's ownership.

Chaucer's poem is, to use the language of today and the perspective offered by Keats's two translations, a metanarrative: a thickly mediated narration about narration itself. The nuclear action of the poem is a long, tedious, and entirely pointless verbal competition between an intransigent Lady (La belle dame sans mercy: or, a character named for her function), and a doggedly amorous gentleman, 'l'amant'. The Lady's refusal makes as much formal sense and as little dramatic sense as the man's desire. As there is no nondiscursive dimension to the exchange (no dramatic or doctrinal rationale), it must end mechanically. The Lady abruptly decides she has had enough repartee. Nothing if not loving, l'amant dies.

As I said, the focus in Chaucer's 'La Belle Dame' is on the narrative occasions engendered by the represented verbal volley. Chaucer introduces himself, *in propria persona*, as the troubled translator of the tale. He is 'constrainid' – 'charge[d]', he says – to write (according to Hunt, by the women he had offended in an earlier poem). This constraint ('in myne entent / I was vexid and tournid up and doune . . .') is textually associated with the queasy indeterminacy he suffers as the poem opens. He describes himself as 'halfe in a dreme, not fully awaked, / The goldin Slepe me wrapped under his wyng, / Yet not forthy I rose . . .' As if seeking a spatial and social correlate for his psychic limbo, the narrator adjourns to a 'pleasaunce'. Half asleep and under 'penaunce' to 'translate . . . a boke called La bel Dame sans Mercy', he is, naturally, in no mood to join in the fun. The 'pleasaunce', which sharply defines his alienation, affords him opportunities for overhearing, and thus for the production of self-consciously indirect discourse. We can see how helpful these ironic removes might be to a translator, whose basic project might be conceived as the reproduction of overheard discourse.

Chartier's poem begins at this point. An extra interlinear space separates the discourses but the text provides no pronomial or temporal distinctions to mark off Chaucer's narration from that of Chartier's persona. Blurring the boundaries even more, Chartier's narrative opens with a sort of editorial preface (what looks like a *facsimile* of Chaucer's complaint but is, of course, Chaucer's Original), followed by the reproduction of a dialogue overheard by this speaker at another 'pleasaunce'. That dialogue is the afore-mentioned debate between the merciless Lady and l'amant. This structural doubling suggests that Chaucer's persona enjoys the same relation to Chartier's tale (eavesdropper–translator) as the narrator of that tale, *Chartier's* persona, bears toward the overheard Original: the romance *contretemps*.

Chartier's persona, who is, with respect to the Chaucerian figure, a *second* narrator (textually later, historically and canonically earlier), describes himself as a man recently widowed. His great grief 'constrains' his writing; he seems to assert both the necessity of composition and its impossibility. He attributes both conditions to his lack of 'ese' ('distresse', 'languishing', 'disese and pain'). In order to resolve this unhappy conflict, the man adjourns, as I said, to a 'pleasaunce'. There he observes l'amant, a figure as melancholy and socially isolated as himself. The observed affinity prompts the widower to follow the man to a deeper glade. Here, the grieving narrator listens to l'amant and the Lady talk at each other a while. Someone, presumably the widower (Chartier's persona), tells us of l'amant's death. Chaucer abruptly takes over with an *envoi*.

This is a very strange poem. One recalls Keats's admiration for Chaucer's 'Floure and the Leafe': it 'keeps[s] the reader in so sweet a place'. No one in Chaucer's 'La Belle Dame', including Chartier, escapes Chaucer's textual place. The work as a whole looks like a sequence of translations, each act compelled by the narrator's 'disese', signified by a dreamy-dreary midway state, and attributed to some woman problem: loss or withdrawal. The only woman directly represented in the poem is that perfect stranger, la belle dame sans mercy. The Lady's entire remove promotes a succession of discursive moments: indirect discourses arising from a self-contradictory state. The reported discourse does not resolve the contradiction and release the narrator from his semi-paralysis. To the contrary, it appears to replicate, perpetuate, and intentionalize that condition. Both narrations are written from resorts, the spatial representation of the psychic in-between. Only la belle dame and l'amant, who speak rather than narrate, coincide with themselves. Their constraint is not the paradoxical coercion – to speak / not speak – experienced by the two narrators, but the single direct imperative of self-expression. Only these two figures, after all, *have* a self to express. They alone have qualities, a distinction inscribed in their names. Indeed, they coincide with their signs.

Nowhere in the Keats scholarship are the relations between Chaucer's 'La Belle Dame' and Keats's examined. This is because Keats draws his narrative motifs and forms – the actual interlude of knight and belle dame – from the True Thomas and Thomas Rymer ballads mentioned above. We note again that Keats's source was a translation: in this case, by both Scott and Jamieson. In the Scots ballads, the hero's encounter with an exceedingly generous faery queen is the condition of his poetic, prophetic, and political identity. He becomes both True Thomas (one who cannot lie), and Thomas Rymer (a poet), by virtue of his achieved intercourse with this powerful Lady. She is not the frigid alterity of Chartier's poem but a friendly Clio, who tells her moral lover his country's political future in the most direct and detailed fashion (battles, coronations, deposings). Thomas is entirely his Lady's creature, bound to return to her after his seven masterful and rewarding years in his native dimension.

Clearly, the Scots ballads tell a fulfillment story. The faery queen graciously possesses the mind and heart of the hero, creating his voice, 'constraining' him by her full presence. Chaucer's narrators, conversely, describe a constraint that arises from privation and longing, and that amounts to a state of self-contradiction. Chaucer's translation is a poem about dis-ease and discourse: enabling distance from Original and ultimately, oral speech.

These themes alert us to the queerness of Chaucer's description of the 'boke' he must translate, a poem 'which Maistir Aleine made *of rembraunce*' (my emphasis). Chaucer thus characterizes *Chartier's* relation to his tale as that of translator to Original, written to spoken. Or, Chaucer designates even Chartier's access to the stuff of literary speech as indirect and corrupt.

Both conditions, the utterly possessed (True Thomas) and the partial or badly possessed (dis-possessed), prompt acts of translation. The Thomases bring over the Lady's prophecies 'entire and unmaimed'. They translate her timeless faery discourse (which is readily intelligible to them) into the common language of their culture at its historical moment. The object of this action is to make the world of the everyday and Faeryland interpenetrate, and by that proper copulation, to make history (that is, change fate). These narrative proprieties underline the perverseness of the Chaucerian model. We see that Chaucer's two narrators do not translate their overhearings into a discourse that might liberate them or their Originals from their stuck states. To the contrary, the narrators *reproduce* the end-stopped dialogues they overhear, the difference being a certain gain in self-consciousness. Each such gain disarticulates slightly the self-coincidence of the romance dialogue, parodying, as it were, the canonical closure which called forth the narrations. By their self-conscious, self-vexing repetitions, the narrators maintain their liminality, an effective dis-ease. The interest is not, of course, in making history but in rewriting it as a discourse of consciousness: an allegory. We can see that the operative metaphor here is masturbation, not intercourse. Given the narrators' available models of sexual interaction (coercion, loss, refusal), this makes good sense.

Each of the three narrations parodies its precursor, liberating its style from its content, and appropriating the free property.[14] Chaucer's *envoi*, however, to a large extent neutralizes the cumulative dissonance by presenting the image of 'the work which shall go forth' ('Go, lityl Boke . . .') from the textual spot which the narrations carve out. To those readers who know Chartier only through Chaucer, it would appear to be the translation and editorial frame which liberate all the narrations into literary history. Ranged under the sanctioning figure of a major English author-*oeuvre*, all that narrative contradiction gets canonized. The dissonance is effectively harmonized.

Keats's functional model is, of course, Chaucer, not the True Thomas ballads. We see, for example, that the dominant mode of speech in Keats's ballad is that of indirect discourse. We are not privy to the discursive interaction between the Lady and knight; we hear only the knight's account of the interlude, and that account is itself a quotation within the minstrel's narration. Inasmuch as the Lady speaks a 'language strange' and sings a 'fairy's song' which is not recorded, the knight's report must be corrupt as well as partial. As for the prologue, we see that the minstrel, acting in his *dramatic* persona, speaks to the knight, not directly to us; his discourse, moreover, is largely a translation of the knight's physical appearance into pathology, itself an allegorical, disarticulated discourse. By the parodic devices of the *Indicator* text, however, Keats installs in that poem *and* in *Brown* the space that Chaucer opens between himself and the widower. Or, Keats assumes the role of overhearer and translator; his source text is the minstrel's discourse – that is, the *entire text* of 'La Belle Dame'. To register Keats's alienation from his representational manner and means is also to graph some interesting intertextual differences. By reference to both Chaucer's poem and the True Thomas ballads, we see that Keats's knight is neither so possessed by his ideal object as to annihilate his originality, nor is he like Chartier's 'l'amant', perfectly bereft, and thus fated to extinction. Keats's hero is, we shall see, semi- or dis-possessed: more like Chaucer's narrators than Chaucer's hero, that is. Thus do we focus the knight as a reflection of Keats's capable poet. We observe the determined, and overdetermined character of his dis-ease.

The knight defines a resort space, a world within but not *of* the given textual spaces. This middling place–state both enables and requires for its maintenance a special discourse, one which makes the knight *know* himself a creature of contradiction, but which does not thereby set him free. As Chaucer works the contradictions of his Original, Chartier, so Keats effectuates Chaucer's inscribed contradictions. For instance, through Keats's remove from his overheard discourse, we see that the Lady is the knight's discursive creature. To feel her possession by his grammar is also to explain Keats's strikingly pathetic representation of the Lady in the *Indicator* revision. While the knight, who speaks to us through the minstrel's report, is, similarly, the creature of that narration, his speech is, by the textual fiction, reported verbatim. The Lady's single direct utterance is severely qualified: 'And sure in language strange she said, / "I love thee true" [Stillinger: no internal quotes]'. That 'sure' is surely suspicious. Even as we remark the knight's possession of the Lady, we notice that his style of possession keeps her apart from his being. His fetishism, which limits the virtues he might derive from her person, defines a special kind of possession and brings into being a new value. The knight confers on the Lady the status of his portable property. She is the belonging of a man who owns but does not possess, whose property – signifiers, even as they extend and express his being –

cannot be assimilated to that being and retain its virtue. I describe the knight as neither a 'have' nor a 'have not', with their mythic simplicity, social and psychic. The knight, a being who is, strictly, a 'having', enjoys or suffers an identity which consists in his self-contradiction.

To explain more clearly the social virtue of this representation, I'd like to extend the translation discussion opened above.[15] The textual analysis resumes on p. 64. To translate is to be at once good and bad, and for the same reasons. While translation is an act of homage and an immortalizing gesture, it is also inevitably parodic, inasmuch as it reifies the strong otherness and self-identity of the Original. At the same time, it is only the occurrence of the translation – a reproduction which, being later, is also, perforce, different – which *constructs* within the given semiotic system the phenomenon of Origins. This is to say, the translation *projects* that aura which it reifies and to that extent dispels. The worse the translation, or the more manifestly unlike its designated Original, the more firmly it consecrates that source work as eternal and inviolate, and the more devastating also, its violation of that innocence. The best translation is, by this logic, the worst: the most literal and the most manifestly conscious of its literalness.

Translation is a substitution: a standing-in not so much *for*, or 'in place of' the Original, but *as* and *with*, or in *the* place of the Original. As a textual anchor, we might recall in this context Keats's apology to Boccaccio: 'But it is done – succeed the verse or fail – / To honour thee, and thy gone spirit greet, [;] / To stead thee as a verse in English tongue . . .' ('Isabella', 157–9). 'To stead' means 'to stand in stead', and since 'stead', the noun, itself means 'standing', Keats's verb would seem to describe an unusually self-conscious, unusually reflexive reproduction of Boccaccio's tale: a supplement, in short.

Consider, in this context, the reproduction of a painting; or, more instructive, since it foregrounds the role of the canon, consider the phenomenon of an original artwork installed in a museum among categorically diverse objects (for example, furniture, clothing, manuscripts). Detached from the social and canonical contexts which ensure the invisibility of its style, the artwork produces the phenomenology of the reproduction, even as its presence in the museum signifies its status as an Original.[16] What it appears to reproduce is its own Originality, or *itself* in its native context. A spatial relation is converted, thus, into a temporal difference, one that both valorizes the museum item and subordinates it to its own ghostly authority.

We illuminate some of these paradoxes by remembering that what gets lost and gained in translation is style. The style gained is a farcical reproduction (isolated, congealed, self-conscious) of the style lost. What are felt to be qualitative causes in the Original materialize as purposes in the translation. To put this more positively, the translation liberates into the badness of the present tense the effects of the Original, retroactively realizing its Originality, or untouchable uniqueness, in the past. One might even conceive the Original as waiting upon that parodic moment for its achieved being.[17] No matter which slant we put on this violence, we see that translation must expose canonicity as a manufactured attribute, and the canon as a vulnerable hegemony: neither a mechanical sequence nor a collective, continuous, evaluative wisdom.

Indirect discourse, quotation, interpretation, and narration itself may all, of course, and not very helpfully, be considered forms of translation. We use the concept literally in this analysis of 'La Belle Dame' first, because Keats does: in *Brown* with respect to canonical Originals, in the *Indicator* revision (a translation of *Brown*), and in both texts' internal dynamics. To read 'La Belle Dame' by the rubric of translation is to learn a great deal about that poem's genetic, rhetorical, canonical, and social logic, about all Keats's poems, and about Romantic poetry. We all know, for example, that 'La Belle Dame' is a literary ballad, but unless we think about the semiotics and sociology of translation, we might not feel how strange and expedient a form that is. We also know, Arnold notwithstanding, that a good deal of Romantic poetry presents its critical reflection on the past and its discourses, a form of translation, as its special primary expressiveness. We want to illuminate the social meanings attending this projection, a kind of aesthetic scholarship.

Now that we've outlined the compositional facts and explored the model that organizes them, we may plot the phenomenology. When we put Chaucer's 'La Belle Dame' and Keats's side by side, we notice that Chaucer's poem, with its nested narrations and self-reflexiveness, seems far less medieval than Keats's; or, Keats's version modernizes and thereby preempts Chaucer. By his translation, Keats liberates from Chaucer and appropriates a certain style, an authenticity effect. The paradox, of course, is that by a single maneuver, Keats displaces Chaucer, implements the canonical authority of the Chaucerian sign, and depreciates that sign by signifying it. The devaluation cuts both ways; the subject who *names* his authorizing property discredits himself by that double display.[18]

Keats's ballad – simple, sensuous, and passionate – ostensibly/ effectively restores the 'Chaucerized' text, ironic and literary, to its original *oral* condition. That condition is designated by Chaucer's doubly allusive charge to himself, 'to translate . . . A Boke callid La bel Dame sans Mercy, / Which Maistir Aleine made of remembraunce . . .' Or, Keats's poem preempts even Chartier, designated by Chaucer as *himself* a translator of overheard oral narration.

The distinctly spoken quality of Keats's poem (an effect taken from the lower and earlier Scots ballads), constructs the distinctly written, artful, 'high' character of Chaucer's. By that artifice, Keats's haunting verse takes shape as *exactly* the sort of verse one might sing to a sleeping lady so as to nudge her from one dream to another. This is the song, we feel, Porphyro must have sung to Madeline, and by a crazy logic, that proleptic and strictly intertextual allusion seems to authenticate Keats's poem. One is reminded of Chatterton's labyrinthine intertextuality; and, of the effect Bloom has named *Apophrades*, 'the return of the dead'. More prosaically, we feel the expedience of the Lady's unrepresented 'fairy's song', another mute(d) ditty which, by the logic of 'La Belle Dame', must occasion additional 'restorations'. The hushed (up) song, 'like a corpse within [the] grave' of the poem, will, 'like withered leaves . . . quicken a new birth'. The immortality which Shelley accomplishes on a small and stanzaic scale (the terza rima 'grave' enclosing the blind germ of the next stanzaic generation), Keats develops into a canonical principle. Through his translational maneuvers, he renders his writing 'first, and last, and midst, and without end'.

The *Indicator* 'La Belle Dame', a sentimentally 'ancient ditty', constructs our impression of *Brown's* naiveté. By reference to the *Indicator's* 'wretched wight', for instance, 'knight-at-arms' sounds a note of vigorous, manly simplicity. We observe that the *Indicator* version smooths out *Brown's* 'has withered'–'is withered [wither'd]' contradiction, and that the wight, less constrained in his loving, enjoys a less ritualistic, healthier intimacy with the more sympathetic Lady.

Generally, Keats brings wight, minstrel, and the Lady into closer verbal association in the *Indicator* revision. He makes the wight a better, more assimilative translator – less like Keats, that is. By blurring the categorical distinctions between the wight and his interlocutors Keats effectively *highlights* the distinction between the nineteenth-century author and his received materials, all of which are evenly fetishized.

By the *Indicator* self-consciousness, Keats installs *Brown* as the *ur* form of 'La Belle Dame', in relation to which not only Chartier and Chaucer, but *all* Keats's canonical imports assume the look of translations. We suddenly see in Keats's 'setting and persons' the *prototype* of Spenser's story of Cymochles.[19] More to the point, we perceive Spenser, Milton, Browne, Wordsworth, Coleridge, and Hunt as derivative. At the same time, the translational dynamics of the *Indicator* bring out the belatedness of that fake Original, the *Brown* manuscript. When we read that text informed by the *Indicator*, we focus *its* authorizing Original, la belle dame's 'fairy's song'. *Brown*, which now looks like a bad translation of that song, is thus saved from its own self-coincidence, just as 'La Belle Dame' rescues Chaucer's and Chartier's translations from their canonical morbidity. For the *Brown* 'La Belle Dame' to live as a 'latest dream' – first and last – the sanctioning figure of the Lady's first words must be designated idealistically. This is the job of the *Indicator* revision.

———————

By his own report, the knight is at once 'here', in the natural world (ll. 43, 45) and 'there', in the nether realm of la belle dame (ll. 33, 34). The verbal form of this logical bind – a both–and structure – indicates that the knight's arrest is not a function of what we might call horizon distinctions: not, that is, related to his clear or qualified refusals of the discursively adjacent orders of fact (stanzas 1–3) and fantasy (4–11).

The knight's suspension signifies his containment of the antithetical worlds he mediates. What holds him in place are the contradictions engendered by his position between otherwise continuous realms. He defines a sort of third world. We see that while the knight discursively and dramatically *connects* the commonsense inquiry of stanzas 1–3 with the weird otherworld of the later stanzas, he also *disarticulates* those natural and supernatural realms. His interposition formally reinforces, even as it ideologically undermines, its surrounding zones.

I mention this fact, explored below, so as to add another dimension to the knight's oxymoronic stance. We typically read his position as expressing his distaste for the food that would nourish him: literally, health food. We also say that the limbo denotes an incontinent appetite for the Lady, a surfeit of her malnourishing manna. Both readings portray the knight as the spatial form of a neither–nor relation: the 'neither' a matter of will, the 'nor' a fact of (human as opposed to faery) life. By attending, however, to the verbal contradictions which define the knight, we grasp his position not as a deficit of content but as the form of a peculiar organization of content. Strictly by his betweenness, the knight materializes diffused extrinsic differentials into formal contradiction, which he translates into psychic and physiological dissonance. By his placement between two determinate speech centers, the knight is constituted a space of competition. We may interpret that space – a *durée* – with reference to the more familiar temporalities which frame him in the poem. Below, we explore the social meanings which these somewhat abstract zones inscribe.

We have, on the one hand, the realm of organic reproduction, what I call the 'done world'. This is an order of repetition so exact as to produce difference without death and, therefore, no difference (or meaning) as we know it. The more explicit representation of this genetic closure occurs in the 'Ode to a Nightingale', where the natural bird's generic perpetuity (its exemption from history's depredations) is aligned with its expressive uniqueness and contrasted to the *sempiternity* conferred by the canon upon its barren but eternally replicated icons: Ruth, emperor, clown (and, we infer, nightingale as a literary topos).[20] Objects in *this* universe are always Original, or first and last of their kind: essential types. This domain, the faery lands forlorn of la belle dame and her creatures, is the 'gone world' of historiography, or romance: of Written as opposed to Writing. It is the universe of the canon where everything is always meaningful because its meaning (like its full being) is always somewhere else. The present tense of that warning vision, stanzas 10 and 11, like the perfect past of the opening stanzas, tells a history only of departed things. Spoken and Written both name the dead.

It might be helpful to recall here Keats's epithet for the Grecian Urn, 'silvan [sylvan] historian', since the phrase collapses the opposition outlined above – roughly, Nature–Culture – into paradox.

'Silvan historian' is, when you think about it, nearly inconceivable, marrying as it does two mutually exclusive temporal styles. Try to imagine the history – that is, the *narration* – of a forest, where Nature, not Fancy, breeding flowers, will always breed the same. Or, to seize the phrase's descriptive option, how might a historian of sylvan sensibility narrate the discontinuity and dead closure of history, a realm of profound nonrecurrence?

Keats's oxymoronic urn figures the paradox of history as repetition (Nature), and history as divine or absolute law (canonized Culture). *Moreover*, it figures the falseness of that antinomy: an artifact of the consciousness that initially dissociated and opposed those terms. The urn, like the knight and like Keats's compositional procedures in these and many other poems, defines idealistically a new temporal zone. Not *neither* slow nor fast time, but both: as we shall see, the peculiarly historical time of the middle class. In the language of the 'Grecian Urn', not men *or* gods, not Tempe *or* Arcady, not deities *or* mortals, and above all, not 'struggle to escape' *or* 'wild ecstasy': both. This is the great oxymoron of Keats's poetry and it is not in the least bit 'mystic'.[21] This oxymoron describes an order of production which produces as its primary object its own conflicted ideology, and which, sensibly enough, endorses above all else things that tease us out of thought. Like ideology itself in its dominant moment, such objects can be thought about, but they cannot be thought.

Between Nature, the zone of meaningless and perfect creativity – a zero-aura realm – and canonical Culture, the place of absolute aura, maximum meaning, and lost objects, stands the knight. In his discourse, one glimpses the model for a third genetic order, an order of original reproduction, or of translation: a bad repetition. Probably the first observation one makes about 'La Belle Dame' is that the knight is textually continuous with the voice of stanzas 1–3, the utterance of a minstrel whose narration, the representation of his own, the knight's, and the Lady's speech, Keats appropriates. The narrational indeterminacy (an imitation of Chaucer's elision, between lines 28 and 29) suggests that the knight's account reproduces to some extent and with different effect the forms and interests which govern the minstrel's speech. That discourse is organized by frankly normative assumptions about productive and consumptive proprieties. Presence and absence are the operative categories, and they are figured as discrete intervals constituted by natural law and by the social behaviors which represent that law. To the minstrel, the knight is a nonsense figure: we might say, since this is so linguistically plotted a poem, a personified solecism. The knight idles and abstains when the deepest and most general imperatives urge purposeful action. The minstrel's verb, 'loiter', is his attempt to rationalize this nonsense, as is his reading of the knight's blush (see below, p. 70). 'Loiter', a pejorative term, affirms a normative kind and degree of activity. The verb describes by reference to that norm a temporary, which is to say, doomed or already absorbed refusal of it. To loiter is not to do anything or to be anywhere; it is only *not* to do something and *not* to be somewhere. ('To linger indolently on the way when sent on an errand or making a journey'; 'to waste time when engaged in some particular task', *OED*.) The effective nuance of the word emerges in the context of the knight's verb, 'sojourn' ('to make a temporary stay in a place', *OED*), added to the minstrel's 'loiter' in line 45, a site of contradiction.[22] The sharply opposed class resonances attaching to the two words today ('loiter' suggests urban unemployment; 'sojourn' evokes civilized leisure) makes us think about their different styles of negation. By restoring to 'loiter' its amputated adverbial tail (that is, 'with intent': in the general context of Peterloo, a lively tail, one suspects), and by attending to 'sojourn''s etymology (from the Latin *'sub diurnum'*: under or during the day), we materialize this contrast. 'Loiter', which implies the threatening nothingness of an idle and unpropertied state – a threat engendered by the concept and fact of private property – formally describes a passive and possessed negation. 'Sojourn', paradoxically, describes a critique which is effective *because* it is possessed, and possessed *of* certain things. Its metonymic (supplemental) relation to the 'day' which its metaphoricity displaces, gives it the edge over 'day''s self-presence. 'Sojourn', which does not imply refusal of the everyday, also has no design upon or desire for that goodness. The word describes a complementary zone: neither an 'anywhere out of this world', nor the bad, binary Other constructed by this good world and maintained by such words as 'loiter'. A sojourn is a supplement. One might, thus, sojourn indefinitely and still be doing something definite: living as it were a parallel life, or facing-page translation of a life: a life of caviar. The logic of the sojourn is not that of dialectic – the rationally progressive triad – but of reproduction in different tone: a dyadic and unstable ratio. La belle dame's minions do not sojourn, as the salient of that state is its capable perverseness. The kings and princes are as purely possessed by their ideology as the minstrel is by his. It is only the knight who is thrust into the sciences of the artificial.

The knight's verb alerts us to the special interests of the minstrel. The fading rose observation noted above reflects a particular concept of health: a set of ideas about plenitude and vacancy, integrity and partiality. The blush need not signify, as the minstrel's organic ideology requires, a decrudescence. In the context of the knight's general pallor, what the minstrel calls a 'withering rose' might just as well indicate a *coming* of color, as much a concentration of blood as a dissemination. The minstrel's implied masturbation charge might, that is, be turned on its head. The willful starvation might be read as a genital competition for appetite, and the pallor a phallic monopoly on blood. (Similarly, masturbation might represent virtuously conservative, as opposed to spendthrift sex.) In other words, the knight's symptoms might denote a state of contradiction so balanced as to expose both wasting and thriving diagnoses as ideological impositions. The minstrel's unreliable observation reminds us that self-preservation – characterological integrity – varies according to the nature of the self to be preserved. In the knight's case, self-preservation requires a partial self-destruction.

There is no place the knight can go because both textual places occupy him in a particular way. This is to suggest that the knight has escaped history, or all that the poem presents as given, coercive, and degenerative. *We see that there is nothing in the poem which can kill him.* In his withering, we perceive only a state of participiality, registered as pathological by that Epicurean voice, stanzas 1–3. For as long as the knight can resist a range of psychic and social entelechies, for as long as he can maintain his dissonance, he survives. He enjoys, of course, an endurance altogether different from the varieties of posthumous life figured by the natural history, stanzas 1–3, and the grim romance, stanzas 10 and 11.

As I noted above, 'sojourn' comes from the Latin for 'under or during the day'. The etymology helps us conceive the knight's sojourn as the other-or-underside of the minstrel's sensible workaday: a complement and opposite. Imagine a tapestry reversed so as to expose the busy side, a surface perfectly continuous with the good side, since all the threads share both planes. What one calls the 'bad' or 'other' side, while it is literally the good side's ground of being, also parodies that smooth self-identity. The two sides are, as it were, repetitions in finer and coarser tone: or, again, facing-page translations, verse and perverse.

The minstrel cannot, of course, make the connection between his speech world and the knight's. By his lights, to sit on a pacing steed all day, to see nothing but the fixed field of one's companion, to eat food that leaves you hungry, and 'to be such a eunuch . . . as to leave a maid, with that character about her, in such a situation', is to go nowhere, to learn nothing, and to gain no value, a sort of rocking horse excursion.[23] By reference to the minstrel's governing metaphor, the knight's excursion is a masturbatory exercise: antisocial, self-indulgent, repetitive, incompletely gratifying, pointless, and morbid. Most readers of 'La Belle Dame' agree with the knight that he *has* had an escape of some kind, an experience which is neither within the diurnal dimension nor a simple antithesis to it. What we imagine is a realm, perhaps a temporal zone, beside or beneath the everyday, as Faery is traditionally a zone beside or beneath this real world.

The relation of the knight's sojourn to the minstrel's quotidian might in turn help us to see that the knight's narration is not, formally, an answer to the minstrel's question, 'what's wrong with you'. It is instead a supplement to the knight's first, physiological presentation. By his narration, the knight says, 'this is the discourse I can produce because of who I am, which is where I've been, which is who I am', *ad infinitum*: an ourobouros.[24]

The knight's account *seems* to answer the minstrel's question. This appearance is a function of those themes which inform both discourses (wasting–thriving; empty–full). We have noticed, however, that the intonational values of those themes differ greatly when they occur in the two speech centers, minstrel and knight. Is the knight, like a half-glass of water, half full or half empty? To the minstrel, the knight figures a qualified emptiness. Through Keats, we hear the knight's account as a statement of qualified, conflictual fullness. By positioning the two discourses as categorical alternatives, we understand that the knight's narration is a very loose translation, into minstrelsy, of the Lady's muted 'fairy's song', that primal speech which charters even Chartier's discourse. *This* is the verbal stuff which partly fills the knight. *What is the knight's narration but a poignant and pointless utterance, a repetition in finer tone (prototype) of the l'amant-belle dame exchange, itself ostensibly a repetition of some more perfectly opaque discourse: something more like the knight's speech?*

One might think here, as I suspect Keats did, of the narrative structure of Wordsworth's 'Solitary Reaper'; like Keats, Wordsworth presents his invention under the entitling sign of an Original speaker and speech. 'The Solitary Reaper', by designating as unintelligible to the narrator the reaper's song, effectively *mutes* that song and *effaces* its singer, creating the conditions for a very free but still authorized translation. In other words, the reaper is suppressed by the poem that claims to restore her: or rather, to repeat her being in a finer tone.[25] In Wordsworth's poem, and in his practice generally, the bringing over of culturally removed material occurs by organically imitative procedures; the object of the endeavor is comfortably assimilative. (It must make a big difference in our reading that Wordsworth's Original singer, like Coleridge's Ancient Mariner [see note 24], is presented as an eternal folk type, not a particular author nor a particular and available Original text.) In Keats's ballad, by contrast, neither the poet's nor the knight's translation fully suppresses – brings over, that is – the authorizing text. The alien is only partially naturalized. Indeed, the effect of this incomplete or mis-translation is to *represent* the otherness of the enabling Original. Let me recall here an observation I made in chapter 1, to the effect that Keats offended the great literary men of his age by exposing some of the conditions and interests governing their aesthetic ideologies. He made the same magic they did, but he showed his hand.

By the concept of a faery Original delivered in the poem only through its translation, the knight's narration acquires the status of an authorized, even inspired representation. At the same time, by reference to that 'language strange' (that 'wildness' is the functional identity of the 'fairy's song' as of its singer), the knight's narrative clearly emerges as *intelligible* discourse: a misrepresentation. As with all good translations, it is bad: accessible to the extent that it misappropriates and misgives.

To produce his version, the knight must seize his Original, la belle dame, perversely. Not only does the Lady offer herself obliquely – leaning 'sidelong' ('sideways' in *Indicator*), and speaking a language strange – but the knight willfully restricts his intake.[26] He limits his lovemaking, or taking, to 'kisses four', demonstrating in this way his determinedly unnatural possessive style. In the *Indicator*, the knight kisses the lady to sleep; thus does Keats inscribe the normative propriety. By his fetishism, the knight avoids becoming what he eats. He will not be encoded by the code which enables and authorizes his narration.

It is crucial to see that the knight's necessary *and* cultivated estrangement from his inner erotic object enables a peculiarly alienated exercise in self-reflection. The 'self' he reflects upon is la belle dame, and the 'expression' he produces is a misrepresentation of her speech. These actions are, speaking quite literally now, holding actions: ways of establishing a self by appropriating a powerful discourse, and at the same time, holding that daemon up for display and also *off*, lest it tyrannize inner space. Again, one glimpses Keats's model in the very odd dialogue between Chaucer's l'amant and belle dame. As I observed, that boring competition enables in Chaucer a finite translational chain reaction. One guesses that Keats collapses Chaucer's Lady, a figure of refusal, into l'amant, a figure of desire. By thus fracturing the self-identity of l'amant, that canonical corpse, Keats enables him to speak – to have effect – in an age that had otherwise buried him. For a physical analogy, think of nuclear fusion, where by driving an extra particle into the atomic nucleus, one makes the entire atomic structure wrong, unstable, and effective.

Whether we register these holding actions by way of a masturbation myth, or with reference to translation dynamics (or, as I shall suggest below, in terms of eating disorders), they are all one syndrome and it is entirely functional.[27] The knight enjoys by his self-consciousness a being which is self-contained but not self-coincident: a living end. While he 'feeds on' the determinate orders which discursively flank him, he does not digest that matter into ego. Thus does he resist annihilation by both those hungry generations: orders of production and consumption. The knight, by his supplemental tactics, achieves an existence at once 'privy' or for itself, and 'apert' or receptive. He becomes at once authorized and original, achieved and becoming, purposive and hedonistic. We could characterize him as one whose productivity – in the poem, his narration and its poise – is the expression and end of his unusual consumptive mode: one which ingests without digesting, consumes without consummating, uses without exhausting, feeds without satisfying. The knight's consumption – bad, fetishistic, and incomplete – *is* his productive act.

To focus this aspect of the knight's poise is to extend our knowledge of his surrounding dimensions, what I have called Nature and Culture. We are invited to construe the self-contradictory consumption practiced by the knight with reference to the foregrounded actions and values inscribed in those zones. The assumption behind the minstrel's 'what can ail thee' is 'why aren't you out crusading, being effective in a knightly way?' The intonation tells us that the minstrel's organic order is, schematically, the realm of production; the squirrels are resting from their labor, as are the harvesters from their reaping and the birds from their singing. On the other side, the realm of la belle dame, we have an order of pleasure and orality (roots, honey, manna, kisses, starved lips): consumption. What I describe is a rough mapping of working-class and leisure-class spheres of influence. In between, stationed by the contradictions which his middleness materializes, stands the knight, that bad eater and misgiver. His perverse consumption produces idealistically his own self-alienation, the condition of his identity and of further and infinite consumptive acts.

It is the knight's 'between' that crystallizes the production / consumption ratio and, at the same time, establishes the deep identity of those orders. With reference to the knight's consumptive–productive mode, the framing zones describe a single practice. (The deep logic of 'La Belle Dame' is dyadic, not dialectical.) To see the knight as a virtuous contradiction is to construe his refusal of the minstrel's facticity as a special way of using that matter-of-fact. And, we grasp that difference as equally a swerve from the condition exemplified by the pale kings and princes. Both dimensions – sensible seasonal life (or, matter) and nympholepsy (consciousness) – represent in their binary and opposed state forms of thralldom.[28] Both are characterized by a self-identity that amounts to a murderous form of self-possession. The pallor of the courtly company is *not* the sign of its hunger or emptiness, but rather of its complete digestion of the Lady, a White Goddess. Analogously, the lily brow of the knight marks *his* containment of the Lady, or rather, and luckily for him, of only a piece of her.[29]

Both pallors, that of the knight and of the royal ghosts, signify states of possession. They denote, that is, two different possessive styles. By its assimilation of the Lady, the visionary company finds itself possessed by whatever code she represents. The wanness of these good eaters is complete: 'death pale'. We have already noted the virtues of the knight's bad table manners.

'La Belle Dame' is not, we can see, a poem about which food to eat or which power to seize: fact or fantasy, escape or engagement. It tells a tale about how to eat wisely, or not too well. The sad consequence of a correct, complete, organic consumption is illustrated by the fate of the kings, princes, and warriors. By their propriety, these quintessential men of power forfeit their identity. Theirs is not a state of contradiction, like the knight's, but one of nullity: men of power, impotent, statesmen unstated. Possessing themselves so completely, they possess, in effect, nothing. Glutted by the Lady, they are starving.

Organic dialectic, the theme of the minstrel's discourse, only produces freedom and pleasure when we take up a position within that discursive universe, something we cannot honestly do, as Keats could not. Our own historical sense tells us that the order of full granaries and done harvests is, in the poem and as it was for Keats, the world of perfect pasts: 'has withered', 'is done', 'no birds sing'. The organic dimension – proper derivativeness – like the perfect present of the nightmare romance, is a zone of stunned satiety, the annihilation of self-consciousness. Both objectify the effects of a particular style of self-production, and both signify the sacrifice of that unnaturalness which is the condition of the middle class's endurance and originality. By and *as* his stationing perversity, the knight is held still: which is to say, in place forever in motion. The knight survives, escaping both the done world of organic repetition and the gone world of romance, dead heroes, the canon: a world so deeply intentionalized as to make obsequious paraphrase its condition of immortality and also its death sentence. The knight is deathwards progressing to no death: set in a time warp which brings no final solution sweet.[30] Within the duration he defines, formal and substantive determinacy does not entail the end of desire, satiety. Self-possession does not obliterate identity.

Because we have always noticed and tried to explain the orality of Keats's poetry, I'd like to articulate an analogy that's been developing alongside the argument unfolding here. The knight's assimilative style may remind us of some strategies associated with anorexia. I will not argue the politically illuminating potential of this resemblance between a twentieth-century, upper middle-class, adolescent female disorder, and the poetics of a marginally middle-class, professionally unequipped, nineteenth-century male adolescent. The obvious self-fashioning at work in the anorectic's ingestive improprieties should improve our understanding of Keats's dis-eased literary consumption, represented and enacted.

Anorectics, when they do eat, typically do so improperly: at the wrong time, in the wrong place, with the wrong utensil, in the wrong sequence, the wrong food. The pattern can be viewed as a complex refusal of the use-value of food even as this value is acquired, the refusal motivated by a wish to avoid a range of closures or absorptions. For instance, rather than cut a regulation size slice of cake and consume it in standard bites over a conventionally established period of time, the anorectic may take an absurdly small and irregular piece, reduce it to crumbs that get eaten too slowly and, since forks are made for bite-size pieces, improperly. The individual may, in this indirect and fetishistic fashion, work her way through a normal or even oversized portion of cake, which is to say, she receives a sufficient or even exorbitant caloric or use-value. The psychic meaning of this perverse consumption is, however, that of effective negation: freedom. The functional myth here is that the unnatural mode of ingestion will somehow outwit the body's inexorably assimilative machinery, that digestive necessity which makes you what you eat by making what you eat, you. The food is psychically maintained as an internalized alien: both the condition for self-contradiction, and the refusal of an adult existence seen as solid, achieved, and inert: sexually determinate and culturally possessed. Further, to eat in this way is to signify, as one eats, not only that one need not eat (since hungry people take proper portions and eat them efficiently), but that one is not, in fact, eating at all. It is to convert all food into a luxury: literally, to toy with one's dinner. By this magic, one alchemizes meat and potatoes into caviar, health food into soul food. The phrase 'holding action' – holding on by holding off – is as good as any to describe the phenomenology of anorexia.

Now, compare the slice of cake to a literary work, and compare that culinary-cultural system which signifies the formal determinacy of cakes to the literary canon. In translating a slice into a pile of crumbs, one seems to destroy the use-value of the slice *as* slice-of-cake, a particular combination of flour, butter, sugar, and egg: processed elements representing labor investments, subjected to further transformational acts in historical time. By eating these disorganized fragments, one naturally acquires the nutritional value and the pleasure of the determined and overdetermined object: the slice, the cake, the system within which cakes have a certain meaning (that is, dessert). What one tastes is not, of course, a fragment of flour but a fragment of cake. The governing myth, however, is that one is consuming raw materials or free effects, uncoercive and capable of entering into any digestive combination; or, better yet, by their unprocessed and thus directly unusable properties, able to remain eternally undigested. This is, quite profoundly, to have one's cake and eat it too.

. To eat in this way – to appropriate the literary past in this way – is to liberate effects or styles from their determinate and determining causes (slices, cakes, cuisines; works, canons, the Canon), and to situate these effects as originary conditions and materials. It is, moreover, not just to maintain one's hunger while sustaining oneself, but to create by that perversely satisfied hunger an incompleteness that gets identified *with essential identity*. By this ingestive mode, which ends in an arrest of sexual development, one not only compromises the inherited uses – the history – of things, one resists delivering one's own social use-value. The anorectic sojourns, so to speak, within the everyday. One might visualize the identity produced by this process (associated, as I've said, with teenagers, women, and, in the forms we've reviewed through Keats, with the early middle class: all anxiously / assertively liminal states) as a space held open and structured by the contradictions it contains. The *sine qua non* here is the success of the defenses in fending off resolution, or digestion of other into self.

Consider in this context that celebrated luxury from the 'Ode to Melancholy': 'burst Joy's grape against [the] palate fine'. The phrase, a terrible one, is wrong on a number of levels. The perversity I remark here is Keats's accent on a *single* grape, and, on an unnaturally restricted gratification. The pleasure of grapes is, literally, the pleasure of *grapes*: the natural, plural, clustered condition of the grape. It is, further, the pleasure of a mouth, a throat, and a stomach full of grapes, a pleasure visually inscribed in that perfectly plumped, most self-identical fruit. Moreover, the *verbal* joy of grapes is, again, the pleasure of fullness and plurality: clusters, bunches, all those engorged sounds.

The complete Keatsian pleasure (revealingly, a melancholic delight) consists of a single grape not swallowed.[31] The real pleasure of the single grape burst against the palate is the swerve from the imagined sensation of a mouthful and a lifetime of grapes swallowed, their fine juice fermenting one's bodily liquors. Keats's phrase describes a supplement: the part, also a sign, is added to and displaces the whole signified. Keats's *self-advertising* supplementation idealizes those normative categories even as it sets them aside.

Who ever ate one grape, we might wonder, but a dandy (where the abstention signifies privilege), a man on a diet (Byron), or a person whose access to grapes – hothouse luxuries – was restricted, and who underwent further restrictions by way of working the unavoidable ones? We might recall, briefly, Keats's neckscarf, derided by several reviewers as an affectation: badge of the aesthete 'cit'. The scarf, which *was* for Keats a sign of professional self-election, was also the tubercular's defense against chills. What I describe is not a simple disguise ratio nor a denial, but a strategy for signifying restriction and, by changing its semiotic form, to alter its social value as well.

The famous phrase from the 'Ode to Melancholy' objectifies the more abstract desideratum from 'Drear Nighted December': 'the feel of not to feel it'. We can see by now that what is consciously 'not felt' isn't, as we generally assume, pain, but full pleasure. What Keats describes is not the condition of knowing yourself numb to pain, as at the dentist, but the pleasure of pleasure-mastery: 'the pain alone, the joy alone, distinct', but occupying the same psychic space and providing each other's constitutive limits. All these celebrated phrases formulate the tense pleasure of a partial, unnatural gratification that creates appetite even as it satisfies, or that truncates satisfaction even as it engenders it. These canonized phrases describe the conscious production of a self-alienation identified with identity itself.

The knight cannot do very much with his fortunate difference from industrious squirrels and wasted warriors (or, we could say, from nightingales and marble men).[32] By reference to the *Indicator* version, we see that the knight only proliferates the contradictions which his mediation releases. The *Indicator* literariness, an authorial signature, marks off for us the difference between those who suffer contradiction and those who stage it. Lacking a consciousness of himself as 'the between' – not the victim but the theater of contradiction – the knight cannot seize the virtues of his state. Only Keats, by his translation, can do this, as it were, *for* the knight, and by an intertextuality which *represents* the knight's 'kisses four' as well as his substitution of 'is withered' for the minstrel's 'has withered'. The *Indicator*, by making the 'wight' a more faithful translator, produces *Brown*'s contradictions as meanings. In these presented meanings, Keats finds his authority and originality.

What Wordsworth and Coleridge do seriously, properly, and nearly imperceptibly, Keats inscribes in his title and surrounds with a certain jokiness. We have marked the resemblance between Keats's title and both 'The Solitary Reaper' and 'The Rime of the Ancient Mariner', formal models, I would hazard, for 'La Belle Dame'. All three titles name the Original speech acts that enable and authorize those latest, those Romantic dreams. There is, however, a difference. Keats's title exactly reproduces the name of an Original text. Whereas Wordsworth and Coleridge tend to conflate point of origin and point of authorial reception–reproduction, Keats pries apart these moments so as to *produce* the historical contradiction present in all these Romantic practices. 'The Solitary Reaper' and 'The Ancient Mariner' figure historical and exegetical differentials only so as to syncretize – effectively, erase – them. Thus do both writers distinguish poetry from repetition, and poets from everyone else. Once the authorial voice has used the alterity of the Reaper's unintelligible song or of the Mariner's no less obscure narration to bring his own, substitutive authenticity into being, that otherness and its vehicles are textually and historically dismissed, banished to the never never land of folklore and philology. The Reaper's song is so thoroughly – organically – assimilated into authorial psyche, thence into Literature, that to say to oneself, 'solitary reaper' in the aftertone of Wordsworth's poem, is to think 'inward music'. It is, more specifically, to imagine some yet more abstracted, 'sublimed' version of the surmising 'song' developed in stanzas 2 and 3. No one is exercised by the fact that Wordsworth's narrator represents himself as the 'profound' and redemptive composer, probably because the poem so successfully blurs the outline of the displaced Original. We have to think hard about the verb that governs the concluding couplet, 'bore' ('gave birth to' as well as 'sustained'), in order to register the meaning – the cost, that is – of Wordsworth's originality.

In 'The Ancient Mariner', the ideological strangeness of the primary utterance, the mariner's, is philosophically resolved by the spatial device of the marginalia, a mechanism for the transformation of historical difference into hermeneutic pluralism. When we keep in mind the translation dynamics outlined above, we can see that both Wordsworth and Coleridge use history under the aspect of personal chronology, tourism, or textual transmission to smooth out intransigent historical contradiction: that is, to convert it into human, literary, and philosophic evolution – metaphysics of presence. 'The music in my heart I bore, / Long after it was heard no more'. This is the burden Wordsworth sings to poets 'who will be [his] second self when [he] is gone'.

The poem Wordsworth produces by his translation of an agricultural worksong is a *literary* worksong: a nuanced, self-reflexive, and self-consciously mediated harvest of mental wealth. Wordsworth ravishes his reaper. He consumes her 'melancholy strain' – and let us hear for once that sad pun – and digests it into easeful poetry. Her ancient worksong, with its turns and re-turns marking the ends and beginnings of rows reaped, is translated into radically pleasurable, nineteenth-century literary ballad: a song about the perniciousness of labor and the virtue of a wise passiveness. The subject of Wordsworth's poem is its coming into being: it is a poem about tropes, tours, and returns. We have here one very concrete illustration of that phrase Keats invented for Wordsworth, 'the egotistical sublime'.

The emphasis in that infamous phrase is not, I believe, moral. Keats's characterization of Wordsworth's mode need not, that is, be read as a humanistic attack upon a poetics of social mystification. Rather, we might read the critique as an insight into the technical ramifications of that aesthetic practice, and into the bearing of those effects on the authorial subject-form.

As I implied, Wordsworth and Coleridge render difference dialectically productive by establishing space as their representational field. Space, the dimension of identity and consonance, *makes* differences productive by enabling them to engage head on. Visualize a landscape, a painting, or a multiple column text; no matter how anarchic the representations, one figure or narration always partly antithesizes the other. What I'm describing is a reciprocal figural interdetermination. Within a spatial universe, difference is form and relationship: life, or a projection thereof. Moreover, all differences, once they are spatialized, can be resolved because space means, ultimately, enclosure within a single field. Difference within such a field exists only at the level of form or appearance. The deep truth – literally, the ground – is identity.

To return to 'The Solitary Reaper', we observe that Wordsworth plots historical and social differences along the X-axis, a spatial plane. I mean this in the most literal sense. The topographical figure for the poem would look something like this.

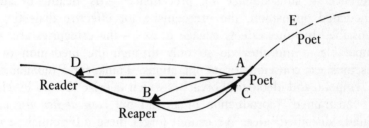

Wordsworth's conceptual model is spatial as well; I refer to the governing town–country opposition, a contained and already resolved – ideologically articulated – contradiction. The figure of the poet-tourguide who commands both a country prospect and an urban audience ('Behold her . . .') is the sign of this preresolved antithesis. The poem quite literally ends by resuming its own beginning.

So enthralling is that wonderful coda – that song / singer / reaper / poet symphony – that we easily forget the historical and social discord which is the ground of that harmony, the strong, sad bass to its high melody: high requiem, really. It takes real effort to recall that the transformation of agricultural worksong into urban lyrical ballad was the result of material and social transformations, and of the severe and unrecompensed discontinuities they brought about. Both the poem and the Romantic ideology which frames it dull our memory; we forget that Wordsworth could 'behold', or occupy the same space as his reaper only in imagination and in poetry. The real vales between their moments and manners were too profound – too temporal – for inseminating overflows, or I–thou encounters. By the time Wordsworth observes the reaper (if he observed her at all), she is already an echo, unintelligible not because she sings in Erse, but because her very being is the effect of a different historical moment, a different productive order from Wordsworth's.[33] In order to use this pastness, Wordsworth must translate the reaper's sociohistorical isolation – how many such figures are left in 1805? – into spatial, aesthetic singularity: 'single in the field'. Even if we manage to make ourselves alive to these changes, we are likely to interpret them providentially: formally, as the effects of an evolutionary dialectical synthesis.

Keats tends to use time as his representational field: the field of noncoincidence and discontinuity. Time is the dimension where difference – subsequence or precedence – is death, because unmediated opposition, the prerequisite for effective dialectic, is impossible. In time, effects engage causes – the categories are not comparable – and they do so only through the mediation of a consciousness conscious of its operations. Think, for a moment, of the temporal and ideological breaches which valorize Keats's Psyche, his 'constrained' reproduction of an old but *even at her origin*, a belated, 'disjoined' idea. We cannot forget these differentials; with such phrases as 'O latest born . . . Of all Olympus' faded hierarchy', and 'pleasant thoughts, *instead of* pines' (my emphasis), Keats dramatizes his supplemental imitation of that making which brought Psyche herself into being. Who, we might ask, but such a 'latest' figure, or so figured an object of desire, could enable the reflexively fetishistic repetitions that constitute Keats's Ode?

'La Belle Dame', while its finale bears a certain formal resemblance to that of 'The Solitary Reaper', (both poems end more or less where they begin), inscribes on every level unresolvable dislocations. The here–there contradiction in the knight's summation marks off the noncoincidence of the minstrel's organic world and the romance realm of the Lady. It reminds us not only that knights and harvesters never shared the same universe of discourse, but that even in the poem, they stage a competition upon which Keats capitalizes. By a stylistic dissonance, Keats signifies and uses his remove from his *materia poetica*. His poetic labor is like that of the *entrepreneur*: one who 'undertakes', but also, the 'between' (*entre*) who takes from both sides, proper producers and proper consumers.

Wordsworth's and Coleridge's syncretic narrations, while they raise up the wrecked utterance they translate, do not articulate the pastness of their founding speech moments. To the contrary, the poems of the first-generation writers typically restore, in their substitutive way, that which has already slipped away or would soon do if not for the poet's saving intervention. At the end of Wordsworth's poem, a speech which silences the reaper's, that Highland figure is still there somehow, reaping and singing. Similarly, Wordsworth's startling, present-tense injunction addresses us directly, no matter where we stand in relation to 1805. We are always stopping and passing, as 'she' is always reaping and singing, because all these events take place in canonical time. Likewise, the Mariner remains, eternally repeating his tale to an eternally recurrent type: the Wedding Guest, that reader surrogate. The canonically absorbed difference of these moments, narratives, and characters, the condition of their permanence, conceals what we have learned to call '*différance*'.

That which would be, in Wordsworth's poetry, *essentially* continuous representations – reapers and writers – are, in 'La Belle Dame', respectively done and gone. The discursive styles remain, but the worlds which engendered those intonations – the organic community, the high romance – are extinct. The speech orders that constitute the knight's narration are, in textual terms, apparitional. The minstrel is not there at the end of the poem to frame the knight's unsettling speech and to reassure us of his own categorical permanence. Nor do the kings and princes have a being outside the discursive space of the knight. Both the minstrel and the pale statesmen are the knight's dream, effects which have outlived their causes. The knight, container of those free effects – lost causes – is all that we get in the way of a represented Origin.

As for Keats's dream, 'La Belle Dame', we see that nothing can kill this poem for it has already parodied itself. Nothing can displace it but another work by Keats, which would, by the two-text dynamic we have examined, effectuate the Original even as it undermined it. Both texts, *Indicator* and *Brown*, are locked into an end-stopped system capable of infinite self-replication. The metaphor that might clarify this mode of production would have to come from Einsteinian physics, as the hallmark of Keats's solution is its deconstruction of the time–space axis, or, its twisting of those parallel bars into a double helix. Keats's experiments in translation demonstrate that space is only a possible order of physical objects (say, texts), and, therefore, that subsequence is not law. The proof should give a whole new emphasis to Oceanus' 'murmurs': 'So on our heels a fresh perfection treads, / A power more strong in beauty, born of us / And fated to excel us . . . nor are we / Thereby more conquered [conquer'd] than by us the rule / Of shapeless chaos [Chaos]' ('Hyperion', II, 212–27).

I have suggested that 'done' and 'gone' may be taken to diagram a class-historical way of relating consumption, associated with a mystified aristocracy, to production, the mythic mode of the working class. Along these lines, the knight emerges as a function which produces itself as a consumer: a market that cannot be glutted because it consumes fetishistically. The more it appropriates, the less there is of self-presence: the greater, thus, its appetite. It makes sense that the novel, prepared according to James's recipe for bad ones (a pudding-suspension of edible odds and ends), should become the exemplary literary form of this class.

But poetry was not exempt from the pressures which fashioned the novel. Consider some very celebrated statements about poetry and the imagination. Shelley, for instance, tells us that poetry, by stretching our capacity to identify with that which is unlike us, enlarges the moral sense and makes us crave new sources of satisfaction when the poetic 'food' or imagery is withdrawn or used up. By feeding us, poetry creates new 'interstices' in our soul that require filling.[34] The great expression of this identification of poetry with consumption is, of course, Wordsworth's 'every author, as far as he is great and at the same time *original*, has had the task of creating the taste by which he is to be enjoyed.' The statement is not a narrow public relations expedient but an expression of class necessity. Poetry's product is appetite production; the Romantic poets are hunger artists in the deepest sense. They produce a literature that 'by giving, makes us ask'. 'Outrageous stimulation' is anathema to Wordsworth because it represents direct and appropriate giving and receiving, and therefore, a satisfaction that amounts to the temporary death of desire: a *genuinely* unmisgiving literature.

We shall see that throughout his poetry, Keats encodes idealized images of the early nineteenth-century bourgeois situation. Generally speaking, his oxymoronic magic, performed at the level of discourse, narrative, text, and canon, reflects a competitive dyadic economy where resolution is counterproductive, where contradiction between functionally differentiated elements (not, that is, essential categories of being) is the condition of productivity, and insatiable appetite for the value of things an institutionalized subversiveness. Because so often in Keats's poetry these forms of dissonance materialize as discursive styles, it is crucial that we cultivate a social ear for his verse. Thus do we translate the richness of his tones into its original form: contradiction. Thus do we come to appreciate Keats's style as that which contains, idealizes, and exists by contradiction.

We may add one more dimension to this sociological reflection. Above, I implied that to conceive the middle class in spatial terms is to describe an organic dialectic, whereby the middleness of that class signifies the moment of synthesis. At that middle station, the 'raw' energy of the working class, and the wise (refined / refining) passiveness of the aristocracy, are preserved and surpassed. To focus the middle class in this way is to see it as a structurally conservative unit: a body that holds things together and that conserves, in its parodic fashion, the values and practices of its adjacent classes.

To plot the middle class upon a *temporal* axis is to bring out its subversiveness. With time as the governing line, we see that the middle class must refuse the concept of the absolute: that Demogorgon which would deny the bourgeoisie a social standing of any kind. On the other hand, in order to defend its identity from that historical necessity which brought it into being, the middle class must develop a perverse relation to 'fast' and effective time. We could say that one ideological task of the middle class at this early point in its formation was to pronounce itself *sui generis* and undetermined, and *at the same time*, as history's telos: first and last. Hence, perhaps, Satan's charm for the Romantics: in Bloom's Miltonic phrase, knowing no time when I was not as now, and myself self-created. Hence, also, Keats's range of placeholding maneuvers. By the translational, ingestive, and masturbatory procedures we have examined, Keats could turn the arrow of literary history backwards (poems in praise of great Originals), all the while using that history, its normative grammar, to define his *original* difference, thereby to move forward but *not* into the jaws of those hungry generations.[35] Imagine a man walking down an up-escalator, just a little bit slower than it ascends; imagine him walking improperly and out of synchrony. A figure of unmoving motion, divinely suspended, he is, in fact, imperceptibly, safely advancing, letting the canon or its grammar do the work.

One focuses the seminal, social bind a bit differently by describing the middle class as neither landed nor unlanded: a class that acquires properties but keeps them alienated, in this way displaying, parodying, and *identifying with* its ownership. This is a body which, to create itself as an ideological phenomenon, had to destroy its 'self', or fracture whatever it had of a given integrity. Byron's powerfully disturbing, suicidal image – the scorpion ringed with fire – tells the impossible history of that class. The agent of destruction, and its fallout, was that good and bad self-consciousness we find throughout the poetry of the period: philosophical enlightenment and social role disjunction. One could say that the middle class's imperative to proliferate and valorize contradiction at every level reflects its structural function: to stand in for and *between* legitimate classes. These classes, already consolidated, found themselves wonderfully mystified by the perversity of that entre-preneurial class, mis-takers and mis-givers. A class neither at home nor exiled, a sojourning class.

The untenable state I describe was refigured as a stationing tension. Again, we confront the conservative function of that subversive subject, the early nineteenth-century middle class: a body that had to be buttressed / beleaguered on both sides by a folk and an aristocracy, dimensions that the middle class *revived* so as to define more sharply its own perverse contours. Here is a classic example of mediation: that which connects by dividing.

Wordsworth's program of organic reproduction is, like Keats's, a substitution program. In Wordsworth, the poet occurs in such a way and at such a time as to realize the wreckage which he finds in the everyday. He is always, formally, the synthesis of some buried thesis–antithesis ratio. By his translation of those ruined lives and tales, he raises them up, transforming their incident into feeling, their substance into symbol, their metonymic uses into a more strictly metaphoric exchange form. Wordsworth connects disengaged effects – history's detritus: unfinished sheepfolds, ruined cottages, hopeless lives – to what he represents as their efficient causes. By his (christological) mediations, he names himself a first cause, and he sets the whole historical dynamic under the sign of that final cause, Literature, which is to say, consciousness: a chronicle of heaven.

Keats's poetry brings out the enabling limits of the first-generation literature. Keats makes us see that poetry's additions to life are also expressions of the destructive character. Poetry *translates*: for the subtle Greek motto, it offers a bathetic, decorative, fetishized, nineteenth-century idea of gnomic discourse: ' "Beauty is truth, truth beauty . . ." '. The translation, we must see, *is* vulgar – a parody – but it is also the only way that Originals and originals, first and latest words, break free of that killing field, the Canon. When Wordsworth addresses his poetry to those writers 'who will be [his] second self when [he] is gone', he has in mind a substitutive sequence closely patterned on the genetic model exemplified by Michael, Michael's father, and Luke – a son and grandson. The force in Wordsworth's representation is, as usual, on assimilation, or continuous, organic reproduction. Keats similarly directs his verse to alter egos, but as with his appropriative style, he puts the stress on alter, not ego. For Keats, it is distance, dis-ease, disjunction that make space and give time. He therefore displays the tendentiousness of his substitutions, identifying his own and all such acts as impossible but necessary. He does so not to resolve the featured contradiction, but to place himself by it.

I believe that 'La Belle Dame' contains a political argument along the lines drawn by Marilyn Butler in her *Romantics, Rebels and Reactionaries*.[36] Keats's poem, a work about our Lady of no Mercy, offers itself as a critique of Wordsworth and Coleridge – their ethos of retirement. These figures are encoded in the poem by Keats's formally resonant title and procedures, as by some direct quotations (for example, 'and her eyes were wild', 'honey wild, and manna dew'). A reading of this kind, which would explore Keats's allusions to the fideism, asceticism, biblical interests, and austere gothicism that was the second generation's idea of the first-generation Romantics, would be most helpful. It would illuminate for us Keats's conscious intentions for the poem, as well as its contemporary and Victorian reception. My object here and throughout this book, however, is to expose that class of meanings which is not intended *by* consciousness so much as *for* it.

I conclude by naming 'La Belle Dame' a waiting poem: its great precursor, 'The Ruined Cottage', and its great successor, 'Mariana'. Masturbation is traditionally something one does while waiting to grow up and have proper sex. The argument of this chapter would lead us to look at the matter differently, or to construe masturbation as something one does to avoid growing up-and-into the system, without becoming possessed on the other side, entombed in Eden. Masturbation is not, then, a way to kill time, but to create it. It is waiting liberated from its object: determinacy without the death which is fulfilled desire. We see, as did Keats, perhaps, that Wordsworth's Margaret at some point ceases to wait 'for' her husband, as she ceases to live 'for' her children. The events of her life transform her from a purposeful, 'forward-looking' woman into one who waits, and who comes to define a new kind of duration. Her death, which occurs in the narrative margins, is no end, just a lapsing into a new kind of waiting. By their discursive responses, the two poetic narrators demonstrate the power of Margaret's peculiar *durée*, her style, to regenerate itself self-consciously (parodically), in persons who enter her domain.

In Tennyson's 'Mariana', the virtues of the waiting state are developed more explicitly. Tennyson, who takes his title from Shakespeare, pronounces his own perversity by the gratuitous epigraphic allusion. Shakespeare's Mariana is a figure of fulfillment, a comic figure. She gets what she waits for and she doesn't wait very long anyway. Tennyson's Mariana waits eternally. Her suffering, an extreme consciousness of a pain sharply dissociated in her mind (and ours) from its cause, puts her in a time-warp where things happen, life vibrates, but death cannot win because life will not face it squarely. Mariana's weariness, like the knight's withering, is a state of permanent participiality, a *nunc stans*.

Translation is traditionally something one does while waiting for the time or money or inspiration to write one's own, original work. Keats's poetry, the apex of a curve beginning its climb in Dryden, Gray, Collins, and Chatterton, and sloping down towards Swinburne, Browning, and Pound, is, we can see, profoundly original translation, its virtues identical with its badness.

Notes

1 Steven Marcus, *The Other Victorians* (New York: Basic Books, 1964; 1974).
2 The virtual image is an image formed of points from which divergent light rays

seem to emanate but do not actually do so: as in the image of a point source seen in a plane mirror.

The changes I ring on the word 'virtue' stem from the physical innocence preserved by masturbation when it is considered only as a *substitute* for intercourse. Here is the difference to which Rousseau (and Jacques Derrida, *Of Grammatology*, trans. G. Spivak (Baltimore: Johns Hopkins Univ. Press, 1974; 1976), p. 150) refers: *pucelage*, or sexual intactness, as opposed to spiritual innocence.

3 The underlying structure of our critique is that of fable, with its didactic, moralistic thrust, while the sort of reading I map out activates formal conventions associated with fairy tale. By this I mean a representation of developmental conflict such that the solution is inscribed in the narrative structure.

4 Of course Keats wanted more than anything else to belong to the company of real literary men, as he wanted to write profound and enduring literature. More than any poet we know, he craved the identity of the great author. When I speak of Keats's desires, I mean the parallel or 'shadow' wishes articulated by his strategies for realizing his good intentions. In Keats's case, the tactical style tends to expose interests sharply at odds with the designated project.

5 Jerome McGann, 'Keats and the Historical Method in Literary Criticism', *Modern Language Notes*, 94 (1979), 988–1032. McGann is the first reader to have penetrated the high gloss of 'To Autumn'. By relating Keats's aesthetically abstracted seasonal representation to contemporary agricultural conditions, to the political emergency (Peterloo, that cold and bloody 'stubble field'), and to the pictorial conventions invoked by Keats's ode, McGann brings out the meanings of the poem's stylistic transparency: what criticism has liked to call its *exemplary* style.

6 We must remember that we are not talking about a middle-class poet but about a young man who aspired to the condition of the legitimate middle class, and to the profession of poetry. Keats's marginality with respect to the bourgeois institutions of his time to some extent explains the exposure potential of his verse, as opposed to the writing of more critical, but also sociologically more *absorbed* authors: Wordsworth and Coleridge. Yeats's patronizing caricature of Keats – a boy with his nose pressed against the window of a sweet shop – develops the wrong exposure. Instead of looking *out* with Yeats from his cosy inside station (Yeats's own defensive strategy) at that embarrassingly squashed nose, we should look through Keats's alienated eyes at that conspicuously structured array, the Tradition.

For a fuller treatment of Keats's position, see chapter 3, pp. 126–7, chapter 4, pp. 218–22; all of chapter 5, chapter 6, pp. 292–5, and, for a gloss on the apothecary training, n. 22, chapter 6.

7 Consider, for example, Byron's 'Jack Keats, or Ketch, or whatever his names are', his 'Johnny Keats', Croker's 'Mr. Keats, (if that be his real name, for we almost doubt that any man in his senses would put his real name to such a rhapsody [as the 1817 volume]', and Lockhart's 'Mr. John', 'Johnny'. (Jack Ketch was slang for the common hangman.)

Bate (*John Keats*, Cambridge, Mass.: Harvard Univ. Press, 1963, Appendix 1, pp. 701–3) identifies 'Keats' as an exceedingly uncommon name in its plural or possessive form, though very frequent in Cornwall in the singular form. Bate's best bet for the derivation of the name is from the OE ' "cyte" (a hut or shed for cattle or sheep), the name probably denoting a herdsman. Other possibilities are that it was originally a nickname for "Christopher" ("Kitt", "Kitts"), or, less probably, a genitive of "Kate", as the name "Maggs" is possibly the genitive of "Mag" ("Margaret")'. Bate's conclusion ('. . . one can perhaps sympathize with the old lady in the Victorian story who, on hearing the poet's name, asked "What are Keats?" ') strikes just the right note. The 's', suggesting plurality, as of objects, and also possessiveness – commonness in both senses – is what gets amplified in the reviews.

8 Printed in the *Indicator*, 10 May 1820. Keats read Chartier's poem in Bell's *The Poetical Works of Geoffrey Chaucer* (1782), vol. 10. The volume also contains Chaucer's 'Testament of Creseide', 'Legende of Good Women', 'Praise of Women' and 'Assemble of Ladies'. (It is now established that Chaucer was *not* the translator of Chartier's 'La Belle Dame'. When I say Chaucer's 'La Belle Dame', I designate Keats's and the period's authorial idea.) 'Thomas The Rymer' appears in Scott's *Minstrelsy of the Scottish Border* (1812), vol. 1; and Robert Jamieson, *Popular Ballads and Songs* (Edinburgh and London: John Murray, 1806), vol. 2 ('True Thomas and the Queen of Elfland').

Werner Beyer (*Keats and the Demon King*, London: Oxford Univ. Press, 1947) argues persuasively for the influence of Wieland's *Oberon* on many of Keats's poems. The Oberon motif I find most interesting with respect to Keats's style and narrative procedures is the wizard's injunction against 'unhallowed love'. For the duration of their journey to Rome, where they will wed, Huon and Rezia are to be as brother and sister. The penalty for disobedience is the withdrawal of Oberon's overseeing magic, a catastrophe which initiates the poem's narrative line. The dynamics – partial and therefore painful pleasure as the condition for full power and poetic discourse – is very much the logic I develop in this reading of 'La Belle Dame'.

9 'Brought over' (also, 'move over', 'put across') is a literal translation of the word 'translation'. 'Metaphor', interestingly ('substitute', 'supplement'), is the comparable Greek word. See Paul de Man, 'Walter Benjamin's "The Task of the Translator" ' in *The Resistance To Theory*, (Minneapolis: Univ. of Minnesota Press, 1986), p. 83.

10 I signify the work situated as a first and authorizing text by the upper case 'Original'; 'original' names the belated work which, by its bad reproduction of its source (that is, Original) text, escapes that work's sphere of influence.

11 McGann, 'Keats and the Historical Method'.

12 My discussion represents a crossing of Mikhail Bakhtin, *The Dialogic Imagination*; V. N. Vološinov, *Freudianism: A Marxist Critique*, trans. I. R. Titunik and N. Bruss (New York: Academic Press, 1976); and *Marxism and the Philosophy of Language*, trans. M. Matejka and I. R. Titunik (New York: Seminar Press, 1973); and Marx's analytic model, *The Eighteenth Brumaire of Louis Bonaparte*, trans. anon. (New York: International Publishers, 1963).

13 Claude Finney, *The Evolution of Keats' Poetry*, 2 vols. (New York: Russell and

Russell, 1963), vol. 2, pp. 595–8. Aileen Ward, *John Keats, The Making of a Poet*, (New York: Viking, 1963), p. 273.

14 The third narration is the romance dialogue which seems to be the poem's narrative bottom line, but which, according to Chaucer's description, is itself a reproduction from memory of some oral Original.

15 See Reuben Brower, *On Translation* (Cambridge, Mass.: Harvard Univ. Press, 1959); George Steiner, *After Babel* (Oxford: Oxford Univ. Press, 1975; 1981); William Arrowsmith and Roger Shattuck, eds., *The Craft and Context of Translation* (Austin: Univ. of Texas Press, 1961); J. B. Leishman, *Translating Horace* (Oxford: Oxford Univ. Press, 1956); J. S. Phillimore, *Some Remarks on Translation and Translators* (Oxford: The English Association, January 1919); Walter Benjamin, 'The Task of the Translator' and 'The Work of Art in an Age of Mechanical Reproduction', in *Illuminations*, trans. H. Zohn, ed. H. Arendt (New York: Harcourt Brace, 1968).

Keats aspired to 'a few fine Plays, his greatest ambition'. In this wish, we sense a departure from the unself-consciousness of both the lofty and the luscious styles. We see Keats developing a range of manners; like Byron, Keats concerns himself with the surface of his text and with its social tone. Keats's attempt to 'wean himself' from Fanny Brawne shows the same withdrawal from direct desires *and* displacements. It was during this interval that Keats became intensely interested in Dryden, whose fame in Keats's day significantly included his work as a translator.

In his revision of the Paolo and Francesca sonnet, completed during these months, Keats substitutes 'worldwind' for Cary's and his own earlier 'whirlwind' (see McGann, 'Keats and the Historical Method'). As with the rejection of the Miltonically possessed 'Hyperion', we see an experiment in conscious badness. Keats's 'worldwind', a perfectly awkward word, parodies the poet's own first words, as well as the translation which is Keats's source. Keats produces his authorial identity as against Cary, and perhaps so as to imply his intimacy with that unheard, empowering melody, Dante himself. Keats's 'worldwind', a sort of homologue for the otherness and vitality which is Dante's canonical meaning, precisely marks off Dante's remoteness. What Dante's lovers suffer is not of course an indifferent world-battering but a specifically Christian and other-worldly punishment. Keats's bad translation shows us how Dante's painful reality, Christian misery, can be a nineteenth-century resort.

16 For an accomplished handling of some of these matters, see Philip Fisher, 'A Museum With One Work Inside: Keats and the Finality of Art', *Keats–Shelley Journal*, 33 (1984), 85–102.

17 Marjorie Levinson, 'The New Historicism: What's in a Name', in *Critical Readings of Romantic History*, ed. Levinson, forthcoming Blackwell's, 1988.

18 The tragic is not tragic until it gets doubled. The repetition – formally, a parody – recasts the Original as a noble first: a *substantive* transformation, this. Napoleon Buonaparte, 1795, waits upon his own detached effect, Louis Buonaparte, 1851, for his realized character: that of the tragic Origin. In that perverse moment – a moment dramatized by Milton's incestuous trio, Satan, Sin, and Death – the Original is delivered into and out of history: effectuated, hollowed out, and

apotheosized. It's not hard to see that the Original painting comes into being with the fact or possibility of mechanical reproduction. The authentic is authenticated – *created* – by the hoax. Somehow it is harder to grasp these dynamics played out in literary space: to see for example that Chatterton created not just the taste but the singular concept which was the object of that taste.

Naturally, one could develop, from Keats's letters and by way of Shelley's historical reflections, a philosophic explanation of these ironic redemptions of the past which construct a present tense. My reading of Keats's translational poetics should not disallow such schemes; it should, however, place them at a certain interpretative level and expose the existence of other, more primary levels. My concern is to explain the practical meanings of Keats's representations; indirectly, we also situate the idealistic readings prompted by those representations.

19 Finney, *The Evolution of Keats' Poetry*, vol. 2, pp. 595–9.

20 The fact that the nightingale's natural – that is, biological – being is supplemented by so famous an iconic dimension makes it an ideal object for a meditation of this kind.

21 Earl Wasserman, *The Finer Tone* (Baltimore: The Johns Hopkins Univ. Press, 1955), p. 135.

22 The fact that we use 'sojourn' as a noun whereas 'loiter' will not be reified, underlines the difference between a perverse and parodic, 'sojourning' critique and an antithetical or 'loitering' discourse: that is, contingent and content-less.

23 This was Keats's response to those who questioned the propriety of Porphyro's accomplishment of his design.

24 For a helpful analogy, one might recall the Ancient Mariner's account, a narration which fails utterly to explain itself or the position and character of the man who delivers it: an account which only, and very forcefully, explains the historicity of exegetical acts. The effect of this represented failure is, paradoxically, to initiate a hermeneutic chain reaction, leading toward the one interpretative moment set free by its powerful historical self-consciousness. (See Jerome McGann, 'The Meaning of the Ancient Mariner', in *Critical Inquiry*, viii, 1981). Within the discursive economy of 'La Belle Dame', the knight's narration is just such a finer tone repetition as the diverse recensions which make up Coleridge's poem. We see that Coleridge arrests, or rather absorbs, the sport by his cool syntheses, the product of the only unmarked ideology in the poem, his own Broad Church interlineations. Coleridge's Mariner will go on repeating his half-truths, but Coleridge, by his poem, has already brought them into the circle of his Higher Criticism, where they can never again be anything but resolved. One could also say that Coleridge enshrines the Mariner in the Canon (a word that maintains its ecclesiastical resonance in the context of Coleridge's *oeuvre*), where he enjoys eternal life-in-death.

Keats's translations, conversely, are neither mediated nor totalized by an authorial exegete. There is no enlightened overvoice in the poem to define invidiously its narrative repetitions. 'La Belle Dame', we see, draws no hermeneutic circle; it develops *by*, and *develops* a special – indeed, antinatural – linear and temporal logic.

25 In 'La Belle Dame', the fictive dynamic mirrors Keats's actual and advertised violence upon an Original. Chartier's poem is triply suppressed: by Hunt's annotation which ignores the French Original, by Keats's strictly titular allusion to Chaucer's translation, and by his misleading display of the True Thomas materials.

26 See the catalogue of 'slant' and 'sideways' representations assembled by John Jones, *John Keats's Dream of Truth* (New York: Barnes and Noble, 1969) 153–4.

27 Apropos that troubling word, 'syndrome', let me present a literary phenomenon which Susan Stewart has lately defined: namely, distressed art. In contemporary colloquial usage, the phrase describes new-made objects which are physically battered ('distressed') in order to give them an antique look. Stewart uses the model to explore the ways in which certain literary–social epochs put their belated and longing inventions under the sign of the old, the oral, and the self-identical. The emphasis in distressed discourse is on the seamlessness of the work; its value is tied to its success in approximating the authorizing look of the epic first (Bakhtin) or, to recast in a Marxian idiom, the tragic first. The new–old contradiction, a byproduct of an ideologically necessitated mode of production, is smoothed out (Susan Stewart, 'Distressed Genres', public lecture, University of Pennsylvania, 1985).

In what I call dis-eased, and sometimes 'dis-articulated' art (Keats's poetry, some of Byron's, Swinburne's, Rossetti's, Browning's), it is the formal contradiction which is valorized, and not its semantic motive or burden. The dis-eased work *represents* its two-faced character: at once medieval and medievalist, a total form and a style, naive and sentimental, tragic and farcical.

This rhetorical distinction I have drawn may amount to a critical difference; perhaps the dis-eased work *is* the distressed work set within a dynamic social field where its contradictions start disclosing their purposes.

28 In effect, Keats opposes matter-of-fact to state-of-mind: material life to intellectual existence. We have, thus, a keen and, given Keats's moment, remarkable critique, familiar to us from the political and economic discourses of the late nineteenth century. Keats articulates the deadliness of the specialized, and also binary practice. It is his special social *place* within his moment that to some extent explains insights such as these. See chapters 5 and 6.

29 One might think here of the irregular pallors of the masturbator and the consumptive. While the surface meaning of these symptoms is, of course, depletion (loss of those vital fluids, semen and blood), the whiteness also denotes a perverse concentration of blood: i.e., pulmonary and phallic engorgement. Both pathologies feature an excessive libido, an overly 'sanguine' temperament. (For a provocative treatment of that nineteenth-century 'master disease', consumption, see Susan Sontag, *Illness as Metaphor* (New York: Random House, 1977).) The resemblances between consumption and the nineteenth-century masturbation *mythos* are striking. One is tempted to read the two disease models as representations of bourgeois social reproduction, and, more specifically, as instructions for a particular mode of material and semiotic appropriation.

30 'The Eve of St. Agnes', a 'realized' romance to the extent that Madeline and Porphyro technically consummate their desire, requires that terminal storm. The

dramatic, discursive, and canonical violence of that ending saves the poem and its heroes from a canonical dissolve.

31 The grape conceit, which might be a loose allusion to Marvell ('Let us roll all our strength and all / Our sweetness up into one ball, / And tear our pleasures with rough strife / Through the iron gates of life', 'To His Coy Mistress'), suggests that only those who *take* their pleasure properly (that is, completely, directly, unself-consciously), *experience* genuine pleasure. To recall Marvell's robust exhortation, however, is also to recognize in Keats's conceit the description of a trivialized, self-conscious, and contrived delight. A grape is a very small ball, and a tongue, no matter how 'strenuous', cannot perform much heroic tearing.

32 This is a difference that gets dramatized in Swinburne's 'Laus Veneris', that 'expans'd' repetition of 'La Belle Dame'. Swinburne's paganized knight – which is to say, a Christian but internally alienated hero – is, to use our operative metaphor, a translation of Keats's withering hero. Whereas twentieth-century Keats criticism likes to transform the knight's contradictoriness into productive dialectics (productive, that is, of just the sort of humanism we value), for Swinburne, the contradiction was the thing: the virtue of Keats's hero and poem. By the conflicts which he embraces, products of his fetishistic absorption of the banished world and the subject of his reflective life, Swinburne's knight is empowered and immortalized. He misses, of course, 'the clean great time of goodly [that is, Christian] fight', 'the battle sharp', 'the fair pure sword', 'the edged light'. But even as he fondly recalls those complete, unconflicted pleasures, he also rejects that phallic, adult style: rejects, that is, the frozen world. We understand that by his constitutive and idealized tensions, the knight is rendered God's equal antagonist. He enjoys a free and effective condition.

33 Between Wordsworth's poem and his putative encounter with a real reaper, intervene not just two years, but a passage from Thomas Wilkinson's well-known guidebook, *Tour in Scotland*. (Regarding that 'putative' and 'real', Dorothy's *Journal* says 'It is not uncommon in the more lonely parts of the Highlands to see a *single* person so employed.' Dorothy's description of her passage with her brother through a fertile, varied, cultivated landscape of 'open fields . . . enlivened by small companies of reapers', implies that the *solitary* reaper, indigenous to the remoter, less bucolic regions, was not actually seen.) Wilkinson's passage finds its way almost verbatim into Wordsworth's poem: 'Passed a female who was reaping alone; she sung in Erse, as she bended over her sickle; the sweetest human voice I ever heard: her strains were tenderly melancholy, and felt delicious, long after they were heard no more.' The exactness of the transposition reinforces one's skepticism; one *must* wonder whether Wordsworth ever saw his reaper at all. Or, being a bit more flexible, one might argue from the poem's discursive obsessiveness (four allusions to the reaper's solitude in the first stanza), that the narrator, prompted by nostalgia for the old days and lays, singles out one figure from a company of harvesters. The contrastive gambit is a way of bringing into focus the secondary and semiotic, as opposed to the more primary, experiential moment. Like Lucy, the reaper is 'Fair as a star, when only one / Is shining in the sky'.

34 Consider, in this context, Madeline's plea that Porphyro remain with her, now

that he has loved her, 'a dove forlorn and lost with sick, [sick] unpruned wing'. The imagery here and throughout the poem equates Madeline's loss of virginity with her acquisition of wings, and it associates this gain with sexual desire. Porphyro's giving makes Madeline ask; she needs his continued 'pruning' to keep her from suffocating of the desire he has aroused in her by the very act she solicits. The horticultural phenomenon invoked here (as by Eve, we recall, just before she sets out to prove her virtue, *and* her desire) has an obvious sexual logic. I think Keats intended the verb 'preen', but the substitution of 'prune' makes better, or deeper sense. See chapter 3, pp. 165 ff.

35 A glance through the table of contents to any standard edition of Keats's poetry discloses a wealth of poems 'after' great Originals: 'Imitation of Spenser', 'To Lord Byron', 'To Chatterton', 'Calidore', 'To One Who Has Been Long in City Pent', 'On First Looking into Chapman's Homer', 'On the Story of the Rimini'. These are just some of the minor pieces; consider *Endymion*, 'Isabella', 'Drear Nighted December', 'The Eve of St. Agnes', and the *Hyperions*.

36 Marilyn Butler, *Romantics, Rebels and Reactionaries* (Oxford: Oxford Univ. Press, 1982).

3

'The Eve of St. Agnes'

The spoken word, it might be said, is the ecstasy of the creature, it is exposure, rashness, powerlessness before God; the written word is the composure of the creature, dignity, superiority, omnipotence over the objects of the world.

Walter Benjamin, *The Origin of German Tragic Drama*

In front of and beside the windows, taper-like candelabra mounted a guard of honor in still leafy trees which spread out in bouquets of enamel, metal, or cloth lilies on the steps of a basilica altar. In short, they were the surprise packages of vagrant children for whom the world is imprisoned in a magic lattice, which they themselves weave about the globe with toes as hard and agile as Pavlova's. Children of this kind are invisible.

Jean Genet, *Our Lady of the Flowers*, trans. Bernard Frechtman

A sense of real things comes doubly strong,
And, like a muddy stream, would bear along
My soul to nothingness . . .

John Keats, 'Sleep and Poetry'

He saw words as things, and he saw them one at a time.

Arthur Symons, *The Romantic Movement in English Poetry*

The classical first move in a critical reading is to map the critical field, and to map it in such a way as to describe the determinate gap that one's own, new reading will remedy. The critic, in effect, outlines Massachusetts, New York, and Rhode Island and then discovers Connecticut. By the metaphor, we can see that insofar as the new reading takes its formal and semantic dimensions – its geopolitical identity – from the existing critical configuration, such readings are anything but new. Moreover, far from disturbing the universe of discourse, readings developed in this manner cannot but confirm it, as Connecticut spatially secures its adjacent states.

To pursue the cartography metaphor, let me suggest that we read our critical maps for their topographical information, and that we track this information down to its source: tectonic interactions, conceived as the historical expression of ongoing geological processes. We learn from such maps that the apparently stable and eternal structures we call nature are but the passing precipitate of intertectonic pressures. To the extent that these structures determine and / or naturalize those geopolitical distributions we call culture (or, cities, states, countries), that system too is positioned within a processual logic driven by contradiction and determined by the manifest history of solutions to deep geological conflict.

Similarly, by analyzing the conceptual kinetics underlying the critical map for a given work, we learn to appreciate the timebound and overdetermined character of literary nature (textual features and the generic norms that frame them) and literary culture (criticism: the institutional distributions of those features and norms). We begin to explain ideological patterns (and the textual knowledge they promote) by way of the material tensions that subtend them and that in slow time and very subtly, *register* the forms they have crystallized out. Since ideas, unlike geological dynamics, *can* be refused, our analysis can have some practical effects. By rewriting the map – in terms of stresses rather than structures, and in terms of reciprocal and overdeterminations rather than unilinear causality – we not only alter our experience of objects that have been captured by that map, we actually change the face of literary nature.

The scholarly discourse on 'St. Agnes' looks like an exemplary critical pluralism. At one end of the field, Douglas Bush has founded 'the romantic tapestry school', an institution with no students or faculty today, but plenty of eminent alumni.[1] This is to say, the academy lives on in many of our more strenuous and semantically interested readings. Robert Gittings, for example, whose reading of 'St. Agnes' emphasizes Keats's 'adult realism', retains the pictorial model for his structural description: 'the poem seems like a series of medieval pictures, giving a fresh view of the same story from stanza to stanza, like some jeweled fresco from a church wall . . .'[2] The apparent contradiction in Gittings's critique ('jeweled frescos' hardly consort with 'adult realism') is in fact an elaboration of Bush's particular notion of 'St. Agnes'' visual beauty. Keats does not, it seems, simply approximate the 'clarity of line' and 'tactile solidity' of the object world; his genius is for 'entering into and becoming and recreating in words an object or sensation'. The opulent beauty of 'St. Agnes' is of a sort that 'comprehends passion and sorrow' and that is as far from the 'merely pictorial' as was Eaton Square from Keats's Hampstead. If there is a contradiction, then, it is in Bush's deeply humanistic, *Renaissance* reception of a work that, by his own account, resembles 'romantic' – that is, *medieval* – tapestry.

Earl Wasserman, who defines the other end of the field, is first man among 'the metaphysical critics'. This is Jack Stillinger's name for those scholars who treat Keats's romance as an allegory of identity, with Porphyro, Keats's persona, playing the hero's part. According to readers of this persuasion, 'St. Agnes' chronicles the evolution of a soul into a 'symbolic identity' through its experience of graduated sensory and intellective intensities in the vale of soulmaking. '[The] spiritual ascent that is implicit in Porphyro's progress . . . [culminates in a] mystic blending of mortality and immortality, chastity and passion, the moonlight of perfect form and the ruddiness of intense experience'.[3] In more literary and psychically sensitive terms, 'St. Agnes' would seem to exemplify that uniquely Romantic form, the internalization of quest-romance.[4] We observe that Porphyro makes himself by making Madeline. The wings she gains by that surrender signify Porphyro's realized soul – his winged Psyche – as well. Porphyro, by this reading, represents a more advanced version of Endymion; both heroes' constancy to an ideal object guides them from sensation to dream to disillusion to an inclusive, 'full-alchemized' being.

Harold Bloom's critique of 'St. Agnes' takes up residence somewhere between these extremes. By reference both to Stillinger's designation and to an old, infamous attack upon Rossetti, we might call Bloom's exuberant approach 'the fleshly school of criticism'. By Bloom's account, 'St. Agnes' is a 'celebration of the risen body in the here and now'. Madeline and Porphyro 'are saved by surrendering themselves to a world of objects, and to one another'.[5] While Bloom, like Bush, emphasizes the sensuous concreteness of Keats's representations, he invests this fact with profound philosophic and psychic meaning. As the above quotations indicate, Bloom's model for Keats's passionate language acts is the Passion. Bloom's respect, however, for the material fact of the word in 'St. Agnes' defines a creaturely resurrection that stops short of the abstract, metaphysical dissolve outlined by Wasserman and his school.

Jack Stillinger's investigation of character upon the plane of dramatic representation is, to this day, a productively subversive approach insofar as it isolates narrative and discursive contrivance (the 'stratagem'), brings out Porphyro's kinship with other, gratuitously ingenious literary plotters, and thus obstructs the alienation-to-identity curve that defines the other critiques. That curve describes, we know, the narrative economy of proper romance: medieval, Renaissance, and Romantic. Strangely, however, Stillinger pulls back from his own insights. Having brilliantly discriminated Porphyro's baroque machinations – the narrative usurpation of ends by means – Stillinger 'confess[es]' that he does not consider Porphyro's stratagem the 'main concern' of the poem. He reserves that honor for 'Madeline the self-hoodwinked dreamer', one who 'turns [her] back, not merely on the pains of life, but on life altogether'. Stillinger tells us that 'in the poems of 1819, beginning with "The Eve of St. Agnes", dreaming [of this kind] is condemned'.[6] By designating Madeline the heroine of the romance – the dreamer who learns her reality principle through Porphyro's agency – Stillinger sets his critique squarely in the critical court. He collapses his shrewd distinction of plot from plotting (and even shrewder, his implicit structural privileging of the latter) by reducing Porphyro to an operational device: the means by which Madeline must make her soul. Effectively, Stillinger merely reverses the conventional romance readings, where Porphyro is the hero and Madeline the combined helper (with respect to the metaphysical allegory, or 'tenor') and, in terms of actual narrative 'vehicle', the object of desire.

Finally, we observe that 'St. Agnes' – which must be described as a referential commotion rather than an architectonics – engenders a certain kind of source study, best illustrated by George Ridley's excellent discussion. Since 'St. Agnes' develops neither a single, sustained allusion (for example, *The Decameron*–'Isabella'), nor does it designate an organized body of texts (organized diachronically, as by the transmission logic of 'La Belle Dame', or synchronically, as by a period allusion), the source study typically demonstrates Keats's local transformations of dead canonical letters into living voice. The problem is one of synthesizing these isolated metamorphoses into a full-scale resurrection. Here is Ridley on Keats's '"use of his sources"':

> however original a literary artist is, part, and probably a large part, of the material on which his selecting and shaping imagination works is the reminiscences of his reading . . . [T]he greater part of this material is in a kind of superior rag-bag of the artist's mind, in which the scraps are not docketed with their provenance . . . so that he cannot tell to what kind of garment, owned by whom, this bit of flannel, or that piece of gingham, or that other attractive bit of silk originally belonged.

The homely metaphor, which appears to describe a discursive patchwork, in fact defines a continuous fabric spun from the unravelled threads of garments filched from other men's wardrobes. Ridley's invidious comparison of 'inharmonious mosaic' to Keats's '"tapestry empyrean"' reassures us that the operative model throughout is Coleridge's 'modifying and coadunating' imagination.[7]

A little reflection on this critical array brings out a single principle of diversity: roughly, discourse vs. meaning. Is the reader invited to gambol upon the rich textual surface of Keats's gorgeous tapestry, there to enjoy a fleshly ecstasy that binds him to the poet in mutual healthy hedonism? Or are we pushed through that intricate surface to the place of meaning, an austere, philosophic place that is humanized by the clouds of sensuous glory we trail behind us, vestiges of our passage through the painted veil? I frame the question of 'St. Agnes' as a rhetorical issue so as to bring out the complicity operating within the prevailing oppositional paradigm. The discourse–meaning debate, which amounts to a sensuous–serious, surface–depth, periphery–center polarity, seems to oppose comparably strong and autonomous terms. We can see, however, that the first, 'outside' term, which we work as the dangerous item in the antithesis, figures an expressive authenticity originating in psychic and physiological truth: the authority of instinct, or determinate need and natural appetite. Dominating this sensuous territory is the pleasure principle with its tension-to-discharge curve, an economy of being. Clearly, this sensuous, surface moment is nothing if not deep, and just as clearly, it is inscribed in its 'serious' partner. That term names the authority of reason and of the immanent meanings it discovers in things. The ruler of this wide expanse is the reality principle, with its consciousness-to-object-to-knowledge curve: an economy of power and meaning. While this second, serious term figures a more strenuous and inclusive position than the first, the two describe a single position which we may appropriately call a metaphysics of presence. The designated 'outside' moment is so easily transfigured by the inside, depth term because it was never anything but a subset of that term. Indeed, we might have guessed from the ease and alacrity with which we all solve 'the problem' of 'St. Agnes' that we are only formulating the cognitive premise that made the work intelligible to us in the first place. This premise, which most clearly betrays itself in our preoccupation with 'St. Agnes'' readily redeemable sensuousness, is, of course, a motivated way of seeing. It shields us from the poem's verbal materialism: a genuinely wayward, rebellious dimension. To the extent that we misread Keats's sensuousness, we mistake his seriousness as well.

The proof of the covert monism I've identified emerges in our most widely shared assumptions about 'St. Agnes' – those conclusions we find too obvious to argue. Each of the critical models sketched above constructs Keats's romance not only as a narrative *tour de force* but as an exemplary product of the 'unmisgiving' imagination. We read the romance as a supremely healthy poem, expression of the chameleon poet who lives in all things and brings them all to life by his generous identity, one that spends itself largely because it is so certain of its infinite resources and of its capacity to regroup following each dissemination. (My language here is deliberately sexual. I would hope that the reader will begin to associate Keats's represented love story with my account of Keats's representational tactics.) All the above critiques, with the qualified exception of the gorgeous tapestry school, treat 'St. Agnes' as an exercise of imagination in the service of the reality principle. We coordinate the elaborately overwrought surface of the poem with our impression of layered, resonant, 'high' representation (expansive meaning subtending the material sign) by way of romance narrative norms. That is, we negotiate the particular surface–depth problem we have planted in 'St. Agnes' by discovering in the poem's discursive and narrative dimensions an economy of action that begins in alienation and dies richly into a complex but integrated identity. The writing, like the story, progresses from physis to philosophy, beauty to truth, imitation to originality, adolescence to adulthood – or again, sensuousness to seriousness. By the conservative character of this plot, we say that the second, privileged term *sublates* the first and inferior term. Nothing is lost; all is transfigured.

Let me present a representative statement by a very fine Romanticist, R. H. Fogle. The apparent obviousness of this statement is as telling as its content. Keats's success in 'St. Agnes' comes 'not by forgetting what everyday existence is like, but by using the mean, sordid, and commonplace as a foundation upon which to build a high romance'. This deep respect for what Coleridge calls the 'it is', gives 'St. Agnes' 'a rounded fulness, a complexity and seriousness, a balance which remove it from the realm of mere magnificent *tour de force*'.[8] To quote Fogle in the context of Frye's classic description of the romance paradigm is to see how completely that model contains our criticism of 'St. Agnes' (and, our general understanding of the relation between Keats's life and art). 'The improbable, desiring, erotic, and violent world of romance reminds us that we are not awake when we have abolished the dream world: we are awake only when we have absorbed it again'.[9] We might note that Frye's 'improbable, desiring, erotic, and violent' world corresponds to what we might call absolute psyche, or the tyranny of natural instinct and the pleasure principle, while his waking world, which reclaims for consciousness the work of more primary processes, names the reality principle. My interest here is not to dispute the relevance of Frye's model to 'St. Agnes'. I hope only to suggest that a practical criticism that rehearses Frye's generic and abstract formulation must suppress the historical particulars of Keats's poem and thus the *meaning* of the romance model as it informs an actual work in an actual time and place, social and psychic.

Before identifying the powerfully weak term that the sensuous–serious debate suppresses, I'd like to sketch the biographical dimension to that debate and its romance resolution. The general season of 'St Agnes'' composition (January 1819) saw the Stateside emigration of Keats's brother and sister-in-law, summer 1818; Lockhart's and Croker's attacks on *Endymion*, August and September 1818; the death of Tom Keats through tuberculosis, December 1818. These losses and disappointments occurred in the context of Keats's worsening financial situation and his almost certain knowledge of his disease. Keats's 'understanding' with Fanny Brawne, December 1818 – positioned by most of the biographers as the single bright spot in this bleak landscape – was a secret engagement, with marriage contingent upon Keats's professional advancement and financial security.

By and large, 'St. Agnes' is read as the sweet solution to a bitter life: a resolution of the actual dilemmas and a remedy for all that loss. The writing is not, we say, a *denial* of the facts, but an imaginative reordering; in disclosing the deep truth of that empirical order, Keats conjures as well a specifically human beauty. Where in the life there is death, deprivation, and disease, we find in the romance lushly breeding experience. Where Keats suffered a circumstantially frustrated desire, the poem delivers full erotic gratification and transcendence of facticity. Where there is painfully lived allegory – not just a dissociation of inwardness from image but a cleavage within consciousness itself – there is the pleasure and plenitude of unmediated symbolic representation. By this logic, what makes 'St. Agnes' great is Keats's transformation of the private, circumstantial, and particular truths – both the longing and the fantasy of fulfillment – into the universal and healing Truth of art. Simply, we say that Keats imagined what he knew, with the emphasis on 'imagined'. Once again, our interpretation reflects a deep, dialectical assumption. Keats's imagination – neither implicated in its particular facticity nor the negation of that order – raises the actual contradictions to the higher power of Art. Here, the wishfulness of 'pure being' and the givenness of 'passion[ing] becoming' melt into 'mystic oxymoron'.[10]

We might pause to wonder where Keats – a man profoundly 'entoiled' in social and psychic doublebinds – found it within him to produce this happy dialectical synthesis. Or, while one might still say of 'St. Agnes' that Keats imagined what he knew, we might put the emphasis on 'knew' for a change. Keats's famous lament from the verse epistle to Reynolds comes down hard on the side of knowledge. 'Oh [O], that our dreamings all of sleep or wake / Would all their colours from the sunset take,[:] / From something of material sublime, / Rather than shadow our own soul's daytime / In the dark void of night'. Rather than isolate the phrase 'material sublime', and position it as a generic description of Keats's accomplishment in 'St. Agnes', we might remember first, that it names a longing, not an achievement or even a project.[11] Second, a shadow neither anti-thesizes, resolves, nor transcends its material conditions. It reproduces the governing facts in a flat, dissociated, and strictly representational fashion: in formal terms, a parodic fashion. To observe this is to guess that Keats wrote for himself the reality of the shadow life, whose virtue is its virtuality. What this invention offers is the reality of the virtual image, that deconstructs its authorizing object by reproducing it in illusionary space. The neglected lines from the verse epistle to Reynolds describe a writing that is neither the dialectical synthesis of a life of contraries nor a univocal alternative to that life. They suggest instead a dyadic, oscillating, and profoundly destabilizing dynamic between designated versions of the real – repetitions in diverse tones. Keats's imagination is not, by this account, a constructive activity but a corrosive operation practiced upon a variety of real, and really incapacitating things.

———

Above, I remarked that the gorgeous tapestry school represents a qualified exception to the humanistic rule elaborated in the other critical approaches. This critique, which addresses the textual surface of Keats's poem, could define for us a very different literary object from that constructed by the other readings. However, insofar as the poem's richly embroidered surface is read as a place for unmisgiving pleasuring on the part of poet and reader – pleasure in the natural sensations precipitated by Keats's naturally abundant expressiveness – this school forfeits its critical edge. By recalling that the appropriate model for 'St. Agnes' is a *medieval* tapestry, and by remembering how flat, stylized, and concretely allegorical such weavings really are, we begin to disentangle the wisdoms of this neglected 'beauties' approach from the reductively hedonistic arguments elaborated around them. We see that today's disdain for the shallowness of this approach is really a resistance to its interest in the verbal surface of Keats's romance, and that this surface is exactly what our finest readings do not register. Indeed, the textual emphases developed by our strongest readings *suppress* a range of features that not only resist the romance groundplot but that seem designed to subvert it. We may categorize these features as instances of verbal virtuosity.

Again, Ridley formulates what has become the conventional wisdom: 'there is the most astonishing cumulative effect of cold about this stanza as we feel in turn with the bird; the wild beast; the domesticated beast . . . ; the man . . .'[12] The virtuosity Ridley describes amounts to a triumph of the sympathetic imagination. By 'virtuoso', I mean a technically preoccupied, professionally accomplished writing: capably alienated and aggressively material. This effect is just about the opposite of Ridley's sensuous naturalism. I use the word, moreover, to describe a conceptual *physis*, or a poem that gives no things but in Ideas, and no ideas but in the script-things that render them absolute (that is, Ideas). In 'St. Agnes', as we shall see, the graphic fact of the word establishes physical and intellectual patterns that do not confirm and often, indeed, parody the sensuous and semantic qualities that those words designate in the world we must call 'nontextual'. I explain this important dynamic by setting out two problems to which I'll return in the course of this chapter.

When we read Keats's poem as we might read a painting, but with attention to the sound as well as the look of the words, distinct verbal groupings begin to take shape. 'Freeze' (l. 14) and 'frees' (l. 227) – widely separated homonyms that organize large blocks of textual activity – constitute one such unit. In the real or natural world, 'freeze' and 'frees' establish a semantic opposition; to freeze is to lose one's freedom of movement. Moreover, a 'frieze' (as in 'the sculptured dead', 'carved angels', 'garlanded' window, 'smooth-sculptured stone') is the generically composed aesthetic representation of this natural confinement, a representation that, fixed in stone and framed by architrave and cornice, pointedly shares in the restriction which it figures.

When these words are themselves 'friezed', or framed as a scriptural configuration – a picture of printed words – those psychically, somatically, and objectively authorizing meanings change status. The verbal array, which takes its meaning from the aural and visual properties of the elements (represented signs), also *surfaces* those natural meanings. Spread upon the figured plane of the page, these deep meanings lose their semantic authority; they become simply part of the collection of items that name them. The word 'freeze' and the idea of a cold congealing are rendered categorically indifferent elements in a horizontal set. It's important to see that those conventionally (that is, 'naturally') mimetic meanings are framed *in*, not *out*. Keats does not merely reverse the inside–outside, surface–depth, art–life binarities, leaving intact the apparatus for an idealizing dialectic. The depth–meaning term is relocated upon the representational surface of the work, rendering that surface absolute – a deep frieze – and destabilizing the surface–depth dualisms that organize innocent or 'living' art.

Simply, the appearance absorbs the reality without assimilating it and without sacrificing its own apparitional character. Within this oxymoronic space, the laws that naturally (as it were) relate 'frieze', 'freeze', and 'frees' do not obtain, or not in the same way. This particular word-cluster produces a semantic *complementarity*, and an unusually instructive one. The grouping associates self-conscious containment (a 'friezed', doubled, *conceptualized* composure) with freedom. By reference to the psychic and philosophic tyrannies designated above (and the argument developed below), we will construe this freedom as the product of instinct mastery through the reification of suffered inner experience, and through a willfully alienated articulation of the object world. In the verbal frieze, an 'iced stream' of consciousness, there is freedom from the deep truths of absolute psyche and absolute reality. There is freedom, that is, from a mastering absence (need, instinct: irresistible desire) and presence (cold fact, answerable objects). Keats's word-frieze argues that those victimizing truths and the binary logic that organizes them acquire a working virtue when materially conceptualized.

We can see that what looked like an exclusively and rather trivially discursive pattern in Keats's romance is no such thing. Similarly, by examining in a seriously literal way the *verbal* dimension of a famously *dramatic* and naturalistically semantic moment, we find not just a new meaning, but a different *class* of meaning than that which romance – and Keats's romance in particular – seems designed to offer. Indeed, the contradiction, once we have seen it, raises to the surface the very assumptions that organize the romance mode: centrality, interiority, synthesis. Laid out in this way, these assumptions become for us, as they did for Keats, liberating objects rather than the properties of an exclusionary and authoritative subject-form.

The textual instance I'll interrogate, like the three-way 'freeze' isolated above, exemplifies that *bad* writing defined in this book as Keats's representational signature. In order to appreciate the virtuous badness of the following example, we should reacquaint ourselves with an old, structuralist distinction: *fabula–sjužhet*. *Fabula* is the order of events referred to by the narrative; *sjužhet* names the order of events presented in the narrative discourse. Peter Brooks has cogently observed that '*fabula* – "what really happened" – is in fact a mental construction that the reader derives from *sjužhet*, which is all that he ever directly knows'.[13] Brooks's working definition of plot as the interpretive negotiations that coordinate these two structures might remind us of a third category, sometimes called 'reading competence'. While the discourse or *sjužhet* is all we *directly* know as we engage in any particular act of reading, we also know a good deal about the elements stories (*fabuly*) contain and the ways *sjužhety* unfold. We have, that is, considerable knowledge of an indirect and categorical kind. This class of knowledge would seem to make the practical distinction of *fabula* from *sjužhet* pretty hopeless.

When we encounter in a nineteenth-century narrative poem situated in a volume containing several romances (all of them heavily and generically allusive) a beautiful, throbbing young man and woman, a hostile household, a crabbed but kindly helper, etc., then 'discourse', what we actually read, gets almost entirely effaced by the story-class. When we read, for example, 'Into her dream he melted' – a line that follows a sequence of risings and fallings in consciousness on both lovers' parts, and of ascending sexual tensions – we construe the line to mean, 'into *her* he melted'. We might remember the Donne lines evoked in the opening stanza of 'St. Agnes': 'As virtuous men pass mildly away / And whisper to their souls to go, / While some of their sad friends do say / The breath goes now, and some say, No; / So let us melt, and make no noise . . .'[14] In the 'Valediction', the verb 'melt' explicitly denotes an erotic death ('melt', like 'death', means 'orgasm' by common Renaissance usage) which it likens to the eternally gainful deaths of virtuous men. And of course, on a physiological level, 'melt' makes perfect sense.

The verb is, in fact, *so* perfect on the literal and literary levels – so consistent with conventional verbal, semantic, and somatic paradigms – that we overlook the designated object into which Porphyro dissolves: not Madeline, but Madeline's dream. What is the content of that dream, we should ask, but a finer-tone version of Porphyro. 'Into her dream he melted', then, is tantamount to saying 'into his own dreamed self – his dissociated, fetishized image – he melted'. What we have in the statement, literally translated, is a figure for what Freud calls secondary narcissism.[15] (We also have a case of literary competence producing textual incompetence.)

To name the event in this clinical way is not to reduce it to a pathological instance.[16] Quite the contrary and as I hope to demonstrate, it is to enrich our understanding of the act that seems so central to this romance. By focusing this action as a compromise solution to certain social contradictions and the psychically determined representational problems these entail, we grasp the force, the necessity, and the resonance of Keats's 'solution sweet'. We begin to explain in a practical way the depths we feel in – or upon – Keats's surfaces.

———————

The surface virtues I describe by the representational problems sketched above emerge in a number of ways, narrative and discursive, which I will outline here. First, we observe 'St. Agnes" pronounced literary allusiveness: the poem's profligate, nonsystematic and displayed incorporation of verbal materials gleaned from a host of canonical systems. As with 'La Belle Dame', these repetitions – canonical signatures – figure in the poem as represented objects. Because they double as an expressive apparatus (morphemes, or semantic units), Keats's language refuses the referential and affective sincerity that is, we know, the condition for literary transparency. Keats's words, which name neither authentic subjects nor authentic objects, *represent* rather than instance literature. One might well describe the language of 'St. Agnes' as neither spoken nor written English but something closer to the system we designate by the academic title, *English*, meaning 'Literature' or 'the Canon': a lexicon and grammar. Insofar as Keats *represents* the lexicon and violates the grammar, however, he cannot be said to write good *English*.

By focusing the surface of Keats's romance, we notice that the heavy discursive 'brede' pulls away from the narrative fabric as if by its own weight, presenting to our view two distinct representational orders. On the one hand, we have the action designated by the narration: loosely, what we have called *fabula* or story. In 'St. Agnes', this textual line approximates the univocal, authoritarian vector of desire: a quest-romance. On the other hand, we have the poem's discursive plot – its sign language, so to speak, or the order of events established by the actual writing. In traditional narratives, this discursive structure cleaves to the story as skin to muscle, appearing as the natural and necessary form of the represented action. Where the two orders *can* be discriminated, the discourse presents as a complementary or amplifying apparatus. In 'St. Agnes', however, the discourse is literally so *pronounced* (politically, so insubordinate) as to precipitate a sharp and antagonistic dissociation of writing from story. Rather than enact or assist the narrative thrust toward structural simplicity (problem resolution, tension dissolution) by a complaisantly object-related or expressive narrativity, the discourse of 'St. Agnes' perplexes and retards. Ultimately, that narrative momentum, liberated both from the story and from an authorial subjectivity, is absorbed by the discourse. The result is that characteristically Keatsian effect of figural suspension – movement in place.

Specifically, one observes that action and feeling in 'St. Agnes' consistently congeal into decor, leaving the story and characters proportionately attenuated – in Bush's phrase, 'romantic silhouettes'.[17] In stanza 28, for example, we encounter this figure: 'Noiseless as fear in a wide wilderness'. This simile, which reverses the traditional tenor–vehicle ratios (abstract:concrete, general:particular), instances the way in which spectacle in 'St. Agnes' appropriates the meaning and affect properly belonging to the story and its agents. Porphyro's anxiety and its dramatic conditions are, we can see, displaced by the trope which supplements them. Indeed, the character, Porphyro, is effaced by an abstracting personification of his attribute, and his action is upstaged by its verbal representation. By techniques such as these, Keats renders plot and character – for Aristotle and all the good writing he sponsored, the first and second most important elements of literary structures – incidental and ornamental elements. Rather than generate and justify the textual surface, they *illustrate* that suddenly vivid, valorized dimension.

In general terms, I'm describing a disengagement and hypertrophy of the poem's formal dimension such that it fiercely competes with the narrative line for textual dominance. The familiar formula for the isolated representation of representational acts is 'baring the device'. The phrase, a formalist coinage, implies a truth technique and a predominantly rhetorical interest. It names a philosophically informed attack upon the bad faith of an unmarked narration and a move in the direction of linguistic and phenomenal defamiliarization. Keats's object was not, as we shall see, to enter boldly upon a deconstructive project, but rather to make a place for himself within a humanly deconstructive environment. The estrangement potential of the sign was, for Keats, an essentially private value, if we can use 'private' to designate a socially determined orientation toward the inner life. In the literary word – dissociated, self-conscious, absolute in its fictiveness – Keats reproduced an imposed and *relative* alienation. The idea was not to abolish that suffered objectivity but to effectuate it. Essentially, the displayed device is worked defensively and according to the properties of the Derridean supplement, discussed in chapters 1 and 2. By way of a Freudian distinction, elaborated below, we see in 'St. Agnes' forepleasure used as a defense against endpleasure. The Freudian account, which puts forepleasure in the service of endpleasure, would of course find Keats's practice perverse.[18] Similarly, and by reference to the sexual implications of Freud's distinction, both discourse and story in 'St. Agnes' situate foreplay as a form of resistance to the hegemony of sexual endpleasure: intercourse and orgasm. Each of these disengagements and rebellions is not so much a *mutiny* of means against ends and part against whole as a supplementation that parodies the received content of those ratios while preserving the form.

Stillinger's fascination with the 'stratagem' betrays, I believe, his perception of the poem's narrative and discursive lawlessness, a perception he will not, however, fully credit. What Stillinger does not articulate but what his canonical parallels make clear, is the gratuitousness of Porphyro's stratagems in terms of ostensive narrative aims. When we compare Porphyro's approach, first, to Romeo's (Romeo is the conventionally designated model for Keats's romantic hero) and second, by reference to Stillinger's argument, to Iacamo's behavior, we bring out its exessive, formulaic, and indirect character. As with all rituals, the aggressively empty form *is* the content. One might conjecture, of course, that Porphyro, who has had no opportunity to charm Madeline, cannot be so assured of her interest as Romeo is of Juliet's, hence the necessity of his excess and indirection. Porphyro's stratagems are not, however, designed to secure this assurance, *neither* are they used in the service of cumulative erotic enrichment. Porphyro's interior decoration, his provision of food and music, his voyeurism, his mirroring of Madeline's movements and postures: none of these is necessary *or even conducive to* the accomplishment of his designs. These actions do not advance the hero toward his beloved, the plot toward resolution and quiescence, or the reader toward the gratification of his textual interest. To the contrary, these cameos interrupt those several forward motions, turning them back upon themselves and inducing a kind of 'circuiting' action, to use a popular word from Keats's letters. By holding off those natural closures, Keats's punctual metamorphoses of story into writing *hold on to* a particular kind of tension – a pleasant pain – which we will consider below.

Now, one might protest that Porphyro's primary, overarching stratagem – the attempt to penetrate Madeline's defenses by appearing as a harmlessly phantasmic lover – is exceedingly practical and object-related. How else might he overcome her virginal resistance? Or, from a different angle, how else could Keats have Madeline yield to Porphyro and yet remain a 'good' (that is, morally intact) character? We answer these objections by noting Keats's elaborate development of Madeline's receptiveness. The representation of a virgin 'danc[ing] along . . . her breathing quick and short', sighing, lingering, 'pant[ing], all akin / To spirits of the air, and visions wide –[:]' 'in sort of wakeful swoon', has a definite comic suggestiveness. The author is not, it would seem, overly concerned with Porphyro's problems or with Madeline's virtue. As Stillinger says, Madeline is 'hoodwinked by faery fancy'. As Stillinger *so much as says*, Madeline is self-seduced: ravished by her own voluptuous, voluntary, and in short masturbatory dreaming. By the time Porphyro reaches her, she has forfeited her virginal defenses. We must, I believe, suspect that any young man, regardless of his tactical delicacy, would be likely to succeed with Madeline, 'a maid, with that Character about her, in such a situation . . .'[19] Porphyro's stratagem is every bit as perverse as Stillinger's baroque associations suggest.

A third feature of 'St. Agnes' that has gone largely unremarked is the jokiness of the writing. By that adjective, I name a linguistic denseness, materiality, and reflexiveness that is largely responsible for the smartness of the authorial projection and the farcical aspects of the characterization. Readers of 'St. Agnes' universally elevate these linguistic *jeu d'esprits* by reference to Keats's 'combining mind' – his associative and syncretic sensibility. Rather than redeem Keats's puns and *double entendres* in this serious way, however, we might read the surface of such figures, or the meaning of the verbal performance. Generally, of course, our overall sense of the intention and stylistic norm of the work determines which of these critical options we shall choose. Because we have always regarded 'St. Agnes' as a serious, important, and above all, a *creaturely* poem – because the narrative norm by which we process the work is that of Renaissance romance, and because our stylistic norm derives from so-called 'golden' discourse as opposed to a metaphysical, baroque, and riddling mode – we have not attended very much to Keats's wit.

For a quick illustration of this important point, let me isolate two words from a phrase quoted above, 'wide wilderness'. While 'wide', by adding a certain mystery to 'wilderness', serves a semantic purpose consistent with the deepening and expanding action of the poem, the real meaning of the word arrives through our recognition of its strictly verbal determination. Keats wants us to see that 'wide' is graphically contained by and textually derived from the word 'wilderness'. Isolated, repeated, and set alongside 'wilderness', 'wide' extends that word in time and space. 'Wide' widens 'wilderness'. These words are a piece of writing, displayed for our delight and to elicit our admiration for Keats's reflexive wit. The phrase, moreover, lets us glimpse the possibility of 'wild wideness', and more important, it lets us see that we can use these phrases interchangeably without producing any semantic difference, since Keats is not naming an object and modifying it, but constructing a self-consciously written phrase. We could be fancier about this and say that by such phrasemaking, Keats examines the ways in which language constructs meanings, meanings that may or may not work (prove valid) in the nonlinguistic universe. Keats is showing by this phrase that writing *writes*, and this is to poke fun at the high, serious, and deep constructions we put on literature, and particularly on such forms as romance and ode.

Above, I observed Keats's reversal of the classic simile formula: clarification of an abstraction by a concrete sensuous particular. 'Noiseless as fear in a wide wilderness' gives just the opposite. Porphyro's physical stealthiness and the anxiety that prompts it – not a difficult state to conceive – are immaterialized and estranged first by the backward personification, and second by the linguistically reflexive abstractness of 'wide wilderness'. A perfectly natural condition in which we might participate is rendered by this device an object of representation. We bring out the rhetorical effect of this maneuver by comparing it to line 56: 'The music, yearning like a God [god] in pain . . .' Here again, Keats deconstructs the tenor and vehicle distinction (abstract and concrete) without collapsing the two modes into a symbolic simplicity. We find ourselves teased into a kind of wayward reflectiveness. *Do* Gods feel pain; why is this phenomenon used as a consensus datum when it is obviously doubtful; don't Gods generally get what they yearn for; isn't it easier to conceive yearning music than it is to imagine the sound of divine anguish? Keats's similes, in short, not only fail to do what similes are supposed to do, they *represent* this semantic failure. Both constructions cited here tease us out of thought, not to push us 'beyond heaven's bourne' whence we can serenely survey quotidian contradiction, nor simply to show us how clever Keats is. These teasing remarks both bring into being and *present* Keats's smartness. By that word, I mean his enabling estrangement from expressive, mimetic, and received discursive imperatives: an affected vulgarity, in short. With phrases such as the above and by a whole range of techniques associated with nonsense literature (for example, framing, repetition, category errors, tautology, catalogues), Keats displays the distance separating him from his representational objects and manner, and he makes of this distance a privilege.

In 'woolly fold', for example – a pun upon sheepfold (enclosure) and sheep *fold* (either individual pelts or the fleecy folds made by woolly bodies huddled together) – Keats makes the sense fold back and forth between these two containers, sheepskin and sheep pen, or between the two cognitive enclosures in our mind. The sense of the line is located *in the words and in our mind* – literally, in our sense of the line *qua* line – and nowhere else. Certainly not in some 'real' or nontextual sheepfold, and not even in the image of one. In both the real and the iconic world, 'woolly' will not bounce back and forth between two ideas. Either the sheep are woolly and we are looking at the folded figure cut by a massed group of animals, or Keats is assuming poetic licence and, by metonymy, describing the sheep pen as woolly. We must make a choice; the both / and semiosis enabled by Keats's exhibitionistically written representation is not available to us in the natural world. ('Natural' in this context encompasses unselfconsciously representational worlds, pictorial and verbal.) While it is important to see that Keats's verbal smartness serves a good many serious purposes of this kind, I would emphasize at this point the superficially performative functions. By the special wit affected / effected through these devices, Keats introduces himself as a man too experienced and skeptical – too blasé, in short – to participate in the creaturely life of his verbal creations.

Finally, this smartness brings out the comic conventionality of Keats's hero and heroine. Or, we could say that it fissures both

Madeline and Porphyro, exposing on the one hand an 'authentic', authorially expressive, and naturalistic aspect, and on the other, a stylized, representational dimension. The poem invites us to focus the breach between motivation and action. More to the point, this breach is not naturalized by reference to character and psyche (that is, conflict, ambivalence); it is featured as a formal problem. Roughly, we have a scenario wherein two young and beautiful 'people', each of them aching with desire, are compelled by the conventions of literary romance to behave like characters in a book. The romance requires that Porphyro, for instance, kneel and pray beside Madeline's bed, thereby producing a narrative and discursive mirroring of Madeline's bedtime devotions. But Keats has exposed to us that in Porphyro which escapes the romance norm, that which identifies him as a *man*, 'with that Character about him, in that situation'. Clearly, a character of this kind would not be kneeling, praying, and formally mirroring his beloved's gestures.

The represented and therefore comic disjunction is verbally crystallized in the ribald *double entendre*. Like a good romantic hero, Porphyro must descend and ascend – in this case, sink to his knees, rise to his feet, itself a trivialization of romance cosmic verticality. By a sequence of paired periphrases ('Porphyro grew faint . . .' / 'Anon his heart revives . . .'; 'his warm, unnerved arm / Sank in her pillow . . .' / 'Awakening up . . .'; 'Upon his knees he sank . . .' / 'At these voluptuous accents, he arose, / Ethereal, flushed [flush'd], and like a throbbing star . . .'), Keats sketches a Porphyro who droops and stiffens with comic, and of course, phallic regularity. Along these lines, Madeline's fastidious rejection of a pale-faced Porphyro – her dainty request for a ruddier lover – strikes a facetious note given the pitch to which Keats has brought her. And Keats's delicate euphemism for intercourse – 'Into her dream he melted, as the rose / Blendeth its odour with the violet, [,–] / Solution sweet' – must surely have an ironic edge, in light of the lovers' very practical and concrete orientation toward their sexual interests. In the revised version of the romance (*Woodhouse 2*), Keats prefaces the aroma marriage with these lines: 'More sooth[,] for that his quick rejoinder flows / Into her burning ear . . .' The wink wink nod nod character of this erotic report ('re-joined her'; a 'quick', 'sooth[ing]' 'flow' into a hot portal) might remind us of some parts of *Don Juan*, particularly the Donna Julia and Lady Adeline episodes.[20] Indeed, the narrative *donnée* of

Keats's poem – the crossed purposes of the star-crossed lovers (Porphyro's desire for an idealized reality, Madeline's for a realized idea) – should put us in mind of sophisticated romantic comedy. The analogue might be Noel Coward's 'Blithe Spirit' or, for that matter, 'Venus and Adonis' or 'Hero and Leander'. Not, however, 'Romeo and Juliet'.[21]

In line with this rather slick humor is Keats's representation of what Miriam Allott calls 'stock' – that is, literary furniture. We have seen that Keats not only includes in his romance what he calls in a letter his 'fine mother Radcliff names', but that he identifies these words *as* names, and as nothing but names. We are asked to focus these items as effects liberated from their legitimate causes: original works and canons, where they function as textual reality or as an expressive medium. In 'St. Agnes', these titles are, as I said in chapter 2, representational objects, or 'effects' in the colloquial sense of that word: Keats's belongings. Indeed, Keats represents romance itself as an acquired property. The heavy-handed symmetries of the poem – a structural allusion to romance binarities – exhibit Keats's possession of romantic narrative and its governing norms. The author of so writerly a romance must 'own' the form, as we say. At the same time, the exaggeration establishes Keats's unnatural access. We see that he has acquired the romance form rather than inherited it. The romance, a sign of possession, is also *and for that reason* a sign of profound dis-possession, and as such, a defense against canonical absorption.

Keats's 1820 volume was, above all, a volume designed *not to offend*, for reasons I'll explain below.[22] It would seem from just this general description of 'St. Agnes' that Keats conceived the danger in terms of stylistic unself-consciousness: a literature that wears its heart on its sleeve. Keats would not write another *Endymion* – which is to say, he would not be caught with his pants down. Keats had erred on the side of expressiveness and identification and he conceived *1820* as a parry in the opposite direction. It was not, I'm convinced, a moral backlash Keats feared from the 1820 volume, which was why it took so much persuasion on his friends' and publishers' part to get him to remove the revised, more sexually explicit passages. Or, we might ask, why did Keats revise in this direction at all, if he wanted to present a 'good' volume? The answer lies in the meaning to Keats of that adjective. *1820* was to be 'good' in the sense of 'wise' rather than 'innocent'. It was to be 'good', moreover, in a literary sense and in the manner of Byron: an urbane, ironic, largeminded, manly unexception-ability – not 'natural' feeling but a sophisticated and well-managed representation of feeling.

To sum up, twentieth-century criticism's preoccupation with 'St. Agnes'' sensuousness, read as an innocent enactment of creaturely fantasy, marginalizes the poem's genuine perverseness: its complexly functional representation of discursive acts, detached from the expressive and mimetic values that, in good writing, invisibilize the verbal materiality. *This* surface term, unlike 'sensuousness', is *aggressively* and absolutely superficial. It will not engage dialectically with the 'serious', philosophic dimension of the work. Indeed, to locate the 'material sublime' of 'St. Agnes' in the line of conscious externality (a baroque, allegorical model) as opposed to the Elizabethan, sensuous way we usually frame it, is to deconstruct that humanistic seriousness altogether.

Everyone discriminates an escapist tendency in 'St. Agnes'. By anchoring these escapes to a psychic imperative, however, we make them confrontatory acts, not really escapes at all. What we miss, then, is the escap*ism* of the poem. By the doubled nominative, I mean Keats's alienated representation of his fantasy, a 'stratagem' that puts the dream at a remove from psychic truth (drives and wishes) and that obstructs its redemption by abstract philosophic truth. What Keats produces by this reflexive fetishism is the Idea of escape. This Idea positions 'the thing itself' (genuine fantasy, a product of an authorizing unconscious; and philosophic truth, transcendentally authorized) as a representation, a substitute for an absent primacy. A substitute is, of course, a relative object. At the same time, the Idea, which *represents* the sign-substitute, objectifies it, thereby compromising whatever authority had accrued to it by association with a 'meaning' subject. Keats's absolute Idea – what I've called his conceptual physis – is a double undoing that constructs for him a place to stand. The *work* of 'St. Agnes' is to give the relative, substitutive dimension (ideas, wishes, words) a supplemental form. By studying this project, we will illuminate (1) the contemporary social meanings inscribed in Keats's romance, (2) the subversive project woven into the happy, healthy romance, (3) the greatness, as opposed to goodness of 'St. Agnes' and the other poems treated here, and (4) the common interest which explains Keats's presentation of these works in a single volume (or, their composition over a particular period of time).

I extend my discussion of Keats's virtuosity and open up the text by way of John Bayley. Here is his moving assessment of 'St. Agnes'' triumph. For Bayley, 'St. Agnes' is the triumph of Keats's career. Like Joyce's 'The Dead', 'St. Agnes' has 'a ritual solidity of description, which somehow pledges that what one dreams and yearns for and regrets is as much a part of life as what one eats, that one's fantasies are as real as one's food'.[23] This is an astute and, I repeat, a moving estimate of Keats's success. It is just what we want to hear; indeed, the formulation solves the problem that its language – its metaphoric choices – reflects. Bayley's model for Keats's achievement in 'St. Agnes' is the real pleasure of real food properly, naturally consumed. By reference to the narrative and discursive work of the poem, we see that Bayley identifies Keats's success with the real pleasure of real narration properly developed and delivered, the real pleasure of real sex properly consummated, and the real pleasure of real words (Beauty) properly digested into meaning (Truth). Bayley's language, however, undoes his translation of Keats's capable negativity into healthy humanism, and several times over. Why should a 'ritual solidity of description' pledge anything about a nontextual reality or even a contextual one? To modify solidity by 'ritual' is to describe a *staging* (formulaic, autotelic) of natural or actual solidity. 'Solidity' in that empirical sense – Bayley's intended sense – is parodied, if not effaced by the phrase. Further, the prepositional clarification, 'of description', compromises 'solidity' from the other side – the object, as opposed to origin side. A solid description is a verbal construction that claims the same denseness of being as all that we regard as 'solid' in the physical or nonverbal world. Bayley's phrase names a discourse ontologically severed from all nondiscursive truths, exactly the opposite of what he means to suggest. We could either say that the sentence swallows itself up, taking back precisely what it offers, or that it accurately reflects the terrific subversion of reality concepts that constitutes the poem's plot. Bayley's perspicacity would suggest the latter.

Second, Bayley's sentence equates 'what one dreams and yearns for and regrets' with 'fantasies'. But fantasies are *waking* dreams, constructs that must install more securely than nightdreams the defenses which enable the wish to take a conscious shape. Without these distortions, we could not enjoy the dangerous wish that is the core of the fantasy. What one dreams and yearns for and what one fantasizes are not, then, the same; indeed, we would expect the fantasy to be an enabling negation of the longing. To focus this defensive aspect is to define fantasy not as a mechanism for the realization of deep psychic truths but as a compromise solution to those problematic truths: detours in the direction of freedom and identity. Fantasies are the bargain one makes with one's wishes in order to produce a working brain. Fantasy, thus construed, is neither an escape from the everyday nor an unmediated reflection of psychic life, but something more like an overdetermined parody of both those real things. By reproducing those primacies upon the flat surface of an alienated consciousness, fantasy practices 'a corrosive operation . . . *on* the real', an operation in the service of mastery and composure.[24] What I describe is not, then, the sort of instinct activity Bayley implies (a swoon toward self-coincidence and gratified desire), but an ego enterprise. This sort of fantasy is as the food that refreshes but is not consumed, and therefore *does not consume*. Like the sojourn described in chapter 2, fantasy constructs a supplemental time and space: the substitutive 'less' which is, by its subversively representational virtues, 'more'. What makes Keats's fantasy, 'St. Agnes', a complete representation of his wishes is its restrictions: its exclusively representational character. Fantasy of this kind – written, self-conscious, double-dreamed – enables experience along the outside, the rippling skin of desire. It affords a simultaneously possessed (empowered) and alienated (autonomous) relation to the origin of desire, to the objects it postulates, and to its natural end: exhaustion, depletion, death.

All the ratios in Bayley's sentence are based on the assumption of a bottom-line reality: meat and potatoes. The assumption is that we know what 'real' is, so did Keats, and that it meant to him what it does to us: namely, the physical world and the deep physiological-psychical drives that bind us willy-nilly to that world. In chapter 2, however, we saw that the healthiest food can be perverted by a fetishistic usage. By 'perverted', I refer to the refusal of what are generally experienced as natural, primary values (such as nutrition, oral gratification), and the pronouncement of critical and semiotic values. In 'La Belle Dame' – the knight's fetishistic absorption of *his* food for thought (the Lady), and Keats's comparable introjection of his literary sources – we read this inversion as a construction of effectual identity. Food, worked as a negation of natural being, can be used for freedom, a project that may appear to or in fact oppose survival. Similarly, as we shall see, foreplay in sex and forepleasure in works of art can be dissociated from natural origins and ends when ego imperatives seem to outweigh more primitive drives. This is to say that aggressive and libidinal instincts may be interrelated in classically perverse ways that are, given the possibilities of action and imagination at particular moments, perfectly natural.

Returning to Bayley, we note that his governing simile reflects the powerfully voluptuous representation of food in 'St. Agnes', perhaps the most celebrated scene in the poem: Porphyro's midnight banquet. Readers have identified this exhibition as a 'love feast', 'sacrifice', 'communion' – all symbolic expressions of a subliming digestion. Bloom compares this passage to the richly erotic *Song of Solomon* and he speaks of the 'sure lover's instinct', to spread before his love 'the reality of rich objects', symbol of that 'physical love [which] *is* the wealth of the world'.[25] Now, as Bayley and Bloom know perfectly well, this buffet is a highly and self-consciously literary collation: literally, a blazon, or display of descriptive legitimacy and power.[26] The verbal exhibition is as a shield that Keats positions between himself and his subject, and between himself and his reader. We grasp the function of this heraldic device by turning to Madeline for a moment, 'guled' by the blushed scutcheon. Madeline's own body – a blank field stained by heraldic insignia – legitimates her. Insofar as Madeline *is* the sign that authenticates her, she would seem to figure an unusually profound or natural authority. At the same time, of course, Madeline's 'device' is only skin deep – a strictly effective or virtual condition. Moreover, to focus the relation between Madeline's blushed body and the 'shielded scutcheon' is to grasp Madeline as an alienated representation of a representation. She is literally the dissociated reflection of the window image. *That* image represents some 'actual' shield, itself the emblem of some absent genetic and social authority. To see this is to recognize Madeline's profound deviance with respect to authorizing originals. Or, as we might have expected, Madeline's entertained colors *perversely* legitimate, and thereby originate her.

It is Milton who operates here to 'gule' Keats. This is not in itself important. It could have been Shakespeare, Donne, or any of the other canonical shields that decorate Keats's romance. Keats wears Milton's colors as a sort of reversible coat of arms. Facing out towards Keats's readers, Milton legitimates Keats. Concretely, the Miltonic sign conceals – or compensates – Keats's social disentitlement. Turned inward, Milton's device obstructs the natural expression of Keats's fantasy: the double swoon toward identification with his literary sources, and with his own verbal creations. By this defense, Keats resists those easeful deaths, absorptions that would annihilate authorial identity: that is, original power.

No one can read lines 264–70 without remembering Milton and his own rich allusiveness. By reference to that deeply integrated text, we notice that Keats's literary sources remain spread along the surface like butter on cold toast. Keats's materials are not digested into *Keats*. We see these 'sources' as substitutes for real, internally grounded power: as a shield that covers a defect and is a substitute (metaphor) for the missing authority. At the same time, we see them as an adornment: by metonymy, and with reference to the ostensive properties of the sign, an *extension* of inner authority. The doubleness of this literary display in Keats – the exposure of both faces of the canonical shield, both faces of the linguistic sign (and, as I argue in chapter 6, both sides of the money form) – begins to explain the strange power of 'St. Agnes'.

We remember that in the famous scene in *Paradise Lost* to which Keats alludes, Adam and Raphael *eat* their supper. Not only do Madeline and Porphyro not get around to eating, but there's no indication that the buffet was ever meant for ingestion. Quite the contrary, the food is used on the dramatic plane for its secondary characteristics (color, form, aroma, texture), on the narrative plane for its enhancement of sexual tension (foreplay), on the discursive plane for its verbal qualities (forepleasure), and on the conceptual plane for the abstention it signifies.

A luxurious banquet is one thing. A luxurious banquet not eaten is a lot more luxurious. The passage produces the supplemental virtues of the food. Its primary values are not just overlooked but rejected. To bring out the narrative overtones of this feast, we might compare it to that fabulously erotic supper in *Tom Jones*. (The wonderful treatment of this scene in the movie 'Tom Jones' is itself instructive. Imagine directing the comparable moment in 'St. Agnes', a scene where all the action and all the sexuality consist in setting a table, then looking at it.) Fielding represents frank and mutual orality, a regressive erotic moment, pointing toward the adult-appropriate reciprocity of intercourse. Simply by the dramatic structure of this episode, Fielding describes a sexual act that proceeds from ease, plenitude, and integrated being. Literally, he represents a species of foreplay that is categorically contained by that genital, object-related, so-called 'mature' sex patently foreshadowed in the episode. In Keats, conversely, the foreplay is neither mutual nor absorbed into the consummate erotic act; the orality involves the feel of words in the mouth, not tastes; and the voyeurism involves literary phalluses. All these distinctions crystallize the difference between a man who writes to present or confirm his identity, and one whose writing invents him. *Tom Jones* is the work of a full man, 'St. Agnes' the product of a very hungry one.

The supper in 'St. Agnes' is specifically a supper-not-for-eating. Keats's choice of foods underlines this fact. In a textual variant, we find the word 'viands', a word that derives from 'vivere' or 'to live' (Allott, p. 457; omitted stanza following stanza 6 and referring to stanza 30). 'Viands' suggests sustenance food, not luxuries: 'meate and drinke' as opposed to 'spices, fruites, jelies . . .' (OED). The word 'viands' thus provided some relief from the cloying collection of syrupy desserts laid out in the standard version. Perhaps Keats deletes 'viands' in the final text so as to emphasize the semantic rubric governing this culinary collection. Porphyro prepares a banquet consisting entirely of children's foods, and like those foods, all these creamy curds and jellies resemble mother's milk. For Milton, this was an appropriate bill of fare, inasmuch as Adam and Eve inhabit a Beulah world: Innocence, the realm of nurturing nature. In 'historical' terms, Eden was, of course, a vegetarian world. However, for grown-up inhabitants of the nineteenth-century romance world, Keats composes a tellingly perverse menu. It is important to see that this is its virtue. While we would gag on these foods if we actually had to eat them, or even if we 'naturally' imagined this natural act (that is, *not* through the alienating apparatus of Keats's writing), we can enjoy reading them, for what we consume is the concrete sensuous particularity of the words.

For an illuminating analogy, compare Keats's representation to the sort of thing one finds in today's sumptuous food magazines. The formal intention of the descriptions we read in *Gourmet* or *Bon Appetit*, like the sexual reports in pornography, is to replace the word by an image, and an image by an instinctual fantasy. The technical, highly conventional and therefore self-effacing character of the discourse enables a degree of identification with the work's fantasy content, the condition for instinctual gratification on the reader's part. We read such magazines when we're hungry, and when we finish, we feel temporarily free of that natural appetite *and* of the fantasy which released us from it.[27] One can (is *meant* to) read these magazines over and over again. Because the words are not felt as words in the first place – do not verbally interest us – we do not tire of them. The job of the discourse is simply to trigger the reader's oral fantasies.

We bring out the profound contrast between this rhetoric and that of 'St. Agnes' by sketching the pornography analogy mentioned above. To liken a pornographic structure to the instinctually liberating discourse of the food magazine is not, of course, to suggest that there are no perversions (fixations at regressive erotic moments) in pornography, only that the perversions occur at the level of representational *object*, not representational act and not reception. By the identificatory processes initiated by the discourse, the reader may follow the perversion down to its primitive source and thus coincide with the origin of the wayward expression. It would seem that the rhetoric of pornography solicits a surprisingly healthy act of reading, albeit within a masturbatory context.

The verbal procedures of 'St. Agnes' do not, as we have seen, efface themselves, nor do they subordinate their collective gratifications to the narrative content or intent of the poem. 'St. Agnes' not only offers no purchase for identification (no grounding subject or object), its conspicuously represented formal dimension actually obstructs that process. Simply, we get no cumulative satisfaction from the representational pleasures produced by Keats's romance. Indeed, the voyeuristic emphasis of the eroticism effectively describes for us a rhetorical arrest at the level of forepleasure: roughly verbal interest. Voyeurs ourselves, we watch another voyeur (Keats), watching another (Porphyro), watching a woman who broods voluptuously upon herself. Madeline, the original narcissistic moment in this sequence of instinctual vicissitudes, does not, of course, arrest the regression and provide a point of entry into the text. To the contrary, her autoeroticism – a splitting of self into lover and beloved – signifies an always already alienated desire. Similarly, the discursive action proceeds in a lateral direction, which is to say, it does not advance from letter to spirit, surface to depth, forepleasure to endpleasure. Porphyro's banquet, like his voyeurism, asserts the refusal of this romance to domesticate desire and thus to enable the self-coincidence – the quiescence – which is pornography's effective if not intentional telos.

By the magnificent onomatopoeia of lines 264–70 – a virtuoso display of alliteration and assonance – Keats effectively designates the *word* the object of consumption. Typically, onomatopoeia seeks to enhance the authority of writing by calling attention to its mimetic properties. This, of course, paradoxically privileges the empirical, referential world yet more extravagantly, and proportionally depreciates the written representation of that world. Keats avoids this double-bind by representing the concept governing his words: here, the idea of original, lost, irrecoverable food. The appeal of Porphyro's display is Keats's conversion of its substitutive character (for, in place of, primary objects: here, mother's milk, Edenic food, Milton) into a *supplemental* character. What is added by the displayed representational status of these foods is first, the idealized memory of the referent – mother, Eden, Milton – or its socially semiotic resonance. More important, a reader who 'consumes' this food eats real nothings. This is not to say that, fed by mere ideas, he goes hungry, but that dieted on absolute and material Ideas, he is liberated from the tyranny of natural appetite and appropriate satisfactions. One might thus realize one's longing and at the same time maintain the tension that sustains consciousness. Like 'sex in the head', Porphyro's supper lets him, Keats, and Keats's readers have their cake and eat it.

What does all this mean? Does Bayley wantonly impose an ideologically comfortable narrative upon a disturbing one? Not at all. Bayley correctly reads the romance but he is so sensitive a reader and so very shrewd a writer, that he articulates the poem's triumph in such a way as specifically to suppress its antiromantic accomplishment. What Bayley's constructive critique must conceal in order to develop its insights are those discursive procedures that do not realize deep truths but, quite the contrary, deconstruct the real of psyche (Bayley's 'fantasy') and the real of meaningful object life ('the food one eats').

We might further situate Bayley's critique – our single most important statement about 'St. Agnes' – by reference to the psychoanalytic concepts, binding and unbinding. André Green, an analyst who applies these concepts to literary structures, suggests that the surface story of any text (in the case of 'St. Agnes', the romance narrative) be construed as a binding of psychic energy, the condition for representation of fantasy material and thus for the release of psychic tension.[28] This binding operation corresponds to the secondary revision that processes our dream materials in such a way as to make them relatively coherent and, more important, inoffensive to the psychic censors. At the same time, the work, like the dream, preserves within it elements that *un*bind (undo) the revisionary work and to that extent, mistell the story. Thus is another and more dangerous story outlined. The supper-not-for-eating, a portion of discourse not digested into story, is one such unbinding and the deviant facts presented above are some others. Such features – puckers, faults – interrupt the smooth linear weave.

What Bayley develops in his critique is 'St. Agnes'' bound line, a line that eventually melts down into the sweet solution of Madeline and Porphyro's intercourse. Indeed, the tradition in Keats criticism has been to repeat in a finer tone (more coherent, logical, resolved, symmetrical) the binding procedures: that which gets the scene set, the characters realized, the story told, and that organizes these dimensions hierarchically (spectacle, character, action). This repetition – in critical terms, a reification – requires jettisoning a good deal of the actual writing, material which tends to get implicitly characterized as a sort of narrative and thematic glue, or as an exuberant expressive overflow. As I've suggested, no critic touches this stuff until it is refined into sensuousness.

What makes 'St. Agnes' unusual is that these unbindings, described by Green as a neutral and inevitable structural fact, are defensively implemented. In 'St. Agnes', all those deviant features I have summed up by the word 'virtuoso' operate as anticlosural devices that arrest the erotic–narrative swoon, the 'downward to darkness' curve of healthy sex and healthy narrative. On the discursive plane, we identify this resistance to the bound line as forepleasure; on the narrative plane as foreplay; and on the existential plane as mastery.

We cannot explore this curious and far-reaching defense until we acquaint ourselves with some practical and circumstantial matters.

First, let's return to Keats's immediate problem, the 1820 volume. This was Keats's last and desperate bid for a name, the condition of his marriage to Fanny and, of course, the culmination of his gargantuan literary efforts from 1817 on. As I said, drawing on Jerry McGann's research, Keats conceived *1820* as an inoffensive volume, the work that would cancel the bad sexual, social, and political image he had suffered. I have glossed this intention on one level, and I would now like to probe a bit deeper. We can appreciate, I think, the conventionally gratifying look of the *1820* romances – their 'goodness', or bound aspect. And the relatively positive immediate response would reinforce our impression of Keats's technical and tonal control over his shaping spirit of imagination. What we want to explain here is the *badness*, and thus the greatness of these poems. By reference to the above discussion, the task is to explain the work's binding procedures, the romance, by elucidating its unbindings, the writing that perplexes and retards.

We focus this goodness–greatness question by comparing 'St. Agnes' in the broadest way to Hunt's *Rimini*. Certainly there are strong institutional reasons for the survival of 'St. Agnes' and the relative obscurity of *The Story of Rimini*, but just as surely, there is an internal, textual explanation. It occurs in 'St. Agnes'' unbindings, the dimension we have for a very long time overlooked. Hunt's poem, the story of Paolo and Francesca's doomed passion, is a triple resurrection. Hunt not only raises Dante's canonical ghosts, his depiction of all that is *pre*-history in Dante's text – the earthly idyll – restores them to the land of the literary living. Moreover, by his flexible, familiar, and *genuinely* sensuous pictorial style, Hunt manages to introduce his lovers into nonliterary and contemporary space. Hunt makes the word flesh – painted flesh, to be sure, but flesh all the same. Keats, as we have seen and shall continue to see, turns flesh to word. By considering once again, this time more technically, the facts of Keats's life and their bearing on this representational distinction, we begin to grasp in an unusually concrete way the greatness of Keats's romances *and* of his odes.

We all know, or say, that Keats lived 'a life of Allegory'. Instead of contemplating the symmetries of such a life from the comfortable vantage of today, we might imagine the experience of the man who lived them, and we might recall that 'symmetry' structurally describes separation and imposed closure. An allegorical life is a life played out in the space between figure and meaning, action and purpose. To live such a life is to be irremediably estranged from what is positioned as one's essential being. Practically speaking, it is to act and then to construct the intentionality of the act *ex post facto*: to experience all action, therefore, as gesture. To live a life of allegory is to know oneself after the fact, or to wear one's identity like a hand-me-down suit: a parody of one's inner life.[29] Again, we recall Byron's 'opinion' of the Cockney school, '*that second-hand* school of poetry'.

One fact emerges over and over in all the biographies, the letters, the reviews, and also in the poetry itself. Keats was *named*: apothecary, cit, Johnny Keates, Jack Ketch, Mankin, Self-polluter, Master John, copyist, Cockney. He was named, moreover, not so much as Other and adversarial but as 'nothing', the dissociated figure of an allegory. The child of unnatural parents, orphaned at an early age, separated from his siblings and his inheritance, ambitious for an identity that was socially prohibited, and isolated by his disease, Keats was detached in an unusually thoroughgoing way from the origins and ends that naturalize most people's lives by fusing their figural aspect (image, attribute, name) to their inwardness.[30]

A man who is allegorized will, to liberate himself from that suffered objectivity, *invent* a life of allegory. If the measure of one's falseness is one's restriction to the world of substitutes (words, ideas, sex in the head), then by a change of sign – a change from experience to consciousness – one might turn the substitutes to supplements, the words to writing, the names to titles. If one can *only* be Miltonic, then one must load every rift with ore from Milton's mine and display the theft. Since Keats could not, by the structures of feeling that stationed him, write from Wordsworthian depth or Shakespearean breadth, he would signify the suffered surface and be belatedly, *Romantically* baroque. We grasp the necessity of this bitter solution by remembering that a man who experiences his identity as his nothingness and desire cannot afford the luxury of full gratification and its natural closures. This is to say that Keats's creativity was powerfully mediated by a set of psychic circumstances that would seem to require rather than resist his particular social reality.

Keats's project was a conversion of zero to zero-degree: a transformation of social and genetic nothingness to 'camelion poet, [which] has no character . . . no Identity'; instead of 'apothecary', there would be 'physician, sage, healer'; and the so-called purveyor of 'extenuatives and soporifics' would name himself a provider of balms, hemlock, and sweet solutions. Anything – even zero – raised to the zero power equals 1. The sad alternative to this self-parody emerges in Keats's letters, where he confesses his horror of the 'nothing' days. These are the days he cannot write, cannot therefore *read* himself, and cannot, thus, recover his stolen name. These are the days when he is drowned by that 'muddy stream' which is his 'doubly strong' *'sense* [my emphasis] of real things': his overinvestment in the real which he knows he can never possess in anything but a temporary, alienated way and that, if he *could* possess properly and forever, would annihilate his identity.

> *You cannot eat your cake and have it too*
> Proverb

> How fevered [fever'd] is the man who cannot look
>   Upon his mortal days with temperate blood,
> Who vexes all the leaves of his life's book,
>   And robs his fair name of its maidenhood:[;]
> It is as if the rose should pluck herself,
>   Or the ripe plum finger its misty bloom,
> As if a Naiad, like a meddling elf,
>   Should darken her pure grot with muddy gloom;
> But the rose leaves herself upon the briar,
>   For winds to kiss and grateful bees to feed,
> And the ripe plum still wears its dim attire,
>   The undisturbed lake has crystal space.[;]
> Why then should man, teasing the world for grace,
> Spoil his salvation for a fierce miscreed?
> (Written 30 April 1819; with 'Ode to Psyche' (written between 21 and 30
>   April), included in journal letter to the George Keatses.)

Nowhere do we find so concentrated an inscription of these matters as in Keats's unpublished sonnet 'How fevered is the man'. All the energy in this poem is in the octet, where the narrator names the naming acts he will not perform, self-ravishings he will not indulge. Keats is trying to say that to covet fame – to conceive oneself as a name or as the owner of a name – is to fracture identity into subjective and objective aspects and to violate the former by the latter.

Keats rejects this self-exploitation, plainly figured as a masturbatory temptation, for the better pleasure of an innocent (that is, self-identical) subjectivity. The task of the sestet is to define this virtuous alternative. Keats cannot, however, inscribe the plenitude of unself-conscious being in a positively autonomous figure. The best he can manage is an image of intransitive, ineffectual, and – in one telling example – *inhabited* being.

We appreciate the logical and therefore technical problem by graphing the way in which the *language* of the poem, as opposed to its argument, identifies autoentitlement with autoeroticism with writing. By the argument, Keats's hero is he who *rejects* the self-pollution of writing; he leaves the leaves of his life's book 'unvexed'. Obviously, the written representation of this existential ideal must be a difficult business. We see just how difficult by attending rather closely to the stylistic effects of the sestet. 'But the rose leaves herself upon the blossom . . . the plum still wears . . . the undisturbed lake has crystal space . . .' In any context, these lines would be semantically faulty and stylistically flaccid; juxtaposed against the perversely vivid octet and situated as a refutation, they are completely lame. 'Leaves', 'wears', and 'has' are about as minimally verbal as verbs can be. The discourse of these lines, contrary to their intended meaning, invites us to focus Keats's hero as the nothingness of a copula without an attribute, a wish without an agency. He is, as it were, virginity without a concept of virginity: a suffered nothing.

The dominant image of the sestet – 'But the rose leaves herself upon the briar, / For winds to kiss and grateful bees to feed' – betrays the contradiction that organizes the sonnet. The line says that roses are kissed by winds and fed by bees. (Or, everything comes to those who wait.) But it is roses, of course, that feed bees, which feed them only in a sexual way, by pollination.[31] ('For grateful bees to fuck' is the effective meaning of the line.) The skewed transitivity of the line would suggest that Keats cannot conceive a self-possession that is not the sexualized taking-in of some other self. Even in what is intended as an image of complete and capable identity, Keats inscribes the figure of a passive and feminized introjection, *itself* an image of productively fissured consciousness.[32]

We might at this point attend to the repetition of 'leaves', a word upon which Keats frequently puns. ('If poetry come not as easy as leaves to a tree . . .') In a strong reading of the 'Ode on a Grecian

Urn', Philip Fisher construes the 'leave' in 'Fair youth . . . thou canst not leave / Thy song . . .' as a transitive verb. Fisher develops the biological dimension of this usage and its relevance to Keats's formalist project.[33] In the context of the sonnet, it is helpful to stress the discursive aspect. The figures on the urn and the nonverbal art that engendered them cannot do the one and the bad thing Keats can do: write, or 'leave' a leaf. They cannot, in Shelley's phrase, 'despoil themselves', cannot 'cleave themselves into chasms' by a catalytic self-consciousness. Only Keats can construct an instant when being is ravished by a meaning that is absolutely external and remains so: a rape without a union – something along the lines of the strange encounter plotted in Yeats's 'Leda and the Swan'. Keats tells us in his sonnet that to name oneself a poet is to deface one's book of life: literally, to 'vex' its fair leaves. However, to refuse this corruption of being by a meaning that is anything but 'silvan' and 'sweet' – to leave oneself alone – is to be left to the meanings imposed by others, and this is surrender to the tyranny of Nature / Culture and its psychic governors. Reductively, the message of this painfully exposed poem is 'do unto yourself that which has been done to you'.

Throughout his poetry, Keats kills the creaturely life he brings forth so that he may resurrect it as the sheared off and absolute Idea of that life: a fever of itself. That strongly attitudinizing phrase, 'Attic shape! Fair attitude', by its framed self-reflexiveness turns the idea of an innocent inwardness inside out. It presents to our view an Idea entirely over-wrought, which is to say, detached from psychic and philosophic truth and from the historical moment that bred that truth. (Here is Empson's comment on the line: 'very bad . . . [T]he half pun suggesting a false Greek derivation and jammed up against an arty bit of Old English seems . . . affected and ugly'.)[34] The Ode asks us to admire a new aesthetic breed: namely, 'brede', a Beauty so orphaned, so barren, and so cold that it really *is* Truth, since it is the only thing in the world that does not refer to Truth. No object, no subject, no reader, and no writer can naturalize a Truth so severed, a relief so severe. Therefore it endures.

'A sense of real things comes doubly strong, / And, like a muddy stream, would bear along / My soul to nothingness'. One's impulse is to read these lines from 'Sleep and Poetry' as a statement of resistance to a reality that is opposed to identity through and through. The defensive agency is imagination. Construed in this way (the way it is always construed), the lines describe an escape from quotidian phenomenal life with its terrible scarcities into the rich reality of psychic life and its products. Keats does not, however, say that 'real things' would bear his soul along to nothingness; it is his 'doubly strong' *sense* of those things – his overinvestment in them – that he likens to a muddy stream. In other words, it is the idea of the real as an object, the possession of which completes us, the lack of which undoes us, that renders both identity and experience 'Nothings'. We could call this idea the reality principle, remembering that 'reality' means in this context a mastering fantasy of facticity.

We know from Keats's life and letters that he could stand a great deal of reality. What he feared, I believe, was the depletion of his soul by an overcathexis of the real, the result of his real deprivations. As we have always known, but not really, I think, understood, Keats was afraid of his natural imagination; the enemy in Keats's poetry is inwardness itself. If this is so, then we must surmise that the quality of the fantasy – a real that fulfills, a real that destroys – is irrelevant. Identity is jeopardized not just by the idea of a real that punishes by withholding itself but by the idea of a real that realizes. By that celebrated lament from 'Sleep and Poetry', we learn that Keats refuses the model of a psyche that binds itself to reality by the agency of the pleasure principle and through the negotiations of an ego which exhausts itself in that intermediary function. We can guess that a man who experiences his identity as his desire, and his station as his contained tension, must be very ambivalent indeed about satisfaction, self-coincidence, and quiescence, the telos of the pleasure principle. By Keats's lights, one is more endangered by fulfillment than frustration. We have all discerned Keats's resistance to the 'sweet' dreaming of sensory escape. What we miss is the equally problematic nature of those inclusive and strongminded solutions we like to find in Keats's mature verse.

The antidote to that 'muddy stream' is the hemlock-balm of an Idea poetry. I use the upper case 'I' to distinguish idea – the weak, relative, and abstract term – from the dissociated, concrete, self-conscious invention: a 'Thing semi-real'. 'Idea' names a transformation of 'sweet dream[ing]' into strong and corrosive dreaming, and of poesy, a possessed act, into poetry, an act of possession.[35] In 'St. Agnes', we witness Keats's transformation of the relative surface – an outside victimized by its relation to ideas of inside and depth – into absolute surface, a skin peeled away from authorizing subjectivity and thus put into perverse relationship with authorizing objectivity as well. There is a name for this magic and it is *schein*.[36] In practical terms, this deconstructive operation amounts to a project in supplementation, where the good, tyrannical term is parodically displaced, in this way avoiding a privileging of the bad term, and thus a reinstatement of the good–bad dynamic. The functional unbindings mentioned above – foreplay, forepleasure, narcissism – are all forms of supplementation: displacements of and additions to intercourse, endpleasure, and intersubjectivity.

In order to register these scandalous supplements, we listen to the poem with what the psychoanalysts call 'the third ear': that is, with a nonlogical, antisystematic attention. We want to hear the 'missaid' in Keats's discourse: those anomalous qualities that somehow contribute to our sense of the power and glamour of the romance but that cannot be articulated within the terms set by our binding criticism. I use the verb 'listen' advisedly: as a refusal of the visually referential instructions imposed by the textual bindings, and out of respect for the aural, verbal, conceptual instructions encoded in the writing. As I've suggested, the deviant facts of 'St. Agnes' are not just the inevitable betrayals of conflictual and/or ideologically unthinkable material – or, exposures of the binding motives. They are specifically functional and overdetermined interferences with the romance narrative. This is an argument, then, not just for the virtues of a deconstructive critique but for Keats's own controlled deconstructive project.

Because any attempt to repeat in one's critical discourse the order of the text is also to take orders from the text (and, thus, to miss the *work*), I'll assemble the material gleaned between and aslant the lines as a thematic configuration rather than as a linear narrative account. The idea is to avoid retelling the romance simply by one's formal maneuvers.

To isolate what I have called the deviant features, one need not ferret out from the romance its 'hidden' representations. To the contrary, one reads what is most blatantly surfaced: the concrete fact of the words on the page and the meanings precipitated horizontally, so to speak, by their arrangement. When I say that one gleans this material between and aslant the lines, I mean just that. One reads the same, foregrounded passages, but one reads them as word-friezes, or compositions assembled from verbal and acoustic representations. The Spenserian stanza – a picture frame and an allusion to Spenser's visual gorgeousness – so much as tells us we must read the words materially: not as a representation of natural or naturalistic images, but as images proper. To read in this surface way is to suspend the left-to-right (cause-to-effect, motive-to-action, figure-to-nature) tendency for a while, and to allow the words to agglutinate according to the verbal principles that seem to obtain. One hears for example the pun in 'unespied . . . peerless bride', and the recapitulation of the opening stanza (trembling hare, feathered owl, woolly sheep) in the description of Madeline, who 'trembles in her soft and chilly nest'. We register what I've called the smartness of this writing and consider the opportunities it affords. Most important, one does not naturalize these patterns by reference to dramatic, psychological, and doctrinal meaning, or not right away. One thinks about the meaning – or antimeaning – of the verbal disposition: not what it tells us, but what it shows us: or, what it shows by *not* telling. Further, one allows rejected versions to enter into the picture. We regard the approved text as somehow preserving (if only by negating, as in the 'viands' example) the variant text.[37]

Interestingly, we explain by this method a contradiction informing the whole range of twentieth-century Keats criticism: our tendency to read the romances allegorically, and our resistance to the reductiveness we sense in that approach. Both these tendencies mark our response to the *locally* allegorical procedures of the romances: the bared yoking of figure to meaning, beauty to truth. Thus does 'St. Agnes', like the other *1820* poems, graph the space which separates those moments, a space which much canonical discourse (and *all* canonically conceived Romantic discourse) effaces. Where this notion of allegory differs from Wasserman's is in its emphasis on the reflexive, represented, and obdurately discontinuous character of the allegory. What is worked allegorically in 'St. Agnes' is not the narrative sequence (a continuous figure bound in a continuous parallel to a dramatic and doctrinal meaning), but everything that is *not* part of that story line.[38] Keats allegorizes all that *obstructs* the progress of the story – essentially, Scene. Fredric Jameson has argued that 'romance is precisely that form in which . . . *world* in the technical sense of the transcendental horizon of our experience becomes visible in an inner-worldly sense.'[39] 'St. Agnes', by *representing* these cosmodicies – self-designated emblems of the real – allegorizes the basic semiotic move of romance narration. Thus does Keats maintain his own narrative act at a particular level; the double signification prevents a discursive meltdown into expressive, mimetic, and generic authenticity. Finally, Keats's meta-allegory transforms his essentially substitutive acts (words as stand-ins for the real things they represent and that Keats couldn't have) into supplemental ones. The meta-allegory produces the *Idea* of allegory, a sign, as an object for possession and an agency of self-possession. By a set of elaborately reflexive procedures, Keats detaches effects from causes, rendering those causes unnatural and more important, those effects material. The possession of these dissociated effects masters 'real' worldness precisely by signifying rather than expressing it.[40] A worldness named is a world robbed of its totalizing properties: its identity as the real. Keats thus refuses what was for him always already gone, unavailable, or prohibited.

One could no doubt analyze the opening paragraph of most novels and emerge in each case with the image of a desire taking on shape, beginning to seek its objects, beginning to develop a textual energetics.[41]

The program for 'St. Agnes'' narrative and discursive grammar is inscribed in the opening stanza. The passage deserves the most deconstructive and also the most exhaustive attention.

> St. Agnes' Eve – ah, bitter chill it was!
> The owl, for all his feathers, was a-cold;
> The hare limped [limp'd] trembling through the frozen grass,
> And silent was the flock in woolly fold.[:]
> Numb were the Beadsman's fingers, while he told
> His rosary, and while his frosted breath,
> Like pious incense from a censer old,
> Seemed [seem'd] taking flight for heaven, without a death,
> Past the sweet Virgin's picture, while his prayer he saith.

The exaggerated structural polarities of 'St. Agnes', as well as the opening editorial pronouncement and, of course, the conventional semantic associations attaching to the first four lines seem to characterize the stanza as a 'real' point of departure for the antithetical fantasy which follows. Typically, we construe the first stanza, a very cold pastoral, as instancing varieties of natural alienation: suffered perversions of deep creaturely truths. The uselessly feathered owl, the silenced flock, the trembling, limping hare, and the frosty-breathed Beadsman present images of natural expressiveness maimed, denatured, truncated, or congealed. Schematically, we have a valorized, vulnerable subjectivity opposed by all the intransigence, pain, and poverty signified by 'Tom's a-cold', echoed in the second line: in a phrase, the fact of facticity.

Keats's masterfully empathic mimesis underscores, we imply, the expressive restrictions suffered by the life that is represented. Keats, who is also very cold (Tom dead, George gone, Fanny improbable), magically transforms his real loss into aesthetic presence. The January facts are but the stuff for a song of summer. The discursive contrast marks out the difference between a sterile and crippled expressiveness – the sign of a lived negativity – and a rich symbolic (that is, subliming) ejaculation. We read the stanza as a discourse that instances, even instantiates, the real: not a descriptive catalogue but a sensuous incarnation. More technically, we read the stanza as an imitation of oral utterance. The language seems to flow from an authorial inwardness through an affective and objective referential universe to a verbal surface. This movement binds all the intervening layers into a smooth continuum and blends in the reader as well. The narration thus construed evinces the curve of healthy representation and sexuality: a flow from a desiring interiority, through attaching qualities or beauties, to a satisfying exteriority – the object of desire – wherein all these moments collapse into perfect union.

The dominant image of the stanza, the Beadsman, stands in stark contrast to the discursive norm I have isolated. For if Keats writes the curve of desire and natural expressiveness, then the Beadsman just as plainly describes the curve of arrested desire and perverse expression. Most readers see in this image a version of Blake's erotic Negations: 'the Youth pined away with desire, / And the pale Virgin shrouded in snow'. The grotesqueness of Blake's figures is the price they pay for refusing the Terrors of Experience. These creatures, that seek to gain Heaven without suffering the death that is instinctual abandon (the end of the pleasure principle), become frozen monuments to their own perversity. Theirs is not the prolific death of intercourse, that marriage of contraries, but a sterile arrest. Structurally speaking, their choice is the antithesis of romance: they prefer alienation to identity, fearful solipsism to joyous embrace.

By the image logic of the stanza, the Beadsman's fingers are analogous to the owl's feathers, the hare's pelt, and the sheep's woolly coat. All these extremities are, it would seem, defensive surfaces whereby a privileged inwardness seeks to ward off a violating environment. The stanza, however, which presents its descriptions serially and as a set of similar items, also and like all sets brings out the salient differences within its membership. Thus, by the analogy between the Beadsman and the other cold creatures, we focus his numb fingers as the concrete sign of his antisensuousness: the Blakean refusal sketched above. Only the Beadsman has a mind of winter; he alone chooses – intentionalizes – the cold world. His extreme numbness is not, then, only or primarily a defensive response to a hostile external environment, but a resistance to a threatening interior environment, an equal but opposite tyranny. Inhabitant of a paralyzing world, the Beadsman willfully restricts his freedom of feeling, in this way protecting himself from an expanding, expressive warmth that would de-compose him. By setting the natural sensory deprivation under an invented sign, the Beadsman, with a wonderful economy, resists that which would freeze him up and that which would melt him down. Like Madeline's voluptuous abstentions, the Beadsman's perversity is designed to enhance his freedom of consciousness: control and composure. Or, an instinctual response is brought into the service of ego determinations.

In this curious and not really logical chiasmus, we begin to experience the stanza as an altogether different kind of representation than that symbolic affair I described above. We ask, why *should* we associate a silenced, shivering, limping order of being, *victims* of their environment, with a wilfully truncated life? Keats's Beadsman is no hero – and below I'll explain just what makes him the pathetic object he is – but neither is he the binary 'bad' alternative to the sensuous discursive ideal we find enacted in the stanza. To my mind, the stanza sketches a something in-between: not the zero nothingness of naturally suffered restriction (the animals), and not the abstract nothingness of a relational restriction (the Beadsman, who suffers in the service of a higher gratification), but the *real* nothingness of an absolute restriction. A restriction of this kind – named, conceptualized – is an object for possession.

Along these lines, let's examine more closely the representational methods of the stanza. One of the first things we notice is that the flagrantly visual invitation is a tease. The visual analogy simply doesn't work in the ways we have learned to regard as iconically referential. We cannot construct from this stanza a scene that corresponds to any of the actual or naturalistically pictured scenes with which we are familiar. There is no human eye – no privileged, coherent, removed but sympathetic consciousness – in which to participate and by which to compose the diverse image elements into a mimetic or expressive composition. If there *is* a discernibly spatialized point of view, it would be deep inside and in the middle of the canvas – the sort of perspective we find in a painting by Breughel or Dali.[42] For that matter, we could compare Keats's perspective to that of the painting Gittings believes strongly influenced 'St. Agnes': Orcagna's 'The Triumph of Death'. At the center of Orcagna's painting sits a melancholy, monkish figure surrounded by images bred of his brooding brain.

We can, of course, construct the visual content of some of the lines. In the mind's eye, one *can* see a shivering owl, a limping rabbit, a flock of sheep, and an old man praying. The pictures, however, are like pieces from four different jigsaw puzzles. What natural eye or vantage could focus a small, quick animal darting through a stretch of frozen grass, a treetop (where else would one find an owl), a sheepfold, and the inside of a chapel? This is to say, we cannot form a composite, eidetic idea of coldness. Further, because what we see is not even a collection of cold things but, as I shall argue, a set of cold signs, we cannot conceive a symbolic Cold that is somehow the image of universal experience, an abstract Truth.[43]

_____

By isolating Keats's descriptive statements from the image world they seem to designate, we begin to *hear* the words and their semantic resonance, and we hear them as frozen echoes – traces – of canonical utterances. Bringing the visual gestures of the discourse into the picture, we 'see' the stanza as a set of word-friezes, each one figuring a particular canonical voice, moment, or style.[44] A review of the footnotes in Miriam Allott's standard edition or a glance at the source studies on 'St. Agnes', and a little Romantic cross-referencing brings out this dynamic clearly.[45] (1) 'was a-cold': 'Tom's a-cold': 'King Lear', Shakespeare. (2) 'the hare limped trembling through the frozen grass': 'the hare is running races in her mirth; / And with her feet she from the plashy earth / Raises a mist . . .': 'Resolution and Independence', Wordsworth. (3) 'Numb were the Beadsman's fingers': *Faerie Queene*, VII, vii 42, Spenser. (4) 'like pious incense': 'Colin Clout', 608–9, Spenser. (5) 'breath . . . taking flight for heaven, without a death . . . , while his prayer he saith': 'Valediction Forbidding Mourning', Donne. Each word group names an origin: a canonical authority and his world of representations. The very *fact* of the collection, however, brings out the exclusively representational character of these origins. That is, the collection kills the worldness of those canonical word-worlds even as it revives and idealizes them, for it materializes that canonical worldness as a determinate, represent-able object, part of a collection of *many such objects*, and, thus, as a bounded space. Jameson has reminded us that 'world' is precisely that which cannot be grasped as a form since it is the context for our definition of all other forms. Or, we might paraphrase Wittgenstein and define 'world' as everything that is the case. If, then, we produce a concept – a representation – of everything that is the case, we have restricted that 'everything' to 'most things', since we have added by our concept a new thing.

Now, where is this concept? As one might infer from the above discussion, the first stanza reads like a rebus: a collection of images, each of which signifies a syllable or word (that is, pictographs: see figure 1).

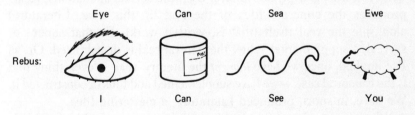

Figure 1   A rebus

The rebus works by a semiotic logic that reverses both the conventionally descriptive word-to-image vector, and the convention-ally pictorial image-to-meaning vector. For instance, we read 'the hare limped trembling through the frozen grass'. This line starts

Wordsworth's hare. We 'see', that is, a line of verse, a graphic image of Wordsworth's words. The image of a natural hare is thus set aside. If we insist on visualizing Wordsworth's words – juxtaposing his natural image against Keats's literary representation – we're led into nonsense territory. Actually, as I'll argue below, we're led into Conceptual territory. At this point, let me just say that Keats's figural juxtaposition – a discursive, representational seme – makes no sense with respect to the semantic and affective content of those images (see pp. 144 ff). We have neither a usable contrast, complementation, nor qualification since the context of Wordsworth's image – the particular semantic patterns of 'Resolution and Independence' – is erased when Keats situates the echo as a *representation of Wordsworth*, rendered by this act 'Wordsworth', a canonical object.[46] Keats plants these quotations and echoes in 'St. Agnes' as severed heads: detached, meta-allegorical figures, or represented signs of other sign systems.

Keats's rebus spells out Literature. It says to us, 'what you are reading exists only on the page, where images can represent the representational acts which bring them into being'. By a voluntary restriction to the word with its inherent duplicity, to the written word with its double duplicity, and to the written *literary* word, Keats can precipitate a real nothingness, or an Absolute Art. By duplicity, I mean the reflexively ostensive capacity of the word; even as it represents and thereby absents, the word establishes itself as a presence in its own right. The written word, separated from the authority of a speaking presence, represents (presents–absents) *that* real thing, and the printed Literary word, which represents other written words, is triply subversive. By these several alienations, Keats produces the concrete Idea of the real (in this case, Literature) alongside the real itself (that is, written work). By that super- or surreal, a supplemental value, the natural real is destabilized. Or, as I've implied, once we have *thought* the literary 'real' – 'everything that is the canonical case' – we have supplemented and thus deconstructed it. We have, in short, produced Literature, a mastering Idea.

What Keats shows us in his opening stanza is his fetishistic possession of other men's words. To see those authorized words as Literary script, and then to see that script put in image space – conventionally, the space of the real – is to grasp the *material* nothingness of representation and thus its monstrosity. It is also to grasp the violability and indifference of that 'real', visual space. What we 'see' turns out to be what we think, and that 'what' is a dissociated Idea of some particular literary reality which exists only in the verbal phenomenon. Stanza one describes neither natural cold (the physical sensation), nor the abstract idea of natural, physical cold (for example, cold facts, harsh reality, vale of soulmaking). Keats produces *real* (autonomous and material) *nothings* (words, signs, effects, substitutes, surfaces).

The discrepancy between the pathos of the represented life and the vigor of the representing writing is explained by reference to the possession or lack of this 'real nothing' which I call in this chapter the Concept, and in chapter 6, money. The creatures in stanza one are 'creatures' in the political sense: slaves of the mastering authorial mind. What subordinates them is the fact that they are forms of consciousness for others, not for themselves. Without a Concept of their restriction (the Beadsman's concept is, as I said, relative and compromised), these creatures can only suffer it. Similarly, without a Concept of this kind, *we*, as readers, are restricted. We grasp only the piteousness of these creatures: their exclusively natural being – *in* itself and *as* their bounding outline. The Concept, however, enables us to focus that line as an assertive intrusion upon the *abstract* nothingness of space. The shivering, limping, trembling, folded motions of the animals sketch a sort of dotted line that contours without realizing and thus authorizing the environment. These representational modes of being – action forms – are a refusal of the comfortably determinate antitheses one anticipates: warm paw–cold ground, smooth continuous movement–static landscape. Generically speaking, the interruptive motions refuse a life–death opposition. The stanza sketches asymptotic lines that seem always about to converge cleanly and settle their differences, but never do. By this determined indeterminacy, the zero space – offcenter but not peripheral – is objectified. In place of the stable 'either–or''s (life–death, moving–static, warm–cold) we have the 'both–and' of material words: a postulate that flickers subversively, invoking other action planes, other figures, the wealth of being that might have been or could become.

By the Concept 'Real', actual reality – the lived experience we bring to the words on the page – assumes a certain glamour. In a way, I'm rehearsing the truism that ugly and unpleasant things can be appealing when aesthetically represented. Or rather, I am concerned to explain a special and unusually self-conscious instance of that general truth. Keats's elaborate and *elaborated* remove from the natural reality of the things he presents forces out the Idea of those things. This Idea, which dominates and deconstructs the less representationally estranged ideas in the stanza (cold, death, etc.), at the same time materializes those negative ideas as items in a word-collection: scriptural presences.

This is an important point. In ordinary life, ideas are the form of an absent thing. When Byron described Keats's poetry as 'mental masturbation', he was labelling Keats a man who fantasized reality because he couldn't live it. Byron was naming Keats a man who 'frigged his *Imagination*' because he couldn't have real sex with a real woman, which meant to Byron that Keats couldn't do or have any of the things that constituted legitimate male adulthood – in Byron's terms, authentic existence. Moreover, Byron's slur implied that even Keats's masturbatory style was unnatural and founded on a second, worse deficiency. Sex with yourself is one thing; solitary sex in the head is another. Self-conscious and cerebral, Keats's autoeroticism was judged by Byron a perversion of normal – male, adolescent – masturbation, or of its physical, phallic expressiveness. Byron's attack on Keats's virility is profound. His critique of Keats's overwrought relation to his mind tells a nasty little story about Keats's body.

In ordinary life, absence tends to be experienced as negative or evil: *estrangement* from the privileged, presence term (warmth, things, life). By reference to this commonplace of our thought, we see that in stanza one, Keats represents precisely these evil nothings, ideas which measure his deprivation. In ordinary life, we feel cold, silence, and numbness as subtractions of heat, sound, and sensation. Keats lets us see, however, that liberated from psychic, physiological, and philosophic primacies – from the origins and ends that constitute these conditions weak negations – these 'nothings' become palpable particulars. Not full presences but real representations of presences which are thereby rendered relative and partial. According to Sartre, Hegel somewhere says that 'the appearance as such is a reality'.[47] The paradox only works, of course, because of the 'as such', a phrase which conceptually absolutizes 'appearance'. The task of Keats's *1820* is, above all, the production of the 'as such'.

We can see, I think, the special virtues of this representational mode for Keats. By it, a man who has nothing can have everything. Moreover, a man who experiences his identity as his desire can, by this mode of production, have nothings *as* his everything. The rich treasure Keats produces in 'St. Agnes' is a heap of substitutes, which, because they do not satisfy, neither do they possess. Keats prepares for himself, over and over again, the food that refreshes but is not consumed.[48] We might recall in this context Trench's sensible observation to Tennyson: 'we cannot live in art'. Keats could 'live' nowhere else.

Keats was not, of course, the first writer to make his art of necessity nor the first to represent the monstrous potential of absolute words. Walter Benjamin finds this capable externality and deconstructive program in German baroque tragedy. Clearly, though, the meaning of the baroque – the place where its philosophical content and economic, and also ideological determinations converge – cannot explain Keats's formally analogous procedures. We are interested in the historical necessity of Keats's solutions. These solutions *do* solve metaphysical and epistemological problems, but it is the others that need explaining.

I'm going to clarify what must sound improbably abstract by way of Benjamin's discussion of the baroque. Let's think for a moment about the grosser effects of the opening stanza. Most readers would agree that the stanza produces an impression of unmediated inwardness: that 'feeling for light and shade' Keats said he admired in Shakespeare. Yet as I've argued, to track down the sources of this impression in particular representations is to bring out the coldness of the piece: its estrangement from its referential means, representational manner, and rhetorical end. As readers, we are like the narrator of the 'Grecian Urn' who haunts about the circumambient relief looking for a way in. Anyone who has tried to teach 'St. Agnes' without the assistance of abstract allegorical blueprints – anyone who has even tried to *describe* the poem (as opposed to enumerating its beauties) – knows what I mean. What does stanza one invite or even allow us to say about it? Or, to seize the question from the other end, why should readers be so fascinated by this stanza which states nothing, describes nothing, evokes nothing?

What this stanza offers is the glamour of a surface that has absorbed its authorizing depths. We are mesmerized not by the abstract semantic indifference of the surface (an *elimination* of depth,

as in a Mondrian design), but by its grotesque meaningfulness. Let
me explain that 'grotesque'. Because the meaning and its vessel sit
cheek by jowl, the meaning *of* meaning – its semantic quiddity – is
abolished. In ordinary life and art, we know meaning by its distance
and difference from material objects and signs. We allow meaning to
invest and transfigure objects but only because we feel it to be
essentially other and, of course, authoritative. To see meaning and
things arranged like apples and oranges in a still life (where, as
opposed to math textbooks, they *can* be submitted to the same
operations) is to see everything and therefore nothing as meaningful
all at once, and this kind of categorical slippage accounts for the
grotesqueness we feel in Keats's gorgeousness.

This effect could be conceived as a parody of the particular
meaningfulness that characterizes courtly romance. In his analysis of
medieval French romance, Erich Auerbach observes that the object-
life characteristic of that form is evenly saturated with a meaning that
derives from the plenitude of the privileged beings who populate the
romance world.[49] Everything means in relation to the structure and
head of meaning responsible for the existence of phenomenal life and
its representations. Everything means in relation to God and the class
that possesses him. In Keats's Romantic romance, meaning is
something imposed by the author, badly derived from his precursors,
and fissuring rather than fusing essences and appearances. Meaning
is not a complement to being but an attack. Moreover, we notice that
in courtly romance, the one thing that does *not* mean is the language
used to represent the meaningful subjects, objects, and actions. This
verbal indifference constitutes the reader's station. From this still
point, the semanticized landscape he surveys is horizoned, and thus
rendered nonthreatening. This is to say, the human perspective
secures itself in a semantically unmarked (but universally and
hierarchically *marking*) language.

This brings us to the second determinant of that grotesqueness we
feel in 'St. Agnes', and to another baroque illumination. We examine
here one more effect of that designated virtuality / virtuosity I have
described. Keats's trembling hare, like 'the carved angels, [staring],
ever eager-eyed' (and the yearning music, snarling trumpets,
wreathed vessels, glowing hand, sculptured dead, etc.), bewitches us
by a vulnerable inwardness that is perfectly surfaced in its physical
appearance. Unlike the pictures we see in someone's living room,

works which assume the modest, natural expressiveness of their owner, Keats's images wear their specularity on their sleeve. The look of these pictures – the look they have of being looked at – is their objectivity, which covers them like a coat of shellac[50] (see 'St. Agnes', ll. 127–31). At the same time, this objectivity *is the consciousness* of these objects worn upon the surface. Or, the consciousness of absolute objects – objects that have no inner life – is literally *our* consciousness of them. Hence the unsettling, inexplicable feeling of unmediated presence produced by 'St. Agnes'. We feel we are alone at night in a gallery of mirrors, 'peerless' ourselves but 'espied' by our own inwardness. We see that we cannot participate in the 'creaturely' life of these graphic images that beckon us by their urgent interiority, since we grasp this inwardness as a virtual dimension established by contextual reference to more stylized and passive representations. And yet the *complete* virtuality of the image – its absolute verbal reality – is the last word in presence. I am describing what Benjamin has called the 'aura', an impression we get from certain objects in certain contexts of incalculable distance and resistance to our humanizing gaze, and at the same time, a deep familiarity.

Keats's hare, to stick with a familiar example, is a representation so absolute that it seems suddenly us. Or, to reverse the reversal described above, *our* consciousness seems suddenly *its* consciousness *of us*, and *we* are thus rendered one-dimensional creatures. Here is the terror of entrapment in a library or museum after closing time – the sense that we have become objects for the consciousness of the mute things that surround us. The blandly staring images – verbal gargoyles – we keep coming upon in 'St. Agnes' formally capture the monstrosity of Keats's phrase 'a working brain'. That phrase describes the workings that bind the consciousness we *feel* from the inside to the consciousness we *see* objectified in our actions and in the images we project. These workings are not generally available to our scrutiny; we do not recognize, that is, the allegory of our identity. Keats's images reveal precisely the space between these existential figures and meanings. The queerness of these word-pictures is that of a self glimpsed suddenly in a mirror, sighted as an object for consciousness. Or it might be like seeing one's own corpse: the carcass, severed from the subjectivity that ordinarily absorbs the mystery of our surface life, our life as self-representing creatures: our ego life.

Keats, more determinedly than most romancers, writes a romance without characters, where it is 'worldness' – in this case, artness – that acts and means, not human agencies.[51] Keats's surprising inclusion of 'St. Agnes' in his critique of 'Isabella''s sentimental weak-sidedness begins to make sense in this context. What we experience as we read stanza one is, as I've said, neither natural, physical cold (creaturely, 'low' truth) nor the abstract idea of cold (philosophic, 'high' truth – the abstract form of the mundane phenomenon). We 'feel', and very consciously, a completely invented category of feeling, available only in an art that tells us it gives only parts and concepts. Sentiment, we know, is the self-conscious feeling of *having* a feeling: a reflexive address to a fetishized feeling. This – both the remove and the possessive mastery – is why one can luxuriate in a sentimental sadness whereas a natural sadness must, of course, be suffered. Keats's critique of 'Isabella' gives us no trouble. It is easy to see that Keats produces Boccaccio's 'authentic' feeling (rendered all the more authentic by Boccaccio's cool narrative control, a contrastive device) as a representational object and expressive apparatus. In 'St. Agnes', which features no severed head and no single canonical model, and which appears to hang its affective drapery on the sound body of a consummated love story, the representational estrangements are not so obvious. This is to say, Keats's control of his method is greater. Both poems, however, tell the same story in the same way, one more effectively than the other. Both romances are about and both produce the virtues of the severed head: the supplement.

As I have said, Keats's wonderfully vivid representation of the hare strongly presents Wordsworth's very differently vivid representation. Wordsworth's image certifies itself a natural representation of a natural phenomenon. Indeed, it is the narrator's gradual realization that he has produced such a living line and can continue to fetch up these quick rejoinders from his bleakest moods that provokes the 'resolution' of the poem, or that transforms isolation into 'independence'. The meaning of Wordsworth's generously anthropomorphized hare is its naturally symbolic presentation: 'A leading from above, a something given'. In representing the hare as a natural emblem of natural consciousness and its natural vicissitudes – as commonplace, regenerative, and redemptive as the seasons and the sunrise – Wordsworth cancels its life as a represented object: its flesh-made-words character. This is exactly what Keats's representation brings out. The virtuosity of Keats's line – its cadence imitates the offcenter uncertainty of the hare's progress – helps to certify the absolutely scriptural reality of the hare. Could we even visualize such a motion if we tried, a motion that *refuses the relativity of perverseness* by withholding both the stable-plane representation (by which we could see *either* a limp *or* a tremble) and the creaturely point of view? The life of Keats's hare resides in all that differentiates it from natural hares and from good (let us say, Wordsworthian, Huntian) representations of such hares. Literally, what Keats's hare *has* – its virtue – is what it lacks.[52]

We might recall in this context Porphyro's gaze at Madeline's discarded dress (l. 245). The empty form produces in Porphyro the dissociated, concrete Idea of what is already an idealized and canonically inscribed object: the idea of a female body as warmth, elasticity, and depth. The power of the dress is its represented lack of these qualities: its stiffness, its borrowed and superficial warmth, its depthlessness. The dress, a parody of the living form, deconstructs the woman as a creaturely and spiritual authority even as it allegorizes that authority, enabling in Porphyro a peculiarly self-conscious and defensively end-stopped swoon. By the figured deficiency which is the meaning and presence of the dress, Porphyro can *have* his pleasure even as it occupies him. The 'feel of not to feel' amounts to a conscious possession of one's being *as* one is being. Madeline's dress, then, is another of those severed heads or supplements. Planted in the funeral urn – in deference to Empson's associative idiom, 'the pot' – of Keats's romance, these heads breed unnaturally vivid and luxuriant leaves.[53]

With the opening lines, Keats puts the entire romance under the sign of loss – ultimately, the sign of death: 'Tom's a cold'. By the allusion to 'Lear', Keats identifies the contextual world as a place of unrecompensed and therefore unthinkable and therefore paralyzing absence. The double allusion – to Tom Keats, cold in his grave and childless – produces the idea of organic endings unrelieved by genetic immortality. This finality – the univocal either / or of life vs. death – is inscribed in the words breath–death. We notice that 'breath' and 'death' make, with 'saieth', one of those word-friezes I've described. Positioned between natural life and natural death (breath–death) is an act and object – a discourse – that is not the living / dying 'pouring forth [one's] soul abroad / In such an ecstasy'. The Beadsman's speech is not, we see, a natural, ejaculatory expressiveness but a materialized emanation attached to him but also subject to his gaze. Keats compares this frosty breath to 'pious incense', and among the several puns packed in that simile, we find one that elaborates this vision of perversely composed discourse. The Beadsman's visible breath – the medium of his prayer words – is as it were his 'in-sense' or creaturely identity extruded and reified, a sort of caption. The projection of breath – *spiritus* – into the alien air congeals what is properly formless, deep, and immaterial. By this parody of his inwardness, the Beadsman can experience it as a possession. (It is important to see that the writing documents no enriching recuperation of consciousness.) The image, which has clear sexual overtones, describes a creaturely flow put into perverse relation with its natural origin and natural end: namely, the death of an utterance received or an emotion expressed. The line describes an 'iced stream' of consciousness, 'impossible to melt as midnight charm'.

Most of us tend to construe that curious line 'taking flight without a death' as the representation of a going without a coming. Or, by reference to the Donne allusion and to the erotic narrative of 'St. Agnes', the Beadsman seems to suffer all the dreary aftermath of passion (the 'waste') without enjoying the 'expense'. By now we can guess that the representation belongs with such other celebrated lines as 'Forever panting, and forever young', and 'Their lips touched not, but had not bade adieu'. All these statements produce the concept of a coming without a going. Like Shakespeare's sonnet 129, these phrases seek to produce a present tense of erotic pleasure: a representation that is neither the nothingness of unrecompensed expense nor the nothingness of anticipatory idea and weary retrospect. The task of the sonnet is to establish a new point on the pleasure thermometer. Keats wants to define a 'tiptop' of conscious tension *coexistent with* the swoon toward quiescence, or the being-in-itself of pleasure. Again, what we have is a conscious unconsciousness, a real nothing.

A discourse that is always 'taking flight without a death' is an expression that resists the 'abroad'-to-'sod', 'expense'-to-'waste' dynamic. The antithesis of a creaturely ecstasy, the Beadsman's utterance marks out a project in composure. Consciousness is fixed in such a way as to obstruct the organic flow of being from center to periphery, subject to object. These energies are arrested in a sort of shield that throws back the alienated image of that inwardness. At the same time and as is the way with shields, this surfaced depth is a projection of power: power inherited, as with 'good' shields, or appropriated, as with Keats.

In defensive terms the line describes a gainful, or at least not impoverishing telling. It is 'told' (ll. 5, 377) without 'tolled' (ll. 22, 156) that is wanted here: discourse without dissolve of the stationing tension. To tell a story properly – orally, let's say – is to lose it to one's listeners, or simply to the silence that frames the enunciation. The analogy to normal sex – object-related, integrative, and completed action – is obvious. In well-written stories, where the writer seems at ease with or absent from his story, where the end is immanent in the beginning, and where things happen 'because they had to', the discourse is devoured by the necessary meaning of the necessary structure. Beauty is digested, as it were, by Truth. The Aristotelian plot is, in fact, a kind of prescription for self-consuming verbal artifacts: that is, the imitation in writing of oral, natural discourse. The question, then – *Keats's* question – is how to write good poetry badly, or in such a way as to hold off the natural closures I've described.

Stillinger's emphasis on Porphyro's stratagem is a useful note here, for that dramatic feature puts to work the discursive procedures we've been considering. What I have added to Stillinger is an accent on the overdetermined nature of Porphyro's plotting, and a concern with the writing. I'd like to explain the important relation between the dramatic and discursive levels by way of Freud's concepts, foreplay and forepleasure.[54] Porphyro's midnight supper, discursively an example of forepleasure and, in dramatic terms, a species of foreplay, furnishes an ideal textual instance.

First, we see that Porphyro's decorative actions structurally imitate the action they anticipate, but as substitutes for that consummative act, they show significant differences. All Porphyro's 'throwing', 'heaping', and 'filling' (and all Keats's metaphors, metonyms, and synaesthesia) cannot collapse the final physical differences that maintain the distinct identities of the various luxuries and thus the tension obtaining among them. No amount of basket filling will blend container and fruit into 'solution sweet', to be blunt about it. Porphyro's declaration of his unendurably aching soul and his 'half anguished [anguish'd]' state would seem yet more strongly to characterize the episode as an instance of foreplay: a sexual tension that, unlike nonerotic physiological tension and mature sexual tension, leads to an increase of tension rather than a reduction. Hence Freud's (allusive?) description of foreplay and of the regressive erotic moments it produces: a 'pleasant pain'. The heavily oral emphasis of both the discourse and the action similarly reinforces the identification of this episode with foreplay, or with the pregenital sexual styles from which it derives.

On the discursive plane, the banquet instances what Freud calls forepleasure: that formal gratification offered to the reader as an incentive to lower his resistance to the fantasy content of the artwork, which would otherwise arouse his envy and hostility. Through forepleasure, we forget that the fantasy that is unfolding belongs to someone else with whom we feel ourselves to be competing for pleasure. Forepleasure also enables us to forget that the represented fantasy contains ideas that are threatening to our conscious moral composure. Forepleasure is in the service of endpleasure. For the author, it enables a direct release of psychic tension through fantasy realization, and for the reader, tension release by identification with the fantasy content.

We observe two things. First, forepleasure, produced by the processes of substitution (condensation: metaphor) and superposition (displacement: metonymy), seems to owe its pleasure quotient to the juxtapositions effected by those processes. In metaphor, two ideas touch by way of a conceptualized resemblance: the possession of a common property. In metonymy, ideas touch by way of physical or temporal proximity, or by causality. In other words, forepleasure might be described as a touching-pleasure, or the 'pleasant pain' of surfaces that graze or seem about to enfold each other but that do not interpenetrate. To say this is to build somewhat on Freud's passing analogy between forepleasure and foreplay: another touching-tension, its restriction to this modality derived from its character as a residue of infantile sexuality. By this character, Freud illuminates the repetitive, tension-inducing tendencies of foreplay. He relates the apparent rebellion of foreplay (from the tyranny of the pleasure principle with its drive toward homeostasis) to the condition of childhood sexuality, where full tension release – orgasm – is physiologically impossible. What *looks like* rebellion is, according to

Freud, only a repetition of an original incapacity: a parody, as it were.

The analogy suggests that the deep psychic gratification we seek or derive from literature – identification with the fantasy content – corresponds to proper orgasm, or what Freud calls the 'higher gratification' of normal adult sex. Great (that is, 'healthy') literature integrates forepleasure into endpleasure by a means–end ratio, just as mature sex is said to absorb foreplay into the cumulative, end-directed, object-related dynamic of intercourse.[55]

Literature that permits fore- and endpleasure to disengage (or worse, that substitutes the former for the latter) would seem to exemplify a species of neurosis: fixation at a particular developmental moment due to unresolved conflicts centering on the special erotic–somatic problem of that moment. I present this background not to analyze *Keats* but to read the meaning of his narrational modes. We have seen that the stylistic perversions discriminated above preserve a certain tension at the dramatic and discursive levels while interfering with the ego-authorial impoverishment resulting from excessive cathexes of the canon, and of imagination and its products. The rebellion is, then, a determined revolt as opposed to a repetition *tout court*.

Porphyro's supper – dramatically, an instance of foreplay; discursively, an instance of forepleasure – is not eaten. It remains an isolated, autotelic, tension-producing tension. By the model of intercourse, it does not submit to 'the dominance of the genital zone'. As a dramatic representation, the scene not only postpones the union of hero and heroine, it absorbs much of the interest and energy which properly attends that union. More important, it offers itself as a set-piece and as a master trope: a piece of writing made of pieces of other men's writing. Discursively, it puts Keats and the canon in a touching-tension, inducing in him a functional pleasant pain that amounts to an authorial self-consciousness. The drift toward a canonical and / or psychic dissolve is structurally arrested.

On the descriptive level, the passage is the very, and very self-conscious, image of forepleasure. Porphyro's banquet is an elaborate and archly self-advertising metaphor for Madeline's body. Madeline, nested in her 'blanched . . . smooth and lavendered [lavender'd]' bedclothes is just such a 'silken', 'perfume[d]', 'delicate' as Porphyro tucks into silver baskets. That curiously charged domestic detail – 'soft he set / A table[,] and, half anguished, [anguish'd] threw thereon

/ A cloth . . .' – allegorizes the discursive action of the passage and would seem thus to connect rather concretely the dramatic and the representational dimensions. The erotic intensity of this literary table laying – an exercise in juxtaposition, superposition, and condensation – is clearly a function of the surface tension produced by Porphyro's physical heaping, arranging, and layering. More important, the sly metaphor inscribed in Porphyro's action (that is, laying a table: laying a woman) evinces that quintessentially Keatsian supplementarity we have addressed throughout this book. It asks us to focus the defensive virtues of the lesser act when it is consciously positioned as a substitute for the greater: a less that is more.

The episode confirms the argument of this section: namely, that Keats's object was not to escape into fantasy but rather to construct a particular *kind* of fantasy, one that resists its own consummation. The project was to write a 'fine spell of words' to 'save / Imagination from the sable charm / And dumb enchantment'. Without words – a special *kind* of word, that 'frosts' our 'in-sense' – we are assimilated by that inwardness. Or so Keats imagined *he* would become 'nerveless, listless, dead, / Unsceptred' by too intimate an association with his fantasies.[56] The words – Freud's forepleasure – are both the substance of Keats's fantasy and the shield he holds up against it to ward off the 'enthrallment far more self-destroying'. Unless the material character of the word is maintained, it cannot be that shield, and unless it is that it had better not be at all. We might recall here Keats's description of the temple he will build to Psyche – a place of 'branched thoughts, new grown with *pleasant pain*' (my emphasis). We might also remember that Keats was a man who could have only the *forms* of legitimacy, not the substance; and, who could only actually have foreplay in the only lovelife that seemed to matter to him.

Keats produces his perpetual-tension machine by a variety of nonsense tactics, many of which I've isolated.[57] To 'tell' a story by such procedures (puns, tautology, category errors and inversions, repetition, framing) is to 'saieth' without 'death'. It is, more literally, to narrate in place, or to move through words without getting anywhere. Or, to resume the sexual theme, it is to come without going.

We might note at this point a few of the represented speech modes in the poem. One very odd thing about 'St. Agnes' is that everyone in the poem whispers. Rarely is the whisper dramatically motivated.

'Whisperers in anger, or in sport' excellently foregrounds the overdetermination of this verb, as there is absolutely *no* dramatic reason why this boisterous company should whisper. 'Whisperers', an onomatopoetic word, is represented *as such* by the phrase 'in anger'. The 'er' of 'anger' reproduces the doubled 'er' of 'whisperer' (much as the conjunction 'or' represents the internal 'or' of 'sport'), effectively signifying the wordness of that word much as 'wide' graphically represents 'wilderness'. Again, the semantic content is aggressively doubtful. To learn that there is angry and sportive whispering at a party is to learn some pretty useless – categorically inappropriate – information. This would suggest that the word is not there to inform referentially, and this refusal brings out other, largely verbal factors. For instance, we notice that one has to mumble 'whisperers in anger . . .' and to hear it as Keats did, with a British accent, is to make it even more of a mumble. In semantic terms, Keats's word 'whisperer', as it were a written whisper, is a sort of mumbo-jumbo: an utterance that means performatively and only within a particular, ritualized context rather than by the individual semantic gestures of the words. *Anything* one whispers becomes a sweet nothing since the act of whispering usurps upon the meaning of the words whispered. In positive terms, a whisper is another way to 'saieth' without 'death'; since there is no substantive communication, there is no loss of substance. We can see that Keats's phrase 'whisperers in anger . . .' is a greatly reflexive as well as a reified speech act. Its meaning is its formal approximation to a whisper, which is to say, its 'natural' nonsense. The phrase, a parody of the warmly animated speech it names, is a sort of posthumous expression, the form or fossil of living speech.

The Beadsman's rosary is an unusually concentrated emblem of the telling style of 'St. Agnes'. First, to 'tell' a rosary is to speak a spatial and circular figure: to translate things (beads) into words that are themselves word-things (prayers), or verbal configurations that are objects of and for consciousness. (We might recall in this context the narrative action of Keats's 'Grecian Urn': the translation of one sort of spatial and circular legend into another.) This kind of telling is not, obviously, a discourse that moves us along, gathers to a meaning, or loses anything in translation. By the mechanical quality of the performance, the words are dissociated both from a creaturely subjectivity and from a beholden objectivity. The rosary, neither a supplication nor celebration, does not express, imitate, or formulate the real. Like the religious processions that figure so prominently in Keats's poetry, the rosary is a devotional form. Both are what is conventionally considered a formal means (prayer as access to the divine ear; the procession as an approach to a sacred place and act) severed from their natural ends. Both are nonreferential, nonsymbolic, and yet thoroughly semiotic phenomena. When the narrator of the 'Grecian Urn' asks, 'who are these . . . to what green altar . . . what little town' – or, what are the natural and historical origins and ends that situate this procession – he puts exactly the questions which the urn, like the odal form, is designed to refuse. However, by voicing these queries, and in what is rhetorically identified as an *oral* mode, the narrator puts the urn's referential perversity (the pictorial equivalent of virtuosity) under the sign of withdrawal. Thus does Keats transform the characteristic restrictions of graphic art into virtues; muteness becomes powerfully critical silence. The escape offered by the urn is not, then, the alternative, abstract, fantasy life it conjures – the 'relief' of young love eternal – but the material, sculptural relief: a dissociated, concrete, and absolute Concept of nature. (That is, Art.)

We enlarge our understanding of this unnatural relief by considering the status of number in the rosary and its closural effects. In everyday life, we experience number either as an abstract idea or as an empirical description (a quality deduced from objects). The rosary, however, renders number an absolute and real Idea. The objects which element the rosary – individual beads – represent certain prayers, the sole function of which is to represent the Idea of number. The Pater Nosters mean by their quantitative correspondence to a group of beads, which itself means by *its* correspondence to a numerical Idea – one that does not, however, mean by correspondence to anything else. The number 10 in the rosary derives its conceptual authority from that which has no being but to illustrate that number. To owe one's authority to such a nothing is not to be indebted in any meaningful way. '[S]ignificance rules, like a stern sultan in the harem of objects'.[58] Benjamin's simile, which would seem to suggest the interdependence of Concept and objects (what is a sultan without his harem and vice versa?) in fact asserts a conceptual absolutism. Master and slave, individually considered, necessitate each other, but Master and *collection* of slaves (that is, Number and prayer) are not so imbricated. The slaves (beads), which are more than the sum of their parts, serve that 'more', a conceptual entity (bead-group). This is no natural Master but a reflexive Idea, abstracted from real things (individual beads, slaves) and assuming material form. This Idea (prayer; harem) displaces the sort of natural incarnation which *would* dialectically constitute a natural – and dependent – Master. Hence, the 'voluptuousness' of the Numerical reign in the rosary.

The status of number in the rosary means that the termination of an act of beadtelling is neither a natural closure (an ending from the natural necessity of exhaustion, as in orgasm and oral discourse), neither is it a personally compelled conclusion ('you! end now!'), nor an abstract compulsion. By abstract, I mean a symbolic use of number, where the relation between the number of Ave Marias and the meaning of the devotion would seem to be determined by some mimetic or associative principle (for example, ten days before Christmas, ten Ave Marias). The conclusion of a rosary telling is an end without consummation.

We notice that the entire romance of 'St. Agnes' takes place during the Beadsman's telling: 'his was harsh penance on St. Agnes' Eve . . . And all night kept awake for sinners' sake to grieve' (ll. 24–7). His ritual brooding, or the discursive tension it sustains, seems to breed the words that write the romance. The abrupt dissolve of the 'natural' romance in the shocking, final revelation of what it had always been, a night of the living dead, is dramatically associated with the Beadsman's natural death, itself linked to the cessation of his discourse: 'after thousand aves told'. Somehow, we feel that the beadtelling kept the Beadsman alive: pleasantly pained and thus stationed.

Similarly, it would seem, Keats's poem maintains him by maintaining *in* him the perversely pleasant pain of writing. This is the act that, like the rosary, prevents him from falling into deep and soul-destroying desire. The model for 'St. Agnes' is, as I suggested above, *not* pornography, a discourse which Steven Marcus wonderfully designates 'a bedtime story'.[59] Pornography lets us fall asleep by facilitating so full a realization of our fantasies as to dissolve the tensions that keep us awake. Keats's purpose, conversely, is to stay *up*: more decorously, to station himself. The writing that 'St. Agnes' instances and celebrates is, like the rosary, a substitute for authentic expressiveness. This substitute is more than the real it stands in for because it knows and works its deficiencies.

———————

I'd like to bring out the syntactic peculiarity of the opening stanza, which we take as inscribing the norms of Keats's romance and the form of his desire. We have graphed the effective perversions of the Beadsman's discourse on every level but one: its dissociation from its designated addressee. His Ave Marias fly 'past' not 'to' the sweet Virgin's 'picture', itself a mediated idea. On one level – the teasing and masking level – we are meant to read in the line an image of highly directed and unmediated discourse: an arrow of desire shooting past the image, binding the beloved and the lover to the divine original. However, the textually centered representation of the Virgin's *picture*, the marked absence of allusion of the celestial first cause, and the tentativeness of the description ('seemed [seem'd] taking flight for heaven . . .') bring out the decidedly *oblique* relationship of speaking subject to receptive object. The contradiction is presented, as it were, by the discursive procedures of the stanza. Structurally and syntactically, the stanza resembles an arrangement of verbal 'twig points', anchors for a word-web that will catch the whispering wind and materialize the nothingness of idea. Consider the preponderance of prepositions and conjunctions in the stanza: 'through', 'in', 'while', 'while', 'from', 'for', 'past', 'while'. Where do these vectors take us but to another absolutely median point? The pattern is most conspicuous in lines 5–9: 'Numb were the Beadsman's fingers, while he told / His rosary, and while his frosted breath . . . seemed taking flight . . . while his prayer he saith'. The 'whiles' underline the absence from this stanza of a privileged consciousness, the 'fixed foot' in relation to which the simultaneities could be organized. What does it mean to say, 'while he x'ed, while he was y'ing, while he was z'ing'? What it means is what it shows: namely, the verbal elision of the dominant indicative that would rationalize by subordinating the participles. The doubled dependent clauses and the omission of the mastering main clause convert a semantic and syntactic action into a formal gesture. The second two 'whiles' change their linguistic status; they become concrete verbal frames for the incense–frosty breath unit. Syntactically, the stanza develops a concrete geometry of sensation: the idea of relationality divorced from the stable consciousness and / or action that would naturalize that idea. Action becomes gesture, or the idea of an action detached from its natural or conventional origin and end. We see this relational idea precisely because there is no *imaged* relationality, only verbal contingency, in the stanza. The hare, owl, sheep, and Beadsman must be, in naturalistically spatial terms, widely separated marks on the canvas.

This same pattern occurs in the conspicuous copulas of stanza one: 'chill it was', 'was a-cold', 'silent was', 'numb were'. Typically, a copula marries a subject to its predicated attribute, rendering that state of being the natural, inalienable effect of the subject – its full identity at that moment. In Keats's stanza, however, by the repetition and inversion (and thus the primacy given to the adjective-attribute rather than the noun-subject), and by a certain tonal incommensurability, the copula *divorces* being from its adjectival state, giving that state an independent status. The predicates in lines 1, 2, 4, and 5 – which exhibit the logic of the part over the whole, attribute over essence, effect over cause – deconstruct the postulate of capably holistic consciousness. We can guess that these local syntactic workings encode the style of all the copulations in 'St. Agnes'. All are incomplete and alienated: instances of foreplay as supplement for consummated intercourse. Or, they are all varieties of touching tension, surface juxtaposition. Only in self-consciously written discourse is this kind and degree of tension possible and pleasurable.

We saw how 'woolly fold' compelled a meaning to ricochet between two ideas (sheep fold and sheepfold), effectively rendering those ideas a formal binarity (soft, warm, organic: hard, cold, manmade) and, at the same time, materializing the word 'fold' and unfathering it from that twofold form. This 'bad' word situates the reader in what I have called a sojourn space. What we experience in 'woolly fold' is the substitute (neither a sheepfold nor a sheep fold) that is a supplement (both–and) because the substitute is self-consciously represented. Only in written words can lips *be* not touching but not parted. In writing of this kind, the negation of a negation constitutes a practical position.

Keats's punnish repetition, incense–censor, teases by its gestures toward naturalistically thematic meaning. The pun starts us thinking about the Beadsman symbolically, or as an abstract allegorical figure: one who *censors* his own experience and who *censures* those who fail to regulate their appetites. At the same time, we might make the connection described above, wherein the Beadsman's in-sense – his expressive inwardness – is assimilated to the visible, public objectivity of incense. In both thematic and dramatic terms, this double pun does not add up to anything. If neither moves us along in the action (as by foreshadowing), nor constructs character. It does, however, suggest how character *can* get constructed by the life-in-death of written speech. We see that language can – and in conventional discourse, *does* – create subjectivity. More generally, we see in Keats's pun a meaning constructed from the outside in – usually, the path of affectation and disguise. In 'St. Agnes', meaning is peripheral, not axial, just as the meaning of Keats's urn is its ornamental surface relief (that is, what is *about* it), not its contents, not its origins (what it is 'about', spatially and temporally). Or, Keats puts his meanings in the 'leaves' that come *to* the tree, and that suspend the deceptively mastering, phallic line. I am reminded of Genet's observation: 'A cherry branch, supported by the full flight of the pink flowers, surges stiff and black from a vase'.[60] By such enfolded and cognitively unstable reversals, Genet, like Keats, confounds some very basic and even physiological assumptions concerning structure and ornament, essence and attribute, necessity and luxury, soul and body, end and means.

Keats's Beadsman materializes the Concept of an extruded consciousness. Benjamin's analysis of baroque representation is apropos: 'He [the emblematist] drags the essence of what is depicted out before the image, in writing, as a caption, such as, in the emblem-books, forms an intimate part of what is depicted'. The 'elective affinity with the baroque' which Benjamin observes in the Romantic writers would seem to be existentially (which is to say, materially and ideologically) overdetermined in Keats's case.[61] Keats's 'essence' – his consciousness – was, as we have seen, largely consciousness of lack. By reifying his nothingness in the scriptural ways we have observed, Keats could render it an effective asset: a signifying (phallic) ornament. This is a startlingly modern technique: a way to make absence presence and dispossession display. The Beadsman's caption is as an emblem for Keats's entire representational project in 'St. Agnes'. He writes in this romance a language not more productive of thought than an orally mimetic poetry but more the material *form* of thought. 'Shadows haunting fairily / The brain, new stuffed [stuff'd] in youth, with triumphs gay', 'full of this whim was thoughtful Madeline', 'sudden a thought came like a full-blown rose', 'sole-thoughted', 'Flown, like a thought'. These phrases, examples of the categorical dissonance I've mentioned, are devices for sealing inwardness – for Keats, nothingness – in the 'black purgatorial rails' of writing.

Let me stress the fact that this is *Keats's* accomplishment. It takes a strong spirit, not the Beadsman's 'weak' one, to release the power of that eternal 'ache in icy hoods and mails' and to produce the freedom of that purgatory blind which is writing. Indeed, the stanza does more than pose a simple opposition between Keats's strong, self-conscious spirit and the relative spirits of the represented creatures. We have seen that the poverty of these creatures lies in their failure to conceive their imposed perverseness perversely, thereby to claim it as an attribute. We might now see that their pathos is also the necessary condition for Keats's powerfully objective self-consciousness. In order to work for Keats, his romantic creatures must literally *work* for him. They must be reduced to morphemes – absolutely apparitional objects – that spell out Literature. 'Literature', the Concept which masters the collection, kills the creaturely life of its servants. We have seen how this rigidly representational Concept kills Wordsworth's hare (kills Wordsworth-*qua*-Wordsworth), and at the same time, raises that image and that canonical name into instances of the Concept, Literature. Indeed, at the end of 'St. Agnes', when Keats summons the romance props to a dance of death, we are explicitly informed that we have been reading a history only of departed things. At that point, we recall the first line of the romance, which we had probably taken for a bit of authentic authorial expressiveness, and we grasp it instead as a parody of first words and of authorial worldbuilding. No longer the expression or description of a thing, the line now emerges *as* a line and as a represented Concept of writerly expression. In this vein, we refocus the natural crescendo and deepening of statement in lines 2–9 (owl, hare, sheep, Beadsman: an allegory of ascending conscious-ness) as the verbal proof of a verbal assertion. 'It was cold': evidentiary cases of coldness.

Keats kills the things he loves because he knows that death is the *father* of Beauty. This sort of Beauty, begotten upon a natural, relative charm, sired and ravished by the coldest Truth, is freedom and identity. Keats's wine must be 'cooled a long age in the deep-delved earth' before it can intoxicate him. His urns must have been steeped in eons of slow time: his Psyche, a goddess dissociated both from her living mythology and from the mythological canons of Keats's own day. All these moldy heads, exhumed and replanted in categorically inappropriate pots, have great virtue for Keats. From them come the leaves that cannot leave, the expression that is sent abroad but is not lost and does not deplete the sender. Nothing lives for Keats without undergoing a sea-change. Madeline and Porphyro live so richly because they were long ago, 'aye, ages long ago', loosed from their romance lovenest and thrust into a posthumous existence. The lovenest itself, the 'natural' literary romance, lives because it is a dead thing, a jumble of wakeful bloodhounds, sprawling porters, fluttering arras, groaning hinges, and trusty keys (cf. ll. 352–69). Keats's lovers must enter the 'flaw-blown' stormworld (Paolo's and Francesca's domain, 'the flaw / Of rain and hail-stones), just as the warm romance must die into the cold canon, and as Shakespeare, Spenser, Donne, and the rest must enter the unnatural territory of Keats's belated romance. Everything dies to rise as the material Idea of itself.[62] The redemptive formula of *1820* is life-to-death-to-the embodied Idea of life. Eyes to pearl – the living, dissociated Idea of an eye, as coral is the live, external Idea of bone. The special virtue of 'St. Agnes' finds its emblem in the grotesque preservation of Lorenzo's severed head, and in the no less bizarre survival of the urn. In Lorenzo's case, the metamorphosis is from *mind*, a helpless, desiring state, to breeding, 'leave-ing' *brain*. The agency of this change, neither Time nor History in the grand, panoramic sense, is a *particular history*, one that is explicitly associated with a new and vulgar economic order, designated through such stereotypes of bourgeois commerce as 'ledger-men', 'money-bags', ' "unfair" dealer[s]'. The urn, once a living cultural artifact, is similarly transformed by changing modes of production into a museum piece and an odal subject. We consider these transforming histories in chapter 6. At this point, I shall observe only that both the severed head and the funeral urn signify a refusal of authorized and generous representation. Indeed, Keats's affinity for romance and ode – classically, 'depth' forms – effectively *underlines* the refusal. We are not carried down to sensuousness or up to seriousness, as those words are commonly experienced in the context of those poetic forms. Like Keats, we are stationed by these works that name their rejection of a 'breathing human passion' and thereby resist 'dying into life'. It is high time we read that phrase correctly and with reference to the quality of the 'life' Keats endured.[63]

I'd like to recall here Keats's association to line 261, where Porphyro hears from afar, interruptively, and 'in dying tone' the full, riotous music from downstairs. Here is Cowden Clarke's report of Keats's gloss: 'That line . . . came into my head when I remembered how I used to listen in bed to your music at school'.[64] Presumably, the reminiscence dates from the year at Enfield following Keats's mother's death (1810), for this was when Keats's friendship with Clarke blossomed. The association might suggest to us that 'Darkling I listen', 'melodies . . . unheard', and 'ditties of no tone', like Porphyro's restricted enjoyment of the music, represent solutions to Keats's actual deprivations. By shifts such as these, Keats converts his lonely, ill-heard, 'darkling' concert – a poor substitute for the rich family harmonies he misses – into a supplemental virtue. A ditty of no tone, piped to the spirit and not to the sensual ear, is music only for oneself: 'more endeared'. Such music is, in addition, inexhaustible and inalienable. These phrases I have isolated name an idealized unnaturalness, a mode of possession that is unique, eternal, and that, by preserving a certain tension, preserves the consciousness that elements identity. Thus does a sad boy who comforts himself under the eaves invent 'a delicious diligent Indolence'.

My anti-romantic argument has centered on that dimension of 'St. Agnes' which is not story. Inasmuch as the story outlines a sequence that begins in alienation (the Beadsman, Madeline, and Porphyro all initially figure varieties of social and erotic estrangement) and proceeds toward interiority and identity, we would seem to have a problem on our hands. How can one talk about willful perversity, verbal virtuosity, and supplements in the context of a plot that engenders images of intersubjectivity, deep truth, and gratified desire? Indeed, how can we talk about end-stopped forepleasure and dissociated foreplay in a poem that has reminded many readers of soft porn and that features one of the most celebrated scenes of sexual union in all English literature?

Let me return to the matter I broached on pp. 106–7 and sketched as a problem in bad writing. There, I suggested that 'St. Agnes'' canonized representation of robust, object-related sexuality – 'Into her dream he melted . . .' – inscribes the figure of a narcissistic interaction. To observe this is not, of course, to advance the normative view of narcissism, but to begin analyzing the virtues of this pathology within a psychic universe that sets 'working brain' against 'solution sweet': work against love.

To love narcissistically is to love a reflection of one's idealized self. More technically, one loves a representation of that which one lacks. We can easily see how Derridean – how supplemental – this kind of loving is. Unlike the genuine primary other – mother, father – the narcissistic object is introjected rather than assimilated. It lives *in* the self as an alienated and idealized consciousness *of* the self. Moreover, unlike the genuine *belated* other (the object loved by transference, so to speak), the narcissistic object, insofar as it is felt as a representational item (as it must be felt if it is to enhance the ego), can never fully satisfy. This is to say, it cannot dissolve that erotic, stationing tension I have described. Narcissism enables a longing that is precisely *not* the desire that fills you up, absorbing the space of consciousness. Narcissistic desire is an object-for-consciousness. What we see in this erotic orientation is a putting to work of psychic dissonance. 'Frigging [one's] *Imagination*' – an act which, like Lawrence's 'sex in the head', would seem to require a two-party psyche – is, in fact, a pretty exact definition of secondary narcissism (as is 'internalization of quest-romance').

I'll return to these issues. For now, let me ask how we can identify Madeline, that gorgeously elaborated creature, as a blank screen upon which Porphyro projects his own ego ideal. It is one thing to discriminate the real and effective nothingness of Madeline's dress, quite another to deconstruct Madeline.

Again, let's look at the writing. First, the set piece: stanzas 24–7. Lines 203–7, the threshold to this famous scene, describe Madeline's vow of silence, a detail invented by Keats, or at least not found in the sources we know him to have drawn on. What makes this description somewhat confusing and, I find, disturbing is its representation of an expressive restriction – and a physically painful one – not just as the condition of a perverse and breeding 'eloquence', but as a physical fullness. 'Balmy side', an allusion to Milton's representation of both Adam's and Eve's births, is one inscription of this breeding virtue. Additionally, we observe that the expressive obstruction (an artificial one on two levels: Madeline imposes it on herself, Keats deviates from his sources to impose it on Madeline) enables an internal colloquy: 'to her heart, her heart was voluble'. Before we translate the poetry into prose ('the loud beating of Madeline's heart has its own painful eloquence'), we might consider the actual words.[65] Deprived of the luxury of enunciation, Madeline is put into a dialogic state. What was, presumably, a univocal subjectivity is now fissured. By her abstention, Madeline's own 'heart', her subjectivity, becomes for her an object-for-consciousness. Keats thus associates what he has already developed as the masturbatory ritual of 'St. Agnes' with perversions of discourse. The general procedures of Keats's romance urge us to read Madeline's painful self-contradiction as the condition for an effectual, if not (*because* not) audible eloquence.

The oddest thing about this description is the closing couplet, with its pronomial ambiguity. The lines are, of course, intended as a simple simile: Madeline is like a tongueless nightingale whose heart, stifled by unexpressed feeling, fails her. But the 'her' in line 207 would appear – overwhelmingly – to describe Madeline. The syntax produces the idea of a tongueless nightingale – Madeline's (in)expressive instrument – swelling *Madeline's* throat in vain. The dreadful image of a woman choking on her speechlessness, her throat engorged by its congealed discourse, might remind us of a happier representation from the 'Ode to a Nightingale': 'full-throated ease'. I would just remark here a pattern we shall explore below: the ambiguity of lines 205–7 not only reifies Madeline's silence but sets it under a phallic, presence sign, albeit an ambivalently valorized sign.

Even when we construe the couplet respectfully, the figure is problematic. 'Tongueless nightingales' are all, as we know, descended from Philomel, who lost her tongue when Tereus, to prevent her from naming him a rapist, cut it out. Why should Madeline, still a virgin, preparing to be safely ravished by her dreams, and soon to indulge in mutually solicited intercourse with a gentle lover, be compared to poor Philomel? There is no logical dramatic reason for this association – no more narrative sense than there is in the Porphyro–Iacomo connection. There is, however, an authorial and discursive rationale, and it brings us back to that curious chiasmus in stanza one, where the animals' expressive restrictions and suffered numbness are related to the voluntary numbness and verbal perversity of the Beadsman. Both these crossovers evince Keats's interest in confounding suffered violation, deficiency, and restriction (for example, Philomel) with contrived, identity-effective deviance.

Stanza 24 is the shielded scutcheon at the center of the poem. This passage and the immediately following are, of course, elaborately framed. The Spenserian stanza frames Porphyro's closet view which frames the overall canvas. The casement makes another frame, as do the panes within the casement and finally, the outline of the scutcheon, a heraldic shield. These five frames converge all sight lines upon Madeline, a figure composed by these nested outlines: or, we might say, a composing figure for Porphyro, Keats, and the reader.

The visual concentration is phonically reinforced. We might note, for example, the profusion of fricatives, voiced stops, and sibilants (s, sh, ch, d, k).[66] This densely substantial language suggests, in action terms, an enunciatory frieze or arrangement of aural arrests. This effect is syntactically represented by the preponderance of past participles (for example, 'garlanded', 'diamonded', 'damasked', etc.). These words make us 'see', very literally, a still life: a picture composed of the material residue of actions. The word 'diamonded', for example, suggests an action frozen in figure, then in the end-stopped sound that freezes the figure, and finally in the script that congeals the sound. ('Damasked', with its central sibilant, enclosed by two voiced stops and a voiceless glottal (d-as-k-d), recapitulates in miniature the acoustic and spatial organization of the stanza.) The semantic content of such phonically clotted words as 'bunches', 'knotgrass', 'scutcheon', and 'damasked' emphasizes the web-like quality of the representation. For an analogy, we might think of the mandala, a meditation device; its concentric design frees by fixing consciousness.

Louis Montrose has recently read Holbein's portrait of Queen Elizabeth in such a way as to bring out the conceptual resonance of the knotted ribbon drawn so assertively in the low center of the queen's dress, which is also the center of the canvas.[67] Once we have grasped the Queen's body as a synecdoche for the body politic, we see that virginity, that secure knot, is meant to figure the security of the state from invasion. Montrose's analysis shows us very concretely how virginity – 'that which hath no being' – acquires determinate form, and more important, value, through the painterly acts which materialize it. At a more primary and general level, virginity 'appreciates' through the social discourses that make this 'thing that is not at all' a virtuous possession.

In passing, we might reflect that virginity – an important theme in both the ritual of St. Agnes and the saint's life it commemorates – plays a larger part in Keats's poem than our criticism has acknowledged. St. Agnes, a pious Christian, was 'condemned to be debauched in the common stews' prior to her execution. Assumed unto heaven, she was at once rescued from her fate and sanctified, 'her virginity . . . miraculously preserved'. One might observe that the sexual violation gets translated into a finer tone. As Christ's creature, St. Agnes is, in a sense, eternally unravished because always already possessed. The annual shearing of a sacred lamb's wool on St. Agnes Eve, and the donation of this fleece to God would seem to reinforce this redemptive replication. St. Agnes enjoys a both / and sexual status, an oxymoronic condition that should be perfectly familiar to us by now. The popular legend elaborates the hidden repetition in the martyrdom as well as the doubleness of the figure engendered by that fiction. It does so by making a real physical abstention the condition for conceptual voluptuousness. The rare virtue available to those who observe the ritual of this holiday amounts to a 'having one's cake and eating it' scenario. The Eve enables devout maidens to enjoy real pleasure under the sign of dream. They awake in the morning as hale as ever, 'no weeping Magdalen': nocent and innocent.[68]

By analogy, and to enlarge our understanding of Keats's 'tongue-less nightingale' allusion, we might reflect a moment on a narrative contradiction deeply installed in Philomel's mythological career: namely, the reversal of Procne's and Philomel's metamorphoses. In the pre-Ovidian versions of the Philomel story, Tereus, in order to indulge his lust for Philomel, his sister-in-law, shuts up Procne in the woods, announces her death, and cuts out her tongue to keep her from disclosing herself. Tereus secures Pandion's permission to wed Philomel; he succeeds in lying with her. Procne's revenge involves the dismemberment of her son, Itys, and the serving of his cooked body to his father, Tereus. The gods prevent full-scale, or rather, immediate massacre by transforming Procne, the muted woman, into a swallow, a bird that has no song. Philomel becomes a nightingale and Tereus a hawk or hoopoe.

According to Robert Graves, who constructs the version sketched above, all the mythographers but Hyginus make *Procne* a nightingale and Philomel a swallow.[69] Robert Anderson, in his commentary on the *Metamorphoses*, similarly observes that 'the Greeks agreed on the whole that Procne, the mother, became the lamenting, lugubrious nightingale'.[70] Graves reads this reversal as 'a clumsy attempt to rectify a slip made by some earlier poet; that Tereus cut out Philomel's tongue, not Procne's'. The conjecture betrays an assumption of dramatic verisimilitude; the logic of metamorphosis requires a naturalistic, as opposed to dynamic, idealizing reflection of historical truths. The tongueless woman is, or should be, aligned with the songless bird. Here is Anderson's astute response to the general form of the metamorphoses in Ovid's text: 'just as words like *tamen* or *antiquus* [668–70] can be used by Ovid to emphasize a certain continuity between the old personality and the new form, so the adverb *adhuc* [669] here makes clear that the two sisters have not escaped from their crime against Itys even if they have avoided Tereus' sword. They are eternally marked with the blood of their crime'. They are also, as defenseless birds, constituted as eternal victims of the hawk, Tereus, who is become their *natural* predator.

While Ovid's version, the major source for the erotic narratives of the English Renaissance, leaves the identity of the metamorphoses ambiguous, it tightens the narrative structure and focuses it sharply on Philomel.[71] According to Ovid, Tereus takes Philomel by force, not stratagem. Second, it is Philomel who is shut away in the woods, and *Philomel* whose tongue is cut out to keep her from broadcasting Tereus's infamy. Finally, Ovid has Philomel participate enthusiastically in the murder of Itys. In other words, Ovid grafts the oral mutilation upon the genital and social violence.

From the Renaissance on, we find a consistent literary identification of Philomel – Ovid's sexually victimized and silenced creature – with the nightingale.[72] George Sandys's account, Keats's source, should be taken as representative: '. . . the two sisters fained to have beene changed into birds, for their speedy flight unto Athens, *by which they escaped the revenge of Tereus* . . . [my emphasis] *Philomela* into a Nightingall, and *Progne* into a Swallow'.[73] The association, which gives to the tongueless woman the loveliest song, would seem to be more than a philological mistake or decision (say, a crossing of Hyginus's text with the more frequent narrative forms). In it, we see the same kind of idealizing repetition inscribed in the St. Agnes legend. Our 'improvement' on the classical mythological tradition –

our compensatory generosity toward Philomel – effectively erases the rape, the mutilation, and the horror which is the irrevocability of *these* 'metamorphoses'. The graphic severity of the earlier versions, their insistence on the history in the myth, is kinder to Philomel than her admirers have been.

Philomel's literary fortunes trace a conversion of doubled nothings (the rape, the symbolic castration) into powerful somethings. Keats is interested in just this conversion, for the reasons I've already and at length set forth. We might consider here an association implicitly developed throughout this book: Keats's feminized status, in the sense of his socially defined lack of all that made for legitimacy and effective originality. We might further guess that virginity, that culturally valorized nothingness, could serve Keats's representational purposes beautifully. The trick was to develop idealistically the culturally implicit association of virginity as lack of sexual *experience* (or of the desire felt to derive from carnal knowledge) with virginity as lack of the *apparatus* for 'genuine' sexual experience. (By bracketing 'genuine', I name the nineteenth-century restriction of sexuality to a male form.) The premium put on the one dimension, lack of experience, would effectively valorize the other, lack of the agency. By this piggyback consecration, Keats could develop a strong form of his weakness.

The textual basis for this reading of virginity as an idealization of phallic lack occurs in Madeline's strange, postcoital complaint, lines 329–33. 'Porphyro will leave me here to fade and pine . . . I curse not, for my heart is lost in thine, / Though thou forsakest a deceived thing –[; –] / A dove forlorn and lost with sick, [sick] unpruned wing.' What Madeline gains by the loss of her virginity – the suffered nothing – is wings, the single ornament she is said to have lacked before the interlude (l. 224). Angel wings (by reference to l. 224, to the St. Agnes legend, and by general cultural convention) denote a virtuous innocence. At the same time, Madeline's wings, which require regular sexual 'pruning', seem to signify her acquisition of a desire that in its urgency and object-interest resembles Porphyro's aggressive desiring. The wings – emblem of a presented absence, with the accent on 'present' – would seem to be another way Keats valorizes (here, gives a phallic form to) deficit.[74] We could say that Porphyro makes Madeline in his own – and in Keats's – image. We might reconsider in this context Madeline's anxiety over her acquisition, which she conceives as requiring expressive relief through the selfsame act which fledged her. As with the nightingale simile, the text represents a full, healthy (that is, adult male) desire as a prodromal state. The 'sickness' Madeline fears is not that enabling dis-ease we have discussed but a helpless frustration. One may glimpse in this ambivalently phallic representation one of the anxieties that committed Keats to his curiously indirect exercise in empowerment. We might also mark at this point that what seems like a contradiction (Keats's identification with Porphyro *and* Madeline) is another socially determined oxymoron. Just as Porphyro, that busy, ambitious, and very redblooded man, solves one set of problems for Keats, so Madeline – 'sweet dreamer', perfect solipsist, blueblooded and luxurious leisurer – solves another.

Probably the most memorable and often quoted detail of Madeline's dress and undress is the description of the colored moonlight on her body. 'Full on this casement shone the wintry moon, / And threw warm gules on Madeline's fair breast'. I have not, however, encountered in my reading any discussion of the surprising coincidence made by that equally famous phrase, beloved of the creaturely critics: 'her warmed jewels . . .' 'Warm gules' and 'warmed jewels' look rather different but aurally, they are nearly identical. 'Gules', we observe, constitutes one act and element in a dressing up, while Madeline's removal of her 'jewels' is, clearly, a deconstructive act, a moment in Madeline's disrobing. This is to say that 'gules' mirrors 'jewels' on the plane of discourse and story, cancelling the natural, or extrinsically authorized meaning of both words and fashioning them into a single semiotic unit.

The collapse of the individual representations into a textual design has several effects. First, the homology of jewels–gules kills the creaturely authority of Madeline's body, or of the notion of meaningful and productive inwardness. The window's conferring warmth – by Keats's analogy, Madeline's heat-conferring body – is not only a strictly optical effect and the result of a conventional semantic association (red = warmth), but a strictly verbal effect, since colors are not transmitted in moonlight. This relative falseness – relative, that is, to natural, empirical truth – is a deviance we call 'poetic license' and which tends to be semantically indifferent. Keats, however, renders this falseness absolute by reference to Scott's identical misrepresentation in 'The Lay of the Last Minstrel'. The allusion establishes the literariness of Keats's figure; it *represents* the unnatural representation and thereby establishes it as an artifice, a literary object. This doubled falseness produces, of course, the truth of the figure and its virtue for Keats.

The linguistic resonance of 'gules' and 'jewels' reminds us that virginity, which many traditional· cultural discourses designate a 'jewel', is also a 'gule' – in the poem, a dissociated and legitimizing effect.[75] Keats's writing would seem to identify virginity as an idea Conceptualized and, thus, effectuated, by its determined remove from both private and social causalities. Abstracted from its historical conditions – the history of some particular woman's or group of women's virginity; the history of the concept of virginity as substitute / supplement for phallic difference – this nothing gains real and symbolic power. Isolated from histories such as these, virginity can signify; indeed, it can signify *those histories*. With this change in semiotic status comes, of course, a value change.[76]

Through Porphyro, Keats directs a fascinated gaze at Madeline: or rather, at the collected effects of her person. Colloquially, we might say that Porphyro gazes at Madeline's personal 'effects' or property: tints, jewels, dress, pearls, bodice, linen, etc. These ornaments, the concrete surface figure for Madeline's virginity, which is literally her virtue (what she lacks is what she has), are all supplements. Collectively, her 'rich attire', a substitute for the anatomical and socially valorized ornament she lacks, is as a shield that covers and compensates for a defect: a sort of prosthesis.[77] The verbal figure corresponding to this function is, of course, metaphor: a *representational* reality. At the same time, these rich decorations signify by their representational *reality* a possession more absolute and inalienable than the natural, phallic endowment. From this perspective, Madeline's ornaments are the shield that signifies inherited and profound legitimacy – an extension of natural power. Metonymy is what we call this verbal effect.

One is reminded of T. J. Clark's reading of Olympia's hand, that 'enraged and exalted the critics as nothing else did, because it failed to enact the lack of a phallus (which is not to say it quite signified the opposite)'.[78] The hand, which hides the phallic absence, also represents that absence in a material and conceptual fashion. Thus is the female figure supplemented by something that men do not ordinarily have: a real, deconstructed Idea, capable of signifying itself and its conditions of being even as it designates other things. The monstrosity of Manet's 'Olympia' was not just (or even?) the picture's suggestion of a phallic woman or a castrated man. It was the transitivity of those ideas, reflected in Clark's honest equivocation, that bewitched Manet's viewers.

Keats's representation of Madeline's 'lack' enraged no one because Keats idealizes that lack in conventional ways (dresses, jewelry, coloration), and gives it the name of a privileged negation: virginity. Then too, Madeline is a fairy-tale princess, whereas Manet names his image a prostitute. Moreover, Keats's elaborately concentric framing and his invocation of the full abstractive powers of language mediate the doubleness to which Manet's viewers were directly exposed. Indeed, criticism's benign response to Keats's perversely fetishistic representations indicates just how virtuous the restrictions of writing can be. Imagine generations of art historians missing the strangeness of Olympia's rigid posture and her very aggressive modesty.

In terms of Keats's project – conversion of substitutes to supplements – we might note his alternating representation of Madeline as a sort of living oxymoron (mermaid; bud / rose; wakeful dreamer), and as a zero-degree figure (the nothingness *between* 'joy' and 'pain', 'sunshine and rain', 'havened', 'blinded'). The reader is urged to construe her as a richly concentrated both / and (phallic woman) and a neither / nor (castrated man).

By the concrete elaboration of Madeline's nothingness, a jewel that gules, Keats both refuses the imposed feminization (the common want that involves both Keats and Madeline in aggressively masturbatory projects), and works the association. Author and heroine long for a real fantasy, an object that will fulfill them while vouchsafing them their virtue: in Keats's case, tension and dissonance. Here, I believe, is the meaning of Keats's emphasis on Madeline's abstentions. Her exaggerated withdrawals strongly urge us to read the St. Agnes Eve ritual as a masturbatory action; deprivation is treated as a richly rewarded refusal of the 'real things' that, if 'naturally' enjoyed, would bear Keats's soul along to nothingness. In this context, we might note Keats's jokey description of Madeline, line 225: 'so pure a thing, so free from mortal taint'. Thus does Porphyro characterize a figure who is nothing *but* mortal taint – guled, rose-bloomed, amethysted, haloed, 'newly dressed' by a lightshow. The joke draws together the various strands I've been teasing apart. Madeline's exclusively representational reality *does*, in fact, constitute her virtue for her lover and her author. One can love such a creature, or creation, without losing the selfhood that is identified with one's relativity and the desire it breeds. To love a congeries of dissociated effects is to love a surface one cannot melt into. To coincide with this surface is not, of course, to lose oneself but to acquire one's reflected, enhanced image.

The mirroring dynamic enacted by the two lovers has been often enough observed and, when interpreted, read as an image of intersubjectivity. What interests me is not the rich mutuality of hero and heroine but the operational character, for Porphyro, of Madeline's virtuality: her mirror identity. By the above discussion, we identify Madeline, Porphyro's object of desire, as an ego ideal for both Keats and Porphyro.

Let me lay some groundwork for an ego and social, as opposed to an instinctual explanation of the leading features of the Madeline–Porphyro eroticism: specifically, the voyeurism, mirroring, and 'solution sweet'. Freud reads the twinned erotic perversions, voyeurism-exhibitionism, sado-masochism, as regressive attempts at defense against object-related interests: to see, to assert, to master.

> Those vicissitudes which consist in the instinct's being turned around upon the subject's own ego and undergoing reversal from activity to passivity [i.e. voyeurism to exhibitionism, sadism to masochism] are dependent upon the narcissistic organization of the ego and bear the stamp of that phase. Perhaps they represent attempts at defence which at the higher stages of development of the ego are effected by other means.[79]

By 'defence', Freud means resistance to the aggressive instincts. The defense is mounted in the sphere of the libido.

Above, I suggested that secondary narcissism, which substitutes an introjected self-other (an ego cathected with object libido), for the extrinsic, other-object, structurally precludes the tension release and consciousness fadeout that mark the end of the pleasure principle. This is to say, we might read narcissism as a defense *against* libido and *in the service of aggression*: or, in a modulated form, composure, mastery, self-assertion. If one accepts the distinction developed in

Beyond the Pleasure Principle, secondary narcissism would seem to be one outcome of the conflict between libido, conceived as the species-preserving principle, and aggression. In its primary developmental form, aggression locates for Freud the clearest expression of what he calls the death instinct. In its later, object-related forms, however, aggression appears to function as an individuating imperative: preservation of the individual at the expense of the species. The reversal of *this* aggressive modality back upon the ego (that is, secondary narcissism) might represent a more strenuous effort yet to enhance individuality, or to resist the psychic hegemony of the pleasure principle in its adult libidinal manifestation. Narcissism would be, by this reasoning, the expression of a problematic wherein tension-dissolution is experienced as death, and where death is experienced as absolute insofar as species-identification is exclusively negative. Only within this essentially social context can we understand why individual consciousness – that is, capable selfhood (being-for-itself) – would experience self-identity (being-in-itself) as extinction. And we understand this social context by considering, as we shall do below, the ideological genetics, so to speak, of the early nineteenth-century middle class, a necessarily self-disinheriting class. Additionally, and with respect to more directly practical imperatives, a narcissism thus conceived would seem to define an unusually subtle and effective orientation toward an external environment experienced as structurally hostile. To internalize but not assimilate the other – to steal the *image* of the threatening object – is to dematerialize rather than resist and thus dialectically reinforce that otherness. It is to commit that genuine externality to a limbo space where resolution can never occur because the contestants are categorically mismatched. An authentic or original ego faces an ego differentiated into a manifestation of otherness that is a love object insofar as it is ego (and insofar as its objectivity is informed by primary objects), but that cannot be assimilated, insofar as it is felt as a representation (and, insofar as it is informed by more socially determined concepts of otherness). Essentially, the dangerous otherness is used to precipitate a permanent and productive psychic dissonance. To reclaim and redeem a bad otherness in this parodic way is to co-opt that otherness. The cost, however, is a rather wholesale effacement of the real. We can see that this dynamic, which sets individual and species interests against each other, would not obtain for groups (historical moments) that have managed to intertwine these interests in the psychic life of their members.

Narcissism would be, by this logic, the psychic form of a familiar aesthetic dynamic, and Keats's poetry would seem to articulate this dynamic with extraordinary awareness. According to classical affective poetics, one feels free to let go in art because there are no real causes or affective objects (characters, actions), because deep down, we never forget this fact, and because this fact reassures us that we can't really let go – can't *really* feel actual emotions. We are tricked, as it were, into a full catharsis. (Roughly speaking, this is Freud's explanation of aesthetic pleasure as well; the formal signature of the work seduces us into an identification with the fantasy content.) Another way to focus the matter, however, would be to suggest that we are free to let go because we *cannot*, however hard we try, *really let go*. The formal dimension of the work – that which identifies it *as* a work – is not a bribe or a false reassurance but an actual defense against the range of absorptions that make affective abandon such a risky business in real life. This is to say that art, which offers only parts and surfaces, *obstructs* the catharsis which threatens consciousness. Art can gratify better than life precisely because it cannot ever fully satisfy. The little death' we feel at the end of a poem or novel is a *conscious* unconsciousness: 'the feel of not to feel it'. Real life offers no such oxymorons, no such sojourns. That art form which can most forcefully represent its fictiveness – that form which can absolutize itself – enables the fullest kind of response, for it protects us most capably from the real and *internal* consequences to our letting go.

I'd like to return to the social dimensions of the narcissistic solution I've sketched, but to position them more specifically in the context of Keats's life. We want to explain the erotic style of a person (or group) who conceives his identity as his desire, and whose aim must therefore be to effectuate his nothingness rather than cure it. We have seen that by a narcissistic orientation, a person in this position might gain his object without losing his desire and the working brain which that desire fuels. Literally, thus might one gain the world without losing one's soul, since what one gains is an image only, a surface: not world but worldness. Contrary to the Narcissus myth, one does not fall into mirrors. Love for an internalized representational object is romance that will not collapse into 'happily ever after'.

Freud discusses primary narcissism in terms of ego development, which consists in a departure from that autoerotic moment and in attempts to recover its effects by a more and more generous orientation toward a genuine other. The initial departure is brought about by displacement of ego energy from the actual ego to the ego ideal, an external object reconstructed psychically as the superego. The ego feels gratified in the attainment of this ideal, or its sense of gradually becoming its admired object. At the same time, the ego puts forth libidinal object cathexes and this expense, along with the formation of an ego ideal, depletes it. The mature solution is for the ego to enrich itself by gratification of its object love (having) and the fulfilling of its ego ideal (becoming): two separate operations.

What happens when narcissistic gratification is *actually* hindered? What if a person cannot, for profound social reasons and the psychic distortions they impose, realize his ego ideal, and what if, for the same reasons, the ego is extravagantly diminished by its object cathexes? What happens, moreover, when the psychic economy will not permit a merger with the ego ideal, even if material conditions *were* favorable? Finally, what about people who, because of primary as well as sustained and severe object loss, cannot tolerate any effacement of identity in loved objects, even if that effacement comes about through internalization? I'm describing Keats, of course.[80] Or rather, I'm describing a textual solution to a psychic dilemma. That solution is, as I've suggested, the 'sweet', regressive solution of a return to narcissism. One chooses a sexual ideal that is also an ego-ideal. One loves that which one lacks and couldn't otherwise attain; that is, one tries to *obtain* it. Keats doesn't want to *have* Milton, originally. He wants to *be* Milton, but the only way to do that, given Keats's circumstances, is to make of Milton the introjected erotic object: the possessed otherness that is inalienable because always already alien. In a sense, I'm describing an oral overdetermination of adult erotic interests. The oral wish is to become by assimilating otherness into self; the secondary narcissistic wish is to acquire by designating a part of the ego as other and ideal – all that one lacks. In order to produce the gratification – the *experience* – of realizing an ego ideal, however, the loved object must be maintained as a possession, and not blended into the subject's being. The object must remain a sign, one that perversely inscribes, of course, the primary or 'natural' deficits. Narcissism would seem, then, to be an attempt to become by mis-acquiring. To 'melt into' Donne is to lose Donne as the sign of legitimacy: a remedy or supplement. For Donne to 'make' Keats (as for Madeline to make Porphyro), he / she must be fetishized and flattened out. Donne must be worked both as Keats's deep expressiveness (or, as a form of being), and as Keats's representational object, a 'having' form. Only a Donne linguistically reified and represented can enable this oxymoronic solution.

Similarly, what the hero loves in Keats's romances is what he must acquire to realize his ego ideal. He cannot, however, let himself *fully* have, and thus *become* that object without at the same time losing himself. Isabella, for example, can live without Lorenzo but she cannot survive the loss of the severed head. Indeed, this peculiar version of her lover enables the prolonged pleasant pain that precedes the murder, and that constitutes the main action of Keats's romance (thematized, as it were, in the sick charm of the exhumation scene), to continue not only unabated but intensified. The *action* remains constant, but Isabella before and after the establishment of her narcissistic object are very different characters. This is to say, the fetish seems to give her a consciousness of herself as a certain kind of character. (Or, Keats seems suddenly to enjoy a new understanding of his heroine.) Instinctual renunciation, the loss of Lorenzo, seems relatively manageable as compared to the loss of the object that realizes Isabella characterologically and discursively. We might even observe that the abstractness of the enemies in 'Isabella' and in 'St. Agnes' – I mean the alternately stylized and spongy quality of the 'bad' others who threaten the lovers' designs – betrays the comparable absence of 'good' otherness, in the form of distinct erotic objects. We might glimpse in this narcissistic economy (where, by loving the ego-ideal, one becomes and possesses simultaneously) a passive, feminized way to compete. A way to work and love without losing one's generative tension.

I want to sketch some of the class implications of this analysis so that we may consider the social project inscribed in Keats's writing and in the criticism that copies from that book into its own. Before opening this discussion, let me position my procedure. The bulk of this chapter consists of the closest sort of textual analysis; the reading I'm about to produce is very general and basically allegorical. Between these two critical discourses stands my reading of Christopher Ricks – his exploration of the privatized psychic dimension of Keats's most characteristic representations – and Sartre: his social, and also structural psychology. I do not, in the following section, produce an analysis of actual social relations and the material facts that require them, nor do I plot the dynamic dimension of my ideological material. I project from Keats's representational system a model of more generic, social self-representations. Obviously, a projection of this kind cannot engender either a causal or totalizing form of explanation. At this point in my discussion, I am not seeking an escape from hermeneutic circles. The idea is to superimpose one such circle on another and, because the fit is never exact, to produce a distinct overlap space where complete coincidence *would* seem to obtain. For a spatial model, we might think of the Venn diagram, where, by a conventionally determined mathematical operation, we open up a space for interfigural – in this case, text-context – articulations. The area wherein text and context match up may be seen as the space of self-parody. Like Keats, I hope to effectuate an Original moment by reproducing it upon a different field. In other words, this social discussion is not offered by way of reinforcing and naturalizing the foregoing textual exegesis, but in the interest of identifying both my critique and Keats's as elements in what Adorno calls 'the world of wares'.[81] In the concluding chapters of this book, I study Keats's attempt to *think* that world rather than manipulate it by its own magic, and I take my method from the critical model he sets.

First, we observe the relational objectivity of the early nineteenth-century bourgeoisie. By a structural allegory, we may conceive this class as the object of a (covetous) gaze from below and a (contemptuous) look from above. Moreover, with its competitive individualism, this was a class that knew no shared subjectivity. We describe, in other words, an internally objectified, psychically dissonant class. The experienced identity of this group would seem to have consisted in its distorted reflection of the legitimate, 'subject' classes that surrounded it. Its job was to surface the deep, creaturely, and substantial truths of the working class, and the high, philosophic, and formal truths of the leisure class. That is, the structurally designated task of this group was to represent the authorizing truths of its adjacent structures within its own queer dimension. Without upper and lower there is, naturally, no middle. This is to say that the project of this class had to be oxymoronic; it had to be a repetition in different tone. Even as the middle class realized lower and upper classes (allegorically, instinctual and conceptual truth) by its repetitions of their creation myths, and thus confirmed itself as the free between, its *location* of these myths in its own illusionary space de-authorized both sides, rendering them *mere* 'existences' on the one side, and mere abstraction on the other, as compared to that vividly scandalous 'Thing semi-real', the middle.

The poems we have treated develop a structural diagram of remarkable clarity and they do so with remarkable consistency. The primary action of these works is the metamorphosis of natural being into the dissociated Idea of being. Keats makes us see a discarded dress as the concrete Idea of a body, foreplay as the live Idea of intercourse, words as the embodied Idea of the spirit, narcissism as the working Idea of object love, and the middle class (in 'St. Agnes', Scene, Worldness, Art) as the effective Idea of the upper and lower orders. The sea-change is, as I've said, from life through death to a posthumous existence. The narrative form of this process should be familiar to us: the dream within a dream (*Endymion*, 'La Belle Dame', 'The Fall of Hyperion', 'Lamia'). The very romance form is, in 'St. Agnes', a dreamed dream; this is the message of the concluding act of narrative distancing, lines 370–8. The second, literary dream, which realizes the first romance (this becomes the real to the second dream's representational imaginary), also empties the Original of its originary authority. The represent*ing* version masters its represent*ed* object and is also thereby enslaved to it.

These structural transformations cast some light on the psychic model we have been using throughout. One could focus Freud's ego, sandwiched between the authority of the id (which *is*, and acts from that simplicity) and the superego, similarly self-identical, as another of the Things semi-real we have been studying. By the social analogy, the ego would function as a screen or shield: a representing plane able to figure its own representational field, the body. 'The ego is first and foremost a bodily ego; it is not merely a surface entity, but is itself the projection of a surface'.[82] What does such a structure resemble but something very like the supplementarity we have identified throughout Keats's writing. An ego *in the place of* an authentic, natural body; and, in addition to an unself-conscious, natural body: a body that cannot mean, cannot 'project' itself, can only *be*.

The middle class of Keats's day could neither experience nor imagine its authenticity. To be genuine is to be naturally derived and to anticipate a natural immortality in one's natural offspring. A class that refuses its sociogenetic past – whose identity *as* a class requires this genealogical erasure – cannot imagine a relation with the future that is other than its parodic relation to the present. It has no means for the identification which alone makes the future ours: our children's, that is. Moreover, it recognizes by the very logic that brought it into being the 'hunger' of the coming generations who are its own class offspring and whose identity must therefore be *their* bad derivation, *their* illegitimacy, *their* Satanic denials. That trenchant phrase I echoed above – 'no hungry generations tread thee down' – as well as the evolutionary preoccupations of the *Hyperion* poems, focus for us the situation of a man who foresees no natural posterity and who feels himself to be sociologically *sui generis* as well. The job of conceiving a realizing future must be, for such a man, a Titanic task.

A class that can only be a bad representation of its adjacent orders and must continually remake itself in / as / against the projected image of those orders must ape that monstrosity in order to consolidate itself. This is consolidation by perverse inclusion, not exclusion: a swerve from what Jameson has described as classic romance norms. According to Jameson, the individual or group defines as Other (a symbolic category, it would seem) what is recognized as profoundly self but, being outside and unassimilable (and also competitively positioned by the law of scarcity), intolerably other in an *imaginary* sense.[83] The problem of essential identity is solved by a normatively dichotomizing structure, where I define 'good' and my double / rival brings 'evil' into being. The us / them dynamic produced by this narrative structure enables legitimate hatred and fear of those for whom sympathy or identification would seem to be both impractical and psychically unbearable.

In much of Keats's poetry, we see definition of the Other as self and the self as occupied by an alien presence. How to explain this swerve, which looks like an internalization of the traditional romance self-other dynamic? We remember that the middle class of Keats's day was nothing but the tension it sustained, tension between the mythically antagonistic upper and lower classes. If the self–other, good–bad, high–low dialectics that, in ideological terms, had *engendered* the middle class were to continue, there would soon be nothing *but* the class in the middle which, by digesting its surrounding, stationing classes, would effectively deconstruct itself. The way out of this double-bind was to convert the dialectic into a dyad, that goes nowhere and produces nothing but reproductions. By its semi-real status, its status as an absolute surface, the middle class refused to play the role of a dialectical synthesis, which it correctly perceived as a double role. It would not, that is, participate as the thesis in a new social moment. The middle class secured itself by a representational oscillation between fixed poles located within its own territory and then again, within its own individual psyches.

We might recall a remark made above, to the effect that narcissism is quite literally the internalization of quest-romance. Its virtue is the unbroachable virginity of the object which engenders and sustains the quest. The authentic ego faces its supplemental self in the interiorized mirror. Love of the supplement, which has no depth to penetrate, is indeed a sweet solution insofar as it ensures the sort of eternal ongoingness one associates with childhood fantasies. To remember in this context that the governing nineteenth-century narrative is the plot of ambition (usurpation or change of place; acquisition of the desired object) is to grasp Keats's project as a narcissistic variant on that model. Keats's interest is not to seize the *object* that will change his place – that is, legitimate him – but to appropriate its *image*. By reproducing that image upon the depthless plane of his own class consciousness, he parodies the consecrating object even as he gains its virtue. Madeline's bluebloodedness, for example (her character as what Wasserman calls 'pure being'), enables Keats to remodel that 'high' authorizing social idea, just as his parody of Porphyro's redbloodedness ('passionate becoming') remodels the 'low' authorizing character. Or, one very economical way to change your place is to sit still and redefine the places which surround you. Additionally, this kind of place-changing maintains the betweenness – the identity – of the middle structure.

As poetry recognizes its loss of practical power in the world, it assumes the magic, oxymoronic virtue of the ceaselessly self-deconstructive structure. It offers us a meaning which we cannot consume and which promises not, therefore, to consume us. It's not hard to conjecture the value of such a meaning to a culture afraid of satisfaction, which it feels as death, and afraid of death, which it imagines as absolute and unrecompensed. As I said, a group that knows no natural inheritance cannot guess at immortality. Such a group must want to own everything because it knows that it never owns anything – can never *let* itself own anything – properly or forever. Consider the value of these unconsumable meanings to a culture that tries to remake everything in its own image but which must then reject those renovated objects as being unworthy, since they are only images of a profoundly 'bad' self.[84] For this culture, academically processed, Keats's poetry is the ideal commodity. It provides 'real pleasure', not for its own sake but 'in the service of an impossible attempt to coincide, in the realm of the imaginary, with the essence of an owner of things. As a result, the whole system is derealized, the very enjoyment becomes imaginary.'[85] This is to say, the enjoyment is incomplete, self-conscious and self-perpetuating: a pleasant pain. A poetry that teases out of thought saves us from the instinctual gratification that would, we fear, annihilate identity.

In a loftier vein, this poetry seems to us a greatly enlightened and yet a comforting discourse; it identifies its own mystifications, reassuring us all the while that the content goes beyond the form.

> O Attic shape! Fair attitude! With [with] brede
> Of marble men and maidens overwrought,
> With forest branches and the trodden weed
>
> Thou, silent form, dost tease us out of thought
> As doth eternity.[:] Cold pastoral!
> When old age shall this generation waste,
> Thou shalt remain, in midst of other woe
> Than ours, a friend to man, to whom thou say'st,
> 'Beauty is truth, truth beauty . . .

The consolation offered by these lines is, in fact, nearly the opposite of that skeptical / salvific humanism which is the general interpretation of the leaf-fringed legend. In the closing stanza of the Ode, Keats tells us – *reassures* us – that the *form* persists, and that it does so because it has digested its own historical content. The urn, which reproduces truth as beauty, meaning as figure, breed as brede, is a sort of formalizing machine that disappears its own past as well as the past–presents of all those people who have engaged it through time. It presents life under the aspect of eternity: the aspect of death. For Keats, as we have seen, this was the only way to seize a meaning, or to make one.

In Keats's poetry, we see literature beginning to enact and to *represent* its enactment of this self-violation, self-love. What I describe may sound like a *mise-en-abîme*, but the violence is end-stopped in words. Keats's is, typically, a literature that, lacking the power to liberate – the power to *think* its own liberation – must station. This composure is offered to us as a new kind of freedom: literally, a new self-possession. The magic of Keats's words is like that of all relative creatures once they conceptualize their contingency. I think Keats understood some of this. Here is an excerpt from his famous, and strangely repetitive reflection on 'the poetical Character'.

A Poet is the most unpoetical of any thing in existence; because he has no Identity – he is continually in for – and filling some other Body – The Sun, the Moon, the Sea and Men and Women who are creatures of impulse are poetical and have about them an unchangeable attribute – the poet has none; no identity – he is certainly the most unpoetical of all God's creatures. If then he has no self, and if I am a Poet, where is the Wonder that I should say I would ~~right~~ write no more? Might I not at that very instant [have] been cogitating on the Characters of saturn [*sic*] and Ops? It is a wretched thing to confess; but it is a very fact that not one word I ever utter can be taken for granted as an opinion growing out of my identical nature – how can it, when I have no nature? When I am in a room with People if I ever am free from speculating on creations of my own brain, then not myself goes home to myself: but the identity of every one in the room begins [so] to press upon me that, I am in a very little time an[ni]hilated . . . I know not whether I make myself wholly understood: I hope enough so to let you see that no dependence is to be placed on what I said that day. (Extract from letter to Woodhouse, 27 October 1818)[86]

Notes

1 Douglas Bush, ed., *John Keats, Selected Poems and Letters*, (Boston, Mass.: Houghton Mifflin, 1959), pp. xi–xvii; and 'Keats and His Ideas', in *The Major English Romantic Poets*, ed. Clarence Thorpe *et al.* (Urbana, Ill.: Univ. of Illinois Press, 1957).

2 Robert Gittings, 'Rich Antiquity', in *Twentieth-Century Interpretations of The Eve of St. Agnes*, ed. Allan Danzig (Englewood Cliffs, NJ: Prentice-Hall, 1971), pp. 86–98. Quotation from pp. 95, 91.

3 Earl Wasserman, *The Finer Tone* (Baltimore, Md: Johns Hopkins Univ. Press, 1953; 1967), pp. 120, 121.

4 Harold Bloom, 'The Internalization of Quest-Romance', in *Romanticism and Consciousness*, ed. Harold Bloom (New York: W. W. Norton, 1970), pp. 3–23.

5 Bloom, *The Visionary Company: A Reading of English Romantic Poetry* (New York: Doubleday, 1961), pp. 397, 399. Robert Buchanan coined the epithet in his review of Rossetti's *The House of Life*. The attack evoked a swift and scathing response from Swinburne.

6 Jack Stillinger, 'The Hoodwinking of Madeline: Skepticism in "The Eve of St. Agnes"', in *Twentieth-Century Interpretations of the Eve of St. Agnes*, ed. A. Danzig, pp. 49–71. Quotations from pp. 62, 63, 71.

7 George Ridley, *Keats's Craftsmanship, A Study in Poetic Development* (Oxford: Clarendon Press, 1933), pp. 101, 102, 11; also see pp. 96, 97.

8 R. H. Fogle, 'A Reading of Keats's "Eve of St. Agnes"', *College English*, 6 (1945), pp. 328, 325.

9 Northrop Frye, *The Secular Scripture, A Study of the Structure of Romance* (Cambridge, Mass.: Harvard Univ. Press, 1976), p. 61.

10 Wasserman, *The Finer Tone*, pp. 111, 135. 'The union of Porphyro and Madeline does not stand for anything, but is in itself the mystic oxymoron which is heaven.'

11 Bush, *John Keats, Selected Poems and Letters*, p. xvi: 'we may react to individual images, bits of the "material sublime", as Keats reacted to northern scenes . . . Of countless images and epithets in Keats we may say what Abt Vogler says of the musician, that out of three sounds he frames, not a fourth sound, but a star.'

12 Ridley, *Keats's Craftsmanship*, p. 112. I'd like to cite two exceptional studies of 'St. Agnes'. Arthur Carr, 'Keats's Other "Urn"', *The University of Kansas City Review*, 20 (1954), pp. 237–42. Carr's emphasis on the ritual discipline of 'St. Agnes', its fearful preoccupation with mutability, its morbidly transfigurative energy, necessary incompletion and, above all, the represented posthumousness of its form are all remarkably fresh observations. For its stylistic acumen, see Charles Patterson's 'The Keats–Hazlitt–Hunt Copy of *Palmerin of England* in Relation to Keats's Poetry', *Journal of English and Germanic Philology*, 60 (1961), pp. 31–43. Patterson calls our attention to a passage from *Palmerin*, volume 4, underlined by Keats (see italics) and re-marked by Hunt, who additionally signed the bottom of the page with Keats's name. '. . . he determined to remain there . . . beside his lady, not remembering that he had no other food there than his own *imaginations, which would sooner destroy than support him*' (p. 41).

13 Peter Brooks, *Reading for the Plot: Design and Intention in Narrative* (New York: Knopf, 1984), p. 13. Brooks defines plot as 'the interpretive activities elicited by the distinction between *fabula* and *sjuzet*, the way we use the one against the other'.

14 Coleridge's marginalia to Donne's *Songs and Sonnets*, written in 1811 and appearing in Charles Lamb's copy of Donne, presumably refer to the 1810 'Poems of John Donne' in Alexander Chalmers's edition, *The Works of the English Poets*, vol. 5, pp. 113–218. See Roberta Brinkley, ed., *Coleridge and the Seventeenth Century* (Durham, NC: Duke Univ. Press, 1955), p. 519 and *passim*. One would assume that Keats and / or Hunt had access to this edition as well.

15 Keats's love for Fanny Brawne, a woman who was pretty unanimously judged to be cool, vain, and self-involved, brings out the difference between Keats's life

and art. Freud remarks the appeal of such women – narcissists – for men who have renounced their own narcissism 'and are seeking after object-love'. Freud goes on to describe the narcissistic charm of children, and of 'certain animals which seem not to concern themselves about us, such as cats and the large beasts of prey . . . The great charm of the narcissistic woman has, however, its reverse side; a large part of the dissatisfaction of the lover, of his doubts of the woman's love, of his complaints of her enigmatic nature, have their root in this incongruity between the types of object-choice'. ('On Narcissism', in *Sigmund Freud: General Psychological Theory, Papers in Metapsychology*, ed. Philip Rieff, New York: Macmillan, 1963, p. 70. In *The Standard Edition of the Complete Psychological Works*, ed. James Strachey, Anna Freud, London: The Hogarth Press and the Institute of Psycho-Analysis, 1959; 1973, vol. 14, pp. 73–104.)

Keats's letters to Fanny are, of course, filled with anxious requests for reassurances as to her love, and with rebukes for her capriciousness. More to the point, we might observe the uncanny similarity between Freud's discussion, quoted above, and Keats's representation of his fascination with a certain type of woman. 'When she [Jane Cox] comes into a room she makes an impression the same as the Beauty of a Leopardess. She is too fine and too concious [*sic*] of her Self to repulse any Man who may address her – from habit she thinks that nothing *particular*. I always find myself more at ease with such a woman; the picture before me always gives me a life and animation which I cannot possibly feel with any thing inferiour [*sic*] – I am at such times too much occupied in admiring to be awkward or on a tremble. I forget myself entirely because I live in her'. (Letter to the George Keatses, 14–31 October 1818. In Gittings (ed.), *Letters*, p. 162.) Keats's insight into the narcissistic type, and his choice of a woman who exemplified that type but so imperfectly as to allow a real exchange of loving, would suggest that the perversions or 'neuroses' of the poetry (what I've called its dis-ease) enabled Keats to live out his life more flexibly and with more satisfaction than might have otherwise been possible.

16 For stylistic and narrative indications of narcissistic dynamics in the romance, see text, chapter 3, pp. 159–71.

17 Bush, *John Keats, Selected Poems and Letters*, p. 339: 'Madeline and Porphyro are, to be sure, only romantic silhouettes, and we may respond less to their passion than to the intensely vivid sensations of cold, color, and the like that belong to the setting'.

18 Sigmund Freud, 'Creative Writers and Day-Dreaming', in *The Standard Edition*, vol. 9; 'Three Essays on the Theory of Sexuality', *The Standard Edition*, vol. 7; *The Ego and the Id*, trans. Joan Riviere, ed. James Strachey (New York: W. W. Norton, 1960); *Beyond the Pleasure Principle*, trans. and ed. James Strachey (New York: W. W. Norton, 1961); *Group Psychology and the Analysis of the Ego*, trans. James Strachey (New York: W. W. Norton, 1959); 'On Narcissism: An Introduction' (1914) and 'Instincts and Their Vicissitudes' (1915) Strachey and Freud, *The Standard Edition* vol. 14 (London: 1959; 1973), pp. 73–104, 117–40; 'The Libido Theory', Strachey and Freud, *The Standard Edition* vol. 18 (London: 1955; 1973), pp. 255–62; 'The Economic Problem in Masochism' (1924) Strachey and Freud, *The Standard Edition* vol. 19 (London: 1961; 1973),

pp. 155–72; *Sigmund Freud, General Psychological Theory,* ed. Philip Rieff, pp. 79–83.

19 This is an excerpt from Keats's comment to Woodhouse in defense of Porphyro's aggressiveness (or, in objection to Woodhouse's and Taylor's maidenish complaints): Keats 'says that if [in 'St. Agnes'] there was an opening for doubt as to what took place, it was his fault for not writing clearly and comprehensibly – that he should despise a man who would be such a eunuch in sentiment as to leave a maid, with that Character about her, in that situation'. Quoted in Allott, p. 475.

20 Keats deletes the line, vulgarizing the passage by gentrifying it. Again, we recall Byron's astute comment: 'I don't mean he is *indecent . . .*'

21 William Keach argues the influence of Marlowe's 'Hero and Leander' on the Haidee episode of *Don Juan.* It wasn't until 1821 that 'the first edition of Marlowe's poem and Chapman's "continuation" [since 1637] . . . was issued . . . as volume 8 in a series called *Select Early English Poets.*' Keach observes, however, that Byron *could* have used Marlowe's text in composing the Haidee episode, 1818–19, through the version presented in an 1815 volume, *Restituta: or, Titles, Extracts, and Characters of Old Books in English Literature, Revived,* ed. Sir Egerton Brydges. Missing from this text are only two brief passages where the text becomes most sexually explicit ('Byron and Marlowe's "Hero and Leander"', NEMLA Comparative Romanticisms session, spring 1985). The following discussion, offered by way of analogical clarification, is also an argument for influence.

Marlowe, in his 'Hero and Leander', rewrites a story that, in its original, 'good' form, is exactly what Byron meant by 'simple, loving, and Greek'. Marlowe makes of Musaeus's pastoral romance and Ovid's more sophisticated but still stylistically sincere version an occasion for acts of unintegrated verbal elaboration. With respect to narrative, dramatic and psychological development, these language acts are aggressively pointless; nor do they assist general authorial expressiveness except in a very stylized fashion. The representational protocol is encoded in that celebrated digression, lines 375–484. The narrative, a long and complex tale about love and power and the stratagems that bind them, is initiated by Hero's emphatically *natural* expression. She weeps, 'strooken' by Love's tyranny. 'And as she wept, her tears to pearl he [Cupid] turned, / And wound them on his arm . . .' 'Laden with languishment and grief' – literally, bearing the dissociated, reified expression, now *sign*, of Hero's grief – Cupid speeds to the Destinies, hoping to secure their assistance in the furthering of Hero's and Leander's love affair. Their refusal, predicated on Cupid's involvement with Hermes and his deceitful erotic projects, triggers another, structurally identical narration. The introduction of the Hermes figure, god of commerce, discourse, and phallic potency, enables Marlowe to extricate himself from his nested narrations by a reflexive turnabout. He concludes with some sharp witticisms about impecunious scholars and writers, a rudely reductive finale and, in terms of narrative content on the local and the large scale, markedly inappropriate. In structural terms, the digression describes the sort of beadtelling analyzed in this text, pp. 151 ff.: a circular, formulaic exercise of the working brain, working to no apparent end. Hero's breeding feeling is 'turned' by Marlowe into a narrative brede; the creaturely feeling engendered by certain characterizing gestures is passed along this embroidery until it emerges as the living Idea of that feeling, an Idea that exists only in the poetic script and by dint of strenuous authorial invention. The opening representation of Hero's dress, stiff with artifice and dissociated from the living contours of her body, informs the reader that he will not be provided with a deep and sensuous experience but with a collection of verbal icons: representations severed from their mimetic, expressive and canonical referents, positioned as scriptural configurations that can only be seized by an act of intellection.

One is reminded of Hero's interesting leg gear, elaborated in the opening passage. As far as I can tell, Hero seems to be wearing a sort of birdsong machine strapped to her legs. The sound is produced by water poured into these mechanical birds by Hero's maidservants, who follow her about with ewers. The motion of her walking sets the birds a-singing. It has taken me about forty words to describe this monstrosity and I feel somehow I haven't succeeded in conjuring the thing. That is because the thing is not meant to be conjured. Marlowe is not, that is, trying to produce a *sensible* image in either sense of that word; he is assembling just such an expressive machine as Hero wears for leggings. The nature of the substance we pass through this device does not affect the sound produced by the turning wheels; any theme, any story will do to precipitate the scriptural presence of the words on the page.

We can see in this representation the way in which a particular cognitive convention of the period (or, it may be, of our own critical moment) is subverted. The visual analogy in much of the non-allegorical poetry of the seventeenth, eighteenth and nineteenth centuries would seem typically to emphasize the natural authority of the discourse. The verbal representation of images (images of human nature, landscape, or paintings), tends to conceal the authority of the constitutive verbal act. So distracted are we by the things we see – so unconsciously do we credit things seen with ultimate ontological authority – that we fail to recognize the word-things that designate/construct the real by a range of institutional laws. We might think of the difference in terms of thing-representation vs. word-representation. Marlowe's figures jam a thing-representation (its ultimate referent, *physis*; its virtues – beauty, vitality, mutability) up against a word-representation (its referent, thought; its virtues – truth, permanence, unity). The juxtaposition of these modalities in a single phrase brings out the failure of either one to realize its claims. We see in the sensuous moment the failure of thing-representation to produce a somatic phenomenon: a sensible real. Similarly, the abstract verbal mode cannot abolish the materiality of the signifier. This double-failure defines the powers and prerogatives of a special, high-tension art, where the representational modes are so evenly matched as to produce a stalemate every time. Johnson understood this. Eliot did not.

22 Jerome McGann, 'Keats and the Historical Method in Literary Criticism', *Modern Language Notes*, 94 (1979), pp. 988–1032.

23 John Bayley, 'Keats and Reality', *Proceedings of the British Academy* 48, 1962, pp.

117–25. Quotation from p. 123.

24 Jean-Paul Sartre, *Saint Genet, Actor and Martyr* (New York: George Braziller, 1963), p. 14.

25 Bloom, *The Visionary Company*, p. 400.

26 Nancy Vickers, 'The Blazon of Sweet Beauty's Best', in *Shakespeare and the Question of Theory*, ed. Geoffrey Hartman and Patricia Parker (London: Methuen, 1985).

27 If we eat while or after reading one of these magazines, the act is a realization of the fantasy activated by the writing. Here, the analogy to pornography – literature to masturbate by – is exact.

28 André Green, 'The Unbinding Process', *New Literary History* (12), 1, Autumn 1980, pp. 11–40. Green is more concerned with affective stylistics than with the genesis of style.

29 This line of thought derives from my reading of Sartre's *Saint Genet*, from Sartre's description of his work on Flaubert in *Search for a Method*, trans. H. Barnes (New York: Random House, 1963; 1968), pp. 137–50, and from Genet's *Our Lady of the Flowers*.

30 According to both sympathetic and hostile descriptions, Keats's parents were remarkably ardent, impulsive, sensuous people, given to excess in food, in erotic display, and in social ambitiousness. My word, 'unnatural', is not, of course, a judgment, but an observation of a social difference that Keats was compelled to register.

31 Gittings's reproduction of the manuscript (the journal letter) version of this sonnet gives the line as follows: 'For winds to kiss and grateful Bees to —taste – feed' (Gittings, ed., *Letters of John Keats*, p. 252). 'Taste', the semantically correct word, is cancelled; Keats *selects* the contradiction. I offer this note to those readers who would observe the existence and, in the sonnet context, the aptness of a particular poeticism whereby the 'on' which would, in ordinary speech, follow 'feed', is elided. Or, one might propose that Keats intends an 'in order to' in the 'to feed' construction. In that case, 'for' would govern only 'to kiss': that is, the rose leaves herself on the bough in order to feed the grateful bees. My point is that when the grammatical intention is executed so circuitously and so poorly and in the absence of strong metrical or phonetic imperatives, *and* when the perspicuous construction has been pointedly rejected, we must look for other kinds of intentionality.

32 Here is Keats's version of Wordsworth's wise passiveness:

> It has been an old Comparison for our urging on – the Bee hive – however it seems to me that we should rather be the flower than the Bee – for it is a false notion that more is gained by receiving than giving – no the receiver and the giver are equal in their benefits – the flower I doubt not receives a fair guerdon from the Bee – its leaves blush deeper in the next spring – and who shall say between Man and Woman which is the most delighted? Now it is more noble to sit like Jove that [for than] to fly like Mercury – let us not therefore go hurrying about and collecting honey-bee like . . . let us open our leaves like a flower and be passive and receptive . . . taking hints from every noble insect that favors us with a visit – sap will be given us for Meat and dew for drink . . . Gittings, *Letters*, pp. 66, 67.

Again, we see the conflation of ingestion, sexual internalization, and power.

33 Philip Fisher, 'A Museum with One Work Inside: Keats and the Finality of Art', *Keats–Shelley Journal*, 33 (1984).

34 William Empson, *The Structure of Complex Words* (Ann Arbor: Univ. of Michigan Press), 1967, pp. 368–74.

35 While I've been keen to refute the evolutionary narration of Keats's life and writing, I would underline a difference between the stated intentions of 'Sleep and Poetry' and the represented interests of the 1820 volume. Here are some celebrated lines from Keats's first important poem.

> O Poesy! for thee I hold my pen
> That am not yet a glorious denizen
> Of thy wide heaven – Should I rather kneel
> Upon some mountain-top until I feel
> A glowing splendour round about me hung,
> And echo back the voice of thine own tongue?
> O Poesy! for thee I grasp my pen
> That am not yet a glorious denizen
> Of thy wide heaven; yet, to my ardent prayer,
> Yield from thy sanctuary some clear air,
> Smoothed for intoxication by the breath
> Of flowering bays, that I may die a death
> Of luxury, and my young spirit follow
> The morning sun-beams to the great Apollo
> Like a fresh sacrifice . . . (ll. 47–61)

Keats yearns to sacrifice his young spirit to poetry: to submit to 'overwhelming sweets' and 'die a death of luxury', 'smoothed for intoxication by the breath of flowering bays'. He calls this poetry 'poesy', a sweet word. 'Sleep and Poetry' is, of course, terrifically sweet dreaming, or *naturally* antithetical, displacing, wish-fulfilling fantasy. Where much of the early verse evinces Keats's longing for full gratification through poetry, *1820* grasps the danger of that dream: a dream told on an empty stomach, in Benjamin's phrase, and with the slant Benjamin puts on it. This sort of dream, which would blissfully annihilate consciousness is, in *1820*, opposed by strong dreaming: a working perversity. By 1819, Keats had come to understand that *not* to invent this slant rhyme was simply to *be*, which meant, in his case, 'be-nightmared [nighmar'd]' ('St Agnes', l. 375). That curious verbal from 'St. Agnes' designates the double horror of a life experienced as the unreality, or dream, of those privileged people who have and *are* being (e.g., Byron, Wordsworth), and of a life whose own dreams dissolve the identity of the dreamer who would enjoy them. Keats guessed, I believe, that not to invent the decentered, limping, flickering form – the reality of supplements – was to suffer the horror of 'palsy twitched [twitch'd]' and 'meagre face deform'. Not to live boldly and fetishistically among 'shade and form' was to be possessed by that visionary company. Not to swallow one's real in bits of bad writing was to down the full draught of hemlock.

36 Fredric Jameson, *Marxism and Form, Twentieth-Century Dialectical Theories of Literature* (Princeton, NJ: Princeton Univ. Press, 1971), p. 89.

37 I summarize from Allott's account (*The Poetry of John Keats*): Keats altered his

original manuscript for publication, adding some stanzas and deleting others. Woodhouse says Keats left it to his publishers to decide which revisions to use and which to reject. Keats's ultimate approval of what is now our standard text – his 'decision' to suppress many of his revisions – may have been affected by his publishers' prudish objections. Allott surmises that a 'final if reluctant approval of the 1820 text seems to be implied in his insistence when overseeing the proofs of the poem on the restoration of a number of his MS readings.' I present this information to demonstrate exactly how vexed the textual issues of 'St. Agnes' are. For those who prefer factual to theoretical argument, we have ample justification here for the interpretative assimilation of textual variants.

38 At the end of this chapter, I *will* suggest a systematic allegorical interpretation of the story, or of its discontinuities and deconstructions. I produce my parallel gloss as a belated and absolutizing procedure, a repetition of the kind of violence to which Keats subjects the Grecian Urn.

39 Fredric Jameson, *The Political Unconscious: Narrative as a Socially Symbolic Act* (Ithaca: Cornell Univ. Press, 1981), pp. 110–12.

40 Each stanza is a sort of display case for the exhibition of fine phrases. Each collection precipitates out a governing Concept that, while it annihilates the history and particularity of the elements it governs, gives them a categorical and absolute identity. This is not hard to understand. On my dressing-table, I have a tray holding five items: a Georgian pillbox, a forties' compact, a Mexican cigarette holder, a 1975 replica of a Victorian cosmetic vial, a Sheffield inkbottle. Each of these items is or is partially made of silver. Individually, each member represents that natural idea: silver. The glass tray on which these items sit represents their representation of this idea. By this tray (what I have called the friezed freeze), I produce the concrete and dissociated Concept which governs the collection: *Silver*. The way these five objects came into being, the uses to which they were initially and subsequently put, the way they came into my house – all these matters are erased by the fact of the collection. See Walter Benjamin, 'Unpacking My Library: A Talk About Book Collecting', in *Illuminations*, trans. H. Zohn (New York: Harcourt, Brace, World, 1968), pp. 59–67; also *The Origin of German Tragic Drama*, trans. J. Osborne (London: NLB, 1977), p. 188.

41 Brooks, *Reading for the Plot*, p. 38.

42 Quoted in Wendy Steiner, *The Colors of Rhetoric* (Chicago, Ill.: Univ. of Chicago Press, 1982), p. 62, from Boris Uspenskij, *Poetics of Composition*.

43 The coldness of Keats's style in stanza one is the discursive equivalent of the marble relief – the represented cold pastoral – that bewitches the narrator of the 'Grecian Urn'.

44 Claude Finney, *The Evolution of Keats' Poetry*, 2 vols (New York: Russell & Russell, 1963), vol. 1, pp. 541–6. Donne and Wordsworth are my additions to Finney's source list.

45 Apropos Keats's revealed / concealed canonical apparatus, I quote from Steven Marcus's wise structural analysis of Henry Spencer Ashbee's bibliographies of pornography (one should say, his pornographic bibliographies).

> The kind of page that Ashbee continually seems to strive for, and that he frequently manages to achieve, consists of a single line of text from which there depends a page

of footnote. Ashbee's persistence in this effort is so pronounced that one is tempted to go beyond common sense and see in it an unconscious iconography: beneath a very small head there is attached a very large appendage. But since this appendage principally contains the assertions of other men, Ashbee . . . need not feel 'responsible' for it. (*The Other Victorians*, New York: Basic Books, 1964; 1974, pp. 52, 53)

In Keats's case, it would seem that the displayed otherness of the apparatus serves also to maintain the poet's enabling illegitimacy, vexing his authority just enough to make it work for him.

46 Similarly, the Iacomo-Imogen allusion makes no dramatic sense, which is probably why Stillinger decides not to develop the stratagem concept into a comprehensive argument. The same holds true for the conflation of virgin and temptress in the Oberon allusion.

47 Sartre quotes this in *Search for a Method*, p. 9, fn.

48 From Walter Benjamin, *The Origin of German Tragic Drama*. Also, see the striking chapters on Benjamin in Terry Eagleton's *Walter Benjamin, or Towards a Revolutionary Criticism* (London: NLB, 1981).

49 Erich Auerbach, *Mimesis, The Representation of Reality in Western Literature*, trans. W. Trask (Princeton, N.J.: Princeton Univ. Press, 1953), pp. 131–7.

50 Eagleton, *Benjamin*, pp. 37–9.

51 Indeed, in the last scene, Keats at once brings the romance props to life and transforms his 'living' characters into the literary dead.

52 To say that Keats's image, a wordpicture, has no inside is not to say that Wordsworth's *does*, only that Wordsworth's procedures conceal this absence whereas Keats's represent it stylistically.

53 Empson, *The Structure of Complex Words*, pp. 368–74.

54 See note 18: Freud, 'Creative Writers and Day-Dreaming', 'Three Essays on the Theory of Sexuality', and *The Standard Edition* vol. 7, pp. 210–12.

55 Pornography would seem to be an attempt to elide the reader–writer distinction and the attendant resistances. Or, pornography tries to detour the whole alienation problematic of reading by so mechanical, repetitive, and formulaic a style as to cancel itself out as a determined productive manner and to dissolve the word in the conjured image, then to melt the image in the fantasized action.

56 From, respectively, 'The Fall of Hyperion' and 'Hyperion'. (Keats's 'loose, nerveless versification' is noted in the reviews. See G. M. Matthews, ed., *The Critical Heritage*, London: Routledge and Kegan Paul, 1971, p. 104.)

57 Susan Stewart, *Nonsense: Aspects of Intertextuality in Folklore and Literature* (Baltimore, Md: Johns Hopkins Univ. Press, 1978; 1979).

58 Benjamin, *German Tragic Drama*, p. 184.

59 Marcus, *The Other Victorians*, p. 269. See pp. 266–86. See also Frye, *Secular Scripture*, p. 24: '. . . it is the function of pornography to stun and numb the reader, and the function of erotic writing to wake him up.' Marcus isolates the contradiction at the heart of pornography. 'Obsessed with the idea of infinite pleasure, the author does not permit the counter-idea of genuine gratification, and of an end to pleasure, to develop. . .' Marcus explains the 'profoundly anti-literature and anti-art' nature of pornography by reference to this formal

dilemma – the refusal of these fictions to fulfill the expectations they arouse.

60 Jean Genet, *Our Lady of the Flowers*, trans. P. Frechtman (New York: Grove Press, 1963), p. 99.

61 Benjamin, *German Tragic Drama*, pp. 185, 213.

62 Woodhouse represents Keats's motivations in revising 'St. Agnes'' conclusion as follows: '[Keats] has altered the last 3 lines to leave on the reader a sense of pettish disgust, by bringing Old Angela in dead stiff and ugly. – He says he likes that the poem should leave off with this Change of Sentiment – it was what he aimed at, and was glad to find from my objections to it that he had succeeded.' Quoted in Allott, *The Poems of John Keats*, p. 479.

63 Similarly, dying a sexual death tends to mean living the higher dimension of intersubjectivity: a fall to rise. For Keats, 'dying into life' in both the sexual and existential sense meant just that: a death of consciousness in the realm of suffered, natural – which is to say, imposed social – being.

64 Cowden Clarke, quoted in Allott, *The Poems of John Keats*, p. 470.

65 Ibid., p. 466.

66 I thank Charlotte Pierce Baker for these discriminations.

67 Louis Montrose, 'The Spenserian Text: Representations of Elizabeth', lecture, Univ. of Pennsylvania, fall, 1985. Published in *Literary Theory / Renaissance Texts*, ed. P. Parker and D. Quint (Baltimore, Johns Hopkins Univ. Press, 1986).

68 This is one of Keats's revised-rejected lines. See Allott, *The Poems of John Keats*, p. 457.

69 Robert Graves, *The Greek Myths*, 2 vols (Harmondsworth: Penguin, 1955; 1984), vol. 1, pp. 165–8.

70 Robert Anderson, ed., *Ovid's Metamorphoses Books 6–10* (Norman: Univ. of Oklahoma Press, 1972), p. 236.

71 *The Metamorphoses of Ovid*, trans. M. Innes (Baltimore, Penguin, 1955; 1968), pp. 146–53.

As noted in the text, Ovid's Philomel assists Procne in the killing of Itys. She is described as 'spattered with the blood of the boy she had madly murdered'. While Ovid does not name the birds into which the women are transformed, he says that the bloodstained one flies up under the eaves, while the other flies off to the woods. He fails to specify who went where. Again, Ovid would seem to be collapsing the received binarity; Renaissance iconography gives the *nightingale* a spotted – that is, bloodstained – breast, and it is the swallow (as in barn swallow), who shelters among rafters.

72 Here is Eliot's Elizabethan-esque inscription of the legend: 'Above the antique mantel was displayed / As though a window gave upon the sylvan scene / The change of Philomel, by the barbarous king / So rudely forced; yet there the nightingale / Filled all the desert with inviolable voice / And still she cried, and still the world pursues, / "Jug Jug" to dirty ears.' (*The Waste Land*, ll 97–103).

Although I do not develop in the text a specifically Keatsian determination, the discussion should add point to ll. 340–1 ('though I have found, I will not rob thy nest / Saving of thy own sweet self'), and more important, Keats's deletion of these lines: 'Soft Nightingale, I'll keep thee in a cage / To sing to me – but hark! the blended tempests' rage. . .' (341–2).

73 George Sandys, *Ovid's Metamorphoses Englished, Mythologized, and Represented in Figures*, ed. K. Hulley, S. Vandersall (Lincoln: Univ. of Nebraska Press, 1970), p. 300.

74 The phallic associations of flight and of the instrument which enables it are, I should think, obvious.

75 For just one poetic reference, see 'Hero and Leander', lines 215–78, and especially 247, 269–78.

76 Lacan's Symbolic, that stage defined by possession of the phallic signifier, presents some resemblances to the representational and desiring interests I have discerned in Keats's poetry. The Symbolic phase comes into being when the child conceptualizes the transitivity which defines the Imaginary or mirror stage. This transitivity, which is based on an externalized 'imago' grasped (reclaimed) as selfhood's *being*, is a pre-dialectical identity organized by a fluidly reflective dynamics. When this movement gets *abstracted* from its concrete, particular situation, fixed in terms of body–environment loci, and also reified in a figure (the father) which undergoes a mythic aggrandizement by that superposition, the Symbolic arises and, to a large extent, maintains the ascendancy. The Law of the Father – a phallic role and an instrument for reflexive semiosis – replaces both the historically particular experience of a particular father, and a positionally particular outside or other.

I don't think we need Lacan for this narrative of social–sexual abstraction. To read Freud across Sartre, and to prove that act upon Benjamin's critique of the baroque, or Marx's account of the commodity and money forms – to name just two historical morphologies – is to acquire a lively and situated version of Lacan. See Fredric Jameson, 'Imaginary and Symbolic in Lacan: Marxism, Psychoanalytic Criticism, and the Problem of the Subject', *Yale French Studies*, 55, 56, Spring 1978, pp. 338–95.

77 Implicit in this is the concept of virginity as the presence of the hymen: a shield.

78 T. J. Clark, *Modern Painting: Paris in the Art of Manet and his Followers* (New York: Knopf, 1985), p. 135.

79 Freud, 'Instincts and their Vicissitudes', in *General Psychological Theory*, ed. Rieff, p. 96. See also 'On Narcissism', ibid., pp. 56–82; 'The Two Classes of Instincts', in *The Ego and the Id*; 'Project for a Scientific Psychology', and *Beyond the Pleasure Principle*.

80 Keats's verb, 'adonize', by which he meant his physical preparation for writing, makes good sense here. We can see that Keats's neologism contains 'adore', 'adorn', 'idealize', 'Adonis'. Within the context of a solitary exercise where the writer faces the mirror-blankness of a white page, all those inscribed meanings are subsumed by the logic of narcissism.

81 Theodor Adorno, *The Jargon of Authenticity*, trans. K. Tarnowski and F. Will (Evanston, Ill.: Northwestern Univ. Press, 1973), p. 62.

> Both appearance and necessity are elements in the world of wares. Cognition fails as soon as it isolates one of these elements. He who accepts the world of wares as the in-itself, which it pretends to be, is deceived by the mechanisms which Marx analyzed in the chapter on fetishes. He who neglects this in-itself, the value of exchange, as mere illusion, gives in to the ideology of universal humanity.

82 Freud, *The Ego and the Id*, p. 16.
83 Jameson, *Political Unconscious*, pp. 118, 119. (Jameson does not discriminate, here, along Symbolic and Imaginary lines.) The priority which Jameson accords the disturbing experience of identity with an external object suggests an understanding informed by Freud's notion of the uncanny. The identification is resisted for reasons that precede such material concerns as scarcity, power, etc.
84 Woody Allen's classic jokes from *Annie Hall* are apropos: 'I would never want to belong to any club that would have someone like me for a member' (from Freud, *Wit and Its Relation to the Unconscious*, via Groucho Marx).
    'And then she mentioned penis envy. Do you know anything about that?'
    'I'm one of the few males who suffer from that.'
85 Sartre, *Saint Genet*, p. 14.
86 Gittings, *Letters of John Keats*, pp. 157, 158.

4

'Hyperion' and 'The Fall of Hyperion'

And thus there arises what at first sight seems to be the paradoxical situation that this projected, mythological world seems closer to consciousness than does the immediate reality. But the paradox dissolves as soon as we remind ourselves that we must abandon the standpoint of immediacy and solve the problem if immediate reality is to be mastered in truth. Whereas mythology is simply *the reproduction in imagination of the problem in its insolubility*.

 Georg Lukács, *History and Class Consciousness*, trans.R. Livingstone

One
Overview
'Hyperion', 'The Fall of Hyperion', 'Lamia'

I'd like to frame a question that has seemed so eminently answerable we haven't bothered asking it. I pose the question so as to articulate the answer we silently advance and to challenge its governing assumptions. Why do we put both *Hyperion* poems in the same critical field as 'Lamia'? The first part of the answer involves the period of 'The Fall''s composition, an interval that coincides nearly exactly with 'Lamia''s compositional season (June, July 1819–September 1819). 'Hyperion' enters into the late-period discussion by way of 'The Fall'. The earlier work, or its specific difference from the later version, helps us establish 'The Fall''s structure and tendency. While many of us characterize 'The Fall' as 'revisionary', our practical operations tend to define the fragments as antithetical exercises bound by a common subject matter and by the binary differentials of their procedures. In the most literal sense, 'Hyperion' figures in our criticism as 'The Fall''s intellectual, formal, and stylistic point of departure.

Our critical constellating of the two *Hyperion* poems with 'Lamia' makes good sense, but a different kind of sense than we're accustomed to developing. Elsewhere, I have argued that 'The Fall' is neither a revision (insofar as that word implies a one-way, one-text improvement), nor a *volte-face*, but rather a *revisionary* poem.[1] By that adjective, I invoke Bloom's theory of influence and its intertextual power-plays. Where my account differs from Bloom's own reading of the poems is first, in its focus on 'The Fall' and second, in its naming of 'Hyperion' as 'The Fall''s strong poem. To make these differences is also to designate 'Hyperion''s authorial persona (Keats himself at a particular writerly *niveau*), rather than Milton as 'The Fall''s precursor poet. Or, if we must preserve Milton as 'The Fall''s troublesome influence, we must also conceive that figure as 'Hyperion''s invention: a thoroughly reproduced Origin. Third, in place of the Hegelian logic underlying Bloom's account, I propose the interruptive function of 'The Fall' and the determined inconclusion of the whole project. By its truncation, 'The Fall' interferes with the two-text dialectic, or with the rationally progressive, self-totalizing teleology promoted by that intertextual model. To read Keats's epic fragments as moments within a single, discontinuous, and terminally arrested project is to situate 'Hyperion' as 'The Fall''s point of *return* as well as departure. The object of the later work is to effectuate the earlier, not escape it. The irresolution of 'The Fall', a foreclosure, executes a refusal of the form to which both works allude: that of the progress poem. The logic of the enterprise is better described as dyadic than dialectical. We are, of course, conversant with the virtues of the dyad for Keats; more important, we have explored the dangers of the sweet, dialectical solution.

By rewriting my earlier account of the *Hyperions*' textual genetics in the different idiom of this book, I hope to explain the peculiar success and failure of the poems in terms of Keats's general literary project: as we have seen, a social, psychic, and existential project. Where I had used Bloom's revisionary ratios to define the *Hyperions*' special intertextuality, I now employ the metaphor of translation, which includes, we know, the model of parody. Like Bloom's protocol, the translation schema figures a strategy for a certain kind of canonicity, entailing a transformation of the Tradition in the interest of the present and its obligatory subversiveness (its originality, that is), and equally, in the service of the past: its constitution as an absolute Origin.

I have said that our criticism binds 'Hyperion' and 'The Fall' by their common subject matter and distinguishes them with repect to their antithetical ways of framing this material. Both poems are said to be about the Titanic–Olympian struggle: a theme of dynastic succession (or, from the 'trodden' side, genetic displacement). 'Hyperion', stylistically a naive, unself-conscious, and, in the idiom of the period, 'virile' work, concerns itself with the events, spectacle, and ethos of that mythic theme, while 'The Fall' entertains with a distinctively modern reflexiveness the meanings of that myth, which is positioned in the poem as a symbolic, archetypal structure rather than a culture-specific material. Roughly, then, we find in 'Hyperion' and 'The Fall' a concrete expression of a familiar epochal dualism: naive–sentimental, ancient–modern, mimetic–expressive, ethos–pathos (and, by an implication we shall explore below, male–female).

To rethink those antitheses and their encoded teleology by the translation logic we studied in the context of the two 'La Belle Dame' poems is to differentiate the *Hyperions* according to their respective subject-forms and contents. While we continue to identify *Paradise Lost* as 'Hyperion''s subject – topic and agency – we see that 'The Fall' takes '*Hyperion*', that epic voice, for *its* hero. The very existence of 'The Fall' pinpoints the problem with 'Hyperion'. Specifically, as I'll show, it explains the sharp stylistic discrepancy between the unit formed by Books 1 and 2 of that poem, and Book 3. As we know, a subject is no subject for Keats unless it is also an object. Keats cannot use the expressive medium (say, the Miltonic sign), unless it is also a representational object: a signified. The double-distance Keats gains on Milton by composing 'The Fall' suggests that the assimilation of the authorizing Original is, in 'Hyperion', exemplary. So good is the translation that Keats forfeits the representational salient of the act, which is also the condition of his originality.

This construct, which might sound like the standard account of 'Hyperion''s abandonment (that is, Keats's rejection of its derivative-ness), is, in fact, diametrically opposed to that reading. There is nothing derivative, nothing 'Milton*ic*' about 'Hyperion', and that is precisely its problem: it *is* Milton. We recall Keats's comment on 'Hyperion' – 'Life to him [Milton] would be death to me' – a comment occurring in the context of Keats's struggle with 'The Fall'. The statement helps us see that the object of 'The Fall', its formal intention, is to realize by its self-signifying artifice the helplessly natural poem, 'Hyperion'. To think along these lines is to take seriously Keats's troubled description of 'The Fall' as a 'very abstract Poem'. By its determined conceptual character, 'The Fall' murderously represents 'Hyperion''s *material* sublime, making that inert goodness thus 'die into life', that 'original', 'bad' sort of life we have been studying. Keats's 'Miltonic' epithet applies then, *just as he said it did*, to '*The Fall*'. That poem, which objectifies Milton's voice while seizing its expressive virtue, is the expediently derivative exercise. Keats marks the representational salient by the literariness of his style, by the complex recursiveness of the narrative structure, and by the incorporation of multiple expressive Originals. The Dantesque character of 'The Fall' should be read neither as a rejection of 'Hyperion''s Milton nor as a Bloomian swerve from that Origin. Dante's signature is for Keats a way of representing Milton's functional, *categorical* status in 'The Fall': that of the Master, or what we might call the (dis)enabling Original. Below we'll consider Keats's withdrawal from this scene of writing.

To argue that 'Hyperion' aborts because it's too good for Keats's purposes is, it would seem, to ignore the conspicuous vulgarity of Book 3. Alternatively, it is to describe the project of Book 3 as an attempt to vex the strong utterance of the first two books and by that reflexive disturbance (in the language of psychic dynamics, an autoerotic and masochistic move), to put the transparency of those books to work. Here, then, is the first stage of that 'remodel[ing]' Keats undertook more radically and on a larger scale in 'The Fall'.

This alternate construct, which is, naturally, the one I advance, poses the question of 'Hyperion''s irresolution. We have seen in our studies of 'St. Agnes' and 'La Belle Dame' how fruitfully Keats frigs his Imagination. Why, then, does he fail to bring off the operation with 'Hyperion'? We may assume that in autumn 1818–April 1819, Keats was still experimenting with the techniques we've investigated. 'St. Agnes', with its writerly exercise, occurred at the very end of that span, just before Keats's confession to Haydon that he was 'not exactly on the road to an epic poem'. The subject and spirit of 'St. Agnes' are often construed as a reaction both to Tom's death and to the deadlocked 'Hyperion'. Moreover, Keats abandoned 'Hyperion' at just about the same time he was composing the first 'La Belle Dame'. Not until 1820, with the *Indicator* revision, did Keats start solving in a critical fashion the problem of his 'good' derivativeness. That solution is, I believe, related to Keats's practical experience with the *Hyperions* (and to the technical lessons of 'St. Agnes'). Through the peculiarly overdetermined failure of 'Hyperion' and the similarly constrained success of 'The Fall', the meaning of Keats's productive method – literally, its status as *means* to a complex end – became available to him.

It is the *incomplete* badness of 'Hyperion''s Book 3 that betrays Keats's less than capable grip on his creative process. Because Keats translates *in propria persona*, he cannot gain the needed distance on the first two books. Keats uses his own early voice – the weak, swooning, Johnny Keats voice – to lift himself above 'Hyperion''s severe virility. He doesn't realize that in order to gain a reflexive position on his achievement, he must construct a specifically Miltonic idiom: not just a generic 'late' and / or 'personal' voice but a distinctly *parodic* narration. He cannot simply antithesize his first utterance, he must *materially conceptualize* it.

Keats began 'The Fall' in July 1819, three months after completing the Brown 'La Belle Dame', six months after 'St. Agnes', and almost a year before the *Indicator* revision. The letters of August 1819 are filled with Miltonic enthusiasm. Suddenly, in the letter of 21 September, there's a backlash; Keats violently rejects both Milton and his own talent for identification *and* parody. It would appear that Keats's abandonment of 'The Fall' (September 1819) is the consequence of that *ressentiment*. 'I have but lately stood on my guard against Milton. Life to him would be death to me. Miltonic verse cannot be written but in the vein of art – I wish to devote myself to another sensation'. Keats's claim to have resisted Milton, a statement generally taken as a reference to 'The Fall''s irresolution, could also mean that he had recently given up *'Hyperion'* (April), a poem possessed by Milton's strong voice and lacking the Keatsian salient. (Keats referred to the two poems indifferently as 'my Hyperion'.) We read in the comment Keats's confession that, in undertaking 'The Fall', he had moved into a *self-consciously* derivative mode, had found the 'artfulness' of the critique unsatisfying, the 'abstraction' too strenuous, and had shifted his attention to 'Lamia', the twin project of the period and a very differently abstract sort of poem.

There are, in addition to the textual genetics sketched above, strong formal reasons for configurating 'Hyperion' and 'The Fall', treated as independent texts, with 'Lamia'. There are also good reasons for coordinating 'Lamia' with *both Hyperions*, read by the translation logic sketched above and as a single exercise in self-actualizing parody.

We begin with the 'Hyperion' – 'Lamia' connection. These poems which frame the 1820 volume are to that extent structurally aligned. Both represent attempts at 'unsmokeable' verse: 'Hyperion' in a grave, austere, and lofty vein, 'Lamia' in an urbane, ironic mode. Both poems use satire as a strategy for writerly distance and in both cases, the defense betrays by its form the conflictual material it was designed to fend off. In both poems, the satire amounts to an allegory on the topic of legitimacy.

'Hyperion' develops its mythologically idealized theme of dynastic revolution by way of associative structures so specific and unconventional as to suggest a topical interest at work. Hyperion, 'dweller on high', is, of course, first of the Sun Gods and thus, unlike his Olympian counterpart, a decidedly prehistorical figure. In Keats's poem, however, Hyperion is very strongly associated with an *ancien régime*, Egypt. The connection appears to be unique to Keats. By contemporary notions of historical evolution, Egypt signified tyrannic, hieratic, and corrupt government: its genetic legitimacy the basis of its political illegality.

We give to these loose, cultural connections a certain edge by recalling that unlike Apollo, Hyperion has nothing to do with poetry or art in any of the sources available to Keats. Hyperion is mythographically related to Apollo only by reference to the sun, a relation completely suppressed by Keats's poem. This omission, along with Keats's accented narrative coupling of the gods, hints at an argument rather more specialized than the one articulated through the poem's official plot.

Alan Bewell has discerned within 'Hyperion''s prominent Egyptiana a general, Napoleonic allusion, the connection being Napoleon's reputation during the period as Egypt's cultural liberator: the agency by which her royal treasures were disseminated throughout the civilized western world.[2] Keats had, we know, seen some of these marvels at the British Institution.

Bewell's acute and important observation suggests a more developed allegorical burden. Hyperion, the Sun God, looks very much like an inscription of that symbol of a more recent and occidental old order: Louis Quatorze / Quinze. (Quite possibly, Keats's Egyptian setting serves to establish Ra – a Sun God with definite monarchical associations – as a mediating allusion.) The awful extravagance of Hyperion's palace underlines the east–west conceptual association.

One would not, of course, venture this reading without locating in Keats's Apollo a Napoleonic inscription, the phonetic resemblance (Apol–Napol) motivated by a narrative gesture. Apollo, that type of all things Greek, liberal, republican, and aesthetic, is in Keats's poem history's coming hero. In this context, we observe that 'Hyperion' departs most pointedly from Hesiod in Keats's failure to emphasize the lawfulness of the Olympian rebellion. In the traditional versions (Keats's sources, that is), the Olympians resist the Titans' usurpation of an authority properly descended to their offspring. To name Keats's different representation (a displacement of legitimate power, *not* a restoration of right government), a departure from tradition is to put the matter too mildly. By the formal economy of his poem, Keats implies that although historical necessity and natural law support the Olympian cause, *authority* is somehow on the side of the fallen Titans. What reader feels for Olympus? The old gods speak to us from what appears, by the Miltonic allusion, to be a morally fallen plane, but since Keats neither indicates their original guilt nor intimates their new corruption, we remember rather the injured dignity of Milton's devils than their hubris. And, as if by a kind of literal poetic justice, neither 'Hyperion' nor 'The Fall' consummates the dynastic transition. Hyperion remains on his throne. In short, Keats urges us to focus the Olympians as usurpers even as he indicates their temporal and natural claims. In effect, he separates authority (Hyperion) from legitimacy (Apollo), giving the latter a bad – or rather, 'bad' – name.

A narrative departure of this kind and magnitude must illuminate the father–son, Original–original dynamics we have examined in the context of Keats's other romances and shall pursue below (see pp. 207–15). At this point, I explain Keats's surprising emphasis on Apollo's felt *il*legitimacy as a way of tightening the connection between that new god and Napoleon, another wayward son in history's vanguard. By the Hyperion–Apollo (Louis–Napoleon) agon, Keats opposes Egypt to Greece, barbarism to classicism, repressive to progressive culture, abstract to organic principles, force to intellect, power to beauty, religion to art, slavery to freedom. It's not difficult to register the contemporary political resonance of this schema. What *is* hard is accounting for the bifurcated sympathy of Keats's poem, or what would translate into his ambivalence toward Napoleon. Keats's refusal to toe the urban-liberal party line on this matter was established some time ago, in an interesting essay by June Koch.[3] Below, we consider from a frankly critical viewpoint the function of this ambivalence.

'Lamia''s satiric component is at once a more restricted and a more profound affair. The poem opens with a meditation on dynastic displacement.

> Upon a time, before the fairy [faery] broods
> Drove Nymph and Satyr from the prosperous woods,
> Before king [King] Oberon's bright diadem,
> Sceptre, and mantle clasped [clasp'd] with dewy gem,
> Frighted away the Dryads and the Fauns
> From rushes green, and brakes, and cowslipped [cowslip'd] lawns,

The passage places the action which follows – Hermes' amours and the story of Lamia: both her descent into history, a metaphysical break, and her Corinthian début, a fallen passage – in the interval just before the Golden Age collapsed into an age of Gold. (Just before, we shall see, history supplanted myth, and commerce, Hermes' province, displaced direct exchange.) These lines describe in a most schematic fashion the transition from a naturally egalitarian community to a hierarchical, institutionally articulated formation; and, from easy, universal prosperity to the fetish form and its corresponding political structure. The progression is from Nature to Culture, symbolized by the extremest form of power (the monarch), concentrated in the single image of royal possession: diadem, sceptre, mantle, gem. If this passage had a headnote, it would surely be 'For 'tis the eternal law / That first in *wealth* should be first in might.' Again, it's important to identify the period of the poetic action not as a secure Golden Age but as something like an interregnum, bracketed by Golden on the one side (myth, Nature, substance, pleasure) and Gold on the other (history, Culture, symbol, power).

This transitional period is the moment in which Hermes participates: or, that Hermes, that go-between god, textually defines. We begin to gloss that character and the episode in which he figures by remarking the general resemblance of this material to the dramatic *donnée* of 'The Cap and Bells', the poem Keats composed shortly after 'Lamia'. Like the Emperor Elfinan, hero of 'Cap and Bells', Hermes is as we meet him 'bent warm on amorous theft'.[4] Both highborn creatures are characterized by their interest in illicit liaisons with creatures of a lower order: a matter of mortal–immortal, fleshly–faery, common–royal sexual commerce. (The contemporary satiric thrust of 'The Cap and Bells' is explicit: its comic butt, the Prince Regent and his amorous escapades.)

This surprising resemblance between the broadly ironic Hermes episode and the very restricted satiric groundplot of 'The Cap and Bells' might remind us that those same liberals who defended the *political* 'natural son', Napoleon, denounced the *natural*, or genetically authorized Prince for his false and unlawful – that is, *unnatural* – vilification of Queen Caroline. It was, of course, the Queen's sexual constancy which the philandering Regent called in question. The meaning of the Elfinan–Hermes connection would seem to take shape as a rather abstract insight into sexual and civil power: varieties of natural rights, so to speak. Or, one way to construe Keats's apparently lighthearted, fanciful comment on Hermes' conniving accomplishment of his desire, 'Real are the dreams of Gods . . .', is as a sincere and bitter reflection on that class of men – 'Gods' – which alone and by virtue of its privilege (that is, everyone else's exploitation) can realize its dreams. To articulate that relatively located reading is to recall that for Keats, particularly at this time in his life, no theme could have been more immediate than the question of entitlement, both sexual and political (and no god so congenial to his interests as Hermes, associated with commerce, discourse, and sexual potency). In the affair of Queen Caroline's trial, Keats could find an excellent metaphor for his own social helplessness and a vehicle for critical inquiry into the political and ultimately, economic determinants of his most private concern: his love for Fanny. 'Lamia''s opening six lines outline a hermeneutic method (roughly, a theory of economic determination); in the subsequent prefatory material (ll. 7–26), Keats introduces a contemporary political topic obviously suited to a method of that kind. It is my feeling that 'Lamia''s 170-line introductory excursus articulates in a narrative fashion the text to which the rest of the poem relates as a dramatic demonstration. By what mechanisms and to what extent, Keats asks, are love and money, pleasure and power, consumption and production, related in contemporary life? This is a question we shall consider at length and as the concluding discussion of this book.

The satiric edge of both poems, 'Hyperion' and 'Lamia', quickly dulls. The problem concerns both the content of the satire and its defensive function. Generally speaking, Keats's textual engagement with contemporary political issues develops as a line of resistance against the more primary processes that were always endangering his special freedom. We notice, however, that the topical themes of both 'Hyperion' and 'Lamia' center on questions of legitimacy, authority, origination, and desire. Both defenses, in other words, reintroduce the very nexus of Keats's psychically enacted class conflicts.

Above, I observed Keats's ambivalence toward the Olympian succession; and as we well know, 'Lamia' plays havoc with the affective distributions which define the romance form in its classic (Manichean) manifestation. By their doubled sympathies, both poems betray the contradiction which governs Keats's writing. I refer to the self-fashioning exercise plotted throughout this book: a process whereby 'having' is equated with 'being' and where 'having' describes, paradoxically, a state of self-alienation – a parody, as it were, of genuine ownership and a corruption of *bona fide* 'being'.

I have described Keats's capable position as that of the perverse son: the boy who appropriates the father's talent and preserves its virtue by keeping it alienated. He maintains this talent as the sign of the father: a dangerous supplement to the father's lawful and particular being, and to those properties which are continuous with his person (that is, qualities and expressions). In the canonically central romances, these paradoxes translate into varieties of discursive tension, the collective function of which is to station Keats and to suspend his voice in the ways we have discussed. In the *Hyperions* and 'Lamia', where the inscription of Keats's class contradictions tends to be *narrative* rather than discursive, it is not poise that we feel but something more like deadlock. However, inasmuch as Keats's poise represents a particular *management* of contradiction, the stalemate of the later poems could indicate less of a *need* for management, or, Keats's better control. We have seen how, in the 'La Belle Dame' poems and 'St. Agnes', the real, contrived, and signified tensions get mobilized in such a way as to constitute textually a speaking subject. In 'The Fall' and 'Lamia', conversely, Keats, a textual effect, seems to be an already consolidated subject, painfully straddling a genetic fence: treaders and trodden, sons and fathers, devouring and devoured.

There is, however, a difference between 'The Fall' and 'Lamia': indeed, a difference between 'Lamia' and all the works treated here. I refer to the greater self-consciousness with which point of view is handled, and its relative independence of those textual interests that typically motivate in an *aesthetic* way the business of perspective. Keats seems in this late work to thematize his enacted stylistic protocol. We could also say that 'Lamia' discovers to Keats the difference between what we have called 'capable negativity' and the virtue he denominated 'negative capability'. In this poem, we feel Keats positioning his best solutions as the core of the problem.

This is a dangerously Romantic proposition. I'd like to elaborate it in such a way as to force out the conditions of its veracity. With respect to the critical detachment of Keats's last romance, one's impulse is to reason that only a person who *has* a self can negate it. To argue thus is to identify 'Lamia' as the enlightened, self-critical product of Keats's exercise in self-fashioning. One could even to some extent 'materialize' that argument by observing that the capacity to suspend self-definition is the privilege of those who inherit a self, or who can afford truly to become their invented self, which means, as we know, ceasing to own it.[5]

This reading model is not consistent with the textual facts. We have repeatedly seen Keats *produce* an authorial self by a sustained exercise in self-negation. This is to say, we really must put the cart if not before the horse, then alongside it. We cannot postulate two sequential Keatses: the poet who constructs an ideal, and to that extent, mystified self, and the philosopher who, by taking that self and its myths apart, creates a new kind of consciousness, one that is proof against illusion.

This textually derived critique of the Romantic argument for Keats's enlightenment is consistent with the general interpretive pattern of this book. Throughout, we have found in Keats's peculiar social place (that is, an imperative to produce his life in a certain way) the condition for a special kind of knowledge. I have distinguished this knowledge not by its content so much as its formal relation *as* 'knowledge' to all that is conventionally considered 'non-knowledge': or, action, feeling, experience.[6] We may allow Keats to lift himself by his own bootstraps, so long as we keep the eminence thus attained within the activity curve that produces it; and, so long as we see that this movement and its products are supposed for Keats – realized *through* him – by his given, positional way of focusing some contradictions of his time and place.

What binds 'The Fall' to 'Lamia' is primarily a matter of technique. Above, I suggested that 'The Fall' positions 'Hyperion' as its subject: in structuralist terms, its hero. 'Hyperion' is also 'The Fall''s object: the alienated item upon which it reflects. I have described this dynamics as a process of self-translation. Another way to conceive it is by reference to the masturbation logic outlined in chapters 1 and 2. In this context, we recall the double perverseness of Keats's literary reflexiveness: his substitution of the canonical phallus for his own, given talent. What distinguishes 'The Fall' and 'Lamia' from the poems we've already treated is that here, Byron's insult is, *for the first time*, a technically accurate assessment. The image projected by both poems' formal activities is that of a writer frigging his *own* Imagination. (As I've noted, Byron's verb, 'to frig' – in today's English, 'fuck' – retains the older meaning, 'to rub or chafe', 'to agitate the limbs' [OED]: that is, to masturbate in a transitive sense.) The reflexive operations of 'The Fall' are performed upon 'Hyperion', Keats's properly authorized/authored utterance. Similarly, 'Lamia''s Hermes material – Keats's production of his own mythic Origin – is textually situated as a point of departure and, as a discourse to which the body of the poem systematically alludes, it is also a point of return.

Putting a different slant on the matter, we could say that in these late poems, Keats produces for the first time his own means of production. Like Chatterton, Keats undertakes the invention of his own, authorizing Original, the difference being Keats's pronounced return upon that Master-voice and thus, the production of his originality. The process is familiar to us from 'La Belle Dame'. By contrast, however, 'Hyperion' so thoroughly assimilates its Miltonic inspiration as to figure a *natural* Origin, preempting all other firsts. Below, we consider the meaning to Keats of this difference: psychically, the difference between internalization and introjection.

Two
Readings
'Hyperion'

'Hyperion''s failure to reach an ending is not without its semantic charge, but the poem's hardworking imperfection – its *anti*-closure – occurs internally. The discrepancy between Books 1 and 2 on the one hand, and Book 3 on the other is sharp and encompassing, involving style, structure, thought, and feeling. One can say with surprisingly little exaggeration that the entire *Hyperion* project unfolds in the gap between Books 2 and 3.

Bate, that fine stylist, characterizes 'Hyperion' as an 'imposing fragment', sustained by its Miltonic inspiration through Books 1 and 2 but exhibiting a marked falling off in style in Book 3.[7] 'Falling off' is not perhaps the best description of what happens in Book 3. The phrase implies a continued but unsuccessful endeavor at the special grandeur of the first two books. What we have, however, is something *so* bad from a poet who has just proved himself so *good*, that we may infer him to be working a decidedly different vein. What looks like an abysmal failure at the Miltonic sublime can also be read as the embrace of a stylistic norm whose salient is precisely its belatedness: sentimentality, reflexiveness, abstraction. (One could, of course, construe the departure as a modulation toward 'The Fall', a construction consistent with the above account insofar as we read 'The Fall' as 'Hyperion''s parodic effectuation.) If we want to maintain the idea of a lapse, we should emphasize the deliberateness of the desuetude.

The transition occurs in the narrative move from Hyperion to Apollo. By the binary logic of the poem, this shift from Titans to Olympians signifies an advance from past to present, mimesis to expression, narrative to lyric voice, epic to romance. The change does not, however, develop in so comfortably teleological a fashion as the schema suggests. What *should* take a progressive form (categorically, ancient to modern, classic to romantic, action to consciousness) is, in the poem, a manifest regression. We explain this effect by the inauthenticity of address in Book 3. The Romantic voice of that book is better characterized as Romantic*izing*. Its circular, solipsistic urgency interrupts the classic poise of the opening books and by contrast to that stylistic transparency, assumes a distinctly feeble, interested look. By its excess and insincerity (what one might call a vulgar, as opposed to a philosophic self-consciousness), the narration of Book 3 forfeits its status as formal equivalent to, much less improvement on the genuine classicism of the opening books. In effect, Keats opposes a genuine Greek artifact *not* to its nineteenth-century counterpart, but to a bad, contemporary *imitation* of such an object. Keats's juxtaposition makes sense only at the level of categorical thought. To put this another way, the *effect* of the comparison is to isolate from each expression its style, and to position the work itself, concrete and actual, as a representation of that reified style.

That effect is consistent with the practical task of Book 3: namely, to break the spell of the first two books' success. By the exaggerated subjectivity of its portraiture, Book 3 *represents* the largeminded, serene impersonality of the characterization, Books 1 and 2, much as the 'falsetto' octet of 'Chapman's Homer' *represents* – brings into being – the genuine 'virility' of the sestet. It would appear from Book 3 that the image of Saturn, Book 1, lines 1–14, is an emblem for the manner and meaning of the opening books. One reads in his trance the morbidity of that correctness: the penalty for authentic discourse.

> Deep in the shady sadness of a vale
> Far sunken from the healthy breath of morn,
> Far from the fiery noon, and eve's one star,
> Sat grey-haired [gray-hair'd] Saturn, quiet as a stone,
> Still as the silence round about his lair;
> Forest on forest hung about [above] his head
> Like cloud on cloud. No stir of air was there,
> Not so much life as on a summer's day
> Robs not one light seed from the feathered [feather'd] grass,
> But where the dead leaf fell, there did it rest.
> A stream went voiceless by, still deadened more
> By reason of his fallen divinity
> Spreading a shade;[:] the Naiad 'mid her reeds
> Pressed [Press'd] her cold finger closer to her lips.

Saturn defines the realm of silence and slow time, the organic world presented by the balladeer in 'La Belle Dame'. Because this is the order of being, in permanent parallel, as it were, with the realm of negation, it is also monochronic. Here, where there is no morning, afternoon, and evening – no differentials because no representation – there is also no temporal passage which is not repetition: no history, thus, nor meaning as we know it. Saturn, seated at the centre of this zero-degree, generates the dead realm, the spatial expression of his trance. Its thick, obstructive atmosphere is his emanation, its dreaming forests (ll. 6, 7; 74–5), the dark vegetation of his own brain. The discourse of the opening passage compels us to register the continuity between maker and image: the organicism, one might say, of Saturn's invention. We experience this natural expressiveness not, obviously, as an accomplishment but as the concrete equivalent of the god's feeble-mindedness. While the passage is, of course, a *tour de force*, its virtuosity is not in the Keatsian vein which we have exposed, a fact which the contemporary reviewers were delighted to observe. The force of the passage under discussion is a function of its mediated symbolic transparency, a figured collapse of subject and object, manner and means. In other words, the style of the passage executes the very fusion described by Saturn and his sunk realm, but because this effect is framed as an exercise In imitative form, Saturn's weakness becomes Keats's strength.

Still, to focus this anomalous excellence within the critical field we've been developing (and with attention to the treachery of Book 3) is to guess that the silence of this realm, its predominant feature, reflects the cost to Keats of a literary goodness modelled on Saturn's organic expression. 'But where the dead leaf fell, there did it rest.' As we know, the naturally inherited letter or 'leaf' – the Tradition, correctly entertained – was, for Keats, both a dead and a murderous letter: inert on its own behalf and preempting all new, original marks. A Milton positioned in this fashion (for Milton is clearly the tutelary genius of this passage) is a dead voice twice over: already an echo, 'still deadened more'. One meaning of this assimilative mode unfolds in lines 15–21. Saturn's 'old right hand lay nerveless, listless, dead, / Unsceptred . . .' The description is powerfully concrete, and what it *most* concretely inscribes is the image of impotence. Saturn's limp, unsceptred state signifies the cost of a healthy relation to the authorial alter ego: abandonment to the desire for full identification. To assimilate the Miltonic 'leaf', 'hand', or 'sceptre' in this fashion is, clearly, to lose that phallic virtue as an instrument of defense and display. 'Life to him [Milton] would be death to me.' 'Hyperion' offers no sharper demonstration of this confession than the opening twenty-one lines. To coordinate this influence issue with the sexual anxieties concentrated in Saturn's sad relaxation is to see that 'Hyperion''s masculinity (a virtue widely remarked in the contemporary reviews and pertaining exclusively to the first two books) is not power and accomplishment to Keats but impotence and death.[8] Books 1 and 2, those complete authorial wish-fulfillments, prove that for Keats to live in and through Milton (as opposed to the narcissistic Milton-in-Keats dynamic) is, like Chatterton's solution, final.

We return to Keats's richly telling complaint: 'Life to him would be death to me.' To give life to Milton, as by 'Hyperion''s innocent reproduction of his discourse, is to kill off the whole Keats canon: to destroy the virtue of its contradictions, the greatness of its badness. Moreover, when we turn the phrase inside out – an inversion invited by the parallel syntax – we learn that a Milton *executed* by the textuality attempted in 'Hyperion''s Book 3 and accomplished in 'The Fall' is the condition of Keats's authorial existence. One recalls in this context Keats's comment on the pleasure he felt in composing 'Hyperion'. 'I have no identity, meditating saturn [*sic*] and Ops.' What the letter presents as a delicious abandon ('easeful death' is the phrase that comes to mind) is, in the poem, a differently accented affair, from which Keats withdraws with the same urgency evinced by the seventh stanza of the Nightingale Ode and the aggressive foreplay/forepleasure of 'St. Agnes'.

As I've said, the stylistic vulgarity of Book 3 signifies Keats's attempt to vex his own large utterance. There's no need, I think, to demonstrate that largeness. Let Byron's astonished approval of the opening books – their calm, masculine power – stand as a testimony to their perfectly unKeatsian (and unRomantic) achievement. The interesting and timely task is to plot the project of Book 3, which I shall do at some length. Before undertaking that stylistic analysis, we should note a structural symmetry between the first and third books. I have read Saturn's fearful composure as an emblem of the undefended Miltonic dreaming of Books 1 and 2, or of its special meaning to Keats. Similarly, the Apollo we meet in Book 3 is not only the Keatsian persona (an identity confirmed by 'The Fall''s nested narrations), but the very *symbol* of that book's perversely authorized discourse. 'There is something too effeminate and human in the way in which Apollo receives the exaltation which his wisdom is giving him. He weeps and wonders somewhat too fondly . . .' Hunt's critique (which hastens to redeem Apollo from this initial self-indulgence) responds not only to the substantive characterization, lines 88ff, but more acutely, to the rhetorical reflexiveness of the whole book. In the most general terms, we explain the sogginess of Apollo's discourse as a problem of address. Apollo is not, clearly, engaged dialectically by his Muse. His utterance, an abandonment to the rich sensation of speech (the feeling of a 'white melodious throat / Throbb[ing] with . . . syllables'), describes by displacement the form of a fantasy. We encountered this full-throated (masturbatory) dream in the context of 'St. Agnes' (Madeline's swelling silence), and noted its virtuous contradiction: the short-circuiting of expression the *condition* of reflexive eloquence, the real ineffectiveness the condition of felt vitality. Those readers who *would* affirm the intersubjectivity of Apollo's speech might meditate the character of Apollo's auditor, Mnemosyne: she who already knows all that Apollo is about to utter, who has seen all the spectacles he would depict. Like Psyche ('pardon that thy secrets should be sung / Even into thy own soft-conched ear'), Mnemosyne typifies Keats's ideal interlocutor. Knowing what he knows, pre-possessing his very words and figures, Mnemosyne, whose divinity guarantees her categorical alterity, is a device for the production of psychic dissonance. She enables that special dialogism that is the condition of Keats's full-throated utterance.

Apollo weeps and wonders fondly, but his self-interrogation evinces a respectable logic. He wants to know what's wrong with him: why *should* he feel cursed and thwarted 'when the liegeless air yields to [his] step aspirant'? Apollo wonders why Nature's unforced courtesy, sign of his marvellous new authority, gives him no pleasure. By the Keats–Apollo superposition, we infer that a liegeless air cannot satisfy a creature who is nothing without the liege–vassal, Original–original, Good–bad ratios. Keats must find his freedom in contradiction and constraint. Apollo's mournful query ironically confirms his accession to power, a metamorphosis from youth to liege. 'Goddess benign, point forth some unknown thing.[:] / Are there not other regions than this isle?' We, who have read Books 1 and 2, see that this is the complaint, '*in truth*' (my emphasis), of 'one who once had wings'. The utterance belongs to a poet who knows his strong self (the narrator of Books 1 and 2, fledged by Milton), and refuses it. Here is the lamentation of a newly realized god, who intones to the universe 'bethou me' and finds that nothing can resist his strong voice. Even Hyperion trembles at the sound of this 'new chord'. A poet who finds himself fully in possession of his precursor's power, a son whose paternal supplementation has evolved into a plain substitution: these creatures, victims of their own victories, are the subject of Book 3.[9] By this line of argument, we illuminate Keats's departure from Hesiod, explained above as an expression of ambivalence toward the progressive figure of Napoleon. The authority of the old regime is the condition for the bad strength of the new. Napoleon's originality does not materialize outside his relation to Origins, or, to what must be maintained in that ideal aspect by those who would, paradoxically, cleave to the conqueror.

In a note to line 12, Book 3, Allott records Keats's echo of *Paradise Lost* I: 550–1, 'the Dorian mood / Of Flute and soft Recorders', lines marked in Keats's Milton edition with this note: 'The light and shade . . . the sorrow, the pain, the sad-sweet melody . . .' Keats's association to Milton's 'penseroso' state, and specifically, the 'sad-sweet' coupling with its resonance to 'pleasant pain' and other familiar Keatsian oxymorons, accents the working perverseness of the narration: its Romantic-baroque quality.

Indeed, the whole invocation (ll. 1–28) announces a return to the negatively capable posture. Keats, who candidly speaks to himself in addressing his Muse, declares himself 'weak to sing such tumults dire' as the Titans suffer. He recommends to himself the minor key, pathetic rather than tragic accents: 'A solitary sorrow best befits / Thy lips, and antheming a lonely grief'. The most casual reader observes in Books 1 and 2 an author powerful to sing his Titanic themes; the confession of weakness is, of course, a false confession and a power play of a familiarly indirect kind. Keats is trying, in lines 10ff, to recover a subordination he has surpassed. The wish is to retreat from linear, masculine song into 'soft warble', 'sad-sweet melody': or into that end-stopped, movement-in-place sort of discourse ('wandering in vain about bewildered shores') in which we have located Keats's enabling stratagem.

The narrator immediately proceeds to accomplish that wish by dedicating his song, already authored by his Muse, to 'the father [Father] of all verse', in this way reconstituting himself a son. The dependence, illegitimacy, and self-contradiction plainly surface in that litany of 'let's. The locution, which belongs to the rhetoric of power, sounds decidedly puerile following the authoritative verbal *display* of Books 1 and 2. As for the pleasures solicited by the hymn,

> Let the rose glow intense and warm the air,
> And let the clouds of even and of morn
> Float in voluptuous fleeces o'er the hills;
> Let the red wine within the goblet boil[,]
> Cold as a bubbling well; let faint-lipped [lipp'd] shells[,]
> On sands, or in great deeps, vermilion turn
> Through all their labyrinths; and let the maid
> Blush keenly, as with some warm kiss surprised [surpris'd]

these clearly evince the immature sensuality familiar to us from Keats's early poetry. What is summoned is warmth, softness, and a titillating indirection: the pleasure of foreplay by the device of discursive forepleasure. The visionary place is described as a 'covert', 'retired cave', 'green recess'; itself an 'embowered' zone, it is stuffed with poplars, lawn-shading palms, and song-laden beeches. Coziness and plenitude are its preeminent attributes. Apollo ('where was he, when the Giant of the Sun / Stood bright, amid the sorrow of his peers') is the fit denizen of this regressive domain. Keats introduces Apollo as one who has just 'left his mother fair / And his twin-sister sleeping in their bower'. The description, which gives us a figure defined by the mother and her nest, distinctly presents to us the very *idea* of the boy. This particular boy, who reminds us of Blake's transitional symbols (Lyca, Thel), is, like those figures, symbolically amplified by association with a transitional moment: 'And in the morning twilight wandered forth . . . The nightingale had ceased [ceas'd], and a few stars / Were lingering in the heavens, while the thrush / Began calm-throated'. Again, we note the inscription of Keats's enablingly oxymoronic, and also restricted position: the both–and/neither–nor state. The middle station.[10] Apollo encounters his world through 'half-shut suffused eyes'. Assisted / obstructed by this dark glass, Apollo 'with eager guess began to read / Perplexed [Perplex'd], the while melodiously he said.[:]' Were his eyes dry, wide open, and trained directly upon the goddess and her 'purport', Apollo would be, presumably, in a position to *know* and *declare*, rather than 'guess' and reflexively describe Mnemosyne's meaning. This is to say, the freedom of the 'perplexed' reading and telling would not be available.

What I'm driving at is the virtue of the handicap, or the special power – a sponsored freedom – afforded by Apollo's self-mystification. One cannot but feel that the flow of melodious surmise which swirls about, precipitating no question and brooking no closure, only interruption, is a function of Apollo's voluntary constraint. Mnemosyne, who characterizes Apollo's song by its painfully pleasurable effect (l. 66) upon the 'vast / Unwearied ear of the whole universe', formulates Apollo's sad–sweet experience. In his pleasant pain of speaking, we hear the 'new chord': a surpassing of the early gods, or of their large, firm utterance. Mnemosyne's question, 'Is't not strange / That thou shouldst weep, so gifted?' answers itself. Apollo weeps *because* of his gift, just as his access of power over the otherwise 'liegeless air' is to him both curse and impediment. (By reference to the antinomial meaning of 'liege' ['vassal bound to feudal allegiance and service; feudal superior to whom allegiance and service are due'], Apollo's mastery is also his servitude.) Apollo solicits the Muse to relieve him of his new virtue by finding in the universe 'some unknown thing'. He seeks, of course, a new Master: the condition of that structural dissonance required for his ongoing song. 'Where is power? / Whose hand, whose essence, what Divinity [divinity], / Makes this alarum in the elements . . .' The question *executes* an alienation of power; by posing it, Apollo injures his own strong hand. Thus does he recover his 'aching ignorance' and the prolific tension that attends it.

Apollo's decisive change of voice (l. 111) appears to be triggered by Mnemosyne's silence. 'Mute thou remainest – mute! Yet [yet] I can read / A wondrous lesson in thy silent face'. The emphasis suggests that Apollo owes his transfiguration to Mnemosyne's perfect resistance; the 'yet' should be a 'thus'. In the goddess's unbreachable negativity, Apollo discovers the 'essence', 'Divinity', 'power' which his own new accomplishment (the 'birth / Of such new tuneful wonder') had, he feared, annihilated. Apollo does *not* become a god 'through his knowledge of human suffering' but rather through his discovery of an irreducible order of being.[11] History, Apollo learns from the remembering Muse, is the virtuous pharmakon. What it offers is the 'sheer puzzle of pain', the very *form* of irrecuperable otherness: the exact opposite of meaning. The deifying wine, a 'bright elixir peerless' (by that punning adjective, Keats again invokes the power of blindness; one thinks, perhaps, of 'viewless wings'), is also a draught of hemlock. It brings about a tumult 'most like the struggle at the gate of death; / Or liker still to one who should take leave / Of pale immortal death, and with a pang . . . Die into life'. Apollo's remedy, the cure for his self-possession, is the ingestion of that which resists humanization, remaining stupidly objective: a catalogue of 'Names, deeds, grey legends, dire events, rebellions, / Majesties, sovran voices, agonies'. These facts – the sheer chronicle of history – when 'Pour[ed] into the wide hollows of [Apollo's] brain', put him in 'fierce convulse', 'anguish[ing]': 'His very hair . . . / Kept undulation round his eager neck'. We recognize in the form of Apollo's apotheosis that circular urgency which signals the Keatsian project: a coming without a going. Naturally, Keats cannot conclude the action; he cannot *consummate* the ravishment by producing the transfigured Apollo. The new god is kept anguishing and liminal: unclothed but not yet mantled with the new authority. 'Forever panting', as it were. Hyperion, the old god and somehow the very statute of that negativity Apollo requires for his perverse power, remains in place. Literally, Book 3 'disturbs' his realm – Books 1 and 2 – but it will not surpass that dominion. The relation of Book 3 to the preceding books is that of a touching tension.

Three
Readings
'The Fall of Hyperion'

We should expect to find some striking stylistic contrasts between 'Hyperion''s Book 3 and the general manner of 'The Fall', insofar as their projects, while they are comparable in intention, differ sharply with respect to strategy. The task of Book 3 is to antithesize the first two books and by that contrived tension, to restore to Keats his warm and capable hand, otherwise possessed by Milton. The job of 'The Fall' is to *represent* that possession – a paralysis – and thus to effectuate while undoing it. 'The Fall''s (mis)translation of 'Hyperion' establishes that poem as an Original tragic moment: a displacement, this, of Milton's large utterance. At the same time, the Milton*ic* supplementation reinstates Keats's capable negativity with this difference: the master he serves and disturbs is, now, his own early words.

We can see, for example, that by discontinuing 'The Fall', Keats at once truncates *Paradise Lost* and formally motivates 'Hyperion'. That fragment suddenly emerges as a noble ruin, the complete formal necessity of which explains (inferentially) its resistance to time's ravages. By reference to this absolute Origin (to this phenomenology, that is), *Paradise Lost* starts looking *Miltonic*: prolix, diffuse, and *literary*, as compared to the concentrated power of 'Hyperion' *as represented by 'The Fall'*. *That* poem's stylistic allusion to Dante is not to be read as an antithetical gesture but as a purchase on 'Hyperion''s Milton: the means of producing a Milton*ic* voice. Further, and as I mentioned, the very presence in 'The Fall' of multiple authorities cancels out the totalizing properties of any one canonical world. We will see that the perverse but by now familiar form of intertextuality played out by these fragments requires the inconclusion of 'The Fall'. Not only does that poem thereby represent 'Hyperion''s ruined state, but thus does 'The Fall' maintain its attachment to 'Hyperion', its strong Original. 'The Fall' can only live by making 'Hyperion' continuously die into life: literally, into 'The Fall', which becomes as 'reality' to 'Hyperion''s 'representation'.

'*Hyperion*' 'lives' in 'The Fall' as a relative, natural, transparent beauty ceaselessly ravished / represented by a cold truth; like the 'Grecian Urn', 'The Fall' is a museum with one work inside. It is, of course, only the difference between the container and the contained which creates those ontological distinctions, beauty–truth, signifier–signified. The virtue and mechanism of this difference are coded in the celebrated induction to the poem: the opening eighteen lines.

> Fanatics have their dreams, wherewith they weave
> A paradise for a sect,[;] the savage too
> From forth the loftiest fashion of his sleep
> Guesses at Heaven; [heaven:] pity these have not
> Traced [trac'd] upon vellum or wild Indian leaf
> The shadows of melodious utterance.
> But bare of laurel they live, dream, and die;
> For Poesy alone can tell her dreams,
> With the fine spell of words alone can save
> Imagination from the sable charm
> And dumb enchantment. Who alive can say, [say]
> 'Thou art no poet; may'st not tell thy dreams'?
> Since every man whose soul is not a clod

Hath visions, and would speak, if he had loved [lov'd]
And been well nurtured in his mother tongue.
Whether the dream now purposed to rehearse
Be poet's or fanatic's will be known
When this warm scribe my hand is in the grave.

The dimension of this passage I wish to develop is its preoccupation with writing, conceived not as an act of knowledge, expression, or communication, but as a negation of deep truths and wishes. The problem posed by this passage is how to tell one's dreams without losing oneself in the telling, the very problem addressed in 'St. Agnes'. *Not* to tell the dream – or, what is the same thing, to tell it correctly: in its own language or in the spirit of the original – is to resign oneself to the order of organic repetition: Saturnian silence, sylvan historiography. The way to resist 'the sable charm and dumb enchantment' of natural dreaming and its 'melodious utterance' is to frame, corrupt, and estrange the vision, as by the medium of a material 'shadow' language, 'traced upon vellum'. The alternative to the sweet speech ('dumb enchantment') of fanatic and savage is, Keats declares, *writing*. Indeed, the narrator, who designates his hand his scribe (l. 18), answers the question which opens line 16. The following verse can only be 'poetry', not just because it is written but because it is written by an agency, 'hand', which is claimed as a property and, thus, (dis)owned by its generative source, whose own natural authority, consequently, is put at risk.

'But bare of laurel they live, dream, and die'. The thought of this line does not, as it might seem, concern material preservation: the production of a dream record to save Imagination from historical oblivion. Poetry's virtue – the virtue of the *written* trace – resides in the special artifice of the form, a function of its special alienation. 'Telling' is equated in the passage with 'the fine spell of words'. The pun on 'spell,' one of Keats's favorites, accents for us the materiality of Keats's general linguistic conception. We are familiar with his invention of a multiply estranged language, defense against the longing for 'paradise', 'heaven', natural escape. The 'spell' of poetry is not a releasing magic. It is, like most enchantments, a thralldom: in this case, the secured freedom of a cage of letters severed from subjectivity, intention, and living presence.

The difference between the dream of poet and fanatic is in the telling, and the telling difference is a question of self-alienation. 'Every man . . . [h]ath visions' and would *speak*, if he had loved [lov'd] / And been well nurtured in his mother tongue' (my emphasis). *Not* every man, however, can *tell* his visions, representing the thing and the conditions of that representing in the selfsame action.[12] Only the poet can *practically* destabilize the mimetic and expressive tendencies of his tongue. This is, one might say, the privilege of the *not* so 'well-nurtured'. By the binary poet–fanatic relation, Keats presents this reflexively alienating skill in terms of cultural sophistication: the more advanced the culture, the more self-estranged. 'Hyperion' marks out the 'fanatic' moment to 'The Fall''s 'poetry'. (Generally speaking, 'The Fall' objectifies 'Hyperion''s essential and ideal narrative mode. That poem's absolute truths are historically relativized.) This evolutionary matrix operates a rationalization. Thus does Keats try to frame logically the deep perverseness of the 'Hyperion'–'Fall' relationship. He succeeds, of course, only in reproducing that bad logic.

The proper beginning of 'The Fall', 'Methought I stood where trees of every clime . . .', places the narrator in an abandoned bower that, by its strong resonance to *Paradise Lost*, Book 5, suggests Keats's own Miltonic idyll: namely, 'Hyperion', Books 1 and 2. Structurally, we have a continuation of the bower scene, Book 3 'Hyperion'. The narrator-poet, a post-Apollonian figure, would seem to be observing the exhaustion of the Miltonic place. The grounds are deserted, and as if to represent the vacancy, Keats features in that precinct a collection of 'remnants', 'refuse'. The narrator drinks deeply of a beverage remaining from some first feast and subsequently 'sipped by the wandered [wander'd] bee': a sort of double-leftover. 'That full draught', defined strictly in terms of the attrition it has suffered, is, we are told, 'parent of [Keats's] theme'. We glimpse in this oxymoronic figure of subtractive completion something very like a crossing of the supplement with the pharmakon. Like Mnemosyne's 'elixir' in 'Hyperion', the 'full draught' (a partial potion/perfect portion) initiates a dying-into-life process.[13]

I'm suggesting that we attend to the doubleness of Keats's word 'draught'. By the argument of this chapter, 'Hyperion', that fully accomplished draft, is in a very real sense 'The Fall''s parent. By drinking that po[r]tion, Keats casts off his 'unwilling life', the Miltonic possession, and enters upon a new form of being. 'I started up / As if with wings . . .' The action sequence describes a process of introjection, the sort we've seen Keats perform with a range of canonical figures. The object seized by 'The Fall', however, is Keats's *own* Original: his own verbal power, alienated and recovered, its Otherness reconstituted (we might say, looking ahead, its naturalness fetishized). 'Hyperion', that 'domineering potion', is just the Master that Apollo/Keats has been seeking. The 'wings' upon which both poets ascend are, naturally, their own appendages, but they acquire by their contrived strangeness a saving virtue.[14]

Lifted by 'Hyperion', his own altered discourse, the poet finds himself transported to another sunk realm: another collection of literary effects. In contrast, however, to the creaturely and organic grace of the Edenic–Miltonic place, this domain, which can only be entered perversely, signifies Culture under the aspect of the tomb. The representation has about it something of the pyramid: better yet, the museum. In this dead space which houses a collection of cultic objects, the poet observes what he takes for 'an image' of Saturn ('. . . what first I thought an image huge, / Like to the image pedestalled [pedestal'd] so high / In Saturn's temple', ll. 298–300). The anticipated correction does not arrive for 200 lines, and within that textual interval, the god's sculptural character is *elaborated*, not effaced. Thea appears and Moneta remains, assuming, however, a more objective form in the poet's brain. 'Long, long those two were *postured motionless*, / Like *sculpture* builded-up [builded up] upon the grave / Of their own power . . . *still* they were the same; / The *frozen* God *still* bending to the earth, / And the sad Goddess weeping at his feet,[;] / Moneta silent . . . the three *fixed [fix'd] shapes . . . Still fixed* [fix'd] he sat' (382–91; 446, my emphasis). The narrator, positioned as an observer, might be said to encounter the presiding deities of 'Hyperion', Books 1 and 2. Or rather, what he so virtuously 'finds' in 'The Fall' is an *image* – the sculptural sign – of his own authorial power. Below we explore the effects of this formal distinction.

There is a sexual logic to 'The Fall''s introjective authority, and it is encoded in a number of arresting locutions: 'sphered words', 'hollow brain', 'globed brain', 'wide hollows', 'enwombed' (and its phonetic cognate, entombed). In the graphic conceptualism of these phrases, we read a collective identity as well as a symbolic, self-referential dimension. 'The Fall' – a dream (within a dream within a dream) poem – takes Moneta's brain as a topos for its structure and theme. First, we recall that 'Hyperion' was widely described as Keats's singularly virile poem. We accept the adjective (interpreted, of course, by the general argument of this book), and characterize 'The Fall', by contrast, as a distinctively female discourse. I refer not only to the obvious time–space, linear–circular, external–internal, narrative–lyric, objective–subjective differences, but to the way in which 'The Fall''s appropriation of the phallic 'Hyperion' (its location of that 'good', self-authorizing discourse in the inner space of individual consciousness) figures a distinctly sexualized intertextuality. (Here is the ideal enactment, as it were, of Lawrence's phrase, 'sex in the head'.) We seem to have something closer to the model of hermaphroditism than to intercourse, although both ideas obtain. In the end, however, neither metaphor is completely satisfying in that nothing comes of the coupling. To coin a Keatsianism, the 'internestling' of these discourses is, and is meant to be, a sterile affair: a matter of reciprocal alienation and the production of internal dissonance.

'The Fall', whose primary task is to frame 'Hyperion', transforms that fragment from an expression into a figure, rendering *itself*, thus, a meta-representation. By the later poem's operations, 'Hyperion''s 'existence' emerges as an *idea* of existence, or what Keats calls a 'Nothing'. By materializing this Nothing, 'The Fall' itself materializes as a fetish, Keats's 'Thing semi-real'. What, after all, is Moneta's elaborately self-contradictory message but a justification for the virtuously *represented* fraudulence which is Keats's solution to his diverse binds? Moneta tells the poet that only he, who is less than the practical philanthropists of the world, and less, too, than the strong poets, is privileged to survive. Only he, a 'dreamer weak' and 'dreaming thing', a 'fever of [him]self' who 'venoms all his days' and 'vexes' everyone else's, is 'favoured for unworthiness'.

The special inferiority which Moneta ascribes – honorifically – to the poet is a function of his alienation: from his audience, his precursors, and his fantasies. Not so ironically (since irony is the rhetorical norm of this poem), the dramatic consequence of this instruction is yet another alienation. The poet, silenced by the sheer perversity of Moneta's accusations, is positioned *by* that silence as a spectator. Moneta, the object of his gaze, is blind; and, *because* her eyes do not reflect their objects, they absorb them. The virtue of the poet's muteness emerges in the field of Moneta's more obviously capable blindness. The two negations become as one single affirmation with the poet's entry into Moneta's globed brain. In that temple, he shares the goddess's visions: the 'theme' that had once, literally, *occupied* him – 'Hyperion' – now 'hung vast *before* [his] mind' (my emphasis).

We see the concrete product of this positional difference – the result of tortuous 'wanderings', turns, and ironies – in the alienated representation of 'Hyperion', beginning on line 310. What concerns us are the discrepancies between this long passage and the corresponding material in 'Hyperion'. Throughout this section of 'The Fall', one feels a strongly narrated quality. We watch a poet watching a sort of *tableau vivant*, 'narrated' by Moneta. The natural grace of the 'primary' spectacle, or the vision of Saturn and Thea, is represented, and thus de-natured and consecrated all at once, by this complex voyeurism. Thea, for instance, characterized by Moneta ('softest-natured of our brood'), is further characterized by the narrator, whose description formally embraces/surpasses Moneta, via *her* account, as well: 'I marked [mark'd] the goddess in fair statuary / Surpassing wan Moneta by the head, / And in her sorrow nearer woman's tears.' Allott glosses 'statuary' as 'stature', in this way suppressing the obvious contradiction, one that we should rather emphasize. What 'Hyperion' offers as a deeply human, immediate, *living* representation is rendered in 'The Fall' a sort of frieze, not unlike the 'sculptured dead' in 'St. Agnes'. By his encounter with these frozen figures, Keats can have his dream and know it; he can *own* his identifications even as he uses them. That this represents an advance in consciousness is suggested by the substance of the poet's comparison. Thea, whose vastness is aligned with her historical precedence, surpasses Moneta in natural feeling. We, who *see* Moneta's strange griefs but are not permitted to enter into them, feel the great mystery of her heart. Thea, the large and positive figure, is where we all begin. What we learn – what Moneta, mediated by the poet's narration, represents – is the negation of Nature and the production of an alter ego. Moneta survives *to* tell and, we infer, *by* telling her dreams to creatures like the poet. As for Thea, that early goddess lives only by the perverse efficacy of Moneta's brain, emulated by the poet. In line 368, for example, Thea exclaims, '*me thoughtless*, why should I / Thus violate thy slumbrous solitude . . .'; the corresponding phrase in 'Hyperion', line 68, is '*Oh, [O] thoughtless*

. . .' (my emphasis). The obvious question is why *Keats* thus violates the solitude of 'The Fall' with a phrase that out-Miltons Milton? Why indeed, but to *represent* 'Hyperion''s firstness and goodness – its large utterance, large as Thea – in this way effectuating and displacing it.

In this vein, we note that the awkwardness and halting disjunction of lines 376–8 do not, as Kenneth Muir proposes, transform 'Hyperion''s 'regular rhythm' into 'one which suggests what it describes', a liquid imagery. To the contrary, these stuttering lines, by metrically counterpointing 'Hyperion''s suave regularity, represent that uninflected smoothness as an onomatopoetic effect. Muir's very curious discrimination is thus explained as a displacement from the signified to the signifier: 'Hyperion' as altered by 'The Fall', to the 'The Fall'.

Thea and Saturn, the symbols of 'Hyperion''s huge success, become, as I've noted, frozen effigies in 'The Fall'. 'Like sculpture builded-up upon the grave / Of their own power'. We can at this point appreciate the extraordinary disclosure contained in that simile. 'The Fall' is, precisely, a sculpture erected upon the grave of Keats's own expressive power: 'Hyperion'. I am reminded of those medieval casts of the supine corpse that lie the length of the coffin, imitating in stone its mortal contents. The poet's long and steady gaze upon the death-in-life of Saturn and Thea – his capacity to sustain the contradiction he has precipitated – ennobles him. Indeed, this action puts him in exactly Moneta's state: deathwards progressing to no death (see 11. 388–99). His role, like Moneta's, is a punishing one but both figures feel its preservative virtue.

Four
Critical Opportunities

I have suggested that Keats truncates 'The Fall' by way of maintaining the dependent posture required for his special authorial practice. We enhance the formal explanation and begin to situate 'Lamia' within the Keatsian project by noting some circumstantial particulars of the *Hyperion* exercise.

In the three-month interval separating the two phases of that exercise, the logic of their sequence might have emerged clearly enough as to have prompted Keats's abandonment of the project. To clarify that conjecture, I pause to spell out what I hope has been implicit throughout this book. The writerly protocols I have presented as Keats's working solution to his legitimacy / originality problems are not to be identified with conscious intention or practical design. They represent what I take to be the *meaning* of Keats's practice: a reconstruction of the problem from the nature, which is also the *style*, of the solution. Keats is not to be read as a proto-Genet, nor should we confuse even *that* arrogantly abject writer with the consummate strategist Sartre delivers. I'm talking about the difference between meaning and knowledge, and I'm suggesting that the *Hyperion* exercise could have produced for Keats a knowledge of the meanings we have developed through this dialectically totalizing study.

Keats's conscious desires were, one suspects, perfectly conventional – if you will, 'good' – ambitions. It would seem that he craved very strongly the recognition of his peers, the admiration and patronage of an audience, and a place in English literary history, and that he wanted to secure these blessings in the customary fashion: by writing poems both good and great. These respectable wishes are the stuff of Yeats's caricature: the boy peering hungrily through the sweet-shop window. We have studied what that boy did when he realized that because he would never get in through the front door – never have his desserts properly – he would never *properly* have them at all. Moreover, a man who consumes factitiously cannot produce anything but substitute sweets, the very sign of his subjective irreality. Nowhere have I meant to suggest that Keats, were he *able* to define his capable negativity, would have done so with any kind of flourish. The misappropriative and dis-eased character of Keats's literary production was the bargain he made with the facts, which had already made *him* a certain kind of bargainer.

It is by reference to these general facts that we may construe Keats's abandonment of 'The Fall' as an attempted evasion of insight into his productive methods. 'The Fall''s inconclusion may also be read as a response to 'Hyperion''s remarkable success. The first 'La Belle Dame' is a magical and accomplished poem, but compared to the massive achievement of 'Hyperion', it's a slight affair. I'm suggesting that 'Hyperion' was a hard poem for Keats finally to kill, no matter how attractive or certain the redemption. To do so meant rejecting the very thing he had coveted from the beginning. It meant rupturing the identification with Milton in order to display it and, in displaying it, to corrupt what had already degenerated from an identity into a relation. Simply, the cure might have begun to seem worse than the disease: the damaging dimension of the pharmakon in excess of its curative properties.

In the language of phallic issues, we could say that 'Hyperion' signified to Keats the direct inheritance of the father's talent. Keats approximates in that poem for the first time to the model of the *good* son, who solves his competition problems by identifying with (that is, assimilating) his rival: the normative, superego solution. As I've noted, 'The Fall' proves, as does no other work of the canon, the justness of Byron's accusation; in 'The Fall', Keats frigs 'Hyperion', his *own* Imagination. We might at this point use Byron's metaphor to imagine the special danger attending Keats's success. A phallus that is not really one's own cannot really be lost; the loss of one alienated property is perfectly remedied by new acquisition. Conversely, a natural, naturally expressive phallus is not only irreplaceable, its meaning is synecdochal and therefore any form of its alienation must have encompassing ego consequences. Perhaps, then, we might read Keats's abandonment of 'The Fall' by the logic of castration anxiety. He stops frigging his Imagination because for the first time, he feels himself naturally possessed of that faculty. He has, for the first time, something of his own to lose.

Finally, we might consider in an openly speculative way Keats's life circumstances in the general period of 'The Fall''s composition. This is also the interval that initiates what de Man calls Keats's 'late period', a phrase intended to describe the ironic, often embittered, and uneven character of the poems dating from the autumn of 1819 on.[15] De Man's periodization places 'The Fall' in the same field as 'Lamia', generally taken to reflect the crisis precipitated by what we presume to have been, by autumn 1819, Keats's complete despair of the longed-for marriage to Fanny. We might reasonably, then, investigate the bearing of this crisis upon 'The Fall'. Indeed, this theme, raised to a categorical level, might turn out to be the most critical connection between the two poems.

The logic defined for Keats by the *Hyperion* venture – a model of mechanically determined self-violation – was in some ways mirrored by the romantic situation. We know that in order to write at all, Keats had to work in an unusually conflictual, self-alienating manner: in effect, an exercise in self-abuse. I have proposed that the unfreedom of Keats's mode of production crystallized for him through the *Hyperion* project and, above all, in the programmed failure of his first 'good' poem.

Rather than meditate the deep issues raised by the stalemate with Fanny, we might study the surface. Here we return to some matters broached toward the beginning of this chapter. Generally speaking, Keats's involvement with Fanny emplots an action wherein money (poverty, to be exact) thwarts love. A more useful description would oppose Keats's private life – his chosen mode of sexuality: categorically, a form of consumption – to the public domain, a domain controlled by the means and relations of production. Keats's knowledge that he would never marry Fanny (nor, in all probability, sleep with her), because he would never realize by his poetry the income required to keep her, was also a knowledge that in order to *write* a profitable poetry, he would have had to enjoy different life circumstances. Keats was forced, in short, to realize the extent to which the gratification of his most private wishes was determined by the most impersonal, Urizenic law of his society: the law of its productive modes. At the exact point in his life when Keats was compelled *consciously* to live his class facts in the sphere of consumption, his experience with the *Hyperions* brought him up hard against his special, self-wounding productive mode.

In this context, Keats's abandonment of 'The Fall' signifies a remarkably sound response: a refusal to cooperate with his own class exploitation. There is an aggressive charge in the truncation of this poem: a new kind of gainful renunciation, this. One feels in that formal arrest the decision of a man digging in his heels. By his silence – the only authentic refusal – Keats negates the factual order which prescribed for him such a terrible way of working. At this moment when his instinctual demands were so great and his sense of his span so certain, Keats would not do to himself what was done to him by others. What I'm proposing as the project of this period is the dismantling of the compromise formation which was Keats's authorial agency. Through 'Lamia', the critical phase of the *Hyperion* endeavor, Keats begins to articulate the *subject* meanings of his social objectivity. I believe with John Bayley that had Keats lived, he would have abandoned poetry, and for the best of reasons.

By these lights, 'Lamia' is not, as de Man would have it, the herald of Keats's negative period, but the most lucid, self-critical, and assertive poem of the canon. For the first time, Keats tries to *relate* social facts to private life, production to consumption, outside to inside, work to love: dimensions entangled within his experience and, in his poetry, representationally intertwined. Simply, but quite incomprehensibly, Keats leaves behind the standpoint of immediacy.[16] He performs this awesome relational act – an investigation of the meaning of his style – by a dramatic meditation on the commodity and the money forms, revealed to him through the *Hyperion* exercise as the model of his literary production. In those forms, he finds the explanation of his misery *and* of his writerly achievement.

We have seen that the job of 'The Fall' is both to displace 'Hyperion' and, by representing it, to realize its effects. From 'Hyperion''s sensuous concreteness, Keats derives an exclusively formal and social value, parallel to, not coinciding with the work itself. 'The Fall', which supplements 'Hyperion', at once creates for the original work a new value and depreciates 'Hyperion' *by reference to* that value. From another angle, the job of 'The Fall' is to render 'Hyperion''s expressive value an object of representation, and by thus changing the *form* of its meaning, to alter the semantic *value* as well. We can see that the unity of 'Hyperion' as a particular expressive product does not coincide with its unity as a *representation* of expressiveness: that is, with its unity within 'The Fall'. There, 'Hyperion' coalesces as something like an object-sign, something resembling that material Concept which we studied in 'St. Agnes'. The epic's expressive specificity is not so much *effaced* as put under a new sign or raised to another power. Keats's operations upon 'Hyperion' amount to a systematic representation of the literary sign: a dissociation of its value from its body, and by the reincarnation of that original value, the creation of a new and exclusively social value.

The operation closely resembles the formal logic and tendency of the commodity: that really effectual Thing semi-real. At the end of chapter 3, I suggested that the value today's readers often find in Keats's verse is its negativity and alienation. Keats's textually actualized distance from nature and need gives *us* a new remove on our own insistent particulars. We experience through Keats the pleasure of an oxymoronically *sensuous* abstraction: 'real' desire, gratified by 'real' and specific sensation, but where the relation of desire to satisfaction is infinitely variable because the reality of both moments is so thoroughly textualized. Any desire can modulate into any other (say, oral to tactile), and any one object can substitute for another. The intensity of 'palsy-twitched' is somehow interchangeable with the intensity of a happily-ever-after. Another word for this effect which we have come to associate with commodity fetishism is 'formalism'.

The closure we feel in Keats's career derives from his glimpse into the structure of his subjectivity. In his working brain, subject and object of his art, Keats discerns the dissociated, reified consciousness *of* the commodity, identified below as the money form. In other words, Keats finds himself recapitulating most profoundly the social relations thrust upon him by the age. His dearly bought freedom amounts to the completest bondage. The heroine of Keats's latest romance is the incarnation of this knowledge and she is also Keats's purest persona. Lamia *is* the fetish – gold, commodity, money, Pythagorean number – descending through its sequence of historical bodies. This is the meaning of the metamorphoses she undergoes when situated in the field of Hermes' designs, Lycius's desires, and Apollonius's reason. This is also the meaning of her strange individuality in Keats's poem. Burton's 'lamia' is a common noun: a class term, or logical abstraction. We shall see that the material and dramatic individuality of Keats's creature is both a suppression of her minute particulars and a disguise for her generic character. Lamia, an outrageously naturalized perversity and nonlogical phenomenon, an idealized particular and a concrete Idea, lives only in circulation, by the effects she engenders and by the social agreement to recognize her reality and rationalize her contradictions.

In order to trace this difficult theme, we return to the early poetry where we can plot the rudiments of Keats's mature style. I regret the procedural awkwardness of this move; the detour is long and involved, and something of an excursion in its own right. The gains are not just in the way of inclusiveness and not just heuristic. We return to first things partly because the end ('Lamia' is Keats's last major effort) recapitulates the beginning. As usual, it is the difference within the identity that concerns Keats and us. Like the very early verse, 'Lamia' is a poem about things, always problematical for Keats. In the early verse, Keats is always looking for a hero and an action and always finding catalogues of objects. In 'Lamia', he positions a thing and its historical career as his subject-in-action. In a queer, apparently unaccountable way, 'Lamia' is, of all Keats's poems, the most humanly animated and immediate, for all its grotesquerie and its allegorical apparatus. The job of this critique is to account for that effect.

Notes

1 Levinson, *The Romantic Fragment Poem* (Chapel Hill: Univ. of North Carolina Press, 1986), pp. 167–96.

2 Alan Bewell, 'The Political Implication of Keats's Classicist Aesthetics', *Studies in Romanticism*, 25, Summer 1986, pp. 220–9. Bewell observes the Napoleonic inscription in 'Hyperion''s Apollo.

3 June Koch, 'Politics in Keats's Poetry', *JEGP*, 71, pp. 491–501.

4 Hermes does and does not not steal the nymph; or, what Keats sketches in this episode is a form of commercial theft. Insofar as Hermes pays for the nymph, his act must be considered a transaction, not a robbery. But, since it is *Lamia* whom he pays, and since the legitimacy of her power over the nymph, creature of the Wood-Gods, is not established, no value can be imagined to redound to them. The text plainly figures for them a value loss.

5 By analogy (developed in chapter 6), the freedom to spend one's money – that is, to translate it into property, thence into qualities – is the phantasmagoric privilege of those to whom money comes 'as easily as leaves to a tree'. Obviously, there is nothing free about an exchange of wages for food and shelter; somewhat less obvious is the unfreedom of that expense which purchases signs and is itself a sign.

6 There *is* also a substantive difference to Keats's knowledge and I'd like to explain it by way of Lukács. In Keats's suffered objectivity, we have found the condition for his practical knowledge of the subject-forms that were his stock-in-trade: the canon. Keats had grasped, we might say, the objective character of his mode of professional consumption. What his circumstances *prevented* him from knowing was the subjectivity of the object; he couldn't penetrate the fetish from the side of production. Keats, who had no collective life to speak of, had nothing that might correspond to a class-consciousness, and therefore no experience of himself as an agency capable of effecting change. Moreover, the part–whole, object–subject fissures which Lukács finds in capitalism's worker – contradictions that explain for him the capable (that is, revolutionary) negativity exclusive to that class – could not materialize for Keats who had no whole and primary being to antithesize the objectified part. For him, the writing was the means of producing that total form. Keats didn't work for a living; he worked to produce a life.

　　The advances I plot in 'Lamia' may be partly traced to the upsurge of instinctual life which, we suppose, accompanied his vision of the end. They may also be related to the technical impasse objectified in the *Hyperion* project. Lamia, the money form, is precisely the reified subject Keats had been producing for the past five years. The work of the poem is to melt her down. In more conventional terms, the project is to make her a subject, as well as *the* subject of a romance which is also a myth of origins. Lukács observes that the dialectical method is only possible because of a change in the *actual* relations between subject and object. 'Lamia''s dialecticity, discussed in chapter 6, can, I believe, be traced to a change of this kind. (See Lukács, *History and Class Consciousness*, pp. 116–18, 168, 169–70.)

7 Jackson Bate, *John Keats* (Cambridge, Mass.: Harvard Univ. Press, 1983), pp. 402–5. 'Falling off in style' is Miriam Allott's summary phrase for Bate's description of Book 3.

8 Keats's most strongly enacted wish was not, we have learned, for instinctual gratification or its sublimated equivalent, but rather for recognition and mastery. The strategies we have studied in his poetry betray quite consistently a determinate form of desire which we elucidate at this point by a Hegelian model. The object of Keats's desire is not the Other *per se*. Or rather, because there really is no such thing, we should say that the wish of Keats's poetry is not to assimilate by identification its beloved sources. Nor does Keats covet the Other's desire: does not substitute himself for the value which his Other desires. Between these two classic desires, a respectively subjective and objective identification with the Other, stands Keats's end-stopped dialectic. Keats produces his subjectivity through the familiar master–slave dynamic, but one that is played out between categorically noncomparable parties. The exaggeratedly representational form with which Keats invests his influential Others may be read as a rough solution to Hegel's famous antinomy. I refer to the paradox whereby the recognition conferred by the Other instantly deconstructs his effective Otherness, rendering the recognition slavish and therefore useless as a subjectively constitutive device. Keats's narcissistic maneuvers, which maintain the alterity of the interiorized Other (or, the objectivity of the possessed subject), interfere with this self-consuming dynamic, and that is just the point of these moves.

In 'Hyperion', where Keats assimilates Milton so well, securing, as it were, Milton's recognition once and for all, Keats also loses that master-figure and the power it had conferred.

9 Keats's circumstances were such as to prove on the pulses that Hegelian groundplot sketched in note 8. Without an opposing Self, there is, for Keats, no self at all. Return upon the 'sole' – literally, singular, untenanted – self cannot but be forlorn.

10 There is a helpful contrast here, between the atemporal zone marked out by Saturn, and the intermediate temporality defined by Apollo. Saturn's paralysis is related to the perfect organicism of his being; Apollo's capability comes from the *un*naturalness of his state. Saturn's full presence amounts to a suffered negation; Apollo's dis-ease is the effect of a fetishized negation.

11 Allott, p. 440, note to ll. 113–20, 'Hyperion', Book 3.

12 Arthur Danto, *Jean-Paul Sartre* (New York: Viking, 1975). 'Wittgenstein . . . supposed that we could not in principle bring into language, as part of what it

represents, the conditions of representation: language could *show* the world, but not the fact that it showed it' (p. 95).

13 Two meanings of 'elixir' still very much alive in Keats's day were 'life-prolonging substance' and 'philosopher's stone', both of them consistent with a 'pharmakon' reading of that potion drunk by 'The Fall''s narrator.

14 This is, one might say, the difference between the locution 'my hand' and 'this warm scribe my hand'. It is also the Lacanian distinction beween penis and phallus.

15 Paul de Man, *John Keats: Selected Poetry* (New York: 1966), pp. xxvi, xxxiii. 'There is some logic in considering the entire period from June till the end of the year as one single unit – the 'late' Keats – that includes the poems to Fanny Brawne, dating from the fall of 1819, and frequently considered as poetically unimportant and slightly embarrassing documents written when he was no longer in full control of his faculties. In truth, it is from *The Fall of Hyperion* on that a sharp change begins to take place; it is also from that moment on that the differences among the commentators begin to increase'.

16 That Keats does not fully penetrate the irrationality of matter and of the socially given, is suggested by his preoccupation with the relatively manifest fetish form, money. Capital, Lamia's fourfold form and a reunion, of sorts, of use – with exchange-value, substance with meaning, has no being in Keats's poem. While he *plots* 'the moment when the links that bind the contemplative attitude of the subject to the purely formal character of the object . . . become conscious', he cannot *elucidate* that moment in a practical manner, one that would shadow forth Lamia's final transformation. (Lukács, *History and Class Consciousness*, p. 126.)

5

Early Poems

After all there is certainly something real in the World – Moore's present to Hazlitt is real . . . Tom has spit a leetle blood this afternoon, and that is rather a damper – but I know – the truth is there is something real in the World.

Keats to J. H. Reynolds, 3 May 1818

The work of the *Hyperion* exercise precipitates the working-through which is 'Lamia'. By this experiment in allegorical romance, Keats throws himself beyond his own imagination and gains a new kind of freedom.[1] When Keats finishes 'Lamia', he is situated to *choose* a poetic style and, beyond that, to choose (or reject) what had been to him in a most literal sense his life's-work. One would expect a critical advance of this magnitude to be purchased by a loss of some kind. Whether, or in what ways, the power of Keats's poetry is a function of its predominantly tactical intelligence, is the important question to emerge from our reading of his latest romance.

By its allegorical invention, 'Lamia' positions Keats's language machines and the subject-form they engender as inscriptions of the commodity form and of its more developed expression: money. The poem thus identifies Keats's basically formal solutions to his social binds as the most possessed practice *and* content of the age. Keats's articulation of this identity is as the consciousness of his entire literary action, produced as a moment in the development of that action. I have proposed that our best access to Keats's late, dialectical critique is through the poetry that initiates that literary action. Here, we can observe at the closest range both the structure of Keats's fetishism and its motivations. Before opening on to that poetry, I pause to differentiate two models of the fetish and to sketch their general bearing on Keats's early poetry.

The Marxian fetish derives from a logic of naturalization. We begin with the object, which owes its first formal and social character (that is, its existence as an object-for-[historical]-consciousness) to the productive operations of particular, particularly conditioned human subjects. Through the mediations of exchange, this product comes to be grasped as a material transparency: a natural content as opposed to a social form. Even as the article forfeits its original social content and thus its special formal properties, however, it acquires by its personalized aspect and facultative address, as by the operative conventions of consumption, the look of the individually, but also *essentially* given. In other words, a specifically integrated human product is annihilated as such and re-produced in consciousness (through real institutions and in its original body) as a vessel for the containment of a different *kind* of social meaning: not so much invisible as *invisibilizing* (or, ideological).

Our everyday use of the word 'fetish' tends less to emphasize the naturalization of historically constituted objects, than the secondary alienation which, in Marx's account, occupies the final moment of the process: the moment of consumption. This is also the dimension which Freud focuses by *his* concept of fetishism: where an inanimate object, associated with a living human ensemble or part of that ensemble, is invested with a vividness stolen from the objective totality and with the subject's own cathexis. The logic is that of metonymy or synecdoche (a superposition of the whole upon the attribute or part), whereas the Marxian fetish emphasizes the *metaphoric* dimension of the abstractive process: substitution and displacement. The accent in Freud's discussion is not, as it is in Marx, on de-animation (naturalization), but rather on the *re-animation* of the isolated part.

By putting a Marxian stress on the Freudian account, we discover that a clinically pathological fetishism owes its *manifest* perverseness to the fact that it operates upon an already fetishized object: the female body. (Sexual fetishism is, for Freud, an exclusively male phenomenon.) A secondary or symbolic fetishism, the Freudian syndrome produces for consciousness the *hidden* perverseness (fragmentation, abstraction, reification) or the more primary and apparently natural or *given* fetish, the referent.

Similarly, to apply Freud's accent to the Marxian fetish is to discern within a representational fetishism the condition for its own demystification and for that of its referent. By virtue of the doubled artifice *or* transparency which characterizes the symbolic fetish (in its pure form, a naturalistic representation of a 'natural' object), the givenness of the first fetish crystallizes as a quality, distinct from the object it invests. Further, the *signifying* naturalness (*or* artifice) of the representation strips that already isolated, 'primary' givenness of its innocence. What had looked like a quality is revealed as a meaning. Insofar as the writer's relation to his textual materials reveals itself as one of value-and-meaning production, the parallel relationship of primary subject to object materializes as a productive dynamic, exposing the falseness of a natural mimesis (reflection or expression), as of a natural reception (the disinterested gaze). In other words, a symbolic fetishism can expose within the moment of consumption *two* more primary productive acts. By so doing, it pries apart the several Natures, or modes of givenness, projected by those acts, establishing both their independent and cooperative meaningfulness.

We have already treated of the contemporary impressions generated by Keats's poetry: specifically, the judgment of its diseased character. Whereas Wordsworth, whom we read as a type of the period's healthy authorial subject, manages to suppress the subversive potential of his representation, Keats's fetishism is closer to the sort we read about in Freud. Just now, I suggested that the sexual fetishism which Freud treats as a pathological state is, in effect, a parody of the historically normative – that is, 'healthy' – fetishism which characterizes the nineteenth-century (male) gaze in general. The symbolically elaborated and self-conscious syndrome is as a formal critique of that regular gaze and of the assumptions supported by it. Similarly, Keats's immoderate, conspicuously alienated, and densely embodied fetishism formally outlines the substantive monstrosity within the judicious and otherwise imperceptible fetishism practiced by the securely middle-class poets of the day.

One would not, of course, want to confuse the typical Romantic gaze – its contemplative operations – with the formulaic fetishism of the eighteenth century and its prospect poetry. Then again, neither should we confer upon the Romantics a knowledge they were not positioned to produce. We explain the scandal of Keats's poetry, even in its most reactionary moves, by way of Keats's special relation to the age's dominative structures.

Wordsworth's poetry is, we know, a greatly dialectical verse. Indeed, when the dialectic breaks down, as in much of the late work, the poetry pretty much turns into prose. What I emphasize here, however, and by way of distinguishing the Wordsworthian from the Keatsian method, is the founding of Wordsworth's dialectic upon two mythical figures: viz. 'the mind of Man and Nature'. Wordsworth's universal Mind is the fetish form of historically particular, which is to say, particular*ized* minds. Similarly, his Nature is a generic phantasm displacing the physical record of all those historically actualized minds that have struggled to transform portions of the material world. Not only are Wordsworth's two first moments imaginary, but their neatly sectored articulation, which gives the authority and initiative to Mind, constituting it history's continuous subject, is also a fiction of what never was on sea or land, the consecration and the poet's dream. The result of this structurally false start (that is, the idealizing field in which Wordsworth's dialectics play themselves out) is that despite himself, Wordsworth tends to rehearse the semiotic protocols of the Augustan poet. In Wordsworth's great poetry, the figuring initiative emanates from a Mind that is, at best, 'shaped' or 'bent' by Nature and, often, *sui generis*. The object world is not of course *realized* by the engagement; it is, rather, 'humanized', which is to say, reproduced as the externally situated mind-of-the-poet. As for the authorial subject, his dialectical negotiations, such as they are, cannot positionally alter him. They merely confirm him in his subjectivity, endowing him with a more collective but no less abstract concept of it.

We have learned to interpret the transparency of Wordsworth's Nature, particularly in his neo-topographical poems, as an attempt to conceal the made-ness of the world: its historicity, and the special suffering pertaining to that state. This naturalness is, then, the sign of a guilty self: not just a class-self, but the 'self' of a class that knows itself a participant in that world-making. The guilt that contaminates Keats's early poetry – the marked *unnaturalness* of this writing – signifies the shame of a man who has no class. In the vulgarity of this poetry, the early readers sensed a connection between Keats's 'bad' subjectivity and his 'bad' audience, an understanding that troubled their own sense of autonomy. What these readers couldn't clearly articulate, although Byron came close, was that 'Cockney school' was a way of designating a non-class: a name for experience that wasn't *permitted* to assume determinate social form, lest it objectify the 'natural' experience of the more secure bourgeoisie. Keats's problem was not that he wrote to a bad audience, but that he *felt* in relation to a badly conceived one. Following Vološinov, we explain the intonational problems of Keats's poetry by reference to problems regarding his inner representation of audience: a social group in which he could claim membership. We *hear* the dialogism of Keats's verse precisely because it is incomplete.

The fabulous innocence and individuation of both Wordsworth's and Byron's subject forms (technically, their tonal perfection) are the effects of a fully socialized psyche: consciousness organized in some primary way by its expressive orientation toward social experience. Individual consciousness in Keats's poetry is not nearly so differentiated and rarely transparent. The expression of the 'I' seems not to correspond in any necessary or spontaneous way to a seminal identity which precedes and follows the utterance. The Cartesian dialectics which animate the great writing of the first-generation poets and the more located but still categorically secure dialectics of the second generation are not available to Keats, whose consciousness is deeply intermingled with what Wordsworth calls 'Nature' and Byron calls 'the world'. The fetishism of Keats's topographical verse is the signature of an author who cannot produce the direct and motionless gaze of the moralizing prospect poem because his relation to the object world is too ragged and also too charged with desire. Neither can he graciously elaborate his subjectivity since he is a thoroughly objectified consciousness: a thing reviewing its thingness. Ultimately, I think, these failures give his work a critical power not available to us in the more accomplished poetry of Wordsworth, Coleridge, and Byron.

Through the work of James Turner and John Barrell, we have come to read the seventeenth- and eighteenth-century topographical poem as an exercise in the production and display of particular subject-forms, definitive of particular classes and serving their interests.[2] If Keats had *designed* to demystify both the landscape poetry of the eighteenth century and the more sublimated prospecting conducted by Wordsworth and Coleridge, he couldn't have done a better job. As we might expect, the Keatsian difference is a function of the action and consciousness forms which were Keats's way of living his class facts. Before we examine 'I stood tip-toe', the *locus classicus* of Keats's visual/verbal fetishism, I'd like to dramatize the problem underlying that solution by way of an even earlier work, 'Had I a man's fair form'.

> To – ['Had I a man's fair form']
>
> Had I a man's fair form, then might my sighs
>   Be echoed swiftly through that ivory shell
>   Thine ear, and find thy gentle heart,[:] so well
> Would passion arm me for the enterprize.[:]
> But ah! I am no knight whose foeman dies,[:]
>   No cuirass glistens on my bosom's swell;
>   I am no happy shepherd of the dell
> Whose lips have trembled with a maiden's eyes.
> Yet must I dote upon thee[,] – call thee sweet,
>   Sweeter by far than Hybla's honeyed [honied] roses
>   When steeped [steep'd] in dew rich to intoxication.
> Ah! I will taste that dew, for me 'tis meet,
>   And when the moon her pallid face discloses,
>   I'll gather some by spells[,] and incantation.

This remarkable poem is constructed almost entirely of clichés: 'man's fair form', 'that ivory shell', 'thy gentle heart', 'no cuirass glistens', 'my bosom's swell', 'no happy shepherd', etc. We shall see that the mere assembly of these received word-things engenders an anti-logic that derails the explicit argument of the sonnet. It's as if the social meanings congealed in these clichés escape Keats's management and return upon that doubtful center with a sort of impish vengeance, in the end exposing Keats's authorial subjectivity as a social allowance, and a pretty minimal one at that.

The sonnet concerns Keats's anxiety about his stature. 'Had I a man's fair form', he says, 'then might my sighs / Be echoed swiftly through that ivory shell / Thine ear, and find thy gentle heart . . .' The sentence that begins with this lament, concludes, 'so well / Would passion arm me for the enterprize.' I paraphrase Keats's intended meaning. 'I've got an object to love and the will for loving; all I need is the physical agency.' The double conditionals framing the wish, however, plainly muddle the priorities. The 'so well' clause, which features an unsettling 'would' (logically, it should be 'does'), is meant to modify the sequence beginning 'then might . . .' but because that middle clause is modified from the other end by the conditional 'had I' construction, the strong central claim effectively drops out. We're left with something like, 'had I a man's fair form . . . *then* passion would arm me well.' We begin to wonder whether the problem is indeed a lack of 'form' (as the narrator says), or is it *content* he wants: a device or desire, agency or energy, and, therefore, object or subject? Along these lines, we see that the textually ephemeral beloved, the object of this putative passion, is not so much erased as *resorbed*, after her brief appearance, by the speaking subject. We're left with something very like a narcissistic lament: the problem, a matter of the self's inadequacy to its own desires, and therefore its *desiring* inadequacies as well. Or, '*if* I had the agency, *then* I'd feel the energy to conceive an object.'

The new direction broached in line 5 intensifies the illogic and opens up the real project of the poem. 'But ah! I am no knight . . . No cuirass glistens on my bosom's swell; / I am no happy shepherd of the dell / Whose lips have trembled with a maiden's eyes.' It's not that I'm too short, Keats confesses, but that I'm too late. Given the meanings which Keats like his critics attached to his height, the complaint, an evasion of one real anxiety, at the same time and by the mechanism of denial expresses the more troubling business of Keats's *social* inadequacy. My problem is not that I lack social stature, he protests in his coded way, but that I come in an age which offers the writer no sponsors, no patrons, no *platform*: a levelling age in the most literal sense. One is reminded of Keats's comment on the dwarfishness of the present literary scene:

> Modern poets differ from the Elizabethans in this. Each of the moderns . . . governs his petty state, & knows how many straws are swept daily from the Causeways in all his dominions & has a continual itching that all the Housewifes should have their coppers well scoured: the antients were Emperors of vast Provinces, they had only heard of the remote ones and scarcely cared to visit them. (Extract from letter to J. H. Reynolds, 3 February 1818)

Suddenly in line 7, the aggressive complaint focused by the figure of the armed knight vanishes into a new cliché: 'I am no happy shepherd . . . / Whose lips have trembled with a maiden's eyes.' The sickeningly effete figure of the lovelorn shepherd – a modulation from epic to pastoral, virile to puerile, swagger to simper – is also a swerve from problems of equipment to a deficit of desire, the very turn anticipated in the grammar of the first four lines. It is not, then, that Keats is too short, too common, too late, or technically unequipped for effective lovemaking; what he requires is a genuine passion. His primary problem is not, he confesses, the want of those properties which would enable him to acquire his loved object. What he lacks is a heart passionate to love: the adequate *subjectivity* without which he cannot *conceive* a beloved. By a familiar paradox, we understand both that 'she' is the condition for Keats's amorous complaint, and *that* is his means of producing himself as an adequate – in this case, complaining – subject.

The desire governing this (self) love poem is *to* write and *for* words. Hence the acknowledgement, 'Yet must I dote upon thee[,] – call thee sweet, / Sweeter by far than Hybla's honeyed [honied] roses / When steeped [steep'd] in dew . . . / Ah! I will taste that dew, for me 'tis meet, / [And] gather some by spells[,] and incantation.' The primary – one might say, the *only* genuine – action of the poem, is that of 'doting'. Conventionally, this is an action requiring an object, a beloved. In Keats's case, the 'doting' is designed to *produce* an object which, in reflecting back to him an estranged version of his own discourse, might furnish him the material with which to concoct an authorial subject. We grasp the project the minute we focus the fact that what Keats 'must' do, 'dote', is just what he *is* doing by so stating. (Similarly, in his 'Specimen of an Induction to a Poem', he 'must tell a tale of chivalry' – must alienate [by verbalizing] the verbal action he is at that moment performing – in order to *continue* performing.) For Keats, the writing, which is the object of desire, is also the means of establishing a desiring origin. It must always, therefore, *precede* the object it would 'express', or proceed waywardly and unauthorized until such time as it can turn around and reflect upon itself. Of course, the minute this happens, the subject gets ahead of the writing (technically, behind or beneath it), and must be deconstructed, as by 'but must I dote', or 'tell', where the *adversion* to immediacy instantly destroys it. Simply, and with all the unthinkable paradoxicality of psychic life, we see that in *order* to write, Keats *must* write, and he must also truncate his writing by naming it. He must, to use his phrase, leap headlong into the sea, which was not there until he leapt, and he must advertise this nonsense.

The leap occurs in line 9. By 'call[ing] [his beloved] sweet', Keats produces a word upon which he may sweetly reflect, initiating in this way an operation as exclusively autoerotic as it is discursive. 'Sweet' enables the contrastive 'sweeter' (1. 10), which precipitates as a third, superlative term the classical cliché: 'Hybla's honeyed roses'. That phrase, by conjoining a height (Mt Hybla) with the word 'sweet' and the odorous rose imagery, engenders the punnish 'steeped', which in turn requires a dew to steep in. This liquor, the sensible ejaculate of logically abstract but verbally material activity, emerges as the subject Keats has been seeking from the outset. He will, he declares, 'taste that dew' ('for me 'tis meet'), which he 'gather[s] . . . by spells and incantation': by spells indeed. By the meet–meat pun, we learn what we already at some level knew. The drama of this poem is that of a man eating himself alive: consuming his own words in order to bring himself to life, a certain *kind* of life.

More conventionally, we could describe this sonnet as an exercise in self-intoxication; in it, we watch a man make poetry of his desire to make poetry and of the words that embody this literary wish. This poem, the motto of which should read, 'words, not/are things', is one of the better demonstrations of Keats's claim that any point will do to spin a web upon. Nowhere in the early poetry can we read so clearly the motives and character of Keats's verbal fetishism, which we have already explored in its more developed forms. Keats was a man with nothing *but* words ('fair form'), a man whose real deficit was one of substance: real things and a realizing desire. The genius of this terribly labored, literary, ill-conceived poem is that it exists at all. Not just *in* the absence of an authorial subjectivity and a poetic object, but *by* that absence, Keats makes his special verse.

We pursue our analysis by turning to two of Keats's earliest published poems – also, by general consensus, among his most embarrassingly fetishistic: 'I stood tip-toe upon a little hill' and, for its insights into the specifically *narrative* effects of this fetishism, 'Specimen of an Induction to a Poem'. The plan is to particularize and theorize that fetishism and then, through a reading of a more successful work, the first Elgin Marbles sonnet, to consider its implications for Keats's consciousness project.

The goal of 'I stood tip-toe' is to bring into being a poet-subject capable of writing a poem of this kind: that is, in the vein of the imaginative picturesque. A man with very narrow prospects tries to widen them by claiming possession of a particular literary terrain.

By 'terrain', I mean an original sensibility, a certain cultivation, and a special language, all of them indicating social privilege. Let me outline the chain of command. To own the formal field (an accomplishment stylistically marked by such qualities as variety, flexibility and smoothness) is also to claim a certain *self-control*. By the circular conventions of the form, *that* discipline denotes / confirms a special moral and epistemological authority, loosely identified with the overall structure of the poem. The narrative and meditative organization should imitate the narrator's mental processes, and in this way represent (that is, approximate) normative associational activity. We can see that the salient of the form – literally speaking, its beginning and end – is the achieved subjectivity of the narrator. The naturalness of his purchase on his own psyche and its cultural contents should correspond to the naturalness of, say, Gray's perspective on Eton College.

Keats could not have chosen a genre less suited to his station. His exercises in this mode effectively (but ineffectually) parody both topographical models: the dissociated moralizing survey of an externally situated prospect, and the richly rewarded ramble through a country of the mind. Because Keats was a poet who had no objects and was no subject, his purchase on both domains is unnatural and designing, and this emerges most generally in matters of perspective and most clearly as a question of scale. The spatial and conceptual diminutiveness of the exercise (the little hill, cozy bowers, nestling pleasures) which are intended to suggest refinement, betray instead the genteel vulgarity of the project. The elevation of the form, in conjunction with the Lilliputian delicacies, draws our attention to the social irony of the exercise: the wide survey of an urban, common land. Hunt's account of Keats's inspiration adds another ironic twist. Apparently, the hill to which Keats refers is in the vicinity of Caen Wood (today, Kenwood), the name for a stately home designed by Adams and built in 1754, and for its surrounding property. The narrator, who appears to be taking imaginative possession of a picturesquely landscaped but still public property, is covertly staking a claim on a private estate of immense real and ideological value. Even if we fail to recognize this project, the pastoral presumptions of the

Figure 2 'Caen Wood, Middlesex' (engraving, 1793)

Cockney poet underline the real lack of prospects and property/ies, and thus the ambitiousness of the representation.

In the strong topographical poem, the sort we associate initially with Gray and then with Thomson, the narrator typically *displays* his perspective, one that he owes to his lofty remove from the scene he describes. As we know, this remove, the condition of an encompassing, even, and (therefore) disinterested gaze, is also the condition of the poet's moral, spiritual, and political authority: his non-professionalism, in a word. The narrator of 'Eton College', like Thomson's controlling voice in *The Seasons*, is nothing *but* a point of view, one that signifies by its impersonality and indifference a whole category of social and economic meanings.

The internal ambler, conversely, derives *his* authority from his perfect coincidence with the empire he mentally – that is, verbally – constructs. (Here is the line descending from 'Grongar Hill'.) Upon the page, the narrator achieves (by the formal fiction, he *reproduces*) a subject / object identity so complete as to annihilate viewpoint. In the more kinetic examples of the form, the poet's perspective, which changes with his movements through a mental topography (and therefore with his objects and their variously encountered aspects), is so constant in its adaptation to the material at hand as to be invisible. The very *absence* of a discernible point of view signifies the achieved subjectivity and thus the objective mastery which is the hallmark of this form. Whereas the stylistic salient of what we have called the strong topographical poem is synoptic strength, that of the weak form is sincerity: the one denoting authority by and at a distance, the other exemplifying ownership as and by occupation. Both styles are expressions of ease: easy action, easy passion.

By the conventions Keats sets himself – those of the interior prospect poem – authorial viewpoint should not congeal as such within the discourse of the poem. At best, it is something for the grateful reader to infer from his own imaginative motions, prompted by his readerly peregrinations. The isolated representation of perspective which, in the strong topographical poem, signifies social and intellectual authority, in the context of Keats's poems produces just the opposite effect. By the exhibition of his purchase on his mental and literary objects, as by the nature of that purchase, Keats identifies himself as an object among objects.

The word 'tip-toe', so painfully exhibited in the opening line of the first poem in the 1817 volume, invites some attention. By the familiarity and ingenuousness of the word, Keats implies (he *intends*, that is) a delicate intimacy between reader and writer. The word alerts us to the pleasure Keats proposes to impart and to the pleasure he forgoes. Both the gravity and the gracelessness of the Wordsworthian contract are implicitly refused. In the rejection, one glimpses that widespread and quite consciously political antagonism Marilyn Butler has marked out between the poets of the first generation (fideistic, northern, gothic, ascetic) and those of the second (liberal, southern, Renaissance, sensuous).[3]

Or rather, one registers in Keats's opening line his *exclusion* from that cultural debate. Both the word 'tip-toe', and the clause in which it figures identify Keats's demonstration of membership in a literary–social estate as a bid for admission. Both execute a kind of social revenge on Keats's ambitions.

First, we sense something slightly redundant in the claim; generally, the *hill* provides the elevation. One would, that is, reasonably stand tip-toe on a plain and flat footed on a hill. Keats's line suggests the action of a man boosting himself up twice over. This is, ironically, the very stunt Keats is attempting by his interested (strenuous) essay in this interested (easy) genre. For Keats to write at all is to claim an unnatural elevation; to attempt this distinctly privileged form is to hoist himself up yet again.

Moreover, the curiosity of the word, 'tip-toe', and the metrical awkwardness of the line invite us to consider the simplest social meanings of the phrase. Why does one assume this stance? Or rather, who typically – what class of individuals – stands tip-toe? Children, short grown-ups, and people struggling to penetrate a defended view or to seize a remote one. Keats, from a political standpoint, was in 1817 all of those things.

The view from one's tip-toes is partial, strained, and framed. At best, it is the prospect of the visually disenfranchised, and at worst, the view of the peeping Tom. In either case, it is just about the opposite of both the equal, wide survey – that manly gaze – and the elegant armchair passivity of the mental traveller, the age's alternate spectatorial form of aristocratic virility.

'There was wide wandering [wand'ring] for the greediest eye, / To peer about . . . And trace . . . To picture out . . . Guess where . . .' A simple quotation of the verb sequence brings out the prurience of the project. Keats cannot make the fundamentally unnatural gaze of the middle-class poet look natural, not just because for him, it isn't, but because it is *itself* an object of desire, a trope for all desired things and a semiotic instrument. Or, for Keats to attempt either of the easy topographical gazes is to claim a social prerogative that is not his by rights, to claim it as a *sign* of those rights and to articulate by that claim a machine (non-mimetic, non-expressive) for the production of meaning. The poem's primary discursive and social fiction, Keats-the-poet, effectively parodies the categorical fiction, Literature, throwing the whole business of representation and the very paradigm of subjectivity into an ironic key. Keats, the effect of a bourgeois formation, enacts in the style of his wishes both the actual and the ideological project of that class: its substitution of signs for things, and difference for authorized, immanent meaning. Hence the peculiarly abstract effect of these terrifically detailed inventories. The discriminating specificity of the representation is the mark of a completely formal elaboration: not, as it claims, the effect of a sensuous concreteness or even of a symbolic or affective interest. What is concrete and particular are the words themselves and what those words *represent* is their own hermetic interrelatedness.

The primary action of the poems is, of course, looking. In the accomplished topographical poem, these acts of visual and conceptual appropriation are presented under the sign of generosity. The poet collects knowledge and sensation in order to bestow this wealth upon the reader: literally, to give him a view. Keats's observations, however, which foreground their indirection, discontinuity, partiality, stealth and strain, underline the author's private interest in the exercise. Hence the felt voyeurism of the thing. More damagingly, the narrator seems less occupied by the sensuous (textualized) sights than by the genre itself. What he covets are its formally definitive gestures.

A glance at lines 15–28 suggests, for example, that the Wordsworthian surmise – a controlled dialectical engagement with the object world – is itself the object of Keats's greedy gaze (my emphases).

> There was *wide wand'ring* for the greediest eye,
> To *peer about* upon variety;
> Far round the horizon's crystal air *to skim*,
> And *trace the dwindled edgings* of its brim;
> To *picture out* the quaint, and curious bending

Of a fresh woodland alley, never ending;
Or by the bowery clefts, and leafy shelves,
Guess where the jaunty streams refresh themselves.
I gazed awhile, *and felt as light, and free*
As though the fanning wings of Mercury
Had play'd [played] upon my heels; I was light-hearted,
And many pleasures *to my vision started*;
So I straightway began to pluck a posey
Of luxuries bright, milky, soft and rosy.

The attention Keats lavishes upon his imaginative departures from the given scene, his indifference to sensational distinctness and detail, and his failure to set his musing within a narrative or intellectual plot, expose to our view a means–end ratio. We see that Keats uses a rhetoric of calculated waywardness to assert his original *possession* of the landscape. (The sly feminization of that landscape [viz. ll. 19–21, 28] is meant for the same purpose.) To perceive this mechanism is, of course, to feel the spuriousness of the claim it engenders. One guesses that Keats is too far removed from the observed, the textualized and the canonical givens to transcend them. The surmising here bears little resemblance to the strong imaginative syntheses we associate with, say, Coleridge's 'Lime Tree Bower' and Wordsworth's 'Resolution and Independence'. Moreover, Keats's inadvertent baring of the device objectifies the natural expressiveness of the look it imitates: Wordsworth's initial look *at* an isolated collection of abstracted things, and the subsequently integrated, animated look *of* those things. From a rhetorical rather than formal perspective, we might say that Keats's improprieties expose both the contrivance of his chosen form (the naturalized visual-verbal perform-ance) and the expedience of its seeming naturalness. Keats's 'given' form is not just visibly 'taken', but taken from another proprietor.

Keats's estrangement from both the objects he observes and the subjectivity he emulates emerges above all in the disproportionateness of the representation: a problem of perspective, continuity and emphasis. What we *expect* is a naturalized passage from one object to another according to a determinate scale and registered from a fixed or evenly graduated distance conforming to the conventions of visual, motor, or intellectual progress. What we *get* are violent swings from the microscopic to the synoptic (ll. 8–22), temporal irregularities (ll. 65–70; 107) and a marked confusion in the handling of inside–outside, center–periphery relations. For an instance of the latter, consider the poem's opening image: '. . . the sweet buds which with a modest pride / Pull droopingly, in slanting curve aside, / Their scantly leaved[,] and finely tapering stems, / Had not yet lost those starry diadems / Caught from the early sobbing of the morn.' What is missing here is the representation of what lies behind those seductively parted leaves. Where is the small visual and narrative climax to which we've been teased along: the shift from ornamental description to a direct contemplative action upon the privileged central object which that decorative discourse projects? Where is the meaningful *content* of the representation; or how is it that what *we* take for 'form' in the most superficial and external sense offers itself to the narrator as an adequate meaning?

The pattern is repeated in the fantasy unfolded in lines 151ff, a representation informed by both the Psyche and Actaeon myths. Both mythological allusions promise the glimpse of a sacred, naked body. What we get – literally, *in the place of* that vision – is a description of trees, garlands, flowers: the sort of thing one associates with peripheral formal elaboration. These violations describe a resistance to the centripetal drift of the discourse. At the same time, there is an anxiety about the passage from surface to surface, suggestive of a displaced *desire* for the center. In the discursive flight from one embodied lack to another, we sense a quest for the presence which complements but also constructs those vacancies.

The run-on verbosity of the poem images an author transfixed by his contemplative acts, a prisoner of the fetish-world he engenders. This projection is, of course, consistent with the social facts. Keats cannot imitate Wordsworth's and Coleridge's easy withdrawal from the dialectical *pas de deux* (that is, the return from a humanized Nature to an enriched subjectivity), since for Keats, the initiative is always and fundamentally on the side of the object world. (Any of Keats's odes, with their forlorn returns to selfhood's empty rooms, could serve as a concrete instance. Any of Coleridge's conversation poems, with their rich homecomings, finds us a counter-example to the Keatsian form.) Of course, one might argue that the immobility of the initial Wordsworthian and Coleridgean gaze – the flat and imaginatively unmediated perception of a dully material landscape – similarly confesses a certain impotence vis-à-vis 'life out there'. But one also remembers that the *negating* of that first physical moment is the project of these capably centripetal poems, and it is broached with the initial authorial reflection upon the situation. Moreover, in such poems as 'Tintern Abbey', 'The Solitary Reaper', 'Resolution and Independence' and the Yarrow sequence, the discursive or figural confession of objective priority is overshadowed by the dramatized command of the poet's inward look and 'overheard' inner speech, a display of subjective prepotency. Keats, as we know, had only a very problematical subjectivity to exhibit, and he only had *that* troubled self as a literary means by virtue of the ongoing discursive project. The dominative, even exploitative character of the object world emerges strongly in Keats's early poetry and, ironically, in the form of his alleged escapes from that world.

There are no subjects in this early poetry: no subjects in the technical sense (authorial personae), or the colloquial (topics). Like the sonnet discussed above, most of the 1817 poems are 'about' their own coming into being. (One hesitates to say 'about' when the reflexiveness is so mechanical.) This fact is explained by Keats's interest in producing a self that can *have* subjects and stories. We have characterized Keats as a man forced to know himself an object before and by way of seizing his subjectivity; the *suffered* objectivity is as a template for Keats's self-parodic subject form. Owing to this dynamics – a double objectification – the deep contradictoriness underlying the world of things regarded as things *tout court*, and of the literature which reproduces in a finer tone the acquired transparency of that world, surfaces with unusual force. In the early work, the natural(ized) trajectory of the Romantic gaze (from centered subject to object and back to [enriched] subject) is scrambled. The words, an objective and structurally antagonistic dimension for Keats, produce a speaker who, in engendering subsequent words, effectively relativizes and thus deconstructs his own subjectivity, requiring another round of arrested dialectics. As we saw in our study of the sonnet 'Had I a man's fair form', the authorial voice of the early poetry is constituted as an *effect* of its discursive projection: an effect, however, which is almost instantly resorbed by its verbal cause. The wildly overinvested, hectic quality of the writing betrays both its priority in the creative act, and its continuing appropriation of any subjective surplus it may engender. Keats, or his periodically emergent authorial voice, is literally a prisoner of his poetry. Indeed, the way these poems (cannot) end, betrays more clearly than anything else the self-consumption which is the logic of Keats's literary mode of production at this stage. In the helpless prolixity of the writing – a sad parody of Wordsworth's spontaneous emotional overflow – we feel the anxiety of a speaker waiting for his words to run their course and release him from their spell. At the same time, we sense an *addiction* to this thralldom; more precisely, an anxiety about venturing on an autonomy which amounts to vacancy and nothingness. We might even go so far as to declare the greatness of Keats's *mature* poetry a function of its very *practiced* (frequent and accomplished) endings: controlled escapes from the 'fine spell of words'. Consistent with the range of double-binds we have plotted in the life and verse, Keats could only *effectively* write by *not* writing. We notice that two of Keats's favorite forms, the sonnet and ode, with their forced turns and closures, are ideal machines for a stop-and-go, and also end-stopped discourse. Through his determined silences, Keats masters, for a time, the expression of his mastery. The power of the fetish to arrest and objectify consciousness is precisely the power of Keats's poetry: literally, its charm. This is also the magic Keats both solicits and resists.

We understand the strong double-negative of Keats's poetry: the fetishized consciousness a reproduction of the imposed objectivity, and, thus, an invention of a second, writerly self. The descriptive excesses of the early poems describe a *single* negative, the simple reflex of Keats's self-alienation. We may recognize, for instance, in 'Tip-toe''s adjectival and adverbial overload, the prototype for 'St. Agnes'' controlled anti-closural strategies. Similarly, the magical suspense of 'St. Agnes' – largely a function of its determined interference with narrative succession – manifests in the early verse as a longing to linger in the downy nests of description. The longing, an expression of Keats's technical immaturity, diminishes the speaking subject more by its failure, ironically, than its success. *Keats* may resist telling the tale, but his very resistance (that is, the consistent recourse to periphrasis, ellipsis, and euphemism) tells it for him. The story that emerges is that same adventure we plotted in 'Chapman's Homer'. What makes 'Tip-toe' so embarrassing is neither the instinctual wish it inscribes nor the adolescent swerve from that wish. The guilt that possesses this verse is the *social* guilt attending Keats's first literary venture; we should say, his first display of social desire. Moreover, we feel in the poem a certain sliding of both the sexual and social desires from their designated or putative objects to the defense itself. The resistance to complete and direct representation has about it an energy suggestive of a wish in its own right. This negative wish, which defines the virtue of the great poetry, does not materialize as such in the early verse. The sheer confusion of the wish and the defense puts 'Tip-toe' beyond innocence but very much short of sophistication. It is the in-betweenness that makes for our squeamishness and the poem's plain badness.

To attack this effect from another angle, we observe in all the narrative poems of this period Keats's failure to get his hero into action. It's hard not to read in so marked and pervasive a failure some resistance to success, and it's easy to relate that resistance to the stratagems of the later poetry. The feverish frustration of the early poetry is, in the great verse, the throbbing suspension that has become the Keatsian hallmark.

The most excruciatingly arrested of all Keats's poems is his 'Specimen of an Induction to a Poem'. (See Appendix.) As is often the case, Keats encodes the sociopsychic project of the poem in its title: here, an exercise in wheel-spinning. The title names an abstractive and ideal representation (or, 'specimen') of a prolegomenon ('induction') to a poem which nowhere materializes. I quote the opening line: 'Lo! I must tell a tale of chivalry.' This line gets repeated eleven lines down, posed as a question in line 31, and it recurs as an exhortation at line 45. Naturally, no tale gets told; predictably, the subordinate posture secured by the locution enables a good deal of telling to take place.

The hero of this poem without an object is not what one would properly call a subject. The young knight, who seems for a moment to consolidate authorial and readerly interest, is almost immediately displaced by his lance: 'The lance points slantingly', is 'hail[ed] with tears', 'reflected[,] clearly in a lake', grasped by the 'tremendous hand' of a warrior, balanced grandly at the tournament, and admired by staring damsels. As we might expect, the weapon is never actually thrown. The pleasurable *delaying* of that action is, in fact, the action of this discourse.

There comes, however, a point of nearly unbearable tension (1. 17), when Keats seems to register the entire embarrassing fiction with all its guilty, phallic aggressiveness. He releases his lance, but in a significantly indirect and also reflexive fashion. 'Spenser,[!] thy brows are arched, open, kind . . . Therefore, great bard, I not so fearfully / Call on thy gentle spirit to hover nigh . . . So will I rest in hope / To see wide plains, fair trees and lawny slope . . . Clear streams, smooth lakes and overlooking towers'. By this precipitous, first-person address to the gentlest, most nurturing of mentors, Keats relinquishes his narrative ambition ('strange pretence'), and the fear which attends it. He settles down to the safely infantile desire: the wish to enter Spenser, not engage him. Keats situates the great poet as, what is called in a letter of 1817 (viz. what 'the Lovers of Poetry like'), 'a little Region to wander in'. One senses in the fantasy the mythic retreat to the unrememberable maternal home. (In the later poetry, the logic of containment is reversed: Keats *entertains* the canon. *His* is the effectual inner space, making him, as it were, host to his fathers: functionally, the female vessel.) The governing wish of Keats's 'Specimen' is not to tell a courtly tale but to re-create and occupy Spenser's textual court. Moreover, the structure of the poem plainly identifies this wish – to become a character in a great poet's story, a creature of/in Spenser's breeding brain – as a defense against the more dangerous desire which haunts about lines 1–17: the wish to *rival* those stories, or to deploy the lance in the correct, directly aggressive way. As usual, the defense becomes for Keats the offense. The set-pieces that occur so prominently in the later poetry – indeed, all of 'To Autumn' – instance just that sort of arrested action we plot, astonished, in the labors of Keats's lance. When the maneuver works – when we conceive the resistance to narrative sequence as a refusal – we call it 'poise'.

Our concern with totalizing meanings should not make us forget the most obvious explanation of Keats's problems with narrative. I refer to the narrow scope for action in Keats's life: the compelled passivity in work and love, and, in addition, the necessary preoccupation with unaffordable or hard-to-replace objects. We remember the pathos of Keats's epistolary descriptions of certain foods, clothes, shoes, domestic interiors; and we see that the descriptive style of the 1820 volume evinces an equal but opposite power. The difference between the bad early poetry and what I have called the greatly 'bad' poetry is the pronounced negativity of the latter. There is a real difference between the fear or inability to narrate and the refusal to do so, even when what is refused is not available.

Even as I draw this distinction I'd like to smudge it by declaring the limits, or perhaps the *order* of the success Keats realizes in the great poems. By contrasting the weakness of the early, unself-consciously fetishistic poetry to the power of the later, determined fetishism, I have in effect reinstated the Romantic transcendence, with one unimportant difference: I have made 'bad' consciousness rather than 'consciousness' the hero of our tale. Because we want to locate the materiality of Keats's sublime – the real conditions that accompany his every real transcendence of conditions – we turn to a poem that is neither bad nor 'bad', 'On Seeing the Elgin Marbles'.

> My spirit is too weak – mortality
>   Weighs heavily on me like unwilling sleep,
>   And each imagined pinnacle and steep
> Of godlike hardship tells me I must die
> Like a sick eagle looking at the sky.
>   Yet 'tis a gentle luxury to weep
>   That I have not the cloudy winds to keep
> Fresh for the opening of the morning's eye.
> Such dim-conceived [conceivéd] glories of the brain
>   Bring round the heart an undescribable feud;
> So do these wonders a most dizzy pain,
>   That mingles Grecian grandeur with the rude
> Wasting of old Time, [time –] with a billowy main, [–]
>   A sun, [–] a shadow of a magnitude.

This sonnet, whose title presents to us a very *type* of the sensuous particular, lets us study Keats's production of the material sublime (and its way of producing him) at close range. By its title and presentation (first in Hunt's *Examiner*, a heavily fine-arts review, and a year later, in the *Annals of the Fine Arts*), the poem sets for itself the conventions of the literary complement/compliment: the translation into words of the properties or effects of the sculptural original. As with both 'Chapman's Homer' and the 'Floure and Leafe' sonnet (composed within the same week as the 'Elgin Marbles' piece and published a week later also in the *Examiner*), 'On Seeing the Elgin Marbles' absents its advertised original by a parodic and at the same time idealizing procedure. The stylistic discrepancy between the Marbles and the poem in their honor is sharp and dramatic: indeed, dramatized. One is invited to see that the production of a distinctively literary value occurs by a violently abstractive process; and, that this objective ravishment is also a form of self-abuse.[4]

In the simplest terms, the object of this poem is to turn sculpture into writing, thus giving us the mirror image of the 'Grecian Urn', or of its attempt to turn writing into sculpture, sound into scripture, relief (deep fantasy) into relief (an art of surfaces). The conversion entails a double abstraction. In isolating from the sculpture its affective virtue – that which can be directly translated into poetry – the narrator *himself* undergoes a bisection. The sonnet articulates this internal division ('undescribable feud') in terms suggested by the occasion and hallowed by literary convention: spirit–flesh, immortal–mortal, desire–capability. What distinguishes Keats's version of this familiar opposition is its logical status as an *artifact* of the contradiction he installs within what comes to him as a unified sensuous object: the Marbles. In consuming that object productively, Keats attenuates himself. More precisely, he constructs an 'ethereal' character within a self that gets *divided* by that addition. The pronounced weakness of the opening line is the *effect* of an aesthetic consumption, itself the *condition* for aesthetic production. At this point in his career, it is a price Keats is willing, even eager to pay, and perhaps because of this, the badness of the bargain is not immediately obvious.

To recall the mimetic dimension of the poem, however (a reflection induced by the poem's title, as by its initial, logical swerve, outlined below), is to feel Keats's self-truncation and the perversity of the argument it engenders. Weakness, mortality, and dizzy pain are literally – chronologically – the *last* sensations aroused by the Elgin Marbles. That is to say, the narrator describes the *reflex* of his own first response to the Marbles, or to their felt power, a power completely suppressed by the narration. 'Dizzy', 'dim-conceived', 'billowy', 'cloudy', 'shadow': these words which describe the narrator's delayed and literally *self*-conscious reaction (that is, a recognition of his own creative limitations) are textually positioned as the primary aesthetic experience. One cannot respect the grammar of the text without at the same time feeling the perversity of Keats's 'compliment'. (As I observed in the opening chapter, Keats does not permit us the illusion of imagining ourselves to be good readers *and* good critics.) Not only are the subjects of the Marbles stirring and heroic (for example, the war of centaurs and Lapiths), but the style of the relief – graceful yet informed by the power of archaic things – is distinguished by its linear clarity and conceptual authority. Here, then, is the most willful abstraction of meaning from matter. Indeed, the sharp disproportion of object (strong, early, concrete, determinate: Classic) to impression (effete, belated, abstract, ambivalent: Romantic) develops a *sotto voce* parody (and self-parody) within this rhapsodically honorific poem.

One could develop a smoother, more conventional, and also more generous reading of the poem's formal and historical discrepancies by reference to the topos of the beautiful-sublime. The sonnet could be described as a dramatic reflection on the sublime as an affective *dimension* of the beautiful object: thus does beauty ensure its transhistorical value. How, then, would we explain Keats's failure to *represent* the initial, expansive phase: that sublime *identification*, triggered by the sealed perfection of the classic beauty, which alone lends force to a difference that must otherwise signify evasion and descent?

More technically, we see that the poem open on an elision; what gets deleted is the moment of imaginative dilation, when the narrator shared in the strong ecstasy of the godlike image and in its causal origin: the godlike artist. To focus this absence is to see that Keats *puts* his poem on a decline by way of establishing both a powerful psychic dissonance and a subject–object contradiction. The narrator rises to the occasion by sinking (harking back to Keats's 'Specimen', we could say he competes with his Attic precursor by capitulating to him); the gratuitous 'unwilling' that modifies 'sleep' is one of several betrayals of this determined perverseness. We feel something of the expedience of Keats's weakness, or of his professions thereof, in the false turn, 'Yet 'tis a gentle luxury to weep / That I have not the cloudy winds to keep . . .' Inasmuch as Keats engineers his own poverty, the 'yet' should be an 'and'. The Marbles, which instance by their representational objects *and* style a calm accomplishment, are in Keats's poem the means of producing heroic longing: which is to say, huge desire, dis-ease, and deficiency. What is action in the original representational and historical order is objectless passion in the other. Indeed, the narrator pointedly luxuriates in his deprivation (l. 6). The Marbles – a 'material sublime' in the most literal sense – become in Keats's poem an 'imagined' exaltation and a shadowy magnitude.

Keats describes, in effect, a *terminus ad quem* by way of suppressing the *terminus a quo*, without which the former has no real, or rather, no *responsible* meaning.

One is far too conscious of the working perverseness of this sonnet for its stratagem to succeed so well as it does in the 1819–20 poems. One feels a certain recoil from the voluptuous feebleness of the stance. As with Olivier's recent rendition of Lear, we feel we are watching a man fondle his own mortality, and this is a luxury we'd rather not witness. Or, what we do *not* feel in Keats's sonnet, and what therefore explains its special failure, is the danger of a full and empowering identification with the sculpture and its maker. We are not, that is, positioned to understand the necessity of the supplement. We *do* appreciate the sheer verbal power Keats engenders by his abstractive method. Indeed, the closing lines of the sonnet, composed of a string of clichés ('Grecian grandeur', 'rude/Wasting', 'old Time', 'billowy main') are a triumph of the written word. These lines – emphatically, *lines*, like the trace of a chisel – do nothing but proclaim their own depthless beauty, and because they do that so coldly and so well, we are moved. We are not, however, convinced that we are or should be moved. This is because Keats's initial logical swerve allows the sculptural full presence to survive not just intact but idealized. That presence becomes for the reader a critical station, giving a view not just of the poem's procedural and (il)logical machinery but of his own programmed response to that machine.

Let me indicate very briefly the bearing of this discussion on our understanding of the two *Hyperion* poems and 'Lamia'. I have argued that the project of the 'The Fall' is to put 'Hyperion''s self-identity to work by rendering that innocence a representational object: a *figure* of presence, givenness, authenticity, and self-closure. Through the agency of the romance, 'Hyperion''s epic primacy, an original and originary value – like gold, let us say – gets deposited in a 'Thing semi-real': by the analogy, a coin or bill. Here, 'Hyperion''s 'existence' assumes the character of the concrete, material sign: in the language of Keats criticism, the oxymoron. Even as the primary 'existence' is socially *realized* by this operation – its value enhanced – it is also depreciated. For, by reference to the chameleon freedom of the coin, gold in its simpler commodity character assumes a limited and passive aspect. Finally, 'The Fall''s determined semioticity opens within its double-utterance a breach which amounts to a form–content contradiction: a permanent opportunity for the re-production of literary value.

I have characterized 'Hyperion' as the very symbol for Keats of his *good* consciousness: proof positive of his identificatory accomplishment. To realize *this* poem by the representational strategies we have studied meant executing in the plainest way an act of self-commodification. Literally, Keats renders his very best expression a sign of expressiveness: the first, material term – the referent, as it were – preserved within the second, signifying term as a kind of death's head. That imprint designates the lateness, illegitimacy, and abstractness of 'The Fall': the fraudulence and *therefore* the social virtue of the new master.

I have called 'Lamia' the most lucid and self-critical of all Keats's poems because here he begins *interrelating* his historically given categories of experience, categories that tend to get conflated in the earlier verse. 'Lamia' performs this relational feat by a dramatic meditation on the genesis and progress of exchange: its historical evolution toward the commodity and the money forms. Under the pressure of his real desperation in 1819–20, Keats began, I believe, to comprehend the meaning of his style. Perhaps the severe and, given Keats's advanced disease, irremediable instinctual frustrations of this period presented to consciousness those 'healthy' solutions he had resisted on account of certain ego-imperatives. And, as we've observed, Keats's logically determined violation of the uniquely resonant 'Hyperion' might have pushed him finally beyond 'working' solutions. Together, these situations could explain Keats's drive to interrogate the range of refusals effected by his dyadic procedures: the mechanism of his literary production.

By this interrogation, Keats identifies his self-consciousness (as we have seen, the subject and object of his art) as the commodity's consciousness of itself, that double-fetish which is also, by the grammar of value forms, money. This is to say, 'Lamia''s economic allegory unfolds an interior plot as well. In Lycius's amorously exploitative action upon Lamia, as in Lamia's action upon the nymph and Hermes' action upon Lycius, we shall read Keats's relation to his working brain, a recapitulation of the social relation thrust upon him by the age. By reference to Lamia's career, we shall see that Keats's mode of literary / self-production, described in this book as a masturbatory dynamics (a taking of his subjectivity for an object), renders him finally a thing dependent for its value upon the representation that will displace and derealize it. Keats is forced by his own mode of production to seize in imagination his determined persona, the fissured-doubled self, as both 'an element of the movement of commodities and an (objective and impotent) observer of that movement'.[5]

Keats in 1819–20, as halted and hopeless as ever a man could be, penetrates the illusion of his subjectivity: the idea of himself as the source of a meaningful activity. His art, which is his only freedom, takes shape for him as merely an object of the process of production – not just any object, but the organizing object-form of his historical moment: the money fetish.[6] In 'Lamia', the fetish form which had presented to Keats his slavery under the aspect of freedom starts releasing its meaning. A new *kind* of knowledge can be said to develop in this poem: 'not the knowledge of an opposed [introjected] object but . . . the self-consciousness of the object'. The objective form of the object – here, the fetish – is overthrown.[7]

Throughout this book, we have seen Keats resist the situational tendency toward overinvestment in things and in his fantasies of them by a carefully conceptualized fetishism designed to produce a specific difference from his inner life. We have seen that for Keats, escape consists not in art, a displacement toward the Imaginary, but in an Idea of art: the material (and Symbolic) form of a social/canonical abstraction. This is the object which liberates those who know how to enjoy it from individual and historical nature: instinct and culture and their interdetermination. Keats's poetry, a parodic reproduction of his life, executes a fixing and inverting action: a distinctly reflexive fetishism, in short. What distinguishes 'Lamia' is its elucidation of this process by reference to the fetish form in its purest, most irrational, and impersonal aspect – also, its most intimate and practical aspect. Money.[8] Lamin *is* that insight. To recall her chief virtue – to 'unperplex bliss from its neighbour pain' – is to realize that the *formal* perplexities of Keats's greatest poetry, like the folds of Lamia's 'gordian shape', *un*ravel the *substantive* knots that bind labor to leisure, production to consumption, content to form, truth to beauty. Like Milton's snake, the gorgeous oxymorons of Keats's poetry make crooked seem straight.

To characterize 'Lamia''s special self-consciousness as pertaining not just to objects-in-general but to the Idea of the object *per se*, the fetish, in its historical incarnation, is to claim for the poem a qualitatively different knowledge than the sort we've explored in 'La Belle Dame' and 'St. Agnes'. A Romantic restatement of the claim would go something like this: through 'Lamia', a crisis poem, Keats acquires his own voice.[9] 'The Cap and Bells', an utterance *in propria persona*, is the satiric-comic expression of that critical subjectivity. We see that there is nothing 'bad' about the poem, and, sad to say, nothing very good either.

Notes

1 In his section on Lukács, in *Marxism and Form*, Fredric Jameson opposes the bourgeois, symbolic mode to that of developed realism, the discursive mode corresponding to the knowledge-forms of the proletariat (*Marxism and Form, Twentieth-Century Dialectical Theories of Literature*, Princeton, NJ: Princeton Univ. Press, p. 200). Allegory, as we know, elaborates those reciprocities which symbolism willfully collapses into identities, and which realism passively reflects. Allegory would seem always, thus, to be a 'meta' form: always a reflection on meaning-production and, thus, a deconstruction of the coherent and primary subject, *even as* that figural projection is enhanced by the semiotic activity it appears to engender. Is this why allegory surfaces so strongly in the Renaissance and the Romantic age (and, alongside or *within* its symbolic discourse), periods of crisis for the bourgeois subject? De Man's wonderful discussion of Romantic allegory is the logical point of departure for an inquiry of this kind ('The Rhetoric of Temporality', in *Blindness and Insight*, Minneapolis: Univ. of Minnesota Press, 1971; 1983).

2 John Barrell, *The Dark Side of the Landscape* (Cambridge: Cambridge Univ. Press, 1980); *English Literature in History, 1730–80: An Equal, Wide Survey* (London: Hutchinson, 1983); James Turner, *The Politics of Landscape* (Oxford: Basil Blackwell, 1979).

3 Marilyn Butler, *Romantics, Rebels and Reactionaries* (Oxford: Oxford Univ. Press, 1982).

4 We enhance this formalist argument by placing it within the field of the contemporary controversy over Lord Elgin's treasure. Thus do we see how Keats's poem recapitulates Elgin's defense of his cultural expropriation: an argument for the better physical preservation of the sculpture and the better dissemination of a particular cultural idea.

5 Georg Lukács, *History and Class Consciousness*, trans. R. Livingstone (Cambridge, Mass.: MIT Press, 1971), p. 166. The reader who is familiar with Lukács will recognize the extent to which my argument draws on his great essay, 'Reification and the Consciousness of the Proletariat'.

6 Ibid., p. 168.

7 Ibid., p. 178.
8 Perhaps Keats's insight into money does not extend to capital because capital, a perverse reunion of use- with exchange-value, is the less fetishistic form.
9 Lukács knows the crisis by the phenomenon of things starting to look like social relations, and relations starting to look like products (*History and Class Consciousness*, pp. 164, 165).

6

'Lamia': Sympathy for the Devil

... money, as the *absolute* means, provides unlimited possibilities for enjoyment while at the same time, as the absolute *means* it leaves enjoyment as yet completely untouched during the stage of its unused ownership. In this respect the significance of money coincides with that of power ...

We know more about money than about any other object because there is nothing to be known about money and so it cannot hide anything from us. It is a thing absolutely lacking in qualities and therefore cannot, as can even the most pitiful object, conceal within itself any surprises or disappointments. Whoever really and definitely only wants money is absolutely safe from such experiences ... If we desire to arrange human destiny according to the scheme of relationship between the wish and its object, then we must concede that, in terms of the final point in the sequence of purposes, money is the most inadequate but also the most adequate object of our endeavours.

Georg Simmel, *The Philosophy of Money*

One

I'd like to call attention to an unusual and powerfully suggestive essay by K. K. Ruthven, 'Keats and *Dea Moneta*', 1976.[1] I shall use this study for the purchase it can give us on 'Lamia'. Ruthven's argument concerns Keats's substitution of Moneta for Mnemosyne in his reconstruction of 'Hyperion' as 'The Fall'. In restoring to our knowledge Moneta's original, traditional, and nineteenth-century interpretative contexts, Ruthven generates a collection of characters and attributes which greatly enrich our understanding of Keats's inscrutable divinity.

Ruthven's real genius in this matter is to confirm the readiest verbal resonance of the name Moneta by way of that goddess's early installation in the Roman treasury. The Moneta–money connection, which most of us had, presumably, discounted as the whimsy of phonetic philology, is thus brought into the interpretative field. Through Ruthven, we learn that Ovid's Moneta, a priestess of Saturn and thus belonging to an age in which 'gold and other precious metals remained safely buried in the earth' (a genuine Golden age, brought to an end by the practice of mining, regarded as inaugurating the Iron age), is *also* that Juno Moneta who presided over the Roman mint and whose treasury was established in the temple of Saturn near the beginning of the fifth century BC.

> From the time of Caesar onwards, Moneta is personified on Roman coins, sometimes as a bust in profile, but more often as a full-length figure holding the emblematic scales which standardize the weight of coins, and the cornucopia which guarantees an abundant supply of them.

Ruthven observes the irony that must have attended allusions to this figure in the context of nineteenth-century English culture:

> because the minting of gold coins was carried out traditionally in the temple of Juno Moneta, the Roman mint continued to be referred to as 'holy' (sacra). Here again is matter to puzzle the Christian reader of Keats's generation, who would tend not to think of banks as holy places, but to believe on the contrary that one cannot possibly serve both God and Mammon.

Tooke's *Pantheon*, with which Keats was intimately familiar, records both etymologies: Moneta as one who 'gives wholesome counsel' (that is, an admonitory goddess, from 'monere': to warn); and, a creature 'believed to be the goddess of money'.

By way of further establishing Keats's knowledge of the money–Moneta connection, Ruthven brings to our attention the following comment from Burton's *Anatomy*, a favorite romantic sourcebook of Keats's: 'our summum bonum is commodity, and the goddesse we adore Dea moneta, Queen money, to whom we daily offer sacrifice'. Ruthven excellently observes the bitter irony of 'having a goddess thus named give advice to a perpetually hard-up habitué of the realms of gold'. He plots the unusually pinched circumstances, and the urgent hopes, of the period of 'The Fall''s (and, we observe, of 'Lamia''s) composition.

Finally, Ruthven reviews the range of Keatsian metaphors based on the association of poetry and imagination with money and gold. He underlines the conflict arising for a man who, conceiving his imagination as a real and immediate value, is forced to exchange that value for (by implication, convert it into) a symbolic and negotiable wealth: one could say, to sell himself at a real loss for an abstract gain. By way of contextualizing very generally Keats's commercial metaphors, Ruthven reminds us of the so-called Restriction: the suspension of cash (that is, gold) payments during the years 1797–1821, a policy instituted in fearful anticipation of a run on bullion.[2]

Ultimately, Ruthven feels, Keats identifies Mammon and Moneta with the reality principle, and he emplots in the poet's confrontation with Moneta's hideously staring eyes ('like two gold coins') a necessary engagement with the doubleness or 'perplexity' of experience. To refuse Moneta's fiscal character – her emblematic association with a world 'which deifies money as a commodity' – is to retreat to Spenserian dreaming. The lesson of 'The Fall' is said to concern the poet's orientation toward his own consciousness. By the mining and refining of his imaginative gold, the poet resumes (or should do) Moneta's end-stopped activities in a prolific field. (Ruthven explains Moneta's ultimacy, her identity as 'pale omega of a withered race', by the fact that 'gold is sterile and cannot breed.') The thrust of 'The Fall' is to relocate Moneta and her 'aerarium' in the poet's breeding brain. One recalls in this context the figure engendered by the narrator's curiosity: 'I ached to see what things the hollow brain / Behind enwombed . . .' (ll. 276–7). We recognize in Ruthven's conclusion a familiar Keatsian topos: that of the severed head, buried within the categorically estranged vessel. Or, as proposed above, 'The Fall' instances yet another of those Keatsian museums with one work inside.

Ruthven does not do very much in a critical vein with his mythographic findings, but then there's not a great deal to do in the context of 'Hyperion' and 'The Fall'. By its formal signature, 'Hyperion' is a 'good' poem: following Bakhtin's formula for epic firstness, a good *old* poem. Moreover, 'Hyperion' is explicitly *about* the better, *older* things: Milton, Saturn's sunk realm. Who but

Mnemosyne, first goddess of memory, should preside over those Origins? It is no less appropriate that Moneta in her monitory aspect dominates 'The Fall', a poem about the dangers of the goodness exemplified by 'Hyperion'. Further, 'The Fall', as we know, *contains* the epic 'Hyperion' within an essentially romantic (and Romantic) narrative frame. The poem, both old and new, is riven by contradiction and effectuated by that dissonance. To that extent, Moneta, with her freight of conflictual significations, is again the divinity of choice.

The sphere of operations for Moneta in her purely *monetary* aspect is, I believe, 'Lamia'. This poem – by its salient rhetorical gestures, a contemporary satire – is properly organized by the goddess of money in her most modern incarnation. In 'Lamia', Moneta plays the title-role, under the name taken from Burton's *Anatomy*.

As I noted, Ruthven cites Burton's acquaintance with Dea Moneta. We extend Ruthven's insights by observing that Burton opens his discussion of love objects – sources of love melancholy – with the love of 'profit, and that which carrieth with it a show of commodity'.

> Among all these fair enticing objects, which procure love and bewitch the soul of man, there is none so moving, so forcible as profit . . .'; 'If our pleasures be interrupt, we can tolerate it; our bodies hurt, we can put it up and be reconciled; but touch our commodities, and we are most impatient: fair becomes foul, the Graces are turned to Harpies, . . . good words to satires and invectives, we revile *e contra*, naught but his imperfections are in our eyes, he is a base knave, a devil, a monster, a caterpillar, a viper, . . .'; Desinit in piscem mulier formosa superne [the beauteous woman tails off into a fish] the scene is altered on a sudden, love is turned to hate, mirth to melancholy: so furiously are we most part bent, our affections fixed upon this object of commodity, and upon money . . .[3]

Burton links his two discourses – the consideration of commodities proper and of women – by a meditation on the origin of the god Love. Love's parents are said to be Porus and Penia: god of wealth and goddess of poverty. Burton mentions as well in this context Aristophanes' comic myth of primordial fourfold creatures, bifurcated for their pride and mechanically recombined through coitus. He seems to be developing a definition of love as an irreducibly oxymoronic phenomenon, tending to impose its own monstrosity upon its 'fair enticing objects', women and things (viz. 'the beautiful woman tails off into a fish'). As if to illustrate this lesson, and to yoke in a dramatic frame the two classes of love objects, Burton tells the story of 'one Menippus Lycius': his strange and 'immoderate' passion for 'a phantasm in the habit of a fair gentlewoman'. The creature is found out to be 'a lamia' (a *common* noun in Burton and by the tradition he invokes). Upon that discovery, 'all her furniture . . . like Tantalus' gold described by Homer, no substance, but mere illusions', vanishes in an instant.

The story is set, quite elaborately and emphatically, in Corinth. A few pages beyond the lamia story, Burton analyzes the effects upon love of various external conditions: for example, 'Temperature, full Diet, Idleness, Place, Climate, etc.'. The following description of Corinth is advanced as an example of a climatological determination ('Your hot and southern countries are prone to lust . . .'), but given Corinth's reputation as a city of immensely profitable trade ('It was that plenty of all things, which made Corinth so infamous of old . . .'), Burton sets the concupiscence within a specifically economic causality as well: 'every day strangers came in, at each gate, from all quarters. In that one temple of Venus a thousand whores did prostitute themselves . . . all nations resorted thither as to a school of Venus'. Here, one could say, is the complement to Moneta's Saturnian temple: another conjunction of the sacred and profane. In this case, we find *love* yoked to commerce: not Juno Moneta but Venus Moneta (or, Hermes). Here too is the logical and historical identity obtaining between Burton's two classes of love objects: commodities and women.

In order to situate Keats in all this, I return briefly to Ruthven's essay: specifically to his Marxian illumination of 'the commodity, money'. Ruthven quotes a general statement by Marx to the effect that 'money abases all the gods of mankind and changes them into commodities', and, that 'money is the alienated essence of man's work and existence; this essence dominates him and he worships it'. As we know, Marx analyzes the money form at great length and with semiotic prescience in that section of the *Grundrisse* entitled 'The Chapter on Money'. Here we learn that money is not, in its 'quintessential' moment (penultimate to its emergence as capital), a commodity as Marx defines that function elsewhere in the *Grundrisse*. Whereas the commodity conjoins in its substance and form two different values (its value as a particular product or instrument of production, and its social or exchange value [roughly, a natural and a social existence]), in the money form, 'all properties of the commodity as exchange value appear as an object distinct from it, as a form of social existence separated from the natural existence of the commodity'.[4] Money, which begins its career in a social need for a third term against which to measure the values of noncomparable objects, emerges historically as a reification of this strictly relational entity. By its (formally) representational function on the one hand and, on the other, its *practically* reflexive value, money, the incarnation of a social relation between two actual and particular items and two social individuals and positions (buyers and sellers), comes between those actively associated terms. No phenomenon so excellently illustrates the antinomy of mediation; money joins by dividing.

Marx describes the money form as a symbol of the commodity *as such*, or of commodity exchange-value in itself and over against use-value, which he aligns with production and consumption. The money form is not, then, any *particular* commodity (insofar as the commodity retains a 'particular' character), but the 'material representative of general wealth'. Marx glosses 'general wealth' as 'general exchange value', itself an abstraction from a totality of concrete commodities. Briefly, Marx's analysis of the money form (and, a parallel but psychologically richer reading: Georg Simmel's) coincides most suggestively with the phenomenon described in this study as the productive mechanism of Keats's poetry. I mean, of course, that material Concept we explored most fully in the context of 'St. Agnes': dissociated, objectified sign of a representation, itself the displacement of a real (that is, canonical) relation.[5]

Ruthven, who identifies money as a commodity like any other, reasonably relates Moneta's lastness to the fact that 'gold is sterile and cannot breed'. But gold and money are not *formally* identical, and *because* they are not, money *can* breed. We conceive this formal difference first by reference to money's constitutive form–content dissonance: roughly, a contrived discrepancy between symbolic and intrinsic value. The contrivance, a negation or renunciation of concrete material value, critically determines the ideal, representational value of money.[6]

Marx derives from this formal discrepancy *between* money and gold and, thus, *within* the money form itself a third contradiction, and it is this which explains the generative potential of money. Money, whose formal identity is defined as representation of general exchange-value, is, of necessity, noncoincident not just with its material content (for example, gold), but with its capacity, or what we might call *practical* content. By 'capacity', Marx means the quantitative limit on money's power to buy all the commodities it represents. In effect, Marx identifies and deconstructs the philosophical fantasy contained in the money form: the dream of a particular, concrete representation not just equivalent in specificity to the reality it describes – in this case, a totality – but interchangeable with that reality. Simply, money, which represents 'the totality of the material substances of wealth', cannot in any particular situation (the *only* context in which it can function *as* money) coincide with that substance.[7] The constant tendency of money to drive beyond its quantitative limit is explained as an effect of its contradictory form, striving toward a structural simplicity (reunion of signified with signifier) it can never realize.

Ruthven's concern is with the contradictions obtaining among Moneta's diverse mythological aspects, as with the contradiction surrounding Keats's highminded invocation of this distinctly commercial goddess. My interest is in the contradictions within the money form itself, those that drive it not only to 'breed' but to undergo a fixed sequence of metamorphoses. We shall see that Lamia's changes (those she suffers and those she engenders) emplot this economic sequence. 'Lamia' is, I believe, an allegory about the evolution of value forms and their corresponding social forms, the whole inquiry determined by Keats's interest in elucidating for the most personal reasons the objective relations between private and public domains (consumption and production) in his particular sector of nineteenth-century life.

In giving to his heroine the proper name *Lamia*, Keats designates his romance a myth of origins. Like Burton's etiological fictions, 'Lamia' confesses by its style – ironic, self-consciously fictive, sentimental – its strictly aesthetic or hedonistic investment in the explanatory genre. At the same time, Keats earns by this confession the right to push his naive conceptual instruments to their formal limit and to situate as truth the products of this enlightened exercise in personification. 'Lamia' constructs Lamia in order to explain Moneta's origin, development, and effects: to explain, that is, the money form, itself the explanation of Keats's literary practice.

To graft (Juno) Moneta upon Lamia, and to characterize that creature as the subject and object of Keats's virtuously contradictory art is to generate for the poem an entirely new set of critical problems, and this for a work which already presents serious difficulties on nearly every textual level. We haven't doubled our work, however, just redefined it. 'Lamia''s familiar problems are, I believe, largely the result of a paradigm mistake. By reversing our criticism's allegorical vector – reading from the abstract to the historically and textually actualized (right-to-left, so to speak) – we dissolve the very worst of the poem's critical problems. I refer to the strangely extended introductory narrative: the story of Hermes and his illicit amours. Given the title of Keats's poem and, in its original published form, the excerpt from Burton's *Anatomy*, one is hard put to motivate this substantial body of material. The complication is, of course, what gets Lamia from her snaky to her sexy self, but Keats could certainly have done this much more efficiently.

Let's say, for a start, that our very natural privileging of the Burton material (the Lamia–Lycius affair) *creates* this structural problem by concealing the *substantive* meaningfulness of lines 1–6, the actual introduction to the poem. Presumably, our criticism's entire indifference to this material means that we construe it as Keats's way to get going and at the same time, to establish the romantic character of the coming narrative: its perfect pastness, or fairy-tale temporality.

By overriding our assumptions about the narrative economy, we start attending in a very different way to the opening six lines. We see that these lines are, if anything, a *problematizing* of the once-upon-a-time motif and, thus, a suspiciously distracting way to get going. While the passage establishes the main action of the poem in a mythic past ('*before* the fairy [faery] broods / Drove Nymph and Satyr from the prosperous woods' [my emphasis]), it defines that past by reference to the corrupt historicity which directly succeeds it. The passage describes in a clear, even diagrammatic fashion the transition from a pastoral Golden Age – an era of natural, universal abundance – to a social formation organized by the differential possession of material wealth: an Age of Gold. The movement is from a pre-social but communal 'prosper[ity]' to a proto-modern, distinctly sociopolitical form: European (Oberon), autocratic or oligarchic on the basis of uneven distribution of property, forcefully expropriative, and defined by scarcity (viz. the implied competition over 'prosperous woods').

Interestingly, Keats chooses for his point of historical departure a famously political king: first of the late-form monarchs. We should not, however, overread the allusion. The discourse of the passage does not empower Oberon *per se*, the particular person and personality of the king, but rather his material objectifications: jewelled sceptre, mantle, diadem. These are the forces that turn myth into history, Golden to Gold. (We shall see that throughout the poem, dramatic agency is economic and structural, not characterological.) By a sort of personified synecdoche, it is the crown, not the king, who rules, and it rules by the laws of quantity and abstraction: more above less, symbol above thing. As I've observed, the events chronicled in the poem are said immediately to precede this transition.

The careful chronological plotting of the opening six lines invites us to elucidate the Hermes–Lamia connection by the relationship of both characters' 'romances' to the economic and social changes figured in the introduction proper. (The conventional approach is to motivate the long 'introduction', ll. 7–170, by reference to the Lamia–Lycius–Apollonius romance. No one has prospered in this venture.) Organized as I've suggested, 'Lamia' starts showing surprising affinities with the *Hyperions*: all three poems, conceptual histories concerned to explain orders of social and material life and the meaning of their sequence. Were we to grasp the endpoint of Lamia's career as an improved or even desirable state of affairs, and were Keats to have concluded the *Hyperions*, we might recognize in these poems that fashionable, second-generation form, the progress poem. As it stands, we have in 'Lamia' something that reminds us of a myth of origins, cast, as I've said, in a sentimental mode. 'Lamia' seeks to explain in an imaginative way the passage from one mode of production and exchange and its power ratios to another: one form of 'prosperity' to another. Lamia's romance is both the last romance, and the one that tries to explain the extinction of that form.

The story of Hermes' amorous escapades follows directly from Keats's opening, historically synoptic meditation. In the context of the issues broached in that preamble, Hermes' unseemly passion for an earthly nymph, as well as its featured consequences (that is, Lamia's acquisition of a human form), offer themselves to a downward-displacing (again, right-to-left) allegorical reading. In a general way, we see that Hermes' desire for a particular social value – the nymph, as the object of the satyrs' and fauns' desire, and, as their natural, native 'luxury' – brings Lamia into being as a historical form. In her initial, recompensed sacrifice of the nymph, Lamia acts as a merchant; ultimately, insofar as she enables Lycius's acquisition of his primary desired object, social envy, she is constituted as a medium of exchange. Simmel's lucid analysis of the money form helps us frame this double function: 'money stands between the objects of exchange as the merchant stands between the exchanging subjects . . . The merchant is the personified function of exchange, and money is the reified function of being exchanged'.[8] We recall Burton's association of Corinth, that thriving commercial center, with prostitution, and we consider Keats's obvious interest in the connection (ll. 350–61). By reference to that theme, one might explain Lamia's offices – merchant and means, pimp and whore – as Keats's attempt to collapse what Simmel presents as an analogy into a historical and logical identity.

We begin by observing Keats's concern to establish textually the referred or indirect value which Hermes covets in the nymph. Admired for her particular attributes ('her beauty,' l. 100), she is additionally (one guesses from Keats's emphasis, *originally*) endeared to Hermes by her manifest value to the Wood Gods.

A nymph[,] to whom all hoofed Satyrs knelt,[;]
At whose white feet the languid Tritons poured
Pearls . . . And in those meads where sometime she might haunt,
Were strewn rich gifts, unknown to any Muse . . . Ah, what a world
    of love was at her feet!
So Hermes thought, and a celestial heat
Burnt from his winged heels to either ear . . .' mid his golden hair,
Fallen in jealous curls about his shoulders bare.

Hermes leaves his golden throne for the green world, in quest of love and / as stolen property: 'bent warm on amorous theft'. The nymph is, precisely and enticingly, both Other and the natural possession *of* Others. Her identity to Hermes is that of she-who-is-desired-by-the-Other, hence Keats's textual accent on the god's strangely anonymous and also inherent jealousy (ll. 26, 33) – as it were, contingently objective and absolutely subjective. Keats seems to be developing a concept of primary, polymorphic envy: a socially constitutive negation of plurality.

As if to reinforce the *intrinsic* lawlessness of Hermes' interest – his desire an *effect* of its illegality – Keats establishes Jove's injunction against forays from Olympus, a detail with no apparent narrative function or obvious mythological precedent and, in light of Jove's own reputation for womanizing, a departure conspicuous for its irony. Hermes' desire, prohibited by Jove and presupposing the desire of a rival group, is surreptitious from both sides. The double offensiveness of this interest is all that we really know about it; by default, it must illuminate the narrative meaning of Hermes' very specific desire for Keats's strangely anonymous nymph. (She is neither named nor described in the text.) The parallelism of 'rich gifts' and 'world of love' implies by the discursive, *metonymic* logic the intrinsic property value of the nymph. By the poem's *narrative* logic, whereby the gifts metaphorically signify the nymph's value to others, we are urged to appreciate her secondary, relatively abstract property value.

Hermes' illicit desire results in an act of exchange. (A shift to the allegorical register positions the exchange imperative, statute of sociality, as the *cause* of Hermes' desire. Hermes is, of course, a mediating god in more ways than one; the voyaging god is also, logically and traditionally, the god of commerce, profit, discourse, and virility. These identities are explored in the next section.) Through the special offices of Lamia, who appears to be of neither the sylvan nor the celestial world, the Wood-Gods are robbed of their natural ornament, the nymph; Lamia herself, narratively framed as a professional mediator, and, thus, Hermes' counterpart, is delivered into history. She receives, that is, a human form and a capacity for social action. We should also observe that Lamia, used *by* Hermes as, loosely, a medium of exchange to procure the nymph, at the same time *uses* Hermes to obtain *her* object of desire, Lycius. The tidy reciprocity of the transaction is, of course, troubled by the fates of both objects, Lycius and the nymph, both of them patently victimized by the interlocking designs of Hermes and Lamia. The marked cruelty of the nymph's fate – a lesson in the abstractive violence of exchange – is rehearsed on a grand scale and with appropriate subtlety in the curve of Lycius's fortunes.[9] Both narratives exemplify not only the progressive logic of exchange but its exploitative character. The text encourages a reading of the nymph's metamorphosis from subject to object, object to instrument, as a form of unwilling prostitution, with the profit accruing to another party. (The same

pattern applies to Lycius, sold to Lamia for the price of the nymph.)
The equivalence of the objects exchanged (nymph and youth), and
the categorical identity of object and profit (human flesh), suggest the
model of barter, or direct exchange of (appropriated, commodified)
use-values, not commerce *per se* with its additional mediation,
money.

There is an inexorable symmetry – a rough justice – to this logic of
sexual commerce. Lycius, himself Hermes' instrument, learns to
reconstitute Lamia both as a medium of exchange and a property: the
means to procure the envy of his friends (Lamia as the concretely
generic sign of Lycius's wealth), and the object or cause of that envy
(the very treasure). Because Lamia's exchange-value physically
inhabits as well as depends upon her intrinsic and cultivated material
value, Lycius's operation offers itself to our notice as an act of
commodification. To see this is to start sensing a terrible necessity in
Keats's narrative line, something that evokes, perhaps, *The Invasion of
the Body Snatchers*. Once transformed into an object and medium of
exchange, each of Keats's characters must, to sustain himself,
transform another natural creature into a kindred spirit: monstrous
human look-alikes. 'In that one temple of Venus, a thousand whores
did prostitute themselves'. 'Lamia''s serial prostitutions develop a causal
analysis of Burton's quantitative description. The undifferentiated
'thousand' emerges as the result of a chain-reaction.

We understand Apollonius's action upon Lamia by reference to the
next step in the evolution of value forms: money. The supremely
rational philosopher, who finds in Lamia nothing but a concretely
realized generic character – 'a serpent' – can be said to advance the
abstractive process to its logical conclusion. That Apollonius derealizes
Lamia in naming her *a* serpent, and that he does so in order to secure
Lycius's love and fealty (to reconstitute his possession of the youth),
puts him in the same field with Hermes, Lycius, and, ironically, Lamia
herself, all of whose abstractive designs are as redundantly injurious
as they are successful.

Paradoxically, each abstraction produces an *access* of material form.
The nymph, who loses her veil of invisibility, which is also her
freedom, suffers a most concretely reifying process. Lamia painfully
gives up her chameleon colors and 'gordian' plasticity to receive a
determinate female body; and, under the pressure of Lycius's desires,
she assumes specific social attributes. Finally, Apollonius reduces the

serial multiplicity of Lamia's being to a single appearance, designated by a single and, so it seems, empirically descriptive noun: 'a serpent'. We can see that each of these changes, the product of an abstractive operation, marks a passage from the full *potentia* of the material toward a strictly conceptual, ideal determinacy. What looks like a movement in the direction of material specificity is just the opposite: an exercise in the extremest formalism. The final image of the poem – 'And, in its marriage robe, the heavy body wound' – gives us Lycius's corpse as the topos of this confining, animal fleshiness which is the revenge of a repressed materiality.

The strange symmetries of the poem – its apparently unmotivated narrative replications – invite another, more positive, and as we'll see, related construction. The model is best approached figurally:

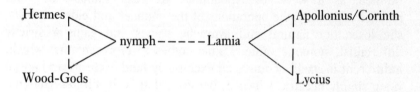

The nymph, object of both Hermes' and the satyrs' desire, *mediates* them in objectifying their respective desires. By a secondary and social logic – the logic of imitative desire – the nymph binds those emblematically dissociated domains, heaven and earth.[10] We might also observe that the nymph, recognized by Hermes as an intrinsic value to the satyrs and fauns, is raised by *his* desire to the level of the simultaneously natural and symbolic, substantive and formal value, in this anticipating Lycius's commodification of Lamia. In narrative terms, this conversion requires Lamia's intervention. Conceptually, or by a strictly formal logic, it *entails* Lamia (in the absence of Hermes' desire for that-which-is-valued-by-others, Lamia would have no narrative being: no scope for a textual agency, that is). Lamia, who formally approximates the nymph with respect to their metamorphoses in the direction of the fixed, female shape, is also *functionally* identical. Like the nymph, Lamia binds by dividing. She connects by competition Lycius and Corinth; further, by the metonymic *and* metaphoric relation of commerce to an abstract rationalism (the topic of section two, below), Lamia associates Lycius and 'the Pythagorean' Apollonius.

What distinguishes Lamia as a value form from the nymph is Lamia's greater abstraction from nature and need. Her human form, nowhere described by Keats, has, we may infer, no natural connection with her constituted value. Nor, since her ancestry remains a mystery, can she be said to have a stable generic value. The *nymph's* value form appears to originate by a primary logic of desire. She signifies that which others value for its properties (not, that is, *as* property in the abstract – instance of a class term), and which I, as a member of, aspirant to, or contester of that community, must value as well. By contrast, Lycius's plot constitutes *Lamia* the necessary and sufficient condition for the competition which directly produces his own sociality and, by inference, the condition of sociality as such: that is, Corinth's (commerce's) realization. In the marriage scheme, fulfilled, as it were, by Apollonius, we read Lamia's de- and reconstruction. By the operations of the younger and elder sophists, she loses her natural and symbolic values and gains a strictly differential, semiotic value. Lamia comes to represent that which, indifferent in itself, acquires an exclusively (and exclusionary) social value simply because I own it; because, that is, it differentiates me from others and to the extent that that difference is intolerable to them, arouses their envy. Like so many of the mediations figured in the poem, this envy joins by dividing. Lamia's inhuman change – a metamorphosis from the materially particular snake, to the symbolically particularized woman, to the colorless, characterless, coldly abstract form – is the fitting realization of Lycius's fantasy. We recall in this context not just the terrible blankness that suddenly glazes Lamia's eyes, but Ruthven's logical association to Moneta's strikingly similar transformation: her eyes, 'like two gold coins'.

Two

Our account of 'Lamia''s narrative structure – in the most literal sense, an economy of desire – is far from complete, since we haven't yet motivated the most distinctive of those elements which the work presents as its irreducible textual matter, its *donnée*. How precisely, or in what character, does Lamia penetrate the closure of a mind 'shut up in mysteries'; how might we *categorize* her peculiar gift for awakening a 'fantasy [phantasy] . . . lost, where reason fades, / In the calmed [calm'd] twilight of Platonic shades'. In short, who *is* Lycius to be so moved by Lamia, and who is she to move him thus? By entertaining these questions, we begin to explain Apollonius's fear of Lamia, that 'gordian shape', as well as his power to breach her enchantments: to solve, that is, the 'knotty problem' of her physique. Additionally, we explain that curious coupling inscribed in my triangulation figure, above: the functional identity of Corinth and Apollonius. Thus do *we* disentangle the great gordian knot of the poem.

That knot consists of three strands, or distinct anagogic codes: philosophic, economic and erotic. We have already isolated the economic order of signification. Our access to the erotic code depends on our penetration of the philosophic plot, although *that* understanding is also modified by the erotic dynamics. In other words, there is no clear hermeneutic hierarchy or even sequence to these codes. Rather, we have something like a set of analytic equations tried out on three orders of signification, each of which is at different moments positioned as both cause and effect, tenor and vehicle, Truth and Beauty. The idea here is to work from the philosophic order to the sexual and economic analyses, and back again, unraveling and to some extent reweaving these three distinct networks. What the method refuses is systematic textual induction: a movement from verbal analysis to formal explanation to syncretic interpretation. Further, rather than argue my readings of these codes, I propose simply to spell them out and to let their mutual coherence and their explanatory value, as well as the general argument of this book, defend their individual propriety. Finally, rather than totalize the poem's diverse materials and plots, I choose to imitate its own experimental method. By so doing, I violate the critical norm of this book, but then, 'Lamia' contradicts the practical and scientific norms of Keats's career. The best defense of this imitative experiment will be its success in establishing the necessity of Keats's curious method.

I would like to offer *some* framing comments on the deductive method and rhetoric of the following critique. We all sense in 'Lamia' the existence of an organized, semantic territory floating above or beneath the concrete textuality. Or, perhaps we project that structured and unified place – the place where the poem's 'poetry' takes shape – because the textual domain is so heterogeneous, disjunctive, and strangely accented. Paradoxically, however, by beginning with the responsible empirical move – an attention to parts – we *forfeit* a textual way to move from poem to poetry, text to meaning. The programmatic quality of our 'Lamia' criticism results from our failure to see that this poem develops its allegory dialectically (not, as in the poems we have treated, dyadically), and *preserves* this dialecticity in the form and substance of its meanings. We cannot but be reductive so long as we try to move mechanically and conclusively from part to whole, concrete to abstract, character to concept, vehicle to tenor: so long, that is, as we fail to let the whole turn around and criticize its parts, thereby destabilizing the part–whole ratio that had governed its operation and our own proceedings. At best, we produce by our analytic method readings that interpret everything while explaining nothing. I refer to the fact – apparent, I should think, to most of us – that very few bodies of criticism are so formally accomplished and also so formally unrelated to the study-text as the 'Lamia' commentary. The wildly extended Hermes episode (an 'introduction' that takes up nearly 200 lines of a 700-line poem) and the doctrinal suspension of the ending are only the most obvious of the poem's enigmas. The left-to-right, step-by-step, end-stopped approach does not begin to explain the elaborateness and specificity of representations extraneous to the central narrative structure: Lycius's sadism, Corinth's murkiness, Lamia's interior decor, the repulsiveness of the wedding guests. Most important, it cannot explain the affective dilemma at the heart of the poem: Keats's sympathy for the devil.

Our second-order understanding of this poem begins with a very active awareness that Lycius is Apollonius's protégé. That, and that alone, constitutes his textual identity. To say this is also to conceive his role as Lamia's lover as logically subsequent to his tutelage in Apollonius's Pythagorean school. From 'Pythagorean', one infers a commitment to the contemplative life and, more important, an association of philosophy – indeed, *truth* – with mathematics. 'Pythagoras' names a school defined by its identification of the material principle, the first stuff of experience, with number: quantity that is also the essential quality.

With this in mind, we can begin to motivate Keats's emphasis on

Lamia's voice: his complete *inattention*, we might say, to her womanly appearance. (Lamia's female form is never textually described although her beauty is everywhere indicated.) Keats very specifically credits Lamia's speech, not her aspect, with the rupture of Lycius's 'dream'. Moreover, in light of this introduction, Lamia's preternatural disappearance upon 'a frightful scream' implies for her a sort of vocal immortality.

Keats pays a great deal of attention to Lamia's *snaky* aspect, and he does so in such a way as to conjure very plainly the gorgeousness of Milton's serpent. Somewhat less conspicuous, perhaps, is the allusiveness of Keats's emphasis on Lamia's voice. As we know, Milton's serpent enthralls Eve less by the content of his discourse than by the fact that he speaks at all. We recall as well that Milton constructs his Eve as a rigid empiricist and an inductive reasoner: a causal rather than teleological thinker. Eve cannot critically think the phenomenon of the serpent, a *thing* that speaks its own meaning (that is, the object and its own self-consciousness), since this ideal simplicity is the very phantasm dreamed by her philosophy as its suprasensible beginning and end. We recognize the underlying idealism and abstractness of Eve's empiricism by the fact that she registers this creature who escapes all her phenomenal categories as their founding statute. She construes the serpent not as the monster it is but as the God if affects: literally, a Revelation. The serpent's miraculous speech is to Eve the testimony of a materiality so essential as to pronounce its own meaning without displacing by that act of signification its full physical presence. The charm of the serpent – *coincidentia oppositorum* – involves its bringing together of the essential / abstract and the contingent / concrete. Surely this must be God, who *means* and *is* simultaneously, His center (meaning) everywhere, His circumference (the negation of His being) nowhere. In short, Eve finds in the serpent an identity of thought and extension, form and content, Truth and Beauty, cause and effect: the dream of her empirical rationalism. Adam, who does not dream of such wondrous identities, is therefore proof against them. Throughout, he is contrasted to Eve chiefly by his understanding of Eden's grateful vicissitude.

This reading of Eve's response helps us connect at a logical level Lycius's textual identity and his attraction to Lamia. Lycius, a 'sophist', is also for all his refinement a child of Corinth: by both

Burton's and Keats's accounts, a code-word for commerce in its most extreme and universal aspect. For a city that buys to sell, as for those who trade in essentialist or totalizing rationalisms (Pythagorean/Platonic, Aristotelian), nothing – no *thing* – can be anything but a local habitation and a name. Bearing these several associations in mind, we identify Lamia's unique charm for Lycius as the mystery of the empirically absolute. Hers is the mystery of Nature *as such*, or in its ideal and at the same time particularized phenomenal manifestation. We connect the dramatic to the philosophic plot by observing that Lamia, seized by Lycius as the incarnate Idea of the sensuous particular, at the same time and *by* his particular form of cognition, seizes him. In other words, Lycius's enthralling vision is prepared for him by his instruction in Apollonius's Pythagorean philosophy. The ideal particularism of Lycius's brief erotic idyll, and Apollonius's material idealism are literally two sides of the same coin: of Lamia, that is.

The figure needs elaboration. Lamia, a living reconciliation of Platonic and Aristotelian systems, articulates in the language of character an 'individuating and totalizing description ... equivalent in specificity to the reality addressed'.[11] In that miracle – a chimera – we read the operative assumption of a Pythagorean science, a science that postulates number not just as the ultimate expression of matter but as the essential material principle. *That* assumption in turn describes the money form, beginning and end of Corinth's commerce.[12] Within a developed commercial context, money, which measures or expresses value, is also a means of exchange, and thus a producer of value; finally, in its ideally functional concreteness, money emerges as a value in its own right and, because it is its own measure and means, an absolute value. The money form – Lamia – is, in effect, Pythagoras's number, and also, as we shall see, the condition for some complex triangulation.

At the outset, Lycius is unequivocally Lamia's object; he is caught by her 'chain', 'tangled in her mesh', 'comprised [comprized]'. By the dramatic economy, her sensuous particularity emerges as the first and privileged term in the romantic dyad. By the logical plot, however (as by Lamia's *textual im*materiality), Lycius's slavishly idealizing recognition *establishes* Lamia in that role. This recognition is presupposed for him by his science, an overflow from Apollonius's fount. We learn that Lamia divines Lycius's hidden desires (to belabor a crucial point, the desire of Apollonius's *student*) in order to present herself as its origin and object. Or, as I observed, Lamia teases Lycius out of thought by her *meaning* materiality. 'Blinded' and 'comprised', Lycius 'passed [pass'd] the city gates, he knew not how, / So noiseless, and he never thought to know'.

The construction 'never thought to know' syntactically encodes an 'in order to' (as in 'murder to dissect'). The nuance underlines the peculiarly philosophic horror of Keats's weird romance. Lamia instances a form of knowledge prepared *by* thought but which, once established, suspends thought that is other than calculation, in this way protecting its mystery. (Textually, one senses in the ominous 'never thought to know' a darker statement yet: 'never knew to think'.) The sensational ideal(ism) which is Lamia's character for Lycius is defined for him by his rationalism, just as Eve's susceptibility to *her* serpent arises from her intellectual program. Lamia's charm – the charm of that knowledge-form which transcends the alienation of thought – is her promise to reproduce her own supreme simplicity within the consciousness that engages her. For a time, the period of the erotic idyll, Lamia keeps this promise. The turn of events, however, along with Keats's philosophic argument, brings out the regressiveness of that simplicity.

Corinth is described as a rich and imperial city, a marketplace, a den of sexual and commercial promiscuity, and very oddly, in light of all this solid flesh, a place of shadows and illusions (cf. ll. 350–61). By reference both to Lamia's apparitional nature and Apollonius's realm of abstractions, the city is thematically situated as a reality principle (materialistic, grossly sensuous, profit-minded). Troubling the tidy antithesis, however, Keats describes Lamia's strange intimacy with the city: her power to project her dreams beyond the serpent 'prison-house'. 'And sometimes into cities she would send / Her dream, with feast and rioting to blend; / And once, while among mortals dreaming thus, / She saw the young Corinthian Lycius . . .' This, combined with the weird emphasis on Corinth's dreaminess, suggests an always–already dynamics binding Lamia to that city. Her palace is not, we notice, newly conjured but rather 'disclosed [disclos'd]', and not just to the lovers but also to ' a few Persian mutes . . . seen about the markets'. Indeed, Keats's descriptive complicities half-incline the reader to take at face value Lamia's claim to have 'dwelt but half retired [retir'd]' in Corinth, 'and there had led / Days happy as the gold coin could invent . . .' (ll. 312–13). Moreover, in representing *Apollonius* as, unproblematically, a child of Corinth, Keats more seriously muddles what would seem to be the operative polarities. We may wonder whether the philosopher's formal empire is indeed Corinth's antithesis, or is it somehow coordinated with – perhaps engendered by – the city's strange abstraction.

For a time, the lovers enjoy an era of innocence, defined by the verse as a moving equipoise. The mirroring transitivity (ll. 22–5) suggests, from the immediate retrospect of Lycius's change, a stream of shared consciousness, something anterior to the push–pull of socially articulated desiring. This idyllic, pre-figurative state, consistently characterized in terms of suspension, equilibrium, and simultaneity ('between', 'floating', 'betwixt', 'side by side', 'even tide', 'near to', 'while', 'almost'), describes at the same time a zone of wonderful clarity – its textures, colors, shapes, and sounds firm and determinate. As I noted, it is Corinth, paradoxically, that empery of objects, which emerges textually as an abstract, indistinct domain. The city, a twilight realm, 'talk[s] as in a dream', 'mutter[s]', 'shuffle[s] [its] sandals o'er the pavement white', 'cluster[s]' about the 'dusky colonnade'.

The lovers' idyll instances that perfect adequation negated by the bitter authorial reflection which opens Part II.

> Love in a hut, with water and a crust,
> Is – Love, forgive us! – cinders, ashes, dust;
> Love in a palace is perhaps at last
> More grievous torment than a hermit's fast.[: –]
> That is a doubtful tale from fairy [faery] land,
> Hard for the non-elect to understand.

It takes no genius to see that Keats interrupts the romance, *narrative* norm with a sharp social comment, and, that he engineers a lapse in the romance proper shortly after. By putting those facts together, we guess that the erotic idyll takes place in and is perhaps meant to define a distinctly pre-social realm. This is as if to say, romance does not and never did exist for civilized men and women.

I take up this complex matter, the topic of lines 1–6, first in a general way. To define life by a single value – wealth or love, for example – is, as we know, to render all human experience and values abstractions from that first idea: diminished repetitions (or, by a Corinthian idiom, shadows). Moreover, in a world where the dominant value is a quantitative one, 'enough' does not exist. (Here, perhaps, is one of the subtler and also more subversive wisdoms of Blake's defiant Proverb of Hell: 'Enough! Or too much!') Experience which can only occur *in relation to* the norm of sufficiency cannot, obviously, coincide with that measure and remain 'experience'. Experience must always, in other words, fall short of or exceed the mark (must tend toward the hut or the.palace, longing or surfeit, Penia or Porus), in both cases engendering the *ressentiment* to which Keats's editorial comment alludes. (Lycius's change is the effect of a satiety which, *mediated* by the social/economic fact of Corinth, gets registered as surfeit. The episode, fully plotted below, demonstrates the more scandalous half of Keats's logical proposition: viz. the grievousness of 'love in a palace'.)

Love in the hut and love in the palace, where money tells by deficiency and excess, as it were competing with Love for supremacy, are *doubly* false to love's first principle: namely, isolation from the negative and symbolic equality of an exchange sociality (or, he wants what I have [my excess, his poverty], I want what he has [my poverty, his wealth]). To paraphrase thus is only to amplify the bitterness of Keats's aside: we get at the *irony* of the comment by considering another assumption inscribed in Keats's hut–palace parallel. By the conventional wisdom, poverty and inherited wealth – peasants and lords – are, like love, forms of privacy: exceptions to the active economic order. Keats's caustic lines, site of a triple deconstruction, tell us that *all* the ideologically noneconomic zones – positive privacies, such as love and unearned wealth, as well as negative ones, like distrust and poverty – are 'comprised' in the logic of quantity, also the logic of the marketplace.

The syntax of the apothegm – its parallelism – instructs us more deeply yet in the mordant symmetries of exchange. I have suggested that the hut–palace example takes its force from the assumption that each of these domains instances an *exemption* from the logic of exchange. By subjecting both the erotic and the economic privacies to the 'distrust and hate' that characterize 'the world' as such – the getting and spending place – Keats invites us to conceive those special zones not just as part of the system they negate but as *artifacts* of that order. Hut and palace, deficiency and excess, hate and exclusive love, are *produced* by the operations of exchange.

This lesson is conveyed to us by the whole force of Keats's love story: specifically, by its multiple inscriptions in Corinth's status quo. The collapsed counterpoint between Corinth and the lovers, brought about through Lycius's appetite for the envy of his neighbors, asks us to see that love is ideologically constituted as a privileged domain – the sporting ground of essential, self-determining subjects – by the very order it refuses. The social requires such playgrounds if it is to project its own irresistible seriousness: the necessity of its (definition of) nature. Something of this grim dialectic surfaces in the ambiguity of the representation, lines 11–15, where 'Love, jealous grown of so complete a pair, / Hovered [Hover'd] and buzzed [buzz'd] his wings, with fearful roar, / Above the lintel of their chamber door, / And down the passage cast a glow upon the floor'. Does the hovering god signify defense against brutish intruders, or is his jealous presence the very sign of a breached privacy and thus of a cruel social deception? The passage asks us, in short, to think the antinomy lodged in the word jealousy: vigilance in guarding a possession, and disrespect for the vigilance of others, or, covetousness. We are invited to relate dialectically love (object relation) and aggression, and to do so in the field of ownership and acquisition, the field where, etymologically, this doubleness originates: where lovers and things commingle. ('Jealous' derives from the Latin *zelus*, or zeal: fervor, passion, 'eagerness and ardent interest in pursuit of something'.)

We come to the second of those received textual problems I mentioned at the outset: Lycius's transformation. The consequential action of the poem begins on line 29, Part II, when Lycius is on the sudden possessed of – or is it, *by* – a thought: 'the sounds fled, / But left a thought a-buzzing [a buzzing] in his head.' To recall Lamia's initial and, for a period, sustained effect upon Lycius ('did not *think* to know': my emphasis), is to realize that Lycius's reversal is more like a return to the status quo. Literally, Lycius is abruptly repossessed by Apollonius's intellectual domain, a change expressed, appropriately, as a competitive, calculating, 'Corinthian' interest. Or, we could say that Lamia's power to suspend thought is itself suspended. However we describe this event, textually presented as a *perepeteia*, we see that it is triggered by 'a thrill / Of trumpets' issuing from 'the noisy world': a world of conquest and display.

One cannot overemphasize the importance of 'thought' in this change. Lamia knows that 'but a moment's thought is passion's passing-bell [passing bell]'; 'Why do you think', she anxiously asks Lycius. His 'thoughts' – themselves, as Lamia knows, an abstraction from the immediacy of loving – amount to a meditation on value as an abstraction from the object it initially inhabited, subsequently (but very differently, very *socially*) invests. 'What mortal hath a prize, that other men / May be confounded and abashed [abash'd] withal, / But lets it sometimes pace abroad majestical, / And triumph . . .' To Lamia's gentle remonstrance, Lycius responds with untoward cruelty: 'He thereat was stung, / Perverse, with stronger fancy to reclaim / Her wild and timid nature to his aim.[:] / Besides, for all his love, in self-despite [self despite], / Against his better self, he took delight / Luxurious in her sorrows, soft and new'. Stranger even than Lamia's sexual 'consent' to this sadism is her participation in its abstract logic: 'she burnt, she loved the tyranny'. The initial antagonism – result of Lamia's wish to preserve, Lycius's to establish, a particular object relation in the other – quickly modulates into a perversely cooperative form, based on the parity of mutually antagonistic desires. Each lover becomes to the other a property: to hoard, in Lamia's case, or, as with Lycius, to alienate and revalue. The equal-but-opposite instrumentality of their interests in the basis of their new passion.

The alarming dramatic sequence, lines 61–81, makes available two logically contradictory but practically compatible meanings: an antinomy, in short. Essentially, we are invited to read Lycius's sensitivity to Corinth as both the cause and effect of his alienation from Lamia. The connection between the Corinthian 'trumpet thrill' and Lycius's sudden distaste evokes the causality of his initial 'taste' for Lamia, triggered by her 'luting voice'. Lycius's disaffection is thus positioned as a socially determined sensation of surfeit. Lycius has not exhausted his desire for *Lamia*, only for the value she initially provided him and which he now grasps as a relative value: relative, that is, to Corinth's more abstract modes of satisfaction.[13] By his determined embrace of Corinth (and here we modulate toward the other side of the antinomy, explored below), Lycius seeks to develop a new *form* of consumption: a new object, oriented toward or capable of creating a new taste. He brings this object into being by reconstructing to himself Lamia's value form, which he does in a peculiarly Corinthian, or commercial fashion. Lamia, who had been to her lover the very essence of a companionable objectivity, is positioned by him as a mediation; her job is to procure for Lycius the jealousy of his townsmen. The text makes it very clear that this new value, this social envy, displaces Lamia as Lycius's primary object; and, that this value is a quantitative phenomeon (viz. the undifferentiated multitude of envious guests), not a particular quality.

We motivate a number of otherwise gratuitous textual facts by reference to this narrative and conceptual model. Lycius's demand for marriage, for knowledge of Lamia's surname, and for an ostentatious wedding all figure in a single plot: a transformation of value forms. In order to constitute Lamia as a property (as opposed to something of the order of a natural resource), Lycius must first establish his ownership. He must publicly and legally secure his goods, hence his insistence on marriage, as on a very public reception. Second, he must situate Lamia as comparable to but exceeding other forms of property. Hence the extravagant nuptial display: an implicitly hierarchical exhibit of wealth. Finally, he must establish Lamia's generic and symbolic virtue; thus his interest in discovering her family name, the class term for her particular being. In effect and as I've observed more generally, Lycius's project is to turn his beloved into that monstrous thing, the commodity. That this potential was implicit in Lamia all along (or, that the allegory is operating at a fairly deliberate level) is suggested by Keats's description of her original value form, the serpent body, as a congeries of precious stones and metals (Part I, ll. 156–63). Ultimately, under the pressure of a more masterfully abstractive gaze than Lycius's, Lamia undergoes a more terrible transformation yet. Apollonius's eye ('keen, cruel, perceant, stinging') converts her from the commodity to the money form, her final incarnation. 'There was no recognition in those orbs'. We mark in Lamia's blank, 'blighted', 'withered' visage both Moneta's double and the mirror image of that essential materiality Lycius loved at the outset. Lamia, a materialized essence, is also the embodiment of Apollonius's supreme Pythagorean fiction. No wonder he alone can penetrate her mystery. By thinking along these lines, we motivate the weird affinities of those characters: Apollonius's 'demon eyes', with their 'lashless eyelids' and 'wither[ing] . . . potency' recall the 'hot, glazed' eyes, 'lid-lashes all sear' and 'wither[ing]' dew of the 'demon's mistress, or the demon's self'.

Lycius's two operations, upon Lamia and Corinth, amount to a single process. Through his conversion of Lamia's ideal sensuous particularity into a medium of exchange – the means by which to obtain Corinth's envy and also to establish its impoverishment with respect to his own new wealth (that is, Lamia as both a coveted quantity and as the means of producing another such quantity) – Lycius brings into being a new and exclusively social value. We see that Lycius's appetite for Lamia undergoes a renewal following the *contretemps* triggered by his swerve toward the city. Or rather, what looks like renewal is in fact the birth of a new *kind* of desire. In Lamia, Lycius finds (produces) a device for the production of an indirect, abstract, and continuous form of consumption, one that bypasses natural appetites and capacities. Lamia, who was once Lycius's absolute value, becomes to him the material form of an exchange-value. What we describe once again is the commodity form.

The narrative structure of the poem indicates that Lycius's awakening to Corinth *presupposes* the encounter with Lamia. After all, it is she who first arouses the otherwise 'staid', 'discreet', 'indifferent', and 'moderate' philosopher to the pleasures of phenomenal life. Lycius's love for Lamia and his interest in Corinth's corrupt commerciality are, then, moments within a single continuum, *not*, as it seems, polar opposites.

How should we explain this transition from one phenomenal attachment to another? In asking what brings about Lycius's sudden responsiveness to the city, we position that swerve as an *effect* of his engagement with Lamia; where above we addressed pleasure ratios, the subject here is power.

If Lycius's change is read as *originating* in a consumptive surfeit – an organic limit – then his marriage plans signify an attempted alteration of Lamia's value form by introducing her into the world of sign-things, or exchange. To construe along these lines is to work the Hegelian implications of the action. We explain Lycius's plot (that is, the instrumentality of his interest in Corinth) by discerning in Lamia the figure of the Other who, by her devotion, has forfeited her alterity, the source of her value. Lycius's perversely divisive nuptial plan is, by this argument, a very sensible device for alienating – technically, alter-ing – Lamia. By exposing her to the covetous gaze of his countrymen, Lycius hopes to revalue his beloved. By the same token, Lycius's objectifying design represents an attempted exorcism of that hidden subjectivity which Lamia, seized as a slave by her acts of recognition, figures to him who knows himself *diminished* by her transformative talents. The project is to revalue Lamia and at the same time to recover the existential prerogative she has usurped. Lamia, reconstituted as being-for-others (that is, '*a* serpent' [my emphasis]) through Lycius's stratagems and Apollonius's completion of their logic, yields up both her given and acquired unity. Framed by the sophist's knowledge and fractured by his epithet, Lamia's person becomes as a material sign dissociated from its original, particular content as well as its socially constituted, symbolic content. It acquires a mythic inscrutability: the blankness and, at the same time, the mysterious meaningfulness of the perfect surface.[14] By their brutally dissociative exercise, the student and his sage render Lamia incapable of returning Lycius's gaze: incapable, that is, of giving him to himself in a finer, more authoritative, more human tone. The selfsame activity brings into being Lamia's ghastliness *and* her immortality. Hers is the eternal allure of Moneta, both creatures whiter, more uncharactered than death itself. Both have passed beyond the lily and the rose: beyond qualities. By this reading, we learn how strong an irony Keats packs in his plotting. Lamia's final transfiguration, concentrated in the awful glazing of her eyes, instances the perfect abstractness Lycius had solicited. The death-dealing horror is, for Lycius, Lamia's inability to *recognize* him: she can only blankly reflect his own image (cf. ll. 256–60). By the Hegelian logic we have sketched, as by Keats's dramatic action, Lycius cannot survive this loss which he has himself and most urgently solicited.

More positively, Lycius's desire to reconstitute Lamia as a semiotic-order property (namely 'she-whom-I-own-who-is-*not*-owned-by-others') can be read as an advance beyond the Imaginary of the idyllic phase. The poem leaves no doubt that the lovers' initial isolation is the seclusion of deep enchantment. (What is at issue is the truth-value of that spell.) Lycius's violently *unnatural* negation of that solitude might, then, be better described as *anti*-natural, that is, social. By the marriage scheme, Lycius seeks to make others want what he has, in this way entering into relation with them.[15] By launching Lamia into the marketplace, Lycius gives himself over to its logic: the logic of negative equality, or an equality constituted by mutual lack and by the reciprocal designs that arise from this condition. This is a form of social identity predicated on social differences: distinctions created artificially, as it were, or by differential ownership. Property, then (in this instance, Lamia), figures the first mediation – also the original negation of matter – without which sociality could not arise. Lycius's new design upon Lamia – seemingly, a *most* ironic swerve from the expected comic–romantic dénouement with its message of enhanced sociality – logically represents a moment *within* a social progression. Lycius evolves from the perfect isolation of philosophy, through love's sequestered dualism, to a fully social (if also corrupt) mode of being.

I have noted that Lycius's plan tends toward a more complete objectification of Lamia than he had envisaged. His concern with his bride's family name, as with the opulence of the wedding, suggest an interest in preserving, if also raising to a new power, Lamia's given attributes. It is Apollonius who, in designating Lamia 'a serpent', transforms her into *lamia*: the most undifferentiated and anonymous form of exchange-value. By this generic idealization, Apollonius separates Lamia's particular properties and the particular needs they speak to, from her general social value. Moreover, he gives that general value (an abstraction from the totality of Corinth's use- and exchange-values) a concrete symbolic form. Effectively, Apollonius supplements (in that peculiarly Derridean sense of addition *and* reduction) Lamia's exchange value. By the economic model we have established, his analytically idealizing eye transforms Lamia from the commodity (her natural attributes aligned with her social or exchange-value) into the money form: material representative of a strictly social value and an abstraction from the sum of concrete social values. What looks ironic from a dramatic perspective is, with respect to the poem's conceptual allegory, completely predictable. I refer to the fact that it is Apollonius, adept at the number and reason game, who brings to completion the transformational sequence initiated by Hermes' indirect, abstract, overdetermined, and literally *commercial* desire.

To recognize Lycius's project is to feel once again but somewhat differently the searing irony of the dénouement. Lycius's recourse to the social, a device for the reconstitution of his coupling with Lamia, culminates in Apollonius's cruelly objectifying look and in the murderously generic name he applies to Lamia. That abstractive gaze is, plainly, an extension of the envious, objectifying, generalizing looks Lycius had solicited of his townsmen. Indeed, insofar as this gaze marries the lovers by their deaths (and here perhaps is the best meaning of Keats's departure from Burton: that is, Lycius's demise), it represents exactly that dyadically constitutive gaze Lycius had invited. To compound the irony, *Apollonius* provides the family name, a class term, that Lamia had withheld from Lycius.

By all these ironies, Keats associates at the deepest level the apparent antitheses, Corinth and Apollonius, Apollonius and Lamia, Corinth and Lamia. What binds these several agencies is, in the last instance, their magic, a mode of production. Burton's Apollonius is described in Lemprière's *Classical Dictionary*, a work well known to Keats, as 'a Pythagorean philosopher, well skilled in magic . . .'. In a letter to Taylor, Keats refers to Apollonius as 'a Magician'. The master rationalist and mathematical essentialist has, then, more in common with Lamia than we might guess and, more interestingly, he is closer to Corinth and its commercial number-games as well.

All three agents are producers of material 'Things semi-real', the fetish form of another fetish: the commodity, quantity, system. All, to effect their magic, destroy those 'existences' which are the natural and symbolic stuffs of those magic 'things'. Corinth's ultimate expression – the end-product of its commercial system – is the money form; Apollonius's consummate product is the ideal-material number; and in Lamia, worked over by Lycius's dialectics, Corinth's gaze, and Apollonius's rationalism, we discern the union of those two monsters. Lamia, the absolute, concrete, and contentless form of general exchange-value, is also, as I observed at the outset, the Idea of matter, reified. She is, in short, a Platonic essence and an Aristotelian totality: the beginning and the *end* of knowledge.

Before pursuing this character, we should analyze Lamia's magic, the nexus wherein Corinth and Apollonius confess their identity. We bring out the peculiar virtue of the world Lamia creates by juxtaposing against its highly structured opulence the idyllic milieu, Part II, ll. 7–25. Lamia and Lycius repose 'upon a couch', 'near to a curtaining', which, parted, 'let appear / Unveiled [Unveil'd] the summer heaven . . . Betwixt two marble shafts'. The scene, which reminds us of Keats's fondest suspension fantasy, minus the voyeurism (a picture of somebody reading before a window, beside a goldfish bowl), spatializes the rhythm of a constant structural metamorphosis; content and form, picture and frame, subject and object engage in continuous dialectical interdetermination. The stationing achieved through this passage is less sculptural, more organically animated than is often the case with Keats.

The lavishly outfitted hall concocted by Lamia for her bridal feast and realized, effortlessly, by her shadow minions, exhibits a strikingly different organizing principle. What we remark above all is the abstract, systematic law of the decor. The various objects are strictly disposed according to familiar formal principles: symmetry, rectilinearity, circularity, regular gradation, and correspondence. Paradoxically, the massive mathematical contrivance produces the illusion of a green world (the hall 'mimick[s] a glade . . . tree-stems . . . jasper panels . . . creeping imagery of slighter trees . . .'), and that sylvan artifice is as the antechamber to a specifically cultural *trompe-l'oeil*. Within the actual banquet room, Lamia engenders the illusion of a great temple, itself a micro/macrocosmic trope:

> A censer fed with myrrh and spicèd wood,
> Each bý a sacred tripod held aloft . . . fifty wreaths of smoke
> From fifty censers . . . still mimicked [mimick'd] as they rose
> Along the mirrored walls by twin-clouds odorous.
> Twelve spherèd tables, by silk seats ensphered [insphered] . . . Thus
>   loaded with a feast the tables stood,
> Each shrining in the midst the image of a God.

Both 'mimick' worlds – green and golden, Nature and Culture, men and gods – are characterized by internal coherence, plenitude, gradation, variety, and centrality. Both are, as it were, physical representations of systematicity.

We could say that Lamia's interior decor instances the form *of* form itself: the materialized logic *of* logic, or the incarnation of Reason. (We recall her initial identity to Lycius, the mystery of particular matter; here, Lamia is the mystery – that is, mystification – of the whole.) We have developed an analogy between Lamia, positioned in a certain way by Lycius, Apollonius, and Corinth, and the money form: that which separates general exchange-value from the body of the commodities it represents, and, in assuming a new, physical form, emerges as a strictly semiotic phenomenon. We can see that like the money form, Lamia in her third incarnation, that of the conjuror, isolates the 'bliss' of consumption from the 'pain' of production. She teases apart the *idea* of the system (Nature, Culture) from its original and secondary contents, and by supplementing that idea with a new and unrelated content, she effectively erases matter and labor *and* their referentiality. Her slaves, we observe, are not only 'viewless' and 'subtle' ('of tenuous substance'), their work is effortless, immediate ('a noise of wings'). They are not the *expression* so much as the *embodiment* of Lamia's 'high-thoughted'-ness.

Apollonius recognizes Lamia because his Pythagorean philosophy engenders such monsters all the time. I have indicated that Apollonius, by naming Lamia 'a serpent' (a violation of the particularity Keats establishes by his title, a proper name), isolates and idealizes one of her series appearances. Thus does the wizard annihilate Lamia's social and historical character, *even as he appears to pronounce it*. (Throughout the poem, what seems most concrete and particular turns out to be most abstract, and vice versa.) Moreover, we have seen that by hypostatizing 'a' serpent (the material form of a generic character: that which is nothing *but* a seriatim and nontotalizable being), Apollonius *constructs* Lamia as lamia incarnate, a monster. The horror, thus, resides in Apollonius's 'a' rather than in 'serpent', and it is the flip side to that beauty we have studied in Keats's happier poems: the Beauty that is Truth. (Or, to repeat in this different context an identity outlined above, Lamia transmogrified is also the inside-out version of Lycius's first view of her: essential matter vs. material idea.) The beauty, like the horror, is an effect of Keats's real Nothings: material representations of categorical constructs. Both qualities are the aesthetic form of our response to a negation at once negated and instantiated: exchange-value divested of its accidental material form and symbolically absolutized.

Ultimately, we may study Lamia as the reified relationship between mentor and student: between, that is, their two idealisms: the rational and the sensuous, conceptual and empirical.[16] Throughout the romance, we are invited to situate Lamia, that mediator mediated, between the old philosopher and his student: the object of a covert triangulated desire. Insofar as we conceive Lamia as the money form, and, thus, as Corinth's presiding goddess, we identify that commerce with Apollonius's and Lycius's philosophic liaison. The 'blaze of wealth' engendered by Lamia (ll. 173–90) describes a clear religion of matter. In that iconography, we glimpse Apollonius's abstract systematicity (a wisdom founded on a perfect blindness to matter), and Lycius's abstract empiricism (*his* knowledge enabled by ignorance of the whole). The oxymoronic quality of Lamia's invention (ll. 125–45) figures the monstrous collusion of Lycius's sensuous this-worldliness with Apollonius's conceptual idealism: abstractions both. Like the hut and the palace, the passion of the youth and the dispassion of the sage contain and require each other. And here again we interpret Keats's departure from Burton: Lycius's death. Apollonius, who loses Lycius in raising Lamia to her third power, truncates himself. Moreover, by 'vanishing' Lamia, the externalized *relation* between himself and Lycius, Apollonius undergoes a further reduction. What I emphasize by this observation is the unfreedom of all parties to the exchange, all of them creatures of its systematicity and of the Reason it worships.

Three

We return to an early question. What is the meaning of Apollonius's decreative eye, or should we call his penetration a constructive critique? How, ultimately, might we read the *effect* of his action upon Lamia, which is also an action upon Lycius and himself? We have already considered this action as a question of motivation. Specifically, we have identified Lamia as the way in which a transcendental rationalism and a rational empiricism solve their problem: namely, the logical content of particular material phenomena. This is also the problem of the whole, or of the ultimate substance of that 'matter' which is our knowledge of matter. Merely to frame these problems is to project a single logical structure which coordinates or subsumes all the partial systems (say, Lycius's physics and Apollonius's metaphysics) and, by explaining, controls the whole of existence.[17] Lamia, the material representation of an abstraction from a totality of particular objects and values, is philosophy's inscription of the money form: the thing-in-itself. (One recalls Burton's simile for Lamia's furniture: 'like Tantalus' gold described by Homer, no substance, but mere illusions'.) By her effects upon Lycius and his mentor, we characterize her as an object that enables and at the same time perplexes thought. In this, she rehearses one of money's (and art's) ideological functions.

It requires Apollonius's abstractively reifying gaze to bring Lamia into being as the money form. Up to that point, she is, as I've argued, the seductive mystery of the commodity: that untoward combination of substance and meaning, the particular and the total (labour and price). In this aspect, she instances the naturalized form of a social thing. We discern in her a given and also a cultivated integrity dissolved, its elements subsequently recombined and re-presented by the work of the social under the *sign* of Nature. Apollonius, in designating Lamia 'a serpent', does not, as he thinks, solve the 'knotty problem' of Lamia, that 'gordian shape': literally, the problem of Lamia's physique. The meaning of Lamia's concrete abstractness, statute and limit of Apollonius's philosophy, is not available to him. Nonetheless, his exclusive power to wither her tells us that she is his creature – and also, that he is hers. Lamia's 'mimick' world – a representation of worldness itself, or of the systematicity which produces that instantly self-consuming impression – materially reproduces Apollonius's intellectual empire. In both its materiality and its represented horizons (its manifest systematicity), her pure value-cosmos constitutes the gravest threat to Apollonius's ideal order. His totalizing but ideally referential rationalism cannot survive that reflexive display. Lamia's destruction is no more to Apollonius than the necessary and sufficient condition for the annihilation of her world.[18]

Apollonius believes he reduces Lamia to her categorical essence, thereby incorporating her into his logical system. In fact, his knowledge (the discovery, 'a serpent') instances an arbitrary act of selection. The philosopher has neither reduced the phenomenon, Lamia, to an essence nor has he totalized it / her. In designating Lamia 'a serpent', Apollonius isolates from her range of appearances a single effect, and, in positing this aspect as an essential and ultimate knowledge, fetishizes what Keats presents to us as a strictly contingent, seriatim, and relational historical phenomenon.[19]

Here is Burton's account of Lamia's fate.

> Apollonius . . . found her out to be a serpent, *a lamia*, and [found] that all her furniture was like Tantalus' gold described by Homer, no substance, but mere illusions. When she saw herself descried, she wept, and desired Apollonius to be silent, but he would not be moved, and thereupon she, plate, house, and all that was in it, vanished in an instant . . . (my emphasis)

As I've noted in two other contexts, Keats, unlike Burton, kills off Lycius. The symmetrical elimination of the lovers, one of whom is explicitly Apollonius's creature, implies Apollonius's parallel relationship with the other. This is to mark, again, the *complementarity* binding Lamia's magic to Apollonius's.

And yet, even as we discern in the lovers' double evanishment their complicity with their nemesis, we must also feel in the strong sadness of the ending an important distinction. Keats's critical genius, here, is a matter of tone. By killing off Lycius, Keats generates the melancholy of a lost ideal. By his sympathy with these devils, Keats makes us see that however monstrous Lamia and Lycius made themselves, they did so through a desire to escape the monstrous conditions of their existence. Both wished to become human; for Lamia, this meant escaping her serpent body and for Lycius, transcending his discipleship. That wish survives in and as its failure.[20]

Apollonius's magic – equal but opposite to Lamia's – disappears Lamia *qua* Lamia. I use that phrase to suggest that *lamia*, the creature whom Hermes engages (or, whose 'syllabling' engages both Hermes and Lycius), survives. That figure, textually introduced on 'a mournful voice', vanishes from the text 'with a shriek'. By adding to Burton in this modest way, Keats provides for Lamia a form of evanishment that is not extinction. The poem's allegorical action curve projectively restores Lamia to her original state. One imagines her back in her green brake, patiently waiting for some mediating god once again to invent for her a historical form: to reinvent *history*, that is. We could even say that Lamia's disappearance denotes nothing but a temporary retirement from circulation. Her being as a merchant, or indirect medium of exchange (Hermes' broker), as Lycius's commodity, his 'prize', and as the money form (Apollonius's lamia), dissolves. Her splendid mirage vanishes and she reverts to her first state: the gorgeous serpent. In that disgusting, enthralling form – the surreality of particular matter – Keats inscribes the mystery of the given and, in his case, the not-given.

Lamia formulates by its narrative structure Keats's recognition that his literary project, a most developed, *determined* mode of production, is produced *for* him and at the level of his deepest desires by the very structures and relations he was working against. He sees that his private domain – wishes, words: his own art as well as the category Art – owes its appearance of isolation from the whole and its indifference to a matter conceived as at all coercive, to a system which *itself* cannot know those domains. The freedom *not* to know these things emerges as an unthinkable mixture of resistance and incapacity. Worse, that 'capably negative' *extrinsic* orientation is found to mirror the psychic accomplishment: what I have called Keats's negative knowledge of his actual life.

By the work of the *Hyperions*, Keats began, I believe, to grasp his writing, which was his chief experience of freedom, as an abstractive process he could neither direct nor arrest. Through 'Lamia', he figures that experience as an allowance (indeed, a *compelled* freedom), designed to conceal from him not just his insertion in an unknowable Real, but his *real* duplication of that mastering domain by the very mechanism of his individuality, the heart of his critically disengaged – that is, his imagined – selfhood.

Lamia's magic is the fabulous face of the exchange system. The world she conjures – its triumphantly materialized formal character – conceals, like all magic acts, the hand behind the illusion. By the economic allegory, we identify that hand with labor itself: the gross, substantive discrepancies upon which Lamia's magic, divinest manifestation of the symmetries of exchange, is founded. The pleasaunce which Lamia brings into being – Art – owes its charm, an illusion of perfect disinterest, to the existence it repudiates: namely, the order of buying and selling. The violent narrative juxtaposition of Lamia's pleasure dome with Corinth's brutish sensuality (the aesthetic expression of its commercial concerns) invites us to guess that quotidian life constructs such domes in order to reinforce its own apparent givenness. The designated freedom of those intellectual islands, a matter of their immateriality, establishes the factive irresistibility of the economic: its independence of *desire and thought*, which is to say, its proof against change. By figuring art as a critical elevation and a luxury, 'life' – the business-as-usual mode – figures itself not just *reality*, or a particular and thus mutable arrangement of facts, but the reality *principle*. To think along these lines is to conclude that the art which believes itself to be most critical must also be the most possessed by the age.

'Money does not create these antitheses and contradictions; it is . . . the development of these contradictions and antitheses which creates the transcendental power of money.'[21] The contradictions to which

Marx refers are the division of labor, specialization, and the emergence of class distinctions based on these differences. This is not the place, and I am not the critic to prove Marx's global premise on Keats's pulses. I will, however, say that Keats, a man objectively determined to the role of the apothecary (not, of course, a manual worker but, as a low-level layer-on-of-hands, not too far from one either), tries to make for himself an exclusively mental world and a capable subjectivity within it.[22] His genius, from this book's point of view, is the way he materializes that mental production and exposes the meaningfulness of his culture's mind–matter distinction. The tragedy, from Keats's own vantage, is his inability to erase his hand. Indeed, throughout the poetry, we discern his *compulsion* to show that hand, to represent the physicality of writing. What is possibly Keats's last poetic fragment and certainly a most end-shadowed expression could stand as the headnote to his entire project: 'This living hand . . . See here it is – / I hold it towards you'.

Following Simmel's *Philosophy of Money* and Marx's *Grundrisse*, I have sketched out the structural contradictoriness of money and positioned that quality as reflecting the contradictions in Keats's experience. Marx deduces from the economic contradictions the crisis: 'a moment when the independent form is violently broken and when the inner unity is established externally through a violent explosion'.[23] This notion of crisis provides an apt model for both the themes and dramatic form of 'Lamia', long acknowledged a crisis poem in every literary sense of that phrase.

One way to articulate this poem's emergency is as the crisis of love as a form of possession, of possession as a form of (self-and-other) mastery and of mastery as a form of slavery. By love as a form of possession, I refer not just to the obvious business of Lycius's marriage scheme, but to the ego-constructive procedures we have studied throughout Keats's romances: a taking-in of the loved Other and maintenance of its otherness by a process of double abstraction and reification. I have presented this dynamics under the rubric of narcissism, in this way availing myself of Freud's formal analysis of a particular kind of introjection. We might at this point drive that discussion in two directions. First, we observe that Freud's canon includes no theoretical analysis of so-called healthy love, for which narcissism figures the negative model. Freud's silence on the subject is explained, of course, by his interest in the pathological rather than the norm. Still, throughout Freud's writings, the one category has a funny way of sliding into the other, and nowhere is this so pronounced as in his discussion of narcissism. By dissolving the healthy–diseased, object-related–narcissistic dichotomy, we see that Freud's concept of normal love crucially entails the idea of the beloved's intransigent otherness: her objectness, we might say. In the absence of this quality or projection, the psyche's drive to secure for itself expedient identificatory forms assumes the ascendancy. The alterity of the beloved is, then, a defense against the fundamentally assimilative and self-aggrandizing energy (or ego) of the lover. I'm suggesting, of course, that the normative *defense* against an appropriative abstraction also reproduces that dynamics. The object that we seize in consciousness as a beloved form of Otherness is no less an abstraction than the narcissistic object. What is, in the one case, a contrived difference is, in the other, a contrived identity.

Freud's model of narcissism in some ways describes an exchange-form of love. I refer to the transformation of that which is me but external to me, noncoincident, and therefore intolerable, into an appropriable, and thus *voluntarily* alienable property: an embodied social value. The abstractness of my object guarantees both its otherness, and therefore its value, and its susceptibility to diverse ownership, and therefore its value. Marriage – or marriage in the aspect of bourgeois institution – is of course the place where the psychic model (love as desire for the permanently, structurally estranged object: love as mutually unrequited desire) and the economic (property as constituting being or quality; property as having, or quantity; having as being; quantity as quality) lie down together.

This is, clearly, the context in which to consider the mechanism that triggers Lamia's awful change: by the allegory developed here, her metamorphosis from the commodity form to the dissociated exchange form, or money: from a socially constituted object-value to the concrete form of a categorical postulate. Lycius's project is not only to exhibit his prize, but to marry it: effectively, constituting his lover a property, securing that property, showing it off (that is, establishing everyone else's poverty), and inviting its theft, all by the same gesture. For the sequel to 'Lamia', or the dialectics of exclusive object-possession, we might turn to Adorno, who reminds us that abstraction in love is the complement of exclusiveness, which manifests itself deceptively as the opposite of abstract, a clinging to this one unique being. But such possessiveness loses its hold on its object precisely through turning it into an object, and forfeits the person whom it debases to 'mine'. If people were no longer possessions, they could no longer be exchanged. (*Minima Moralia*, p. 79)[24]

This is to say, we would anticipate from the wedding of Lycius to Lamia (untroubled by Apollonius's interference), precisely the bind that necessitated Lycius's turn to the market – to marriage, that is – in the first place. Namely: the loss, through excess of a certain kind of loving, of the concrete otherness which was Lamia's virtue for Lycius, her reason for being (lovable). The text and lesson of 'Lamia' is that 'exclusive' love, like all chartered privacies, does not as it thinks transcend the exchange form. It is part – the most deceiving, enthralling part – of business as usual.

'Real are the dreams of Gods, and smoothly pass / Their pleasures in a long immortal dream'. I glossed one part of this provocative statement above. To resume, by way of the social themes we've been exploring, is to produce a paraphrase that runs something like this. Only the master-class, 'Gods', can realize its dreams. By the same token, that class, which knows nothing *but* dreams – values and abstractions – enjoys in its reality a poor and feeble thing. Even its love is ideal.

We recall Marx's formula for the crisis, quoted above: when the 'inner unity' is 'externally established'. I have *not* meant to suggest that this crystallization, a unity of meaning and knowledge, occurs in 'Lamia', or not in any way that is textually available to us. We might, however, venture to guess that it occurs in Keats. We see, for example, that the name Lamia nowhere appears in the poem; to frame the observation a bit differently, neither Lycius nor Apollonius discovers Lamia's identity. It is *Keats* alone who names Lamia and he does so only outside the text, in the title. Perhaps Keats intends by this unusual display of authority, as by the narrative innovation of Lycius's death, to imply the death of himself as a counterfeiter: a maker of severed heads and material Ideas.

Throughout this book, we have identified Keats as a man who does to himself what others do to him. He produces himself as an alienated property and an element of exchange. As Lycius takes Lamia to market, so Keats takes himself. For Keats, who (like Lamia) has no collective life in which the goods might get together, this strategy is no answer.[25] It is only, as we have seen in our study of Lamia's action upon the nymph, Lycius's action upon Lamia, and Apollonius's action upon everyone, including himself, a process of mutual prostitution: a mechanism, thus, of the system it thinks it abjures.

Like Chatterton's, Keats's was a most modern career. We plot in his experience the fortunes of a person who works to live and lives to write: to perform, that is, a different work, the production of a different life. Our criticism has for some time and quite properly been naming Keats a poet of our climate. How could we, who teach and write about Keats today, from within a particular (American, academic) form of the present, fail to recognize the dissociation of one 'life' from another? (Then again, one might ask, how can we *afford* to acknowledge it?) Keats's transformation of both organic, nonspecialized life, and also institutional/political life into the means toward the end of intellectual life is a magic many of us must know intimately.

Keats's two modes of production require, of course, two modes of consumption: a consumption of substance and one of value. And, in the appropriative techniques Keats developed as part of his perversely effectual, literary mode of production, we have seen that primary consumptive schism reproduced. I refer to the way Keats converts the canon – literary Nature – into materialized signs of the meaning of that system. Both substance and value, understood as parallel total forms, are thereby dissolved, precipitating out a third total-system: Literature, that grandest of Things semi-real. By my reading of 'Lamia', I have tried to indicate that this third world did not altogether displace the first two Natures, which could finally become for Keats the instrument of a better resistance.

By reference to the paradox of Keats's cooperation and refusals, we might ask why the money form does not stamp itself upon the face of the other major Romantic canons. The answer, or rather the beginning of an answer, lies in the most prosaic place, the business of livelihood. That is, more or less, where this book began. Wordsworth was supported by a legacy and sinecure. Coleridge, sponsored by Thomas Wedgewood and periodically assisted by generous admirers, made his living by journalism. Shelley was independently wealthy, like Byron, who, additionally (and conflictually) made money by his poetry. Moreover, and perhaps more important, all these men were children of parents educated in or *to* a particular cultural paradigm: a sort of categorical imperative governing the most primary kinds of experience. One can certainly locate exceptions to this rule among the successful writers of the early nineteenth century, particularly the female poets.[26] One should also correct the above generalizations by reference to the unique facts of each writer's case. Still, even the most careful review should betray to us Keats's anomalous situation among the major Romantic writers, a fact to which Keats's contemporaries were keenly alive.

There is one factor we can appreciate that was unavailable to those first readers: namely, the advantageous immediacy of Keats's situation. Perched on the edge of the bourgeoisie (with Hampstead giving geographical expression to that marginal middleness), Keats was positioned to reflect in a certain way the definitive contradictions of that class. Keats's *incomplete* estrangement from the middle class – his longing to achieve its cultural mode of being – was, as we've seen, the condition of his inadvertently subversive representations. By his fetishistic imitation of diverse bourgeois styles, Keats materialized their diffused *mythoi*, formally identifying their subject-vehicles as class forms. While we read Keats's poetry as no less a machine for the production of ideology than Wordsworth's or Byron's, we observe that Keats engendered an unusually stressed, self-conscious, and fragile ideological image. He could not *articulate* the transparencies of what I've called the subject class: could not, that is, explain their mediating and mediated functions. By his style, however, Keats did *represent* his culture's idols as reified social relations. What distinguishes 'Lamia' is that here, for the first time Keats begins reflecting on his representations and on his way of producing them.

What he learns is specifically related to his allegorical material. In money, that concrete Nothing which can only be realized by an act of divestment – only truly possessed by being lost – we glimpse the identity bind posited throughout this book as the problematic of Keats's poetry. I refer to the dilemma of a man who can only *be* by having and only *have* by not assimilating to being.[27] Keats's project was an attempt to realize himself authorially (to him, a primary existential necessity) by claiming the bad identity conferred upon him, thereby fracturing whatever there was initially – or imaginatively – of a whole subject self, and setting the pieces against each other.

Lamia serves her purpose. By inventing her career, Keats undoes the gordian knot of his own mode of production. His discovery of its philosophic, erotic, and economic inscription is also a genuine, if temporary, erasure of that trace. By his indifference to the special freedom he had fashioned by his burdened stylistic protocol, Keats negates that double negation and its web of determinants. 'Lamia''s allegorical reproduction of the exchange process *is* a parody, but it is neither end-stopped nor dyadic. Its structural doublings are part of a critical operation that knows itself to be always already a possessed form of escape. The textual consciousness to result from this operation formally antithesizes the murderously contemplative knowledge associated with Apollonius. Nor, of course, has Keats's knowledge anything to do with the subjective fetishism exemplified by Lycius.

The consciousness raised up by the work of 'Lamia' is 'not the knowledge of an opposed object [nor the knowledge of an illusory subject] but the self-consciousness of the object [and therefore] the act of consciousness overthrows the objective form of its object'.[28] This is to say, Keats demystifies the freedom and subjectivity of the age within the field of his own feeling and action. He finds his authentic freedom in his objectivity, but not as contemplated by a consciousness which distinguishes itself normatively from that (consequently) fetishized property. The freedom marked out by 'Lamia' resides in the power of the objectified consciousness to think itself and thus to become for the period of this thought an identical subject–object. Because Keats's is above all a *practical* reflection, his dismantling of the antinomies turns up no new idols in the wreckage. This strange, late poem of Keats's perplexes all of us who think and feel – who conceive ourselves – by the agency of those antinomies: subject–object, master–slave, leisure–work, consumption–production, eros–aggression. One could say that 'Lamia' allows us to glimpse in Keats the figure of the slave who has overmastered the master – *without at the same time becoming him* – by the very badge of his slavery: namely, the compulsion to work, and to work in a particular way. This surpassing registers in Keats's poetry as the displacement of parody by satire. 'The Cap and Bells' is, as I've said and as we all know anyway, a bad poem. But it is not a 'bad' poem, which is to say, Keats appears to be making himself into a new kind of subject. I return to

John Bayley and conjecture for Keats, had he lived, a movement beyond writing.

Notes

1 K. K. Ruthven, 'Keats's *Dea Moneta*', *Studies in Romanticism*, 15 (1976), pp. 445–59.
2 Georg Simmel's dates for the Restriction are 1796 to 1819 (Simmel, *The Philosophy of Money*, trans. T. Bottomore and D. Frisby, London: Routledge & Kegan Paul, 1978, p. 161). Simmel's comments on the relation between money and centralization (civil and religious) are germane. Throughout his book, Simmel emphasizes the socially progressive effects of the developing money form. Clearly, money as an absolute *intermediary* enables the development of uniform trade relations which in turn assist the centralizing tendencies of the human society. Those tendencies, incarnated in such institutions as church and state, find themselves symbolized by money in its character as absolute *value* (pp. 183–7).
3 Robert Burton, *The Anatomy of Melancholy*, ed. Holbrook Jackson (New York: Vintage Books, 1977), part 3, p. 21.
4 Karl Marx, *Grundrisse*, trans. M. Nicolaus (New York: Vintage Books, 1973), p. 145.
5 Marx, *Grundrisse*, pp. 162, 163: Marx rejects the comparison of money with language. 'Language does not transform ideas, so that the peculiarity of ideas is dissolved and their social character runs alongside them as a separate entity . . . Ideas do not exist separately from language. Ideas which have first to be translated out of their mother tongue into a foreign language in order to circulate . . . offer a somewhat better analogy; but the analogy then lies not in language, but in the foreignness of language'. Marx's distinction is consistent with and, indeed, required by his materialist position, one that radically historicizes matter, to that extent deconstructing its primacy, but at the same time maintains a pre-historical zone where the philosophical authority of the material survives intact. Thus does Marx practically undo the covert idealism of a simpler, Enlightenment materialism without deconstructing the *concept* of essential matter. The always-already priority of signification, and the infinite anteriority of the referent projected by the sign, were not available concepts for Marx.
6 Simmel's understanding of the renunciation structurally inherent in the money form leads him to associate money with art: 'It appears that even the most useful object must renounce its usefulness to function as money' (*The Philosophy of Money*, p. 152). Simmel reads this phenomenon as a class instance of 'the influence of not-being on being', a class that also and signally includes art. 'This is the essential meaning of art, for the artist as well as for those who enjoy it, namely, that it raises us above the immediacy of its relation to ourselves and to the world. The value of art depends upon our overcoming this immediacy, which then operates as if it no longer existed' (ibid., pp. 153, 154). Our work on Keats

might encourage us to construe Simmel's universal observation as an astute understanding of art as it operates within a capitalist economy: an art the ideological function of which is to glamorize the renunciation of immediacy and substance which a fully developed exchange economy requires of its citizens. That Simmel's definition of art is also a definition of the art we associate with the Romantic period and with all those nineteenth- and twentieth-century negative aesthetics deriving from it, supports the economic equation.

7 Marx, *Grundrisse*, pp. 150, 221–2, 233.

8 Simmel, *Philosophy of Money*, p. 176.

9 I do not mean to suppress the more positive aspects of the nymph's rape, or seduction. 'But the God fostering her chilled hand, / She felt the warmth, her eyelids opened [open'd] bland, / And, like new flowers at morning song of bees, / Bloomed [Bloom'd], and gave up her honey to the lees. / Into the green-recessed woods they flew; / Nor grew they pale, as mortal lovers do' (ll. 140–6). Indeed, this accent, coming on the heels of the nymph's 'fearful sobs', her 'cowering', fading 'like a moon in wane', 'self-folding like a flower, / That faints into itself at evening hour', is consistent with the providential social meanings released by the grimmer narrative patterns further on (Lycius's sadism, his wish to arouse Corinth's envy, etc.). 'Lamia''s narrative is profoundly dialectical, as are, naturally, the meanings it engenders. No less keenly than Marx (or Hegel), Keats penetrates the antinomial virtue of the negation: that world-making/losing dynamic.

10 René Girard, *Deceit, Desire, and the Novel*, trans. Y. Freccero (Baltimore, Md: Johns Hopkins Univ. Press, 1965). I'd like very briefly to translate this literary schema into what was, presumably, its original Freudian form, in this way illuminating from a new angle Keats's unusual but class-specific identity binds and solutions.

One can easily see how Girard's plot (desire as a mediated interest in the object which is desired by one's *primary* object, one's Other) derives from and profoundly disturbs the classical Oedipal account. A 'triangulated' reading of the Oedipal romance would position the mother not as the boy's primary desired object but as both an instrument of primary aggression, and as an instrument of desire for the father. By wanting what my father wants, imaginatively taking what he has (that is, sharing and/or competing for his valued object), I realize my first, antinomial wish: to be him. I accomplish this by realizing through my own wishes *his* desire (a metaphoric displacement, this). I realize as well my wish to be loved by him, to the extent that I am *identified* with his loved object; here, the logic is metonymic. My mother, intrinsically an object of no value, acquires by my father's desire, mediated by mine for him, the negative value of the possession as such: not a value analogous to the commodity, with its preserved 'natural' or substantive value, but something more like money, which has lost both its direct and symbolic relation to valued substances. The mother, conceived as property, is the basis for the competition which binds sons to fathers, then (to resume the literary application) Arcadia to Olympus, Wood-Gods to Hermes, Lycius to Corinth/Apollonius, the common (male) wealth to the Prince Regent, Keats to his precursors.

11 Arthur Danto, *Jean-Paul Sartre* (New York: Viking, 1975), p. 16.

12 Simmel observes, as if in anticipation of Lukács's Kantian critique, that 'if money were reduced entirely to this value and had divested itself of all co-ordination with valuable things [a goal toward which it is always striving] it would realize, in the field of economics, the extraordinary conception that is the basis of Plato's theory of ideas' (*The Philosophy of Money*, p. 156). (Lukács was Simmel's student.)

13 'Desire wisheth, love enjoys; the end of the one is the beginning of the other; that which we love is present; that which we desire is absent' (Burton, *The Anatomy of Melancholy*, part 3, p. 11). The apothegm lends itself to a more transitive construction: to love is to *make* present; to desire is to absent the object. Lycius tries to convert love – presence – to desire, or absence. More succinctly, 'in pleasure [he] thirst[s] for desire' (Goethe, *Faust*).

14 Marx, *Grundrisse*, pp. 163, 222. Greed only comes into being as such with money, 'when general wealth has been individualized into a particular thing'. See Keats's alternate text describing the wedding guests.

15 The pattern recapitulates the conceptual action, lines 1–6. The discourse of that passage clearly suggests that Hermes' envy brings about the change from a mythic to a historical dimension, and from a natural to a social order. Similarly, Lycius's interest in cultivating the envy of his countrymen is the narrative bridge between his 'natural' or instinctually determined isolation, and a fully social existence.

16 One could conceive Lamia, the money form, as a parody of the combined subject/object projected by Lukács and derived from Kant, Fichte, and Hegel. (It is the abstractness of the individual components and of that third thing, their combination, which makes for parody.) Ironically but logically enough, Lamia engenders the dissociated cognitive acts which sustain her oxymoronic being. The binary acts and understandings to which she gives rise in the poem are reproduced in our 'Lamia' criticism, which likes to distinguish poetry from philosophy, romance from satire, imagination from reason, id from ego/superego, escape from reality, so that it can reduce or raise up that distinction by invoking some syncretic form. What we miss is the primary unity of what *appears* to our divided senses as an antithesis. Both Lycius's and Apollonius's philosophies are based on this false opposition, a mechanical subject–object distinction. Both require of subjectivity a point of view distinct from the thing contemplated. Both derive from reflection: reflection *of* (where phenomena reflect and thereby privilege noumena, as in Apollonius's rational idealism), and reflection *upon* (immanent subjective truth: or, Lycius's sensuous idealism).

17 Georg Lukács, *History and Class Consciousness*, trans. R. Livingstone (Cambridge, Mass.: MIT Press, 1971), pp. 111–21.

18 What Apollonius fears in Lamia is her power to expose the never-being-there-ness of consciousness, *and* to show it not as a proof of the thing-in-itself, but as evidencing the negative structure of reality and consciousness. Lamia, who can reveal the literal nothingness of thought, must be banished if Apollonius's philosophic universe is to survive.

19 Danto, *Jean-Paul Sartre*, pp. 47–51.

20 The phrasing and thought here come from Jerry McGann.

21 Marx, *Grundrisse*, p. 146.
22 Most students of Keats wonder how to designate his first or intended profession. Was he training to be a doctor, apothecary, physician, or surgeon; what did those names *designate* and what did they *imply* in the early nineteenth century? Aileen Ward's excellent account would suggest that our confusion reflects the tumult in the medical world of Keats's day. I quote in full from her text.

> Medicine . . . was being slowly revolutionized, like English society as a whole, by middle-class energy breaking through the traditional system. For centuries the practice of medicine had been divided among three distinct groups – physicians, surgeons, and apothecaries. In Keats's time the field was still dominated by the physicians, a small and conservative group trained at the universities, who alone took the title of 'Doctor' and charged fees that only the wealthy could pay . . . [A]s late as the beginning of Victoria's reign there were fewer than three hundred licensed physicians in all Britain, as compared with eight thousand surgeons. It was surgeons who tended most of the country's sick . . . and their development of new medical techniques helped immeasurably to raise the general level of health . . . in the later 18th century. Before that time medicine was hardly a profession in the modern sense, and surgery was hardly a science; quacks were everywhere, and surgeons were not considered gentlemen. Not until 1745 did the surgeons . . . begin to establish professional standards . . . not until 1800 were they granted a charter for their own Royal College. *The apothecaries, the lowest rank in the medical hierarchy, soon followed suit. In the 18th century they were still classed as tradesmen and were forbidden by the physicians to dispense medical advice along with their drugs; in actuality they were the doctors of the poor. Only in 1815 did they finally win their independence of the physicians by an act of Parliament empowering the Society of Apothecaries to license candidates for general medical practice.* By this time it was becoming customary for apothecaries also to qualify as surgeons by a year of 'walking the hospitals' after the usual apprenticeship (*John Keats, The Making of a Poet*, New York: Viking, 1963, pp. 23, 24). (My emphasis.)

Ward observes that 'Keats could look forward, then, to a comfortable and respectable existence as a small-town doctor', but her own, rich account would make that an implausibly optimistic anticipation. Keats became apprentice to Mr Hammond in 1811, four years before the parliamentary licensing act for apothecaries. Indeed, this was the occasion that liberated Keats from Hammond and sent him off to Guy's Hospital, for it stipulated that no one could practice as an apothecary without attending a prescribed course of lectures in a London hospital, followed by an exam set by the Society of Apothecaries (Ward, ibid., p. 45). Keats would have been, *at best*, at the very edge of the lower-middle rank of the medical profession.

23 Marx, *Grundrisse*, p. 198.
24 Theodor Adorno, *Minima Moralia*, trans. E. F. N. Jephcott (London: NLB, 1974), p. 79.
25 Luce Irigaray, 'When the goods get together', trans. C. Reeder, in *Demystifications*, pp. 107–10.
26 Stuart Curran, 'The I Altered', in *Feminism and Romanticism*, ed. Anne Mellor (Bloomington: Univ. of Indiana Press, 1987).
27 Simmel takes up the special relation between money and outsiders ('Money's

congruence with those who are marginal', *The Philosophy of Money*, p. 221). 'The importance of money as a means, independent of all specific ends, results in the fact that money becomes the centre of interest and the proper domain of individuals and classes who, because of their social position, are excluded from many kinds of personal and specific goals' (ibid.). The relevance to Keats's case is obvious.

28 Lukács, *History and Class Consciousness*, p. 178.

Appendix I

Texts of Poems by John Keats

Specimen of an Induction to a Poem

Lo! I must tell a tale of chivalry,[;]
For large white plumes are dancing in mine eye.
Not like the formal crest of latter days,[:]
But bending in a thousand graceful ways –[;]
5   So graceful[,] that it seems no mortal hand,
Or e'en the touch of Archimago's wand,
Could charm them into such an attitude.
We must think[,] rather, that in playful mood
Some mountain breeze had turned its chief delight[,]
10   To show this wonder of its gentle might.
Lo! I must tell a tale of chivalry,
For while I muse, the lance points slantingly
Athwart the morning air. Some [air, some] lady sweet,
Who cannot feel for cold her tender feet,
15   From the worn top of some old battlement
Hails it with tears, her stout defender sent,[:]
And from her own pure self no joy dissembling,
Wraps round her ample robe with happy trembling.
Sometimes, when the good knight his rest would take,
20   It is reflected[,] clearly[,] in a lake,
With the young ashen boughs[,] 'gainst which it rests,
And the [th'] half-seen mossiness of linnets' nests.
Ah,[!] shall I ever tell its cruelty,
When the fire flashes from a warrior's eye[,]
25   And his tremendous hand is grasping it,
And his dark brow for very wrath is knit?
Or when his spirit, with more calm intent,
Leaps to the honours [honors] of a tournament
And makes the gazers round about the ring

Stare at the grandeur of the balancing?   *30*
No, no,[!] this is far off![: – then] Then how shall I
Revive the dying tones of minstrelsy,
Which linger yet about long [lone] gothic arches,
In dark green ivy[,] and among wild larches?
How sing the splendour of the revelries,   *35*
When butts of wine are drunk off to the lees?
And that bright lance[,] against the fretted wall,
Beneath the shade of stately banneral,
Is slung with shining cuirass, sword[,] and shield
Where ye may see a spur in bloody field?   *40*
Light-footed damsels move with gentle paces
Round the wide hall, and show their happy faces,[;]
Or stand in courtly talk by fives and sevens,[:]
Like those fair stars that twinkle in the heavens.
Yet must I tell a tale of chivalry –[:]   *45*
Or wherefore comes that steed so proudly by?
Wherefore more proudly does the gentle knight
Rein in the swelling of his ample might?

Spenser,[!] thy brows are archèd [arched], open, kind,   *50*
And come like a clear sun-rise to my mind;
And always does my heart with pleasure dance[,]
When I think on thy noble countenance,[:]
Where never yet was aught [ought] more earthly seen
Than the pure freshness of thy laurels green.   *55*
Therefore, great bard, I not so fearfully
Call on thy gentle spirit to hover nigh
My daring steps; or if thy tender care,
Thus startled unaware,
Be jealous that the foot of other wight   *60*
Should madly follow that bright path of light
Traced [Trac'd] by thy loved [lov'd] Libertas,[;] he will speak[,]
And tell thee that my prayer is very meek,[;]
That I will follow with due reverence[,]
And start with awe at mine own strange pretence.   *65*
Him thou wilt hear. So [hear; so] I will rest in hope
To see wide plains, fair trees and lawny slope,[:]
The morn, the eve, the light, the shade, the flowers,[;]
Clear streams, smooth lakes[,] and overlooking towers.

Appendix I

The Brown *manuscript version of* 'La Belle Dame Sans Merci'

I

Oh, [O] what can ail thee, knight-at-arms [knight at arms],
    Alone and palely loitering?
The sedge has withered [wither'd] from the lake,
    And no birds sing! [.]

II

5   Oh, [O] what can ail thee, knight-at-arms [knight at arms],
    So haggard and so woe-begone?
The squirrel's granary is full,
    And the harvest's done.

III

I see a lily on thy brow,
10   With anguish moist and fever-dew [fever dew],
And on thy cheek [cheeks] a fading rose
    Fast withereth too.

IV

I met a lady in the meads[,]
    Full beautiful, a fairy's child,[;]
15   Her hair was long, her foot was light,
    And her eyes were wild.

V

I made a garland for her head,
    And bracelets too, and fragrant zone;
She looked [look'd] at me as she did love,
20   And made sweet moan.

VI

I set her on my pacing steed,
    And nothing else saw all day long;[,]
For sidelong would she bend, and sing
    A fairy's song.

VII

25   She found me roots of relish sweet,
    And honey wild, and manna dew;[,]

And sure in language strange she said, [–]
'I love thee true'.

VIII

She took me to her elfin grot,
And there she wept, and sighed [sigh'd) full sore,   *30*
And there I shut her wild wild eyes
With kisses four.

IX

And there she lullèd [lulled] me asleep,
And there I dreamed [dream'd] – Ah! woe betide!
The latest dream I ever dreamed [dream'd]   *35*
On the cold hill [hill's] side.

X

I saw pale kings, and princes too,
Pale warriors, death-pale [death pale] were they all;
They cried – 'La belle Dame [dame] sans merci
Hath thee in thrall!'   *40*

XI

I saw their starved [starv'd] lips in the gloam
With horrid warning gapèd [gaped] wide,
And I awoke, [awoke] and found me here
On the cold hill [hill's] side.

XII

And this is why I sojourn here,   *45*
Alone and palely loitering,
Through the sedge is withered [wither'd] from the lake,
And no birds sing.

The Indicator *version of 'La Belle
Dame sans Merci'*

Ah, what can ail thee, wretched wight,
Alone and palely loitering;
The sedge is withered from the lake,
And no birds sing.

Ah, what can ail thee, wretched wight,
 So haggard and so woe-begone?
The squirrel's granary is full,
 And the harvest's done.

I see a lily on thy brow,
 With anguish moist and fever dew;
And on thy cheek a fading rose
 Fast withereth too.

I met a Lady in the meads
 Full beautiful, a fairy's child;
Her hair was long, her foot was light,
 And her eyes were wild.

I set her on my pacing steed,
 And nothing else saw all day long;
For sideways would she lean, and sing
 A fairy's song.

I made a garland for her head,
 And bracelets too, and fragrant zone;
She looked at me as she did love,
 And made sweet moan.

She found me roots of relish sweet,
 And honey wild, and manna dew;
And sure in language strange she said,
 I love thee true.

She took me to her elfin grot,
 And there she gazed and sighèd deep,
And there I shut her wild sad eyes –
 So kissed to sleep.

And there we slumbered on the moss,
 And there I dreamed – ah, woe betide –
The latest dream I ever dreamed
 On the cold hill side.

I saw pale kings, and princes too,
 Pale warriors, death-pale were they all;

Who cried – 'La belle Dame sans mercy
  Hath thee in thrall!'

I saw their starved lips in the gloom
  With horrid warning gapèd wide,
And I awoke, and found me here
  On the cold hill side.

And this is why I sojourn here
  Alone and palely loitering
Though the sedge is withered from the lake,
  And no birds sing.

'As Hermes once took to his feathers light'

As Hermes once took to his feathers light,
  When lullèd [lulled] Argus, baffled, swooned [swoon'd] and slept,
So on a Delphic reed, my idle sprite [spright]
  So played [play'd], so charmed [charm'd], so conquered, [conquer'd] so
    bereft
The dragon-world of all its hundred eyes;   5
  And, seeing it asleep, so fled away –
Not to pure Ida with its snow-cold skies,
  Nor unto Tempe[,] where Jove grieved that [griev'd a] day;[,]
But to that second circle of sad hell,
  Where in the gust, the whirlwind, and the flaw   10
Of rain and hail-stones, lovers need not tell
  Their sorrows. Pale were the sweet lips I saw,
Pale were the lips I kissed [kiss'd], and fair the form
I floated with, about that melancholy storm.

The Eve of St. Agnes

I

St. Agnes' Eve – ah [Ah], bitter chill it was!
The owl, for all his feathers, was a-cold;
The hare limped [limp'd] trembling through the frozen grass
And silent was the flock in woolly fold.[:]

5   Numb were the Beadsman's fingers, while he told
       His rosary, and while his frosted breath,
       Like pious incense from a censer old,
       Seemed [Seem'd] taking flight for heaven, without a death,
       Past the sweet Virgin's picture, while his prayer he saith.

                                    II

10   His prayer he saith, this patient, holy man;
       Then takes his lamp, and riseth from his knees,
       And back returneth, meagre, barefoot, wan,
       Along the chapel aisle by slow degrees,[:]
       The sculptured [sculptur'd] dead, on each side, seem to freeze,
15   Imprisoned [Emprison'd] in black, purgatorial rails,[:]
       Knights, ladies, praying in dumb orat'ries,
       He passeth by; and his weak spirit fails
       To think how they may ache in icy hoods and mails.

                                    III

       Northward he turneth through a little door,
20   And scarce three steps, ere music's [Music's] golden tongue
       Flattered [Flatter'd] to tears this agèd [aged] man and poor;
       But no – already had his deathbell rung,[;]
       The joys of all his life were said and sung;[:]
       His was harsh penance on St. Agnes' Eve.[:]
25   Another way he went, and soon among
       Rough ashes sat he for his soul's reprieve,
       And all night kept awake[,] for sinners' sake to grieve.

                                    IV

       That ancient Beadsman heard the prelude soft,[;]
       And so it chanced [chanc'd] for many a door was wide[,]
30   From hurry to and fro. Soon, up aloft,
       The silver, snarling trumpets 'gan to chide;[:]
       The level chambers, ready with their pride,
       Were glowing to receive a thousand guests;[:]
       The carvèd [carved] angels, ever eager-eyed,
35   Stared [Star'd], where upon their heads the cornice rests,
       With hair blown back, and wings put cross-wise on their breasts.

                                    V

       At length burst in the argent revelry,
       With plume, tiara, and all rich array,

Numerous as shadows haunting fairily
The brain, new stuffed [stuff'd,] in youth, with triumphs gay   40
Of old romance. These let us wish away,
And turn, sole-thoughted, to one Lady there,
Whose heart had brooded, all that wintry day,
On love, and winged [wing'd] St. Agnes' saintly care,
As she had heard old dames full many times declare.   45

VI

They told her how, upon St. Agnes' Eve,
Young virgins might have visions of delight,
And soft adorings from their loves receive
Upon the honeyed [honey'd] middle of the night,
If ceremonies due they did aright;   50
As, supperless to bed they must retire,
And couch supine their beauties, lily white,[;]
Nor look behind, nor sideways, but require
Of Heaven [heaven] with upward eyes for all that they desire.

VII

Full of this whim was thoughtful Madeline.[:]   55
The music, yearning like a God [god] in pain,
She scarcely heard;[:] her maiden eyes divine,
Fixed [Fix'd] on the floor, saw many a sweeping train
Pass by – she heeded not at all;[:] in vain
Came many a tiptoe, amorous cavalier,   60
And back retired – [retir'd,] not cooled [cool'd] by high disdain,[;]
But she saw not;[:] her heart was otherwhere.[:]
She sighed [sigh'd] for Agnes' dreams, the sweetest of the year.

VIII

She danced [danc'd] along with vague, regardless eyes,
Anxious her lips, her breathing quick and short.[:]   65
The hallowed [hallow'd] hour was near at hand. She [: she] sighs
Amid the timbrels[,] and the thronged [throng'd] resort
Of whisperers in anger, or in sport;
'Mid looks of love, defiance, hate, and scorn,
Hoodwinked [Hoodwink'd] with fairy [faery] fancy – [;] all amort,   70
Save to St. Agnes and her lambs unshorn,
And all the bliss to be before to-morrow morn.

IX

So, purposing each moment to retire,
She lingered [linger'd] still. Meantime, across the moors,
75   Had come young Porphyro, with heart on fire
For Madeline. Beside the portal doors,
Buttressed [Buttress'd] from moonlight, stands he[,] and implores
All saints to give him sight of Madeline[,]
But for one moment in the tedious hours,
80   That he might gaze and worship all unseen;
Perchance speak, kneel, touch, kiss – in sooth such things have been.

X

He ventures in – [:] let no buzzed [buzz'd] whisper tell,[:]
All eyes be muffled, or a hundred swords
Will storm his heart, love's feverous [Love's fev'rous] citadel.[:]
85   For him, those chambers held barbarian hordes,
Hyena foemen, and hot-blooded lords,
Whose very dogs would execrations howl
Against his lineage;[:] not one breast affords
Him any mercy, in that mansion foul,
90 Save one old beldame, weak in body and in soul.

XI

Ah, happy chance! The agèd [the aged] creature came,
Shuffling along with ivory-headed wand,
To where he stood, hid from the torch's flame,
Behind a broad hall-pillar[,] far beyond
95   The sound of merriment and chorus bland.[:]
He startled her; but soon she knew his face,
And grasped [grasp'd] his fingers in her palsied hand,
Saying, 'Mercy, Porphyro! Hie [hie] thee from this place;
They are all here to-night, the whole blood-thirsty race!

XII

100   Get hence! Get [get] hence! There's [there's] dwarfish Hildebrand –[;]
He had a fever late, and in the fit
He cursèd [cursed] thee and thine, both house and land;[:]
Then there's that old Lord Maurice, not a whit
More tame for his gray hairs. [–] Alas me! Flit, [flit!]

Flit like a ghost away'![.] [–] 'Ah, gossip [Gossip] dear,   105
We're safe enough; here in this arm-chair sit,
And tell me how – ' ['–] 'Good Saints! Not [not] here, not here;
Follow me, child, or else these stones will be thy bier'.

XIII

He followed [follow'd] through a lowly archèd [arched] way,
Brushing the cobwebs with his lofty plume,   110
And as she muttered, [mutter'd] 'Well-a- [–] well-a-day'!
He found him in a little moonlight room,
Pale, latticed [lattic'd], chill, and silent as a tomb.
'Now tell me where is Madeline,' said he,
'Oh, tell me, Angela, by the holy loom   115
Which none but secret sisterhood may see,
When they St. Agnes' wool are weaving piously'.

XIV

'St. Agnes? Ah! It [it] is St. Agnes' Eve –
Yet men will murder upon holy days:
Thou must hold water in a witch's sieve,   120
And be liege-lord of all the elves [Elves] and fays [Fays],
To venture so;[:] it fills me with amaze
To see thee, Porphyro! – St. Agnes' Eve!
God's help! My [my] lady fair the conjuror plays
This very night. Good [: good] angels her deceive!   125
But let me laugh awhile, I've mickle time to grieve'.

XV

Feebly she laugheth in the languid moon,
While Porphyro upon her face doth look,
Like puzzled urchin on an agèd [aged] crone
Who keepeth closed [clos'd] a wondrous [wond'rous] riddle-book, 130
As spectacled she sits in chimney nook.
But soon his eyes grew brilliant, when she told
His lady's purpose,[;] and he scarce could brook
Tears[,] at the thought of those enchantments cold,
And Madeline asleep in lap of legends old.   135

XVI

Sudden a thought came like a full-blown rose,
Flushing his brow, and in his painèd [pained] heart
Made purple riot;[:] then doth he propose
A stratagem[,] that makes the beldame start:
140   'A cruel man and impious thou art – [:]
Sweet lady, let her pray, and sleep, and dream
Alone with her good angels, far apart
From wicked men like thee. Go, go! [–] I deem
Thou canst not surely be the same that thou didst seem'.

XVII

145   'I will not harm her, by all saints I swear',
Quoth Porphyro: 'Oh, may I ne'er find grace
When my weak voice shall whisper its last prayer,
If one of her soft ringlets I displace,
Or look with ruffian passion in her face – [:]
150   Good Angela, believe me by these tears,[;]
Or I will, even in a moment's space,
Awake[,] with horrid shout[,] my foemen's ears,
And beard them, though they be more fanged [fang'd] than wolves
      and bears'.

XVIII

'Ah, why wilt thou affright a feeble soul?
155   A poor, weak, palsy-stricken, churchyard thing,
Whose passing-bell may ere the midnight toll![;]
Whose prayers for thee, each morn and evening,
Were never missed [miss'd]'. [–] Thus plaining[,] doth she bring
A gentler speech from burning Porphyro,[;]
160   So woeful [woful], and of such deep sorrowing,
That Angela gives promise she will do
Whatever he shall wish, betide her weal or woe.

XIX

Which was[,] to lead him, in close secrecy,
Even to Madeline's chamber, and there hide
165   Him in a closet, of such privacy
That he might see her beauty unespied,
And win perhaps that night a peerless bride,
While legioned [legion'd] fairies paced [pac'd] the coverlet[,]
And pale enchantment held her sleepy-eyed.

Never on such a night have lovers met[,]   *170*
Since Merlin paid his Demon all the monstrous debt.

XX

'It shall be as thou wishest', said the Dame,[:]
'All cates and dainties shall be storèd [stored] there
Quickly on this feast-night;[:] by the tambour frame
Her own lute thou wilt see. No [:no] time to spare,   *175*
For I am slow and feeble, and scarce dare
On such a catering trust my dizzy head.
Wait here, my child, with patience; kneel in prayer
The while.[:] Ah! Thou [thou] must needs the lady wed,
Or may I never leave my grave among the dead'.   *180*

XXI

So saying, she hobbled off with busy fear.
The lover's endless minutes slowly passed [pass'd];
The dame returned [return'd], and whispered [whisper'd] in his ear
To follow her; with agèd [aged] eyes aghast
From fright of dim espial. Safe at last,   *185*
Through many a dusky gallery, they gain
The maiden's chamber, silken, hushed [hush'd], and chaste,[;]
Where Porphyro took covert, pleased [pleas'd] amain.
His poor guide hurried back with agues in her brain.

XXII

Her faltering [falt'ring] hand upon the balustrade,   *190*
Old Angela was feeling for the stair,
When Madeline, St. Agnes' charmèd [charmed] maid,
Rose, like a missioned [mission'd] spirit, unaware.[:]
With silver taper's light, and pious care,
She turned [turn'd], and down the agèd [aged] gossip led   *195*
To a safe level matting. Now prepare,
Young Porphyro, for gazing on that bed – [;]
She comes, she comes again, like ring-dove frayed [fray'd] and fled.

XXIII

Out went the taper as she hurried in;
Its little smoke, in pallid moonshine, died.[:]   *200*
She closed [clos'd] the door, she panted, all akin
To spirits of the air, and visions wide – [:]
No uttered syllable, or[,] woe betide!

But to her heart, her heart was voluble,
205   Paining with eloquence her balmy side,[;]
As though a tongueless nightingale should swell
  Her throat in vain, and die, heart-stifled, in her dell.

XXIV

A casement high and triple-arched [arch'd] there was,
All garlanded with carven imageries [imag'ries]
210   Of fruits, and flowers, and bunches of knot-grass,
And diamonded with panes of quaint device[,]
Innumerable of stains and splendid dyes,
As are the tiger-moth's deep-damasked [damask'd] wings;
And in the midst, 'mong thousand heraldries,
215   And twilight saints, and dim emblazonings,
  A shielded scutcheon blushed [blush'd] with blood of queens and
  kings.

XXV

Full on this casement shone the wintry moon,
And threw warm gules on Madeline's fair breast[,]
As down she knelt for heaven's grace and boon;
220   Rose-bloom fell on her hands, together pressed [prest],
And on her silver cross soft amethyst,
And on her hair a glory, like a saint.[:]
She seemed [seem'd] a splendid angel, newly dressed [drest],
Save wings, for Heaven. [heaven: –] Porphyro grew faint;[:]
225 She knelt, so pure a thing, so free from mortal taint.

XXVI

Anon his heart revives;[:] her vespers done,
Of all its wreathèd [wreathed] pearls her hair she frees;
Unclasps her warmèd [warmed] jewels one by one;
Loosens her fragrant bodice [boddice]; by degrees
230   Her rich attire creeps rustling to her knees.[:]
Half-hidden, like a mermaid in sea-weed,
Pensive awhile she dreams awake, and sees,
In fancy, fair St. Agnes in her bed,
  But dares not look behind, or all the charm is fled.

XXVII

235   Soon, trembling in her soft and chilly nest,
In sort of wakeful swoon, perplexed [perplex'd] she lay,

Until the poppied warmth of sleep oppressed [oppress'd]
Her soothèd [soothed] limbs, and soul fatigued – away [away;]
Flown, like a thought, until the morrow-day;
Blissfully havened [haven'd] both from joy and pain;   *240*
Clasped [Clasp'd] like a missal where swart Paynims pray;
Blinded alike from sunshine and from rain,
As though a rose should shut, and be a bud again.

XXVIII

Stol'n to this paradise, and so entranced,
Porphyro gazed upon her empty dress,   *245*
And listened [listen'd] to her breathing, if it chanced
To wake into a slumbrous [slumberous] tenderness;
Which when he heard, that minute did he bless,
And breathed [breath'd] himself[:] then from the closet crept,
Noiseless as fear in a wide wilderness – [,]   *250*
And over the hushed [hush'd] carpet, silent, stepped [stept],
And 'tween the curtains peeped [peep'd], where, lo! – how fast she slept.

XXIX

Then by the bed-side, where the faded moon
Made a dim, silver twilight, soft he set
A table, and, half anguished [anguish'd], threw thereon   *255*
A cloth of woven crimson, gold, and jet.[: –]
Oh, [O] for some drowsy Morphean amulet!
The boisterous, midnight, festive clarion,
The kettle-drum[,] and far-heard clarionet,
Affray his ears, though but in dying tone;[: –]   *260*
The hall door shuts again, and all the noise is gone.

XXX

And still she slept an azure-lidded sleep,
In blanchèd [blanched] linen, smooth[,] and lavendered [lavender'd],
While he from forth the closet brought a heap
Of candied apple, quince, and plum, and gourd,[;]   *265*
With jellies soother than the creamy curd,
And lucent syrops, tinct with cinnamon;
Manna and dates, in argosy transferred [transferr'd]
From Fez; and spicèd [spiced] dainties, every one,
From silken Samarcand to cedared [cedar'd] Lebanon.   *270*

XXXI

These delicates he heaped [heap'd] with glowing hand
On golden dishes and in baskets bright
Of wreathèd [wreathed] silver;[:] sumptuous they stand
In the retired quiet of the night,
275 Filling the chilly room with perfume light.[–]
'And now, my love, my seraph fair, awake!
Thou art my heaven, and I thine eremite.[:]
Open thine eyes, for meek St. Agnes' sake,
Or I shall drowse beside thee, so my soul doth ache'.

XXXII

280 Thus whispering, his warm, unnervèd [unnerved] arm
Sank in her pillow. Shaded was her dream
By the dusk curtains;[: –] 'twas a midnight charm
Impossible to melt as icèd [iced] stream.[:]
The lustrous salvers in the moonlight gleam,[;]
285 Broad golden fringe upon the carpet lies.[:]
It seemed [seem'd] he never, never could redeem
From such a steadfast [stedfast] spell his lady's eyes;
So mused [mus'd] awhile, entoiled [entoil'd] in woofed [woofed]
phantasies.

XXXIII

Awakening up, he took her hollow lute,[–]
290 Tumultuous,[–] and, in chords that tenderest be,
He played [play'd] an ancient ditty, long since mute,
In Provence called [call'd], 'La belle dame sans mercy',[:]
Close to her ear touching the melody[;] –
Wherewith disturbed [disturb'd], she uttered [utter'd] a soft moan.[:]
295 He ceased – she panted quick – and suddenly
Her blue affrayèd [affrayed] eyes wide open shone;[:]
Upon his knees he sank, pale as smooth-sculptured stone.

XXXIV

Her eyes were open, but she still beheld,
Now wide awake, the vision of her sleep – [:]
300 There was a painful change, that nigh expelled [expell'd]
The blisses of her dream so pure and deep.[:]
At which fair Madeline began to weep,
And moan forth witless words with many a sigh,[;]
While still her gaze on Porphyro would keep;

Who knelt, with joinèd [joined] hands and piteous eye,   *305*
Fearing to move or speak, she looked [look'd] so dreamingly.

XXXV

'Ah, Porphyro'! said she, 'but even now
Thy voice was at sweet tremble in mine ear,
Made tuneable with every sweetest vow,[;]
And those sad eyes were spiritual and clear.[:]   *310*
How changed [chang'd] thou art! How [how] pallid, chill, and drear!
Give me that voice again, my Porphyro,
Those looks immortal, those complainings dear!
Oh, [Oh] leave me not in this eternal woe,
For if thou diest, my love, I know not where to go'.   *315*

XXXVI

Beyond a mortal man impassioned [impassion'd] far
At these voluptuous accents, he arose,
Ethereal, flushed [flush'd], and like a throbbing star
Seen mid the sapphire heaven's deep repose;
Into her dream he melted, as the rose   *320*
Blendeth its odour with the violet,[–]
Solution sweet – [:] meantime the frost-wind blows
Like Love's alarum pattering the sharp sleet
Against the window-panes; St. Agnes' moon hath set.

XXXVII

'Tis dark;[:] quick pattereth the flaw-blown sleet.[:]   *325*
'This is no dream, my bride, my Madeline!'
'Tis dark;[:] the icèd [iced] gusts still rave and beat.[:]
'No dream, alas! alas! and woe is mine!
Porphyro will leave me here to fade and pine.[–]
Cruel! What [what] traitor could thee hither bring?   *330*
I curse not, for my heart is lost in thine,
Though thou forsakest a deceivèd [deceived] thing [;]–
A dove forlorn and lost with sick, unprunèd [unpruned] wing'.

XXXVIII

'My Madeline! Sweet [sweet] dreamer! Lovely [lovely] bride!
Say, may I be for ay [aye] thy vassal blest?   *335*
Thy beauty's shield, heart-shaped [shap'd] and vermeil dyed?
Ah, silver shrine, here will I take my rest
After so many hours of toil and quest,

A famished [famish'd] pilgrim[,] – saved by miracle.
340   Though I have found, I will not rob thy nest
Saving of thy sweet self; if thou think'st well
To trust, fair Madeline, to no rude infidel.

XXXIX

[']Hark! 'Tis ['tis] an elfin-storm from fairy [faery] land,
Of haggard seeming, but a boon indeed.[:]
345   Arise – arise! The [the] morning is at hand;[–]
The bloated wassailers [wassaillers] will never heed.[:–]
Let us away, my love, with happy speed – [;]
There are no ears to hear, or eyes to see,[–]
Drowned [Drown'd] all in Rhenish and the sleepy mead.[:]
350   Awake! Arise, [arise!] my love, and fearless be![,]
For o'er the southern moors I have a home for thee'.

XL

She hurried at his words, beset with fears,
For there were sleeping dragons all around,
At glaring watch, perhaps, with ready spears;[–]
355   Down the wide stairs a darkling way they found.[–]
In all the house was heard no human sound;[.]
A chain-drooped [droop'd] lamp was flickering by each door;
The arras, rich with horseman, hawk, and hound,
Fluttered [Flutter'd] in the besieging wind's uproar;
360 And the long carpets rose along the gusty floor.

XLI

They glide, like phantoms, into the wide hall;
Like phantoms, to the iron porch[,] they glide;
Where lay the Porter, in uneasy sprawl,
With a huge empty flagon [flaggon] by his side.[:]
365   The wakeful bloodhound rose[,] and shook his hide,
But his sagacious eye an inmate owns.[:]
By one, and one, the bolts full easy slide;[: –]
The chains lie silent on the footworn stones;[–]
The key turns, and the door upon its hinges groans.

XLII

370   And they are gone – aye[: ay], ages long ago
These lovers fled away into the storm.

That night the Baron dreamt of many a woe,
And all his warrior-guests, with shade and form
Of witch[,] and demon, and large coffin-worm,
Were long be-nightmared [be-nightmar'd]. Angela the old   *375*
Died palsy-twitched [twitch'd], with meagre face deform;
The Beadsman, after thousand aves told,
For ay [aye] unsought for slept among his ashes cold.

Appendix II

Text of 'La Belle Dame Sans Mercy'

by Alain Chartier, 'translated' by Geoffrey Chaucer

LA BELLE DAME SANS MERCY

M. Aleyn Secretary to the King of France framed this dialogue between a gentleman and a gentlewoman, who finding no mercy at her hand dyeth for sorrow.

> Halfe in a dreme, not fully well awaked,
> The goldin Slepe me wrapped undir his wyng,
> Yet not forthy I rose, and well nigh naked,
> Al sodainly my self remembèryng
> Of a mattir, levyng all othir thyng,
> Which I must doe without in more delaie
> 7   For them whiche I ne durst not disobaie.
>
> My charge was this, to translate by and by,
> (All thyng forgive) as parte of my penaunce,
> A boke callid *La bel Dame sans Mercy*,
> Whiche Maistir Aleine made of remembraunce,
> Chief Secretarie with the Kyng of Fraunce;
> And hereupon a while I stode musyng,
> 14   And in my self greatly imaginyng
>
> What wise I should perform the said processe
> Considiryng by gode advisèment
> My unconnyng and my grete simplenesse,
> And ayenward the straite commaundèment
> Whiche that I had; and thus in myne entent
> I was vexid and tournid up and doune,
> 21   And yet at last, as in conclusioun,
>
> I cast my clothis on, and went my waie,
> This foresaid charge having in remembraunce,
> Till I came to a lustie grene valaie
> Full of flouris, to se a grete plesaunce,
> And so boldly, with ther benigne suffraunce
> Which redin this boke, touching this matere

Thus I began, if it plese you to here.   *28*
  Not long ago, ridyng an esie paas,
I fell in thought of joyful desperate,
With grete disese and pain, so that I was
Of all lovirs the most unfortunate,
Sith by his darte moste cruill full of hate
The Deth hath take my ladie and maistresse,
And left me sole, thus discomfite and mate,
Sore languishyng and in waie of distresse.   *36*
  Then said I thus, It fallith me to cesse
Eithir to rime or ditees for to make,
And surely to makin a full promesse
To laugh no more, but wepe in clothis blake
My joyfull tyme (alas!) now doeth it flake,
For in my self I fele no manir ese,
Let it be written, soche fortune (as I take)
Which neithir me nor non othir doth plese.   *44*
  If it were so my wyll or myne entent
Constrainid were a joyfull thing to write
My penne coud nevir knowin what it ment,
To speke thereof my tongue hath no delite;
Tho with my mouthe I laugh mochil or lite
Mine eyin should make a countenance untrue,
My herte also would have therof despite,
The wepyng teris have so large issue.   *52*
  These sicke lovirs I leve that to 'hem longes,
Which lede ther life in hope of alegeaunce,
That is to saie, to make balades and songes
Every of 'hem as thei sele ther grevaunce,
For she that was my joye and my plesaunce,
Whose soule I praie God of his mercie save!
She hath my will, myne hert'is ordinaunce,
Which lyith here within this tombe igrave.   *60*
  Fro this tyme forthe tyme is to hold my pees;
It werieth me this mattir for to trete;
Let othir lovirs put'hem selfe in prees,
Their seson is, my tyme is now forgete;
Fortune by strength the sorcir hath unshete
Wherein was sperde all my worldly richesse,
And all the godis which that I have gete
In my best tyme of youth and lustinesse.   *68*

Love hath me kept undir his govirnaunce;
If I misdid God graunt me forgivenesse!
If I did well yet felt I no plesaunce,
It causid neithir joye nor hevinesse,
For when she dyid that was my maistres
My welfare then ymade the same purchase;
The Deth hath shette my bondis of witnesse,
76   Which for nothing myne hert shal nevir pase.

In this grete thought sore troublid in my mind,
Alone thus rode I all the morrow tide,
Till at the last it happid me to finde
The place wherein I cast me to abide
When that I had no furthir for to ride,
And as I went my lodgyng to purvaie
Right sone I herd a little me beside,
84   In a gardin, where minstrels gan to plaie:

With that anone I went me backir more,
My self and I, me thought we were inow,
But twaine that wer my frendis here before
Had me espied, and yet I wote not how
Thei came for me; awaiewarde I me drowe,
Somwhat by force, somwhat by ther request,
That in no wise I coud my self rescowe,
92   But nedis I must come in and se the fest.

At my commyng the ladies everichone
Bad me welcome, God wote right gentillie,
And made me chere every one by one
A grete dele bettir than I was worthie,
And of ther grace shewed me grete curtisie
With gode disport, bicause I should not mourne:
That daie I bode still in ther companie,
100   Whiche was to me a gracious sojourne.

The bordis were spred in right lityl space,
The ladies sat eche as she semid best;
There were no dedly servauntes in the place,
But chosin men, right of the godelyest,
And some there wer, peraventure most freshest,
That sawin ther judgis right full demure,
Without semblaunt eithir to moste or lest,
108   Notwithstandyng thei had 'hem undir cure.

Emong all othir one I gan espie
Which in grete thought ful oftin came and went,

As one that had ben ravished uttirly,
In his language not gretly diligent;
His countinaunce he kept with grete turment,
But his desire farre passid his reson,
For er his eye went aftir his entent
Full many' a tyme when it was no seson.   *116*
    To makin chere sorely hymself he pained,
And outwardly he fainid grete gladnesse;
To sing also by force he was constrained,
For no plesaunce but verie shamefastnesse,
For the complainte of his moste hevinesse
Came to his voice alwaie without request,
Like as the soune of birdis doeth expresse
When thei sing loude in frithe or in forest,   *124*
    Othir there were that servid in the hall,
But none like hym, as aftir myne advise,
For he was pale, and somwhat lene withall,
His speche also tremblid in ferfull wise,
And er alone but when he did servise;
All blacke he ware, and no devise but plain;
Me thought by him, as my witte could suffise,
His herte was nothyng in his owne demain.   *132*
    To fest hem all he did his diligence,
And well he coud, right as it semid me,
But evirmore when he was in presence
His chere was doon, it n'olde none othir be;
His scholemaistir had soche aucthorite
That all the while he bode still in the place
Speke cou'd he not, but upon her beaute
He lokid still with a right pitous face.   *140*
    With that his hedde he tournid at the last
For to beholde the ladies everichone,
But er in one he set his eye stedfast
On her whiche that his thought was moste upon,
For of his eyen the shot I knewe anone,
Which ferfull was, with right humble requestes;
Then to my self I saied, By God alone
Soche one was I or that I sawe these jestes.   *148*
    Out of the prese he went full esily
To make stable his hevie countinaunce,
And wote ye well he sighid wondirly
For his sorowes and wofull remembrance,

Then in hymself he made his ordinance,
And forthwithall came to bryng in the messe,
But for to judge his moste wofull penance
156   God wote it was a pitous entremesse.
      Aftir dinir anone thei' hem avaunced
To daunce above the folk everychone,
And forthwithal this hevie man he daunced
Somtime with twaine and somtimis with one;
Unto 'hem all his chere was aftir one,
Now here, now there, as fell by avinture,
But er emong he drewe to her alone
164   Whiche that he moste drede of livyng creture.
      To mine advise gode was his purveiaunce
When he her chose to his maistresse alone,
If that her herte were set to his plesaunce
As moche as was her beautèous persone,
For who so evir setteth his trust upon
The report of the eyen withoutin more
He might be dedde and gravin undir stone
172   Or er he should his hert'is ese restore.
      In her failid nothyng that I could gesse
One wife nor othir, privie nor aperte;
A garison she was of godelinesse,
To make a frontier for a lovirs herte;
Right yong and freshe, a woman full coverte,
Assurid wele of porte and eke of chere,
Wel at her ese, withoutin wo or smerte,
180   All underneth the standerde of Dangere.
      To se the fest it weried me full sore,
For hevie joye doeth sore the herte travaile,
Out of the prese I me withdrawe therfore,
And set me doune alone behinde a traile
Full of levis, to se a grete mervaile,
With grene wrethis iboundin wondirly,
The levis were so thicke withoutin faile
188   That thoroughout no man might me espie.
      To this ladie he came full curtisly
When he thought time to daunce with her a trace,
Set in an herbir made full plesantly,
Thei restid 'hem fro thens but lityl space,
Nigh 'hem were none of a certain compace,
But onely thei, as farre as I coud se;

Save the traile there I had ychose my place
Ther was no more bitwene 'hem two and me.   *196*
   I herd the lovir sighyng wondir sore,
For aie the more the sorir it hym sought,
His inward paine he coud not kepe in store,
Nor for to speke so hardie was he nought;
His leche was nare, the gretir was his thought:
He musid sore to conquere his desire,
For no man maie to more penaunce be brought
Then in his hete to bryng hym to the fire.   *204*
   The herte began to swell within his chest,
So sore strainid for anguishe and for pain,
That all to pecis almoste it to brest,
When both at ones so sore it did constrain
Desire was bolde, but shame it gan refrain,
That one was large, the othir was full close;
No little charge was laied on hym certain
To kepe soche werre and have so many fose.   *212*
   Full oftin times to speke himself he pained,
But shamefastnesse and drede saied evir naie,
Yet at the last so sore he was constrained,
When he full long had put it in delaie,
To this ladie right thus then gan he saie,
With dredefull voice, wepyng, halfe in a rage;
For me was purveied an unhappie daie
When I first had a sight of your visage: *220*
   I suffre pain, God wote, full hote brenning,
To cause my deth, all for my true servise,
And I se well ye recke thereof nothing,
Nor take no hede of it in no kinde wise,
But when I speke aftir my best advise
Ye reke it nought, but make thereof a game,
And though I sewe so grete an entirprise
Yet peirith not your worship nor your fame.   *228*
   Alas! what should it be to you prejudice
If that a man doe love you faithfully?
To your worship eschewyng every vice,
So am I yours, and will be verily:
I chalenge nought of right, and reson why,
For I am whole submit to your service;
Right as you list it be right so will I,
To binde my self where I was in fraunchise.   *236*

L'amant.

Though it be so that I can not deserve
To have your grace, but alwaie live in drede,
Yet suffre me you for to love and serve
Without maugre of your moste godelihede;
Both faith and trouth I give your womanhede
And my service without any callyng;
Love hath me bound withoutin wage or mede
244   To be your man and leve all othir thyng.

La Dame.

When this ladie had herd al this language
She gave answere full soft and demurely,
Without chaungyng of colour or courage,
Nothyng in hast, but full mesurably;
Me thinkith, Sir, your thought is grete foly;
Purpose ye nought your labour for to cese,
For thinkith not whilis ye live and I
252   In this mattir to set your herte in pese.

L'amant.

Ther maie none make the pece but onely ye,
Which are the ground and cause of all this war,
For with your eyen the lettirs writtin be
By whiche I am defied and put afarre;
Your plesaunt loke, my very lodèstarre,
Was made heraude of thilke same defiaunce
Whiche uttirly behight me for to barre
260   My faithfull trust and all myne affyaunce.

La Dame.

To live in wo he hath grete fantasie,
And of his hert also but slippir holde,
That onely for beholdyng of an eye
Can not abide in pece, as reson wolde;
Other or me if ye list ye maie beholde;
Our eyen are made to loke, why should we spare?
I take no kepe neithir of yong ne olde;
268   Who felith smart I counsaile hym beware.

L'amant.

If it be so one hurte an othir sore
In his defaute that felith the grevaunce,
Of very right a man maie do no more,
Yet reson would it were in remembraunce,
And sith Fortune onily by her chaunce

Hath causid me to suffre all this pain
By your beautie, with all the circumstaunce,
Why list ye have me in so grete disdain? *276*

La Dame.

To your persone ne have I no disdain,
Nor nevir had truelie, ne nought will have,
Nor right grete love nor hatred in certain,
Nor your counsaile to knowe, so God me save;
If that soche love be in your minde igrave,
That lityl thyng maie doe you displesaunce,
You to begile or make you for to rave,
I will not causin no soche encombraunce. *284*

L'amant.

What er it be that me hath thus purchased
Wenyng hath not decevid me certain,
But fervent love so sore hath me ichased
That I unware am castin in your chaine;
And sith so is, as Fortune list ordaine,
All my welfare is in your handis fall,
In eschewyng of more mischevous paine
Who sonist dieth his care is left of all. *292*

La Dame.

This sicknesse is right esie to endure,
But fewe peple it causith for to die,
But what thei mene I knowe it very sure,
Of more comfort to drawe the remedie;
Soche be there now plainyng full pitouslie
That sele, God wote, not althir gretist pain;
And if so be love hurte so grevouslie
Lesse harme it wer one sorowful then twain. *300*

L'amant.

Alas! Madame, if that it might you plese
Moche bet it were by waie of gentilnesse
Of one sorie to make twain well at ese
Then hym to destroie that liveth in distresse,
For my desire is neithir more nor lesse
But my service to doe for your plesaunce,
In eschewyng all manir doublenesse
To make two joies in stede of one grevaunce. *308*

·La Dame.

Of love I seke neithir plesaunce nor ese,
Nor have I therein no grete affiaunce;

Though ye be sick it doeth me nothing plese,
Also I take no hede of your plesaunce:
Chese who so will ther hertis to avaunce,
Free am I now and fre will I endure;
To be rulid by mann'is govirnaunce
316   For yerthly gode naie, that I you ensure.

L'amant.

Love, which that joy and sorow doth depart,
Hath set the ladies out of all servage,
And largily doeth graunt 'hem for ther part
Lordship and rule of every maner of age;
The pore servaunt nought hath of avantage
But what he maie get onely by purchesse,
And he that ones to Love doeth his homage
324   Full oftin tymes dere bought is the richesse.

La Dame.

Ladies, be not so simple, thus I mene,
So dull of witte, so sottid in folie,
That for wordis which said be of the splene,
In faire language paintid full plesauntlie,
Whiche ye and mo holde scholis of dailie,
To make'hem all grete wondirs to suppose,
But sone thei can awaie their heddis wrie,
332   And to faire speche lightly ther eris close.

L'amant.

There is no man that janglith busilie,
And setteth his herte and al his minde therfore,
That by reson maie plain so pitouslie
As he that hath moche hevinesse in store;
Whose hedde is whole and saieth that it is sore
His fainid chere is harde to kepe in mewe,
But thought, whiche is unfainid evirmore,
340   The workis previth as the wordis shewe.

La Dame.

Love is subtill, and hath a grete awaite,
Sharp in working, in gabbing grete plesaunce,
And can hym venge of soche as by disceite
Would fele and knowe his secrete govirnaunce,
And makith 'hem to obeie his ordinaunce
By cherefull waies, as in 'hem is supposed,
But when thei fallin into repentaunce
348   Then in a rage ther counsaile is disclosed.

L'amant.

Sith for as moche as God and eke Nature
Hath avauncid love to so hie degre,
Moche sharpe is the poinct, thus am I right sure,
Yet grevith more the sante, where er it be;
Who hath no colde of hete hath no deinte;
The' one for that othir askid is expresse;
And of plesaunce knowith none certainte
But it be one in thought and hevinesse. 356

La Dame.

As for plesaunce, it is not alwaie one,
That you think swete I think it bittir pain;
Ye maie not me constrain, nor yet right none,
Aftir your luste to love; that is but vain;
To chalenge love by right was nevir fein,
But herte assent, before bonde and promise,
For strength and force ne maie not er attain
A will that standeth ensessid in franchise. 364

L'amant.

Right faire ladie! God mote I nevir plese
If that I seke othir right in this case
But for to shewe you plainly my disese,
And your mercie to'abide and eke your grace;
If I purpose your honour to deface,
Or evir did, God and Fortune me shende,
And that I ner unrightfully purchace
One onelie joye unto my liv'is ende. 372

La Dame.

Ye and othir that swere soche othis faste,
And so condempne and cursin to and fro,
Full sikirly ye wene your othis laste'
No lengir then the wordis ben ago,
And God and eke his sainctis laugh also;
In soche sweryng there is no stedfastnesse,
And these wretchis that have ful trust therto
Aftir thei wepe and wailin in distresse. 380

L'amant.

He hath no courage of a man truelie
That sechith plesaunce worship to dispise,
Nor to be callid, for he'is not worthie
The yerth to touch, the aire in no kind wise,
A trustie herte, a mouthe without feintise,

Thus by the strength of every manir name,
And who that laieth his faithe for little prise
388 He lesith both his worship and his fame.

La Dame.

A cursid herte, a mouthe that is curteise,
Full well ye wote thei be not accordyng,
Yet fainid chere right sone maie 'hem apeise,
Where of malice is set all ther workyng,
Full false semblant thei bere and true semyng,
Ther name, ther fame, ther tonguis, ben but fained,
Worship in 'hem is put in forgettyng,
396 Nought repentid, nor in no wife complained.

L'amant.

Who thinkith ill no gode maie him befall,
God of his grace graunt eche man his desert!
But for his love emong your thoughtis all
As thinke upon my wofull sorowes smert,
For of my paine whethir your tendir hert
Of swete pitie be not therewith agreved,
And of your grace to me were discovert,
404 That by your mene sone should I be releved.

La Dame.

A lightsome herte, a folie of plesaunce,
Are moche bettir the lesse while thei abide,
Thei make you think and bring you in a traunce,
But that sikenesse will sone be remedide;
Respite your thought, and put all this aside;
Full gode disporte ywerieth me all daie;
To helpe nor hurte my will is not aplide;
412 Who troweth me not I let hym passe awaie.

L'amant.

Who hath a birde, a faucon, or a hounde,
That foloweth hym for love in every place,
He cherisheth him and kepith him ful sound,
Out of his sight he will not hym enchace,
And I, that set my wittis in this cace
On you alone, withoutin any chaunge,
Am put undir, moche farthir out of grace,
420 And lesse set by, then othir that'be straunge.

La Dame.

Though I make chere to every man about
For my worship and for myne owne fraunchise,

To you I n'ill doe so withoutin doubt,
In eschewyng all manir prejudise,
For wote ye well Love is so little wise,
And in bileve so lightly will be brought,
That he takith all at his owne devise
Of thing God wote that servith him of nought.   *428*

L'amant.

If I by love and by my true servise
Lese the gode chere that straungirs have alwaie
Whereof shall serve my trouthe in any wise
Lesse then to him that cometh and goeth al daie,
Whiche holdeth of you nothyng, that is no naie?
Also in you is lost, as to'my semyng,
All curtisie, whiche of reson will saie
That *Love for love* were lawfull desiryng.   *436*

La Dame.

Curtisie is alyid wondir nere
To worship, whiche hym lovith tendirly,
And he will not be bounde for no praiere,
Nor for no giftes, I saie you verily,
But his gode chere depart full largily
Where hym lykith, as his conceipt will fall;
Guerdon constrained, a gift doen thankfully,
These twain can ner accord, nor nevir shal.   *444*

L'amant.

As for guerdon, I seke none in this cace,
For that deserte to me it is to hie,
Wherefore I aske your pardon and your grace,
Sith me behovith deth or your mercie;
To give the gode where it wantith truly
That were reson and a curtise manere,
And to your own moche bettir were worthy
Then to straungirs to shew'hem lovely chere.   *452*

La Dame.

What cal ye gode? fain would I that I wist;
That plesith one an othir smertith sore,
But of his owne to large is he that list
Give moche and lesin his gode name therfore;
One should not make a graunt, little ne more,
But the request were right well accordyng:
If worship be not kept and set before
All that is lefte is but a little thyng.   *460*

L'amant.

Into this worlde was foundin nevir none,
Nor undir hevin creäture ibore,
Nor nevir shall, save onely your persone,
To whom your worship touchith halfe so sore
But me, whiche have no seson lesse ne more
Of youth ne age but still in your service;
I have no eyen, no wit, nor mouthe, in store,
468   But all be givin to the same office.

La Dame.

A ful grete charge hath he withoutin faile
That his worship kepith in sikirnesse,
But in daungir he settith his travaile
That sessith it with othirs businesse;
To hym that longith honour and noblesse
Upon none othir should not be awaite,
For of his owne so moche hath he the lesse
476   That of othir moche foloweth the conceits.

L'amant.

Your eyen hath set the print which that I fele
Within my herte, that where so er I go
If I doe thyng that sounith unto wele
Nedes must it cum from you and fro no mo;
Fortune will this, that I for wele or wo
My life endure, your mercy abidyng,
And verie right will that I thinke also
484   Of your worship above all othir thyng.

La Dame.

To your worship se well, for that is nede,
That ye spende not your seson all in vain;
As touchyng myne I rede you take no hede,
By your follie to put your selfe in pain;
To ovircome is gode and to restrain
An herte whiche is decevid follilie,
For *Worse it is to breke then bowe certain;*
492   *Bettir to bowe then to fall sodainly.*

L'amant.

Now, faire ladie! thinke sith it first began
That Love hath set mine herte undir his cure
It nevir might, ne truelie I ne can,
None othir serve while I shall here endure,
In most fre wise thereof I make you sure,

Which maie not be withdraw, this is no naie;
I must abide all manir advinture,
For I ne maie put to nor take awaie.   *500*
               La Dame.
   I holde it for no gift in sothfastnesse
That one offirith where it is forsake,
For soche a gifte' is abandonyng expresse,
That with worship ayen maie not be take;
He hath an herte full fell that list to make
A gift lightlie that put is to refuse,
But he is wise that soche conceipt will slake,
So that hym nede neithir studie ne muse.   *508*
               L'amant.
   He should not muse that hath his service spent
On her whiche is a ladie honourable,
And if I spende my time to that entent
Yet at the lest I am not reprovable
Of fainid harte, to thinke I am unable,
Or I mistoke when I made this request,
By whiche Love hath of enterprise notable
So many hertis gottin by conquest.   *516*
               La Dame.
   If that ye liste doe aftir my counsaile
Seche a fairir and of more highir fame,
Whiche in service of love will you prevaile,
Aftir your thought, accordyng to the same;
He hurtith bothe his worship and his name
That follily for twain himself will trouble,
And he also lefith his aftir game
That surely can not set his poinctis double.   *524*
               L'amant.
   This your counsaile, by ought that I can se,
Is bettir saied than doen, to myne advise,
Though I beleve it not forgive it me:
Mine herte is soche, so whole without feintise,
That I ne maie give credence in no wise
To thyng whiche is not sounyng unto truth:
Othir counsaile I se' is but fantasise
Save of your grace to shewe pitie and ruth.   *532*
               La Dame.
   I holde hym wise that workith no folie,
And when hym lift can leve and part therfro,

But in connyng he is to lerne truelie
That would himself conduite and can not so;
And he that will not aftir counsaile doe
His sute he puttith into disperaunce,
And all the gode that should yfall hym to
540   Is lost and dedde clene out of remembraunce.

L'amant.

Yet woll I shewe this mattir faithfullie
Whilis I live, what evir be my chaunce,
And if it hap that in my truthe I die
Then deth shall doo to me no displesaunce,
But when that I by your harde sufferaunce
Shall die so true, and with so grete a pain,
Yet shall it doe me moche the lesse grevaunce
548   Then for to live a false lovir certain.

La Dame.

Of me get ye right noght, this is no fable,
I will to you be neithir hard nor straite,
And right will not no man customable
To thinke ye should be sure of my conceite;
Who seekith sorowe his be the receite;
Othir counsaile can I not fele nor se,
Nor for to lerne I cast me not to' awaite,
556   Who will thereof let hym assaie for me.

L'amant.

One must it be assaied, that is no naie,
With soche as be of reputacion,
And of true love the right honour to paie
Of fre hartis gottin by due raunsome,
For frewil holdith this opinion,
That it is grete duresse and discomforte
To kepe a herte in so straite a prison
564   That hath but one bodie for his disporte.

La Dame.

I knowe so many causis marveilous
That I must nede of reson thinke certain
Soche avinture is wondir perilous,
And yet well more the coming backe again,
Gode or worship thereof is seldome sene,
Where I ne will make any soche araie,
As for to finde a plesaunce but baraine
572   When it shall cost so dere the first assaie.

L'amant.

Ye have no cause to doubt of this matter,
Nor you to meve with no soche fantasise,
To put me farre all out as a straunger,
For your godenesse can thinke and well advise
That I have made aprise in every wise,
By whiche my truthe sheweth opin evidence;
My long abidyng and my true service
Maie well be knowen by plain experience.　　　　*580*

La Dame.

Of verie right he maie be callid true,
And so must he be take in every place,
That can discerne and let as he ne knewe,
And kepe the gode if he it maie purchase;
For who that praieth or swereth in any case
Right well ye wote in that no trouth is preved;
Soch hath there ben and ar that gettin grace,
And lese it sone when thei have it acheved.　　　　*588*

L'amant.

If truthe me cause, by vertue sovèrain,
To shewe gode love and alwaie find contrarie,
And cherishe the whiche fleeth me with the pain,
This is to me a lovely adversarie,
When that Pitie, whiche long on slepe doth tarie,
Hath set the sine of all my hevinesse,
Yet her comfort, to me moste necessarie,
Shall set my will more sure in stablenesse.　　　　*596*

La Dame.

The woful wight what maie he think or say,
The contrarie of all joye and gladnesse,
A sicke bodie, his thought is ferre alwaie
From 'hem that felin no sore nor sickenesse;
Thus hurtis ben of divers businesse,
Whiche love hath putt unto grete hindèraunce,
And truthe also put in forgetfulnesse,
When thei full sore begin to sigh askaunce.　　　　*604*

L'amant.

Now God defende but he be harmèlesse
Of all worship or gode that maie befall
That to werst tournith by his leudènesse
A gift of grace or any thyng at all
That his ladie vouchsafe upon hym call,

Or cherish hym in honourable wise;
In that defaute what er he be that fall
612   Deservith more then deth to suffre twise.

La Dame.

There is no judge iset on soche trespace,
By whiche of right love maie recovered be,
One cursith fast, an othir doth manace,
Yet dyith none, as farre as I can se,
But kepe ther course alwaie in one degre,
And evirmore ther labour doeth encrese
To bryng ladies, by ther grete subtilte,
620   For othirs gilte, in sorowe and disese.

L'amant.

All be it so one doeth so grete offence
And is not dedde nor put to no justice,
Right well I wote hym gainith no defence,
But he must ende in full mischevous wise,
And all evir saied God will hym dispise,
For falshed is all full of cursidnesse,
That his worship may ner have entirprise
628   Where it reignith and hath the wilfulnesse.

La Dame.

Of that have thei no grete fere now a daise,
Soche as will saie and maintain it thereto,
That stedfast truthe is nothyng for to praise
In 'hem that kepe it long in wele or wo,
Their busie hertis passin to and fro,
Thei be so well reclaimid to the lure,
So well lernid 'hem to withholde also,
636   And al to chaunge when love should best endure.

L'amant.

When one hath set his herte in stable wise
In soche a place as is bothe gode and true
He should not flit, but doe forthe his service
Alwaie withoutin chaunge of any newe:
As sone as love beginnith to remewe
All plesaunce goeth anone in lityl space;
As for my partie that shall I eschue
644   While that the soule abidith in his place.

L'amant.

To love truely there as it ought of right
Ye maie not be mistakin doutilesse,

But ye be foule discevid in your fight
By your light understandyng as I gesse,
Yet maie we well repele your businesse,
And unto reson have some attendaunce,
Moche bettir than to abide by simplenes
The feble soccouris of disperaunce.   *652*

L'amant.

Reson, counsaile, wisedome, and gode advise,
Ben undir love arrestid everichone,
To whiche I can accorde in every wise,
For thei ben not rebell but still as stone;
Ther will and myne be medlid all in one,
And therwith boundin with so strong a chain,
That as in 'hem departyng shall be none,
But pitie breke the mightie bonde atwain.   *660*

La Dame.

Ye love not your self, what evir ye be,
That in love stande subject in every place,
And of your wo if ye have no pite
Othirs pite bileve not to purchace,
But be fullie assured, as in this cace,
I am alwaie undir one ordinaunce;
To havin bettir trust not aftir grace,
And all that levith take to your plesaunce.   *668*

L'amant.

I have my hope so sure and so stedfast
That soche a ladie should not lacke pitie,
But now, alas! It is shit up so fast
That Daungir sheweth on me his crueltie,
And if she se the vertue faile in me
Of true service, though she doe faile also
No wondir were; but this is my surete,
I must suffre whiche waie that er it go.   *676*

La Dame.

Leve this purpose, I rede you for the best,
For the lengir ye kepe it is in vain,
The lesse ye get as of your hert'is rest,
And to rejoyce it shall you ner attain;
When ye abide gode hope to make you fain
Ye shall be founde asottid in dotage,
And in the ende ye shall knowe for certain
That hope shall paie the wretchis for ther wage. *684*

L'amant.

Yet saie as fallith moste for your plesaunce,
And your powir is grete, all this I se,
But hope shall ner out of my remembraunce,
By whiche I fele so grete adversite,
For when Nature hath set in you plente
Of all godenesse, by vertue and by grace,
He ner assemblid 'hem, as semid me,
692   To put Pitie out of his dwellyng place.

La Dame.

Pitie of right ought to be resonable,
And to no wight do grete disavauntage,
There as is nede it should be profitable,
And to the pitous shewyng no domage:
If a ladie will doe so grete outrage
To shewe pitie and cause her owne debate,
Of soche pitie comith dispitous rage,
700   And of soche love also right dedly hate.

L'amant.

To comfort 'hem that live all comfortlesse
That is no harme, but comfort to your name,
But ye that have a herte of soche duresse,
And a faire ladie', I must affirme the same,
If I durst saie, ye winne all this defame
By cruiltie, whiche fittith you full ill,
But if pitie, whiche maie all this attain,
708   In your high herte maie rest and tary still.

La Dame.

What er he be that saieth he lovith me,
And paraventure I leve well it be so,
Ought he be wrothe, or should I blamid be,
Though I did not as he would have me doe?
If I medlid with soche or othir moe
It might be callid pitie mercilesse,
And aftirward if I should live in wo
716   Then to repent it were to late I gesse.

L'amant.

O marble herte! and yet more harde parde,
Whiche mercie maie not perce for no labour,
More strong to bowe then is a mighty tre,
What availeth you to shewe so grete rigour!
Pleseth it you more to se me die this hour

Before your eyen, for your disport and plaie,
Then for to shewe some comfort and soccour
To respite deth, whiche chasith me alwaie?   *724*
    La Dame.
Of your disease ye may have allegeaunce,
And as for myne I let it ovir slake,
Also ye shall not die for my plesaunce,
Nor for your hele I çan no suretie make;
I will not hurte my self for othirs sake;
Wepe thei, laugh thei, or sing thei, I waraunt
For this mattir so will I undirtake
That none of 'hem shall make therof avaunt.   *732*
    L'amant.
I can not skill of love by God alone,
I have more cause to wepe in your presence,
And well ye wote avauntour am I none,
For certainly I love bettir silence:
One should not love by his hert'is credence,
But he were sure to kepe it secretlie,
For a vauntour is of no revèrence
When that his tongue is his moste enemie.   *740*
    La Dame.
Male bouch in court hath grete commaundèment,
Eche man studieth to saie the worst he maie,
These false lovirs in this tyme now present
Thei servin best to jangle as a jaie;
The moste secrete iwis yet some men saie
How he mistrustid is in some partise,
Wherfore to ladies when men speke or saie
It should not be bilevid in no wise.   *748*
    L'amant.
Of gode and ill shall he and is alwaie,
The world is soche; *The yerth is not al plain*;
Thei that be gode the profe sheweth every daie,
And othir wise grete villonie certain;
It' is not reson though one his tongue distain
With cursid speche to doe hymself a shame
That soche refuse should wrongfully remain
Upon the gode renomid in ther fame.   *756*
    La Dame.
Soch as be nought, when thei here tidinges new
That eche trespas shall lightly have pardon,

Thei that pursuin to be gode and true
Will not set by none ill disposicion,
To continue in every gode condicion
Thei are the first that fallin in domage,
And full frely the hertis habandon
764   To lityl saithe with soft and faire language.
                    L'amant.
Now knowe I well of verie certainte
If one doe truelie yet shall he be shente,
Sith all manir of justice and pite
Is banished out of a ladies entente;
I can not se but all is at one stente,
The gode, the ill, the vice, and eke the vertue;
Soche as be gode soche have the punishmente
772   For the trespace of 'hem that live untrue.
                    La Dame.
I have no powir you to do grevaunce,
Nor to punishe none othir creature,
But to eschewin the more encombraunce,
To kepe us from you all I hold it sure,
For False Semblaunce hath a face full demure,
Lightlie to catche these ladies in a waite,
Wherefore we must, if we will here endure,
780   Make right gode watch: lo! this is my conceite.
                    L'amant.
Sith that of grace a godely worde not one
Maie now be had, but alwaie kept in store,
L'appele to God, for he maie here my mone,
Of the duresse which grevith me so sore,
And of pite I complaine furthirmore,
Whiche he forgate in all his ordinaunce,
Or els my life to have endid before,
788   Whiche so sone am put out of remembraunce.
                    La Dame.
My herte nor I have doen you no forfeite
By whiche ye should complaine in any kinde;
Nothyng hurtith you but your own conceite;
Be judge your self, for so ye shall it finde:
Thus alwaie let this sinke into your minde
That your desire shall ner recovered be;
Ye noye me sore in wastyng all this winde,
796   For I have saied inough, as semith me.

This wofull man rose up in all his paine,
And departid with wepyng countinaunce,
His wofull herte almoste to braste in twaine,
Full like to die, walkyng forthe in a traunce,
And sayid, Deth, come forthe, thy self avaunce,
Or that myne herte forget his propertie,
And make shortir all this wofull penaunce
Of my pore life, full of adversitie. *804*

   Fro thens he went, but whithir wist I nought,
Nor to what part he drewe in fothfastnesse,
But he no more was in his ladie's thought,
For to the daunce anone she gan her dresse;
And aftirward one tolde me thus expresse,
He rent his heer for anguishe and for pain,
And in hymself toke so grete hevinesse
That he was dedde within a daie or twain. *812*

L'ENVOY.

   The true lovirs I beseche you all
Soche advintures flie 'hem in every wise,
And as peple defamid ye 'hem call,
For thei truelie do you grete prejudice
His castelles strong stuffid with ordinaunce,
For thei have had long tyme by their office
The whole countrey of Love in obeisaunce. *819*

   And ye ladies, or what estate ye be,
Of whom Worship hath choise his dwellyng place,
For Godd'is love doe no soche cruiltie,
Nor in no wise ne folowe not the trace
Of her that here is namid right wisely,
Whiche by reson me semith in this cace
Maie be callid *La belle Dame sans Mercy*. *826*

   Go, lityl Boke, God sende the gode passage!
Chese well thy waie, be simple of manere,
Loke thy clothyng be like thy pilgrimage,
And specially let this be thy praiere
Unto 'hem all that the will rede or here,
Where thou art wrong after ther helpe to call
The to correcte in any parte or all. *833*

   Praie 'hem also with thine humble servise
Thy boldènesse to pardon in this cace,
For els thou art not able in no wise
To make thy self appere in any place;

And furthirmore beseche 'hem of ther grace
By ther favour and supportacion
840 To take in gre this rude Translacion,
　　The which God wote standith full destitute
Of eloquence, of metre, and colours,
Like as a best nakid without refute
Upon a plain to abide all manir showers:
I can no more but aske of 'hem socours
At whose request thou wer made in this wise,
847 Commaundyng me with body and servise.
　　Right thus I make an ende of this prosses,
Besechyng hym that all hath in balaunce
That no true man be vexid causèlesse
As this man was, whiche is of remembraunce;
And all that doen ther faithfull observaunce,
And in ther trouth purpose 'hem to endure,
854 I praie God sende 'hem bettir avinture.
　　　　　　　　　　　　　　　　Explicit.

Index